voice(s)
of hope

voice(s)
of hope

Latter-day Saint Perspectives on Same-Gender Attraction—
An Anthology of Gospel Teachings and Personal Essays

Compiled by Ty Mansfield

DESERET
BOOK

SALT LAKE CITY, UTAH

Library of Congress Cataloging-in-Publication Data
Voices of hope : Latter-day Saint perspectives on same-gender attraction : an anthology of gospel teachings and personal essays / Ty Mansfield, editor.
    pages cm
  Includes bibliographical references and index.
  ISBN 978-1-60641-338-8 (paperbound)
  1. Homosexuality—Religious aspects—The Church of Jesus Christ of Latter-day Saints.
I. Mansfield, Ty. editor.
  BX8643.H65V65 2011
  261.8'35766—dc22   2011010014

Printed in the United States of America
Publisher's Printing, Salt Lake City, UT

10 9 8 7 6 5 4 3 2 1

Wherefore, whoso believeth in God might with surety hope for a better world, yea, even a place at the right hand of God, which hope cometh of faith, maketh an anchor to the souls of men, which would make them sure and steadfast, always abounding in good works, being led to glorify God.

ETHER 12:4

Contents

Introduction

"A Seal of Living Reality"

Ty Mansfield

Homosexuality is a sensitive and complex issue that Latter-day Saints are learning to face with increasing openness and candor. Few issues of our time are proving as difficult to respond to in the way I believe our Eternal Father desires of us: with both heartfelt compassion and uncompromising devotion to eternal principles. President Gordon B. Hinckley affirmed, "Our hearts reach out to those who struggle with feelings of affinity for the same gender. We remember you before the Lord, we sympathize with you, we regard you as our brothers and sisters."[1]

We live in a world where the stories of those quietly striving to live the gospel get lost in the crossfire of sexual politics and where popular perception increasingly is that if you experience same-gender attraction, the only way to live true to who you are is to pursue a gay or lesbian relationship. Because of this, it's more important than ever for Latter-day Saints dealing with these issues to seek as much understanding as they can and to hold up hopeful alternatives that are consistent with the teachings of The Church of Jesus Christ of Latter-day Saints.

Furthermore, as disciples of the Lord Jesus Christ, Latter-day Saints covenant at baptism to "mourn with those that mourn . . . and comfort those that stand in need of comfort" (Mosiah 18:9) and to "succor the weak, lift up the hands which hang down, and strengthen the feeble knees" (D&C 81:5). We can more effectively fulfill that

1

covenant responsibility to succor all of our Father's children, including those who experience same-gender attraction, as we feel their humanity by hearing their individual stories firsthand. This volume contains such essays of men and women who are living in harmony with the gospel of Jesus Christ and the teachings of His prophetic witnesses in relation to the eternal order of sexual expression, marriage, and family.

Our Need

Several years ago, President Hinckley identified three things every convert to the Church needs as he or she matures in the gospel: "a friend, a responsibility, and nurturing with 'the good word of God' (Moro. 6:4)."[2] I first heard President Hinckley's remarks while I was serving a mission, and I thought about his words often as they related directly to the work in which my companions and I were engaged.

In the years since that time, I've come to feel that President Hinckley's counsel is vital not just for converts but also for every son and daughter of God. Each of us yearns for a sense of community and belonging through close friendships with those who share various aspects of our life experience, we long to feel a deep sense of purpose and that we have something meaningful to contribute to the lives of those around us and toward the building up of Zion, and we all need a constant dose of the life-giving and regenerating power of God's eternal Spirit.

Sheri Dew confirmed the powerful impact of having these three needs met in her own life as a single, adult member of a church where family is everything. Reflecting on her experience, Sister Dew said:

"I have often been asked why I feel so comfortable as a never-married member in such a family-oriented Church.

"I do not understand this question, which implies that I would be happier if I were not a member of the Church. It also implies that happiness comes only to those whose lives are ideal, which would make, incidentally, for a very small group of happy people. So perhaps the question on some people's minds is really, How does someone in

2

nontraditional circumstances feel a sense of belonging in The Church of Jesus Christ? . . .

"As I have reflected on my experience in the Church and on the reasons I have felt so at home within this divinely inspired organization, I have concluded that it is because I have been blessed to have [President Hinckley's] three essential ingredients since the time I was young. . . .

"If there is anywhere in the world where every one of us, regardless of our personal circumstances, should feel accepted, needed, valued, and loved, it is within our Church family. And every one of us can reach out to others and help them feel a sense of belonging."[3]

As a thirty-something Latter-day Saint who has experienced same-gender attraction and who has wrestled to find answers concerning this complex issue, I understand what it is like to find oneself in "nontraditional circumstances" in the Church. Over the past several years as I've contemplated the reasons I feel so hopeful and happy, I have felt to echo the words of Sister Dew as my thoughts have repeatedly returned to these principles outlined by President Hinckley. Neither pen nor tongue can tell the gratitude I feel for the love I've received from family and friends who value me for all that I am, for a strong sense of spiritual mission that keeps me both grounded and growing in my faith in Jesus Christ, and for the eternal peace I've felt as the life-giving Spirit of the living God has nourished my oft-thirsty soul.

My Background

This was not always the case. There was a time when I felt growing discouragement and doubt that living gospel teachings was a realistic possibility for me. I wasn't sure I could continue on in the Church given the deep longings that persisted despite some very helpful work with a great LDS therapist. Because the few people I could find who also experienced same-gender attraction were either openly gay, living double lives, or simply didn't seem happy in what appeared to be white-knuckled efforts to live Church standards, I began to wonder if it was even possible to live the kind of life in the Church I had always hoped for. Eventually, I started to explore the possibility of a committed same-sex relationship despite my deep testimony of the gospel and my understanding that such a choice was inconsistent with what I knew to be true. I started to feel as though I didn't have any other choice for a happy life, and I longed for the strength and encouragement I believed could come from others who had dealt with similar issues but who were faithfully living the gospel and were willing to talk openly about it.

While I understood that there are legitimate reasons that people may choose to address these issues privately, I still longed to *really* know that there were faithful Latter-day Saints who were happy and successful in healthily addressing their feelings. The lack of these open voices, combined with the fact that the most insistent and prominent voices were telling me that the life I wanted with a thriving temple marriage and a family was simply unsustainable (and unfair for the Church to ask of me), left me feeling increasingly discouraged and hopeless.

All I could find on this issue from a faithful Latter-day Saint perspective seemed to be almost exclusively scientific or clinical in nature. In addition, it focused on how to overcome these feelings, with success stories ("success" usually being pretty narrowly defined) either artfully vague or safely concealed behind pseudonyms and broad clinical statistics, all of which perpetuated the shame with which I already struggled so much. I longed to hear the real, lived experiences of real, live Latter-day Saints—flesh-and-blood people who had been where I was. And when I grew weary of the polarized clinical rhetoric and political debates, I often sought solace with trusted teachers and leaders with whom I could talk about the issue from a more gospel-focused perspective. I wanted to believe that peace, at the very least, was possible, since "change" didn't seem to be happening as quickly as I would like. So even as I started to more openly explore the possibility of a gay relationship, I continued to attend meetings and activities where I hoped the Spirit would be present and give me some desperately needed personal guidance and comfort.

It was during one of these times that I had some sacred,

heart-changing spiritual experiences that reignited my rapidly fading hope for resolution and helped to reground me on a gospel path with a more optimistic and eternal perspective. I felt enveloped by the Spirit as it taught me that whether I ever married or achieved my desired transformation in this life, I was infinitely loved and accepted of God. My responsibility was to continue to live one day at a time while seeking and following the guidance of the Spirit. As I did so, I was assured that I would eventually receive every promised blessing of the gospel, including eternal marriage, whether in this life or the next. Something about that direct and divine communication to my heart liberated me. I felt a hope and joy and freedom in Christ that I hadn't felt in years.

This Book

As I was contemplating this experience, the idea for this book was born. Though I had found (and continue to find) good therapy helpful, it was the basic eternal truths of the gospel and Christ's Atonement, communicated to my heart through the power of the Holy Spirit, that soothed my soul and gave me renewed energy to keep moving forward with faith. I dreamed of a book with a collection of gospel teachings by respected inspirational writers that would speak of widely applicable gospel principles but be targeted directly toward LDS individuals and families dealing with issues related to same-gender attraction. My hope was that those teachings might facilitate further spiritual insight and encouragement for others.

In addition, in the years since that time, my initial yearning to meet Latter-day Saint men and women who have committed their lives to the gospel and who have experienced peace and resolution in that choice in various ways has been richly realized. Their stories and their tutoring examples—and in some cases, their personal support and friendship—have lifted and inspired me. I've longed for some kind of forum where their stories might benefit an even wider audience.

Although the idea I had for compilations of gospel teachings and first-person stories seemed like two very different projects, they came together when I recalled a lesson I had learned years earlier. For three years after returning home from my mission, I worked as an instructor at the Missionary Training Center in Provo, Utah. During my time there, I often heard referenced in talks and training some inspired counsel from Elder Bruce R. McConkie, who suggested that as we teach the gospel, "perhaps the perfect pattern . . . is to teach what is found in the scriptures and then to put a seal of living reality upon it by telling a similar and equivalent thing that has happened in our dispensation and to our people and—most ideally—to us as individuals." There is something inspiring, he taught, about having "stories of real people who faced real problems and who solved them in a way that was pleasing to the Lord."[4] I would add that equally valuable are the stories of those whose problems *aren't* fully solved, who may have yet to find the much sought-for resolution but who continue to exercise faith in the Lord—being "led by the Spirit, not knowing beforehand the things which [they] should do" (1 Nephi 4:6), and trusting that they will be led to their promised land "according to his own will and pleasure" (Mosiah 7:33).

It has been with Elder McConkie's pattern as a guiding principle that I have compiled this collection of gospel teachings and personal essays. The compilation is organized along loosely defined themes, with an introductory chapter expounding broadly applicable gospel teachings related to each theme. These chapters are written by some of the Church's seasoned teachers, who elaborate on the concept as they find it in the scriptures, the writings of latter-day prophets, and their experiences with LDS culture and perspectives. These authors do not personally experience same-gender attraction. Following each of these chapters is a handful of shorter, first-person essays by those who have wrestled directly with the issue of same-gender attraction in their lives, whether themselves or as parents, spouses, or priesthood leaders. These essays broadly correspond with the given themes, adding the "seal of living reality" Elder McConkie spoke of. "Unless our religion is a living thing," Elder McConkie said, "that changes the lives of people in whose nostrils the breath of life is now inhaled, it has no saving power."[5] My desire is that ever more Latter-day Saints will have opportunities to share their witness of how God's love and sustaining power have been made manifest in their lives.

In many ways, the selection of personal essays has been the most difficult part of this process. First, there are many men and women whose heroic stories of faith and commitment deserve a wider audience, and there simply hasn't been enough room in one volume to include them all. Second, I wanted to highlight a wide variety of ways to understand and respond to this issue while remaining firmly anchored within the umbrella of faithful adherence to core doctrines and standards of the Church. I may not have been entirely successful in that effort, but I hope that each of these essays will help our faith community piece together a broader, more textured approach to this issue, carving out a more compassionate place for all who strive to follow the Lord, regardless of their mortal circumstances.

Parenthetically, in discussions of homosexuality in our broader culture, we typically also hear about what are commonly referred to as *transgender* issues—feelings of disconnection or incongruence between a person's biological sex and the person's internal sense of gender. Gender incongruence is distinct from homosexual attraction in that few men and women who experience same-gender *attraction* desire to actually *be* the opposite sex, and men and women who experience feelings of gender incongruence may or may not experience sexual or romantic attractions to the same sex. While this collection of teachings and essays primarily addresses the Latter-day Saint experience with homosexual attraction, virtually untouched in faithful LDS literature are the stories of individuals who have struggled with gender identity or transgender feelings. There are untold numbers of Latter-day Saints who have struggled with these issues who are as equally in need of the love and sympathy and understanding of their brothers and sisters in the gospel. Within this collection is an essay by a man (John Alden) who is dealing with this distinct issue, although he doesn't experience homosexual attraction.

My Hope

My hope is that both the widely applicable gospel teachings and the narrative personal essays can serve readers of every background. Elder Richard G. Scott has taught, "As you seek spiritual knowledge, search for principles. Carefully separate them from the detail used to explain them. Principles are concentrated truth, packaged for application to a wide variety of circumstances. A true principle makes decisions clear even under the most confusing and compelling circumstances."[6] In the case of the principle-themed chapters, personal application is a clear imperative, but in the case of the narrative-focused essays, readers are invited to mine deeper nuggets of truth, "separate them from the detail used to explain them," and seek the Spirit for guidance concerning how those principles might be appropriately applied to their unique situations. It's also important to note that not everyone's story is the same, and the presentation of one person's story is not meant to suggest that it is the only right way.

I also hope that this collection might offer something akin to each of the three key human needs President Hinckley taught: that as readers hear the stories of others they will know that they are not alone either in their feelings or in their efforts to live the gospel, that they will gain a deeper appreciation for the truth that they belong in the Church and that they have a vital role in the growth and perfection of the Lord's kingdom, and, finally, that they will feel loved, nourished, and empowered in the life-giving word of Jesus Christ.

A Unique Approach

The approach to same-gender attraction in this book is unique among other traditional LDS approaches, and there are four broad concepts that have informed and framed the lenses through which I've taken this approach. Sadly, they are concepts that I feel have often been neglected in conversation about homosexuality in the LDS community and that I believe are critical to continuing dialogue.

Concept One: Rooted in Jesus Christ

Aside from doctrinal and ecclesiastical positions articulated by Church leaders, the bulk of what has been written about homosexuality from a faithful LDS perspective, or that has been promoted in the LDS community, has been scientific or clinical in nature, often with a focus on changing attractions and behavior. There is a place for helpful literature within that frame of reference, but it is only one thread of a much larger conversational tapestry.

Without minimizing the importance of continued research that the various scientific and social disciplines provide on this issue, or the place they have in LDS discourse, I have collected these chapters and essays with the primary intent to provide messages of gospel-centered hope in the work of Christ in which we are all engaged. As more and more voices share their personal experiences and perspectives, the more help we will have in ministering more effectively to the individuals and families dealing with these sensitive issues. As a practicing therapist and as one who has benefited from good therapy, I have strong convictions of the value of the human sciences and the healing professions. Nevertheless, when it comes to the issue of "change," I find even greater value in the wisdom of President Boyd K. Packer's teaching that "true doctrine, understood, changes attitudes and behavior." He added, "The study of the doctrines of the gospel will improve behavior quicker than a study of behavior will improve behavior."[7]

Although many men and women, including many of the authors of the personal narratives in this book, have experienced a significant shift in the nature of their attractions, this book isn't advocating one particular path or perspective of change. Among those authors who have experienced various types of change, change did not happen in the same way, and those authors who haven't (yet) experienced the types of change they hope for are still maintaining their gospel covenants. The common thread running through each of these essays concerns the spiritual change and the holistic transformation—a change in heart that is linked to becoming a disciple of Christ, whether or not it is accompanied by a change in orientation or attractions—that takes place when we center our lives in Christ and allow Him to consecrate all difficult circumstances for our gain (see 2 Nephi 2:2).

Affirming the importance of faith and testimony in response to same-gender attraction is not to endorse a shallow "pray the gay away" approach. What it does mean, however, is that even as we fully and humbly acknowledge all the complexities of our humanity and of life in a fallen world, we must bring those complexities to the altar of God, seek His guidance, and willingly surrender our entire hearts to Him and His work and glory (see Moses 1:39). Again, resources that help individuals explore the human dynamics of homosexuality are useful to many, but I believe that they are secondary to the spiritual capacities we cultivate as we surrender our hearts and lives to the Lord. Whatever other resources we may seek, whatever other helps or truths or programs we benefit from, President Packer has also taught that any truth not connected to "the very root of Christian doctrine"—the truth of Jesus' infinite love and atoning sacrifice—is insufficient. If branches of truth "do not touch that root, if they have been cut free from that truth, there will be no life nor substance nor redemption in them."[8] The call of Christ is to become *holy* before it is to become heterosexual.

Efforts to change or live in harmony with the behavioral standards of the Church that are disconnected from the Spirit-born faith, love, and "perfect brightness of hope" (2 Nephi 31:20) offered us by our Savior are at best insufficient and at worst empty and void of true life. And, I would suggest, they are at times even harmful. One young man said to me, "I had become so consumed with changing my sexual orientation that my relationship with my Savior kind of got pushed to the back. Things weren't in balance. I continue to do all that I can to experience a healthy shift in my sexuality, but as I've been able to reshift my primary focus back to the Savior, I've felt able to turn the timetable over to the Lord. I realize I need to focus instead on living my life such that I feel His presence, just as everyone else is trying to do."

Understanding the gospel of Jesus Christ is more than simply connecting a host of doctrinal dots that underscore a variety of behavioral dos and don'ts. The gospel of Jesus Christ is "the power of God unto salvation to every one that believeth" (Romans 1:16)—a power that runs in and through us, empowering us to do what we cannot do by ourselves. I still have much to learn about the Savior's Atonement, but according to my experiences thus far in life, the promise of the Atonement is as much a promise of peace and sustaining grace *during* our mortal challenges as it is a promise of deliverance through and from them (see Mosiah 24:10–16). It's important to understand that the redemption and transformation promised through Christ's Atonement far surpasses anything that can ever be fully realized in a fallen world.

I believe the mortal challenges of *all* people will be transformed through the power of Christ's redemption, but I also believe that those who promise through some spiritual platitude or therapeutic program that the Atonement will change them in this or that way may misunderstand the true nature of the Atonement and limit its power. Some seem to think of the Atonement more as a *tool* to be *used* than as a *power* to be *accessed*—a power that is God's alone to dispense. And it will be dispensed according to a mind and will and plan that is much bigger than any of us can fathom in our mortal myopia.

The promise of the Atonement, as I understand it, is that all the effects of the Fall—whether manifested intellectually, emotionally, physically, spiritually, or sexually—can be transformed through the power and grace of Christ either in time or eternity. Yet our human tendency, it seems, is to want to make the transformations we desire happen in our own time—which is usually yesterday—and we condition our faith in and allegiance to Christ and the Church upon it. As Elder Neal A. Maxwell observed: "When we are unduly impatient with an omniscient God's timing, we really are suggesting that we know what is best. Strange, isn't it—we who wear wristwatches seek to counsel Him who oversees cosmic clocks and calendars."9

As I strive to keep my focus on Jesus Christ and stay attuned to His life-giving Spirit, I experience His power. It's what keeps me going every day. And the more I've come to access and understand that power, the more my feelings resonate with one Christian author who stated:

"There are few things quite so boring as being religious, but there is nothing quite so exciting as being a Christian! Most folks have never discovered the difference between the one and the other, so that there are those who sincerely try to live a life they do not have, substituting religion for God, Christianity for Christ, and their own noble endeavors for the energy, joy, and power of the Holy Spirit. . . . They are lamps without oil, cars without gas, and pens without ink. . . .

"There are those who have a life they never live. They have come to Christ and thanked Him only for what He did, but do not live in the power of who He is. Between the Jesus who 'was' and the Jesus who 'will be,' they live in a spiritual vacuum, trying with no little zeal to live for Christ a life that only He can live in and through them."[10]

It is the truths of eternity, infused by the living Spirit of the living God, "not in tables of stone, but in fleshy tables of the heart" (2 Corinthians 3:3), that ultimately provide the hope and grace and divine tutelage men and women need to return to the Father's presence. It is also that same Spirit that may potentially guide them to seek professional assistance for particular temporal concerns. In my own experience, it was specific promptings from the Holy Ghost that led me to some of the best therapeutic help I've yet received and that made a healthy marriage to my beautiful and supportive wife a meaningful reality. But even with that said, it was an eternal perspective and the empowering companionship of the Spirit that have most inspired me to stay on (or return to) the path of discipleship during the times I was most discouraged.

One of my concerns with a disproportionate focus on the changeability of sexual orientation is that men and women who experience unchosen and often confusing feelings frequently come to believe that they are not worthy Latter-day Saints, even if they obey the laws of the gospel. They may also believe that they are not worthy of love and acceptance from the Saints below and God above—unless and until they can eliminate their homosexual attractions. At the same time, there are still many differences of opinion regarding tentative and evolving scientific theories about homosexuality. Such differences need not concern Latter-day Saints because they aren't nearly as important as the larger truth that obedience to the gospel and genuine happiness and peace through the Comforter are possible when we have anchored our lives and perspective in the revealed plan of our Heavenly Father. And the variety of therapeutic options, even though many may seem contradictory, means that if one approach isn't helpful, an individual is free to try another. We can be flexible in our personal response so long as we are firm in our covenants.

Too often the message that comes across is that unless and until an individual can be heralded as an example of complete reorientation, he or she cannot exist in a faithful Latter-day Saint context. "Those who have completed their change," this attitude implies, "are now welcome into the fold of true Latter-day Saint respectability." The many heroic stories of faith and commitment of those who are still striving, who believe in the ideal but haven't achieved it yet, seem to have had rare place in LDS discourse on this topic. And too often, when men and women have given so much of their emotional and temporal resources in sexual-reorientation efforts and then do not succeed as soon or as easily as they had hoped, they tragically conclude that God has rejected them. Such people can so thoroughly lose hope that they succumb to some of the worst forms of self-destructive behavior.

Of course it is wise to seek benefit from the best that modern helping professions can offer, provided that it is consistent with the gospel and helps individuals live more fully in harmony with their covenants and attain greater peace, fulfillment, and sense of individual worth. It's important to note, however, that if an individual's therapeutic work doesn't provide the anticipated results, that individual still has full access to the sustaining and redeeming power offered us through the Savior's atoning sacrifice. Even the best of practitioners, as finite mortals, have had clients beyond their reach. My testimony is that such people are never beyond the Savior's reach. Therapists, family members, friends, and others may fail them, but the Savior never will.

Thus, the "change" I desired to be the focus of this collection of gospel teachings and personal essays concerns the choices over which we have full control regarding keeping our behavior in line with our covenants. This collection also focuses on the change of desires in the spiritually reborn heart that comes through the gift and power and grace of Christ. My testimony is that if you keep your covenants, follow the Lord's servants, and endure to the end, then you are a worthy Latter-day Saint who is destined to inherit the celestial kingdom even if you experience homosexual attractions until your dying day. Some, like Paul with his "thorn in the flesh" (2 Corinthians 12:7), may have the gift and blessing of learning to trust that God's grace is sufficient for them.

In a book I was recently reading by a Buddhist psychotherapist, the author talked about how most religious traditions hold place for what she called "sacred pause."[11] I reflected on my own experiences with "sacred pause" in the temple, in prayer, and in quiet meditation. During those times, when my heart has simply been quiet for God, when I've slowed down enough to really listen to my feelings and attractions—not to fight or run or avoid or overcome but to merely listen without judgment—I've found that I'm taught those things I most need in order to grow in Christ and fulfill the measure of my creation. Through all that I've learned, same-gender attraction has become less my "struggle," my "problem," or my "cross." Rather, it has become more my teacher and my friend. I no longer hate my attractions as an enemy to be conquered; I honor them as a mentor—as a divinely orchestrated spiritual tutor—and as one of the greatest blessings the Lord has granted me. Without that mentor, I would never have been brought to my knees as I have been or brought to know Him as my Savior and Redeemer as I do.

I believe that if we had eyes to see the blessings that come through an honest and open engagement with all aspects of our complex human experience, we would echo the words of the prophet Brigham Young. If members of the Church had the eternities in full vision before their minds, he said, "there is not a trial which the Saints are called to pass through that they would not realize and acknowledge to be their greatest blessing."[12] We would see how the difficulties and tensions we experience in mortality refine and enlarge our souls for the greater good

Christ offers us and how they give us the greatest opportunity to exercise our agency in developing faith and the attributes of godliness. Elder Orson F. Whitney similarly taught, "No pain that we suffer, no trial that we experience is wasted. It ministers to our education, to the development of such qualities as patience, faith, fortitude and humility. All that we suffer and all that we endure, especially when we endure it patiently, builds up our characters, purifies our hearts, expands our souls, and makes us more tender and charitable, more worthy to be called the children of God."[13]

As a final point, the restored Church of Jesus Christ is a living church guided by living prophets (see D&C 1:30, 38). To be firmly rooted in Christ is to be firmly rooted in the living witness of His living oracles (see Mosiah 15:10–11). "Whether by mine own voice or by the voice of my servants," the Lord declared, "it is the same" (D&C 1:38).

While science can inform our understanding of sexuality as part of the broad spectrum of our human experience, it is still far from conclusive on the origin and development of sexuality in all its qualitative variations from person to person. And it will never be sufficient to frame the eternal lenses through which we see our potential and guide our life's choices.

It's important for us to understand that the Lord's prophets need not be experts in all things human in order to be a prophetic medium for things divine. In a 2004 interview with television host Larry King, President Hinckley stated that he didn't fully understand all the complex issues associated with homosexuality. "I'm not an expert on these things," he said. "I don't pretend to be an expert on these things."[14] We will continue to learn much about the human dynamics associated with homosexual attraction and the myriad potential factors influencing its development through the scientific disciplines, but God's living oracles have spoken clearly and with divine authority regarding the order and appropriate bounds of sexual expression. If the findings of modern science appear to contradict the teachings of the living prophets, our proximate understanding is either incorrect or incomplete.

The late Hugh Nibley, a respected Latter-day Saint scholar, wrote:

"The words of the prophets cannot be held to the tentative and defective tests that men have devised for them. Science, philosophy, and common sense all have a right to their day in court. But the last word does not lie with them. Every time men in their wisdom have come forth with the last word, other words have promptly followed. The last word is a testimony of the gospel that comes only by direct revelation. Our Father in Heaven speaks it, and if it were in perfect agreement with the science of today, it would surely be out of line with the science of tomorrow. Let us not, therefore, seek to hold God to the learned opinions of the moment when he speaks the language of eternity."[15]

Concept Two: Proximate vs. Ultimate Hope

An outgrowth of living faith in the living Christ—and another of the central themes running through the chapters and essays in this volume—is hope. *True* hope keeps us going when the right choices are the hard choices. It enables us to see something beautiful and sanctifying on the other side of adversity. The prophet Moroni wrote, "Wherefore, whoso believeth in God might with surety hope for a better world, yea, even a place at the right hand of God, which hope cometh of faith, maketh an anchor to the souls of men, which would make them sure and steadfast, always abounding in good works, being led to glorify God" (Ether 12:4).

Generally, there seems to be two polar approaches to homosexuality, both of which condition hope and happiness on the possibility (or impossibility) of "change." First, there are those who insist that homosexual orientation is inborn; they see a life of faith and devotion to the Church as incompatible with happiness for individuals with same-sex attraction. They insist that the only way for same-sex-oriented people to be happy, healthy, and well-balanced is to leave the Church or to demand that the Church alter its teachings and practices in a way that will make room for gay or lesbian relationships. They do not allow for the possibility that for some individuals, sexual orientation may be sufficiently fluid or flexible to allow for satisfying, heterosexual relational intimacy. For those who affirm the teachings of the Lord's prophets and apostles regarding heterosexual marriage and sexual expression, the problems with this approach are clear.

On the other side of the spectrum, some people, as a well-intentioned means of offering hope to those seeking resolution to their feelings, focus on environmental and relational factors in the development of homosexual attractions to demonstrate the possibility of their elimination. These people continually promote stories of those who have done so. The problem with this approach is that it often leads people to anchor their hope in change of sexual orientation rather than in Christ. And then if efforts to change don't work or don't work as quickly as expected, this approach actually has the potential to increase despair rather than hope.

The stories of those who have experienced a meaningful and lasting shift in the nature of their attractions are valuable—this volume includes many of them—but they must be placed within a larger conception of the spectrum of faithful responses to homosexuality. When therapist-mediated reorientation is promoted as the only means of offering hope, and when the only messages people hear are how their attractions will go away if they just apply the right formula—the right therapy, the correct application of a set of temporal and spiritual practices, and so forth—then these therapies and formulas, if they don't work, have the unwitting potential of doing spiritual and psychological harm.

The gospel of Jesus Christ is a gospel of change, of course, but some people in their eagerness to help or provide hope make promises the Savior never did. And when we make promises the Savior hasn't made in order to instill a hope that only He can offer, we do a disservice both to Him and to those who seek to follow Him with faith built upon an eternal foundation. Hope conditioned on sexual reorientation is like the house built upon the sand, while the hope promised through the eternal vision offered in Christ—the only hope that saves—is the rock upon which we must build our lives. "If in this life only we have hope in Christ," the Apostle Paul declared, "we are of all men most miserable" (1 Corinthians 15:19).

Just as the first principle of the gospel is not faith alone but rather faith *in the Lord Jesus Christ,* so it is not hope alone that anchors our souls but rather hope *in Jesus Christ.* Elder Maxwell was clear to distinguish between "ultimate hope" and "proximate hope." Every one of us may hold tightly to the truth that we *all* can have ultimate hope in Jesus Christ—a hope that growth and transformation and transcendence of all the effects of the Fall are assured and extend even beyond the grave—while proximate hopes are more temporal in nature and may not always be realized. Elder Maxwell wrote:

"Having ultimate hope does not mean we will always be rescued from proximate problems, but we will be rescued from everlasting death! Meanwhile, ultimate hope makes it possible to say the same three words used centuries ago by three valiant men. They knew God could rescue them from the fiery furnace, if He chose. 'But if not,' they said, nevertheless, they would still serve Him! (Dan. 3:18.) . . .

"Though 'anchored' in grand and ultimate hope, some of our tactical hopes are another matter. We may hope for a pay raise, a special date, an electoral victory, or for a bigger house—things which may or may not be realized. Faith in Father's plan gives us endurance even amid the wreckage of such proximate hopes. Hope keeps us 'anxiously engaged' in good causes even when these appear to be losing causes (D&C 58:27)."[16]

The hopeful message I pray comes through this volume is that individuals who experience homosexual attractions can find happiness and fulfillment in the Church and that they can find joy and meaning in their journeys through mortality, even before they have completely resolved their feelings of same-gender attraction. While growth and change are inevitable when we submit our lives to the Lord, we cannot hold the Lord hostage to an arbitrary timetable or qualify our faith in Christ and devotion to His Church upon some dangerously narrow characterization of what change should look like. The mixture and degree of influencing factors of homosexual attraction—whether biological, psychological, emotional, or relational—are so different for everyone that "one size fits all" explanations or formulas simply cannot account for all the variety encountered.

"As for why you feel as you do," Elder Jeffrey R. Holland reported saying to one young man, "I can't answer that question. A number of factors may be involved, and they can be as different as people are different. Some things, including the cause of your feelings, we may never know in this life."[17] But, he stated on another occasion: "I do know that this will not be a post-mortal condition. It will not be a post-mortal difficulty. . . . I want that to be of some hope to some."[18]

With an eternal hope offered through the Spirit, we understand that for every blind man who experiences the miracle of sight (see John 9:1–7) there is at least one Paul who pleads for the transformative power of Christ only to be given the simple assurance that Christ's grace is sufficient, even as human weakness and struggle remain. Ultimate hope—*saving* hope—is grounded in an eternal perspective, with reliance upon the promise that whatever burdens the Lord doesn't remove He will lighten, even to the point that we "cannot feel them upon [our] backs" (Mosiah 24:14).

Concept Three: "Standing As Witnesses of God" —Passing the Baton of Primary Voice

One reason I believe the inclusion of personal essays in this volume is important is that they give the witness of lived experience where it belongs: to those with lived experience. For too long, those who don't have personal experience with same-gender attraction have dominated the discussion around these issues. While those perspectives are highly valuable, we're long overdue for those voices to step back and assume a more supportive role to those who understand these issues firsthand.

Perhaps a valuable metaphor for this idea can be found in the words of LDS convert Roger R. Keller, a former Presbyterian minister and current professor of Church history and doctrine at Brigham Young University. At the "Worlds of Joseph Smith" conference in 2005, where both LDS and other respected scholars gathered to commemorate the Prophet's life and work, Brother Keller noted the value of having those from outside Mormon tradition share their perspectives of Mormon faith and practice. He also noted that this value has inherent weakness. "I know the limitations of [this] approach," he said, "having . . . stood outside of [Mormon tradition] myself at one point in my life. No matter how hard I tried then to be fair to Joseph Smith and Mormonism . . . as an outsider I can never articulate another's tradition quite the way that a practitioner of that particular faith could or would. I might come close, but there will always be something I overlook or do not completely comprehend."[19]

As a Latter-day Saint, imagine what your understanding of yourself and your faith would be like if you had to rely solely upon outside scholars who didn't share important aspects of your life experience. From the perspective of many who experience same-gender attraction, too much of the discussion of this issue has been like that. While there is great value in the work and perspectives of other concerned voices who have devoted much of their time and resources to assisting those who have struggled with homosexual feelings, those perspectives can never be as salient as the perspectives of those who have dealt with these issues firsthand.

We live in a time when popular cultural discussion of these issues is becoming increasingly strident and uncivil. It is more important than ever for individuals of faith to share their stories and bear witness in a way that has potential to build bridges of understanding and present positive alternatives to the increasingly narrow polemics that dominate public discourse on homosexuality today. More than ever before, those striving to live in harmony with the gospel of Jesus Christ need to step out of the shadows and let their voices be heard. If their voices are obscured through anonymity, mediated by clinicians, or shielded by spokespeople, they will simply never match the credibility or impact of the numerous first-person accounts that dominate the broader cultural discussion and that do not understand the eternal truths for which those who have contributed to this volume stand.

In order for more faithful Latter-day Saints to be willing to share their perspectives, we need to create space where these men and women can authentically share their experience and witness of Christ without fear of judgment or retribution. A friend of mine, a lifelong and seasoned member of the Church who has experienced significant resolution to his homosexual feelings, shared with me the following as he contemplated how open he should be when sharing his story: "When I made the final decision to use my real name, knowing the potential for backlash, I decided that there is a war being waged, and our side is losing while gay cultural ideologies are winning. We are losing because people like me feel the need to hide and pretend. I pretend not out of fear of the gay community; I pretend out of fear of the negative reaction I will get from people in the Church." There is something clearly problematic in our traditional approaches to this issue when committed disciples can't share their authentic witness of Christ or tell their personal stories of hope and faith and transformation without fear of backlash and retribution from fellow believers.

As cultural battles continue to wage ever more passionately, and as the restored gospel of Jesus Christ continues to go forth to every nation, kindred, tongue, and people, the Church's teachings regarding homosexuality will increasingly affect how people respond to our message. I suggest that in addition to the continued witness and teachings of the Lord's prophets and apostles on this issue, there will be an increasing need for "a cloud of witnesses" (Hebrews 12:1)—Latter-day Saint men and women who have personally dealt with these issues.

I was recently contacted by a bishop in California who was choking back tears as he expressed his gratitude for the growing number of Latter-day Saints who are willing to add a real face and name to this issue in their efforts to live faithful to the gospel. Just months prior, same-gender attraction had been simply an issue he dealt with as a priesthood leader or as it related to California's Proposition 8 campaign to stop same-sex marriage. Then his son confided in him regarding his own private struggle with feelings of same-gender attraction. In an instant, the issue took form in one of the people he loves most in his life. Not being aware of any nonpolitical resources that addressed homosexuality from his faithful perspective, the bishop, as he went looking for help, said he wanted to believe that there were real people, believing Latter-day Saints, who had worked through their feelings and had come out on the side of active faith in gospel teachings. For him and his family, to find a host of such Latter-day Saints brought him and his wife to their knees in gratitude before the Lord.

As Latter-day Saints prayerfully decide how open they should be, it's important to understand two potential extremes to which many are tempted, both of which are inconsistent with the gospel of Christ. The story of Adam and Eve's garden narrative serves as a valuable metaphor. After Adam and Eve had partaken of the fruit of the tree of the knowledge of good and evil, Satan shamed them, telling them to hide from God's presence. God had other plans, however. He called them out of the bushes, out of darkness and hiding—their proverbial closets, if you will—and into His light. He didn't chastise or shame them. Their mortality would play an essential role in their eternal progression. Yet He didn't tell them to go marching in the "mortal pride parade." Rather, He called them to the altar of covenant. While fully acknowledging their mortality and the associated blessings and weaknesses it would bring, God taught them of redemption and eternal possibilities, for which they rejoiced and praised His name (see Moses 5:5–12). He then called them to be witnesses of both His love and His law.[20]

I suggest that there is a contemporary equivalent to how God would have us respond to issues associated with same-gender attraction. Hiding in shame or fear is no more God's way than are rainbow festivals or pride parades—both are distortions that grow out of the same dark spiritual and emotional shadows. And those who choose or advocate for either extreme serve only those same ends Satan sought in Eden—to keep us from fully embracing the true light and consecrated life of the Holy One. As we come to understand and similarly learn from Adam and Eve's divine tutorial, we are opened up to a sacred spiritual and emotional space where neither shame nor pride exist.

We understand that all difficult aspects of our mortal experience can be for our eternal growth and good if we will but relate to them more as teacher than tormentor. Then, from the altar of covenant, as we rejoice in the promises of reconciliation and exaltation in Christ, God calls us to stand as authentic and open witnesses of His love and redemption "at *all* times and in *all* things, and in *all* places that [we] may be in" (Mosiah 18:9; emphasis added). And if that witness is rejected or ridiculed, we know we stand with the Apostles of old, who rejoiced "that they were counted worthy to suffer shame for his name" (Acts 5:41).

Concept Four: Our Covenant to Mourn and to Comfort

The fourth broad concept framing this collection concerns each of us in the Latter-day Saint community at large, whether or not we personally deal with homosexual issues or are close to someone who does. By giving a human face to the issue through first-person narratives of real people with real feelings, I hope this collection will help members of the Church learn more about what it feels like to experience these challenges firsthand and thereby exhibit a greater sense of compassion and understanding. For Latter-day Saints to more effectively fulfill their covenant responsibility to "mourn with those that mourn . . . and comfort those that stand in need of comfort" (Mosiah 18:9), to "succor the weak, lift up the hands which hang down, and strengthen the feeble knees" (D&C 81:5), we need to spend time with others, seeking to understand the depth of their humanity.

Not all issues surrounding mortality, including homosexuality, are as clear-cut as we would like them to be. Even when we may not always agree with what others have to say, we should not be afraid of sincerely opening our minds and hearts to simply listen—to understand the length and breadth of what it means to be human from the perspectives of others whose mortal experiences, challenges, or beliefs have been different from our own. We need not compromise revealed doctrines or inspired convictions in doing so. In fact, such explorations may provide us with opportunities to more fully discover the godly heart and the divine nature—whereby we come to know more fully of the Savior's infinite love for each of our Father's children. The Savior had to go to people where they were. Often, those sheep were wandering, lost in the mountains. We, as His emissaries, must do the same. And we cannot find people until we know where they are.

Suppose a same-sex couple were to walk into an LDS church with the desire of learning and worshipping with everyone else. How would we respond to them? Would we tell them they are not welcome? Would we shy away from them and avoid interacting with them? Or would we recognize that everyone has eternal value and spiritual needs, regardless of where they are in their personal journey back to our Heavenly Father? Would we reach out to them, talk with them, befriend them, sit with them, and let them know that they are welcome in our midst? Would we encourage them to live as many principles of the gospel as they are willing to live and to learn and grow and seek the guidance of the Spirit in making important decisions about their lives?

One of the hallmark witnesses of President Thomas S. Monson's prophetic leadership has been the importance of personal, one-on-one ministry. We must make sure that "issues" never lose their human face. Elder Stephen L Richards taught that while Jesus Christ brought the gospel to humanity, "it is *our* duty to bring humanity to the Gospel."[21] Members of the Church, who cannot realistically be expected to master all the science behind the causes of and therapeutic responses to homosexual attractions, can nevertheless transform the shame and burden associated with this issue through the everyday practice of unfeigned love and compassion.

President Dieter F. Uchtdorf stated that of all qualities Latter-day Saints have the potential to be known for—from images of clean-cut missionaries to friendly and family-oriented neighbors who don't smoke or drink—the most important is to be known as a community that embodies divine love. "Because love is the great commandment," he taught, "it ought to be at the center of all and everything we do in our own family, in our Church callings, and in our livelihood. Love is the healing balm that repairs rifts in personal and family relationships. It is the bond that unites families, communities, and nations. Love is the power that initiates friendship, tolerance, civility, and respect. It is the source that overcomes divisiveness and hate. Love is the fire that warms our lives with unparalleled joy and divine hope. Love should be our walk and our talk."[22]

Regrettably, when it comes to how many in our community have historically responded to the issue of homosexual attraction or men and women who experience it, love and compassion are not the first words that come to mind. That said, we've improved immeasurably over the past several years. When Church historian Elder Marlin K. Jensen of the Seventy was interviewed for the 2007 PBS documentary *The Mormons,* producer Helen Whitney asked if he felt that there had been a change in how Church members have approached the issue of homosexuality. "Yes, I do," he replied. "We're more enlightened. We're more accepting in the sense that we understand this is a condition that some people are dealing with and that even if it needs changing or even if it needs controlling, that can't be done without our support, our love, our empathy, our interest in them as people. That's much different, I'm sure, than it was in my youth."[23]

My own experience is that this support, love, empathy, and interest Elder Jensen speaks of is more spontaneously and abundantly offered than ever before by the collective Church body, and we continue to grow ever more Christlike in this way. I'm encouraged that those growing up in or joining the Church today will find much more empathy and sensitivity as they seek to understand and respond healthily to their feelings than perhaps those of earlier generations. Even so, there is room for growth, and the Lord's prophets have offered inspired instructions in that regard. In an article on assisting those who struggle with same-gender attraction, Elder Holland stated, "Some members exclude from their circle of fellowship those who are different. When our actions or words discourage someone from taking full advantage of Church membership, we fail them—and the Lord. The Church is made stronger as we include every member and strengthen one another in service and love (D&C 84:110)."[24]

President Uchtdorf similarly counseled:

"Unfortunately, from time to time we . . . hear of Church members who become discouraged and subsequently quit coming to and participating in our Church meetings because they think they don't fit in. . . .

"I hope that we welcome and love all of God's children, including those who might dress, look, speak, or just do things differently. It is not good to make others feel as though they are deficient. Let us lift those around us. Let us extend a welcoming hand. Let us bestow upon our brothers and sisters in the Church a special measure of humanity, compassion, and charity so that they feel, at long last, they have finally found home. . . .

"I am not suggesting that we accept sin or overlook evil, in our personal life or in the world. Nevertheless, in our zeal, we sometimes confuse sin with sinner, and we condemn too quickly and with too little compassion. We know from modern revelation that 'the worth of souls is great in the sight of God' [D&C 18:10]. We cannot gauge the worth of another soul any more than we can measure the span of the universe."[25]

In this battle for souls, as homosexuality becomes an increasingly prevalent social and political issue, more and more Latter-day Saints are being seduced by cultural ideologies that are inconsistent with the truths of the Restoration. Often it's not just individuals dealing with the issue who are leaving the Church but also their LDS friends and family members. My hope is that the more we live the harmonious balance of covenant discipleship and unfeigned love and compassion, the more likely it will be that those who struggle to reconcile the Church's teachings on homosexuality with their perception of homosexuality will seek to find the peace and resolution they desire within the protective walls of Christ's church and kingdom. For those who struggle with such reconciliation, Elder Joseph B. Wirthlin counseled:

"To you who have strayed because you have been offended, can you not set your hurt and anger aside? Can you not fill your hearts with love? There is a place for you here. Come, join the fold, consecrate your abilities, talents, and skills. You will be better for it, and others will be blessed by your example.

"To those who have strayed because of doctrinal concerns, we cannot apologize for the truth. We cannot deny doctrine given to us by the Lord Himself. On this principle we cannot compromise. I understand that sometimes people disagree with doctrine. They even go so far as to call it foolish. But I echo words of the Apostle Paul, who said that sometimes spiritual things can appear as foolishness to men. Nevertheless, 'the foolishness of God is wiser than men' [1 Corinthians 1:25; see also 1:18]."[26]

There have been and will continue to be times when Latter-day Saints will be an active voice in the cultural debates about homosexuality. There will be times when we must, as the Lord has directed, teach and "reprov[e] betimes with sharpness"—that is, with clarity and boldness. Even so, that is only the first part of our gospel stewardship. After those times when we—of covenant necessity—must teach and preach hard truths, we are then called to act with "an increase of love toward him whom [we have] reproved, lest he esteem [us] to be his enemy" (D&C 121:43). My concern is that we've perhaps given too much heed to the first part of that call without equal heed to the second part, and our efforts have thus been perceived more as prejudice masquerading as principle than as a demonstration of God's perfect love and eternal plan for all of His children. Unless we give ever more emphasis to truly cultivating and expressing God's gift of divine love, we may be perceived more as a hateful enemy than as a loving witness.

As we share the message of the restored gospel of Jesus Christ, not all will be ready to receive it in the timetable we would like. But through the practice of true friendship and unfeigned love, we might do much to soften hearts, heal wounds, and change perspectives. In an 1896 letter to his missionary son, President Joseph F. Smith offered wise counsel regarding the attitude and approach we would do well to emulate: "Kindness will beget friendship and favor, but anger or passion will drive away sympathy. To win one's respect and confidence, approach him mildly, kindly. No friendship was ever gained by an attack upon principle or upon man, but by calm reason and the lowly Spirit of Truth. If you have built for a man a better house than his own, and he is willing to accept yours and forsake his, then, and not till then, should you proceed to tear down the old structure. Rotten though it may be, it will require some time for it to lose *all* its charms and fond memories of its former occupant. Therefore let *him,* not *you,* proceed to tear it away. Kindness and courtesy are the primal elements of gentility."[27]

A friend of mine who worked with a wilderness survival program for troubled teenagers told me about one teen who was so angry about being in the program that as soon as she got a chance, she bolted from the program's office. Two staff members who were going to be walking the trail with her followed her. She got into a dry cement canal and started running down it. The staff started running with her. The girl was running without her shoes, and rocks and glass started cutting up her feet. The two staff members removed their own shoes and continued running with her. Her heart was eventually softened by their actions. She realized that the pain she was experiencing was because of her own rebelliousness, yet here were people not scorning her, not trying to force her to make the right decision, but instead willing to experience the pain along with her. The actions of the staff members left an indelible mark on her.

Those I'm personally most grateful for are those who, in my own times of ignorance or rebellion, have taken off their shoes and walked with me and loved me. While maintaining full fidelity to the principles of the restored gospel, I hope fervently that this volume will better equip Latter-day Saints to reach out with ever more empathy and compassion—to likewise remove their shoes—to a group who most desperately need to know of the Savior's love and grace. I hope that as individuals and as a collective community we can truly reflect the nature and love of Christ to men and women who experience same-gender attraction. I firmly believe that those who love most and love longest will be the ones who win the hearts of God's children. As one friend of mine has said, "If they feel the most love in the gay and lesbian cultural community, that community wins; if they feel it with God's covenant people, then we win."

Conclusion

I hope you will find the teachings and essays in this volume beneficial. If you personally experience same-gender attraction, I hope the Spirit will impress upon you the depth of God's love for you, that you will know you belong in His church and kingdom, and that you will know there are many who walk this journey of faith with you. If you are a family member, friend, or ecclesiastical steward who loves someone dealing with these issues, I hope you will feel even greater empathy and capacity to support your loved one in a way that will inspire that person either to remain faithful to gospel covenants or to eventually return to his or her spiritual roots in Christ. Finally, if you are simply seeking a greater level of understanding, for any reason, I hope you will feel greater empathy and capacity to reach out with love for all of God's children. With all of my heart, I thank you for reading.

Chapter 1

Seeing the Big Picture

Brad Wilcox

As I have had the opportunity to serve in various Church leadership positions, it has been my responsibility and privilege to interview many people. In those private, confidential moments, sensitive issues are often discussed and personal questions often asked. Of all the questions, one of the most difficult to answer is "Am I gay?" It comes from those who are worried or struggling. It sometimes is not even verbalized. Instead, the question is seen behind insecure and frightened eyes. The question has come from young and old, married and unmarried, male and female, active and inactive Latter-day Saints.

I once heard the question from a young woman who was concerned that she was getting older and was still unmarried. She felt rejected and overlooked by men. The few dates she had were not positive experiences. When she began realizing that she felt closer to her female roommates than she did to any of the men in her ward, she began to wonder about sexual orientation.

Another time the question came from a young man who had been involved with some sexual experimentation with other boys in his neighborhood at sleepovers when they were deacons. Years later the experiences haunted him and made him question his sexuality.

Another young man asked me the question after his mission. Despite all the warnings of priesthood leaders, he had become involved with pornography and found himself curious about viewing men as well as women. As he compared his body to those in the pictures, he began to wonder if such comparisons were normal.

Similarly, one boy felt much guilt as he sized up other boys in the locker room. Even something as simple as a "shirts" vs. "skins" basketball game at church left him feeling great shame because he felt that he shouldn't be noticing the physiques of the other boys, and yet he was.

The question came from a young man who had been sexually molested by an older male. His parents told him the abuse was not his fault, and he accepted that. Still, deep in his heart he carried unspoken fears about his sexuality because when he had been touched, his body had responded. Since he didn't stop the man quickly, this young man still felt that he was partly to blame.

I was asked the question from a young man who had always felt rejected by other males. He had a sensitive nature, a tender heart, and many artistic talents that sometimes made him a target for teasing. A popular boy his own age finally offered the acceptance and friendship for which he had longed but also introduced him to homosexual practices. Soon the young man felt trapped into trading sexual favors for continued association with the popular boy.

The question came from a man who had absolutely no history of molestation, abuse, pornography, or sexual experimentation. He came from a strong and happy family. He said, "Whatever factors have led to the development of these feelings and attractions have been so subtle that it is difficult to put my finger on any one thing. Perhaps it had to do with attachment issues or my own self-concept, but my earliest attractions were always toward other boys, and I worry how they might affect my ability to develop a healthy and meaningful relationship with a woman."

Others may have similar stories but hesitate to ever voice their private concerns for fear of how they might be viewed or labeled. They simply bottle up the past and refuse to address it. Shared or not, the question "Am I gay?" is difficult to answer because *gay* has come to mean so many different things to people in our society.

Some of us still remember when the word *gay* meant happy. We sang songs in elementary school that used the word. Now the same songs can't be sung without snickers from even the youngest children. Parents used to name their children Gaye or Gaylan, never dreaming that such names would be problematic.

Today *gay* refers to homosexuals, but even that definition is unclear and misunderstood. Are we talking about homo-emotional needs common to everyone, or are we talking about homosexual tendencies felt by some and not others? Are those tendencies due to natural curiosity and early sexual experimentation, or do homosexual temptations increase as a consequence of prolonged interactions with those who have chosen that lifestyle? When we speak of homosexuals, are we talking about a unique gender or a sexual preference that develops over time due to a variety of factors? Does the word *gay* refer to a person, an act, an instinct, or a feeling? For every question there are many answers representing multiple viewpoints. Such confusion often leads to bitter arguments in which people on all sides of the issue can easily feel misunderstood, hurt, or offended.

I don't pretend to have answers to such complex issues. However, when people have asked me, "Am I gay?" some have felt relieved to learn that homo-emotional needs are real and acceptable. The word *intimacy* is often associated with sexual acts, but it doesn't need to be. Nonsexual intimacy is essential to our growth and development at all ages of our lives. We all need to love and be loved by both women and men. Meeting that need in healthy ways is one of the foundations of happiness as well as mental and emotional wellness. Often the feelings and attractions we have toward others are evidence of a deep need within us. Once recognized, it is up to us to fill that need in ways that are in harmony with God's plan for our lives and relationships. Similarly, hunger lets your body know of a need for food, but we must choose to meet that need with a healthy and nutritious diet rather than with potato chips or french fries.

Often I have explained that sexual experimentation at young ages, though not condoned or encouraged, is a phase through which many children and teenagers pass. "Playing doctor" with those of the same or opposite gender is considered quite normal and does not need to be a source of guilt and self-doubt.

Many young people have felt relieved when they learn that natural curiosity about the human body is not limited to the opposite sex. The human body can be considered beautiful and appealing to the senses no matter the gender. Taking notice of someone else's body during a sporting event or in the locker room does not indicate a fixed sexual orientation. Even when such notice involves an emotional charge, a physiological response, or even sexual arousal, such responses are quite normal—especially in the young and inexperienced. Perhaps more hurtful in the long run than the curiosity is the shame that young people feel because no one has ever explained that their feelings can often be chalked up to normal adolescent development. It is the shame associated with such feelings that gives rise to fears and anxiety that can affect future choices.

Some who have been molested and who understand that they were without fault still experience needless guilt about "feeling good" during the experience. Within marriage, sexual experiences are supposed to feel good. Imitating those experiences outside of marriage is wrong, but our bodies will respond whether they are touched by a spouse, a friend, or a stranger. Those who have been molested should not feel guilty or responsible for having normal, healthy bodies that respond naturally. In the same situation, anyone's body would have responded the exact same way.

Others feel guilty because of sexual explorations well beyond childhood. Again, while such behavior is not condoned, it is understandable. When curiosity is mixed with normal hormones, it can lead to explorations. Our bodies are ready for sexual experiences long before our minds, hearts, and spirits are mature enough to handle them correctly. When such explorations occur with those of the same gender, do such behaviors qualify as gay or indicate a permanent lifestyle? Couldn't we just as easily attribute such behavior to youth and immaturity and feeling more comfortable with those of the same gender? Such moments do not need to define, limit, or bind us. Such transgressions can be repented of and do not need to affect future choices.

One woman felt confused when she read an article in which the author described homosexuality as a genetic variation. I responded that even if some people may be born with genetic or temperamental factors that predispose them toward homosexual feelings, those factors don't remove their agency or responsibility to make appropriate choices. Similar articles report genetic variations that are believed to make certain people more likely to overeat or have lower metabolisms. Such a situation may explain certain tendencies or behaviors, but it doesn't excuse them. In any facet of life, certain healthy choices may be harder to make for some than others, but they are important for all of us. Those who make them never regret it. Those who don't almost always wish they had.

"Am I gay?" When I am asked that question I no longer attempt to determine what that word may or may not mean to that particular person. Instead, I usually respond by saying, "You are a child of God." The questioners sometimes feel that I am avoiding the issue, but that is not the case. I am simply trying to lift their vision beyond society-shaped words and conflicting definitions to see a broader picture. Seeking an eternal perspective will allow us to understand God's ultimate desire for us, the Savior's redeeming role, and the perfect and infinite love of the Father and the Son.

God's Desire for Us

In Genesis we read, "God created man in his own image" (Genesis 1:27). An entirely new perspective awaits those who see God's own image as the eventual end as well as the beginning. Christ prayed that we might be one with Him as He is with the Father (see John 17:11; 21–22). That heartfelt desire went way beyond a plea for unity. He was speaking about sameness.

Christian writer John Stott wrote, "We are not interested in skin-deep holiness, in a merely external resemblance to Jesus Christ. We are not satisfied by a superficial modification of behavior patterns in conformity to some . . . sub-culture which expects this, commands that and prohibits the other. No, what we long for is a deep inward change of character, resulting from a change of nature and leading to a radical change of conduct. In a word we want to be like Christ and that thoroughly, profoundly, entirely. Nothing less than this will do."[1]

Sincere Latter-day Saints not only share this desire but also know how it can become a reality. We know what Jesus has asked of us in order to make such a transformation possible. From childhood we learn of faith, which includes repentance and making and keeping covenants. We demonstrate faith by receiving from those having authority essential ordinances and the gift of the Holy Ghost to guide and sanctify as we endure to the end.

God gives these requirements—not in an effort to control us but rather to transform us. His expectations are not about punishment or payment but rather about practicing living as He lives. Some say God's goal is to bring us safely home, but that sentiment does not express His complete desire. Not only does He want us home, but He also wants us to be able to feel at home. If simply being in God's presence is the ultimate goal, why did we ever leave in the first place? In the premortal existence we were already with God, but we were also painfully aware that we were not like Him physically or spiritually. We wanted to be like our heavenly parents and knew it was going to take a lot more than just dressing up in their clothes the way little children do. We needed to fill their shoes and not just clomp around in them. The ultimate goal is not just being *with* God but being *like* God.

This perspective changes how we view difficulties. It allows us to see them as opportunities for refining and soul-expanding growth rather than simply as challenges to be dealt with or crosses to be carried. This perspective allows us to see the Fall and all its consequences as a blessing instead of a curse and mortality itself—as difficult as it can be—as an ideal learning environment rather than a tragic mistake. We can see God's commandments as positives instead of negatives, freedom instead of bondage.

Members of many religions have rules. The knowledge that sets

Latter-day Saints apart is the reason for the rules. The Restoration was not a restoration of rules. The Ten Commandments and the Sermon on the Mount had survived the long night of apostasy. What the world had lost sight of was why God gave rules in the first place. In Alma 12:32 we read, "Therefore God gave unto them commandments, *after* having made known unto them the plan of redemption" (emphasis added).

Commandments without the perspective of the plan of salvation can easily be seen as hollow and meaningless ends in and of themselves. When we know God's ultimate desires for us, living the commandments becomes the means to an end more glorious than we can hardly imagine. "Eye hath not seen, nor ear heard, neither have entered into the heart of man, the things which God hath prepared for them that love him" (1 Corinthians 2:9).

Both Christ and Satan desire us to become as they are, and each choice we make takes us in one direction or the other. When someone asks, "Am I gay?" perhaps the response should be, "How do you want to live your life?" We can make choices that will help us feel the guiding and sanctifying power of the Spirit in our lives, or we can distance ourselves from it. We can keep striving to be like Christ and Heavenly Father, who don't want us to trade eternity for an instant, or like Satan, who wants us to focus only on the here and now. Satan thinks nothing of asking us to exchange all we have and might become for what is, in the eternal perspective, a few fleeting moments of mortality. Christ, on the other hand, gave all that He had so that those fleeting moments could educate and enrich us rather than condemn us. He opened the door for all of us to reach our potential.

The Savior's Redeeming Role

Still, some days that potential seems like an impossible dream. We see where we are now and how far we have to go, and we feel that there is just no way it could ever really happen. At these low moments some people give up and turn away from the Savior. It seems easier to try to justify and rationalize poor choices instead of humbly trusting Christ's enabling power—not just to save but also to redeem (see Romans 8:12–13). If saving were all we needed, Satan's plan could have worked. He offered to get us back safely. It is the redeeming we would have missed—the possibility of having Christ's image in our countenance.

Most of my life I have thought saving and redeeming were synonymous because that is how they are most often used. However, the second question in the temple recommend interview is, "Do you have a testimony of the Atonement of Christ and His role as Savior and *Redeemer?*" The words describe two separate roles, and having a testimony of both is essential. By definition, a redeemer is one who buys or wins back, one who frees us from captivity or debt by the payment of ransom, one who returns or restores us to our original position. However, there is an additional dictionary definition we must not overlook: A redeemer is one who changes us for the better.

Once, after a lesson about how Jesus had suffered for all of us, a young man said, "I never asked Jesus to do that for me. If anyone has to suffer for my sins, I will do it for myself." This young man was ignorant of the amount and degree of suffering we are talking about. In a revelation to the Prophet Joseph Smith, the Lord said that His "suffering caused myself, even God, the greatest of all, to tremble because of pain, and to bleed at every pore, and to suffer both body and spirit" (D&C 19:18).

But along with not understanding the extent of the suffering, this boy was also ignorant of just what suffering can and cannot do. Doctrine and Covenants 19:17 makes it clear that those who do not repent and accept Jesus' Atonement "must suffer even as" He did. So will that teenager be able to suffer for his own sins and then waltz into the celestial kingdom and live with God and his family eternally? Will he be beaten "with a few stripes, and at last . . . be saved in the kingdom of God"? (2 Nephi 28:8). No. The Book of Mormon makes it clear that such an idea is false, vain, and foolish (see 2 Nephi 28:9). While he can meet the demands of justice by suffering for his own sins, such suffering will not transform him in the same way Christ's redemptive power can. Just as a criminal can pay his debt to justice by doing time in prison and walk out no different, suffering alone does not guarantee change. Real change can only come through Jesus. We must accept Christ, not because it will save us some pain down the road but because it is the only way we can become new creatures (see 2 Corinthians 5:17; Mosiah 3:19).

The name *Emmanuel* means "God with us" (Matthew 1:23). Is there a better definition of grace than that? God is not waiting at the finish line. He is not waiting for us to do "all we can do" by ourselves before He helps us (see 2 Nephi 25:23). Rather, He is "with us"—ready, willing, and able to help us every step of the way.[2] In redeeming us, Christ does not just make up the difference. He makes all the difference.

The Atonement of Jesus Christ does not just provide a way to clean up messes; it provides the purpose and power to avoid making more messes. The Atonement allows us not just to ignore our appetites and pretend they don't exist but also to educate and elevate them. The Atonement can transform—not in a narrow way from *gay* to *straight* but in an all-encompassing way from human to divine. Such a transformation is a process that began long ago. Here on earth we continue the process, which includes many trials, but we don't face them alone. Christ suffered alone so that we would never have to. With God's help, our burdens can be made light (see Matthew 11:30; Mosiah 24:21).

One young man who had struggled with same-sex attraction in the past wrote, "In my self-loathing, I thought, *When I am over this and have conquered it, then I will accept the Atonement and put it all behind me. How could I possibly deserve the Atonement in the current state I'm in?*" This type of thinking is devastating. He wanted to overcome his struggles on his own so that he could then be "worthy" to turn to Jesus, but it just never worked. He wanted to be strong and independent and take care of himself. He wrote, "The problem was that I thought I knew more about myself than the Lord does, and that is painfully far from the truth."

Their Perfect Love

God's great desires for us would be impossible dreams without the Savior's Atonement. In the same way, the transforming power of the

Atonement would be incomplete if it were not available continually. So what keeps us going day after day when we know that transformation and sanctification will take a lifetime and beyond? The only answer is the love we feel for God and Jesus and the perfect love they feel for us.

"But that's the problem," one friend said. "How could they love me when I have done so many things wrong? How could they love me when I have said, 'I will never do it again' and then I still do it? How could they love me when I have made covenants and broken them?"

My friend forgets that the love of God and Christ is not like a good grade to be given to those who earn it. They love us—not because we are always good but because *they* are. It is part of their character. They love those they serve and succor, and they serve and succor each of us without ceasing. Their love is not limited to here and now. There is no veil over their memories. They remember our sweet associations in the premortal existence. They know who we were then as well as who we are now.

A mother of a convicted criminal was asked how she could love her son when he was guilty of such serious crimes. She responded, "I don't love what he has done in recent years any more than you do, but I have known him longer than you have. You see only a criminal. I see a little boy who used to bring me flowers and offer to help me wash the dishes."

In the classic tale *Beauty and the Beast,* the townspeople desire to kill the beast because they don't know him the way Beauty does. They feel threatened, and in their fear they make a quick judgment based only on appearances. Beauty knows differently. She has spent time with the Beast and knows his heart. She can see goodness that the townspeople can't because she has known him longer.

It is the same with God. While we only see our current beastly selves, God sees our eternal beauty. While those around us may make quick judgments and harsh condemnations, God and Jesus know us better. We are loved perfectly because we are known perfectly.

The Big Picture

No one can overestimate the power of eternal perspective. True faith, according to Joseph Smith, is not just believing in the Supreme

Being. It is knowing His attributes and our relationship to Him. It is knowing His plan for us and that we are living our lives in accordance with that plan. That kind of vision changes us forever.[3]

On the day of Pentecost, the outpouring of the Spirit, combined with an encounter with the resurrected Lord (see Acts 2), transformed a group of insecure disciples into fearless and confident witnesses of truth, who in turn changed the world.

This is precisely the vision God wanted to share with the early Saints in this dispensation when He commanded them to complete the Nauvoo temple even as they were being forced to abandon it. In the temple, God could lift their gaze away from current struggles and persecutions and give them a broader perspective. In the temple, God could remind them that, as sore as their trials were and would yet be, His plan for them was far greater than anything they had imagined and that they were greater than they realized.

Suddenly, mobs and persecutions, injustice and pain, wagons and oxen were all put into proper perspective—an eternal perspective. This vision didn't just provide a temporary shot in the arm but rather a long-term motivation that allowed those early Saints to endure with hope, patience, and strength.

The same vision calls to us today. If we can step away from the confusing voices and contradicting viewpoints of the world long enough to seek God, who sees the entire view, we will be able to endure as well. Seeing the big picture will give us the perspective we need to deal positively with all temptations, sins, mistakes, and challenges (see Alma 37:33).

A national journalist once reported that despite the success and good works of the Mormon Church, it was a terrible environment for women, blacks, and gays. The statement troubled me deeply. I know many women, blacks, and people who have experienced same-sex attraction who would strongly disagree with the journalist's words. They know that The Church of Jesus Christ of Latter-day Saints offers them blessings they could never find elsewhere and a perspective large enough to allow them to disregard the world's labels, stereotypes, and unsupported generalizations. Only in the Church do we learn true doctrine about what God desires for us and about the redeeming role of Christ. It is the only place where the perfect love of God and Jesus can be felt—not momentarily but continually through the covenant relationships we have with them.

The Church is not about drawing a line to exclude certain people but instead about drawing a circle to include all people. It is not about fitting a mold but instead about being molded. For those who have eyes to see, the Church of Jesus Christ is not just a good place for women, blacks, and gays; it is the only place for everyone who truly accepts Christ's invitation: "And he inviteth . . . all to come unto him and partake of his goodness; and he denieth none that come unto him, black and white, bond and free, male and female; . . . and all are alike unto God" (2 Nephi 26:33).

One Man's Story

One man who had struggled with homosexual temptations in the past shared how keeping a long-term perspective helped him make better choices. He wrote:

"In high school, I listened closely to the world around me and heard the word *gay* being thrown around. Like every teenager, I was trying to figure out who I was. When I looked at the people who were being labeled as gay, I identified with many of their qualities. I decided that if the shoe fit I might as well wear it. I adopted the label and distanced myself from the Church and my family. In my mind it seemed easier to accept a culture that approved of what I was doing than a Church that didn't.

"But as time went on I realized that what is easy is not always best. I look back on that time in my life and realize I was shortsighted. It was like I was taking a shortcut to finding out who I was. I found a shoe that came pretty close to fitting, so I tugged and pulled and did whatever I had to in order to make it fit. In retrospect, it didn't fit. I see now that I jumped to the gay conclusion quickly and erroneously. It felt good to know there were others out there who were similar to me, so I gravitated toward these men because I didn't want to be alone. They were accepting, but their acceptance involved lustful moments of immediate gratification that left me feeling more alone than ever.

"If what I was doing was really 'me' and as 'natural' as everyone kept telling me, why was I so unhappy? If the shoe really fit, why was I left with such painful blisters? I started rebuilding my relationship with my parents and returned to church.

"My friends told me it would be impossible to reconcile my 'gayness' with the teachings of the Mormon Church. I told them there was indeed a way to reconcile the two, and it was called repentance. With the help of my bishop and others, I began the healing process available only through the Atonement of Jesus Christ. It has taken a long time, but I have found that the only shoe that fits perfectly is truth. When I accept the truth, then my choice is confirmed by the Holy Ghost and I feel peace, comfort, and joy—not just when I live that truth perfectly but as I plod along toward that goal."

One Leader's Journey

One bishop experienced great changes in his attempts to help others as he began to see a bigger picture. He admitted that he didn't even know what to say the first time a man spoke with him about same-sex attraction and homosexual experiences. The first words that came to his mind were, "Well, just stop feeling that way. Stop doing those things"—as if those solutions had never occurred to the struggling member. The bishop said, "I was glad I held my tongue. If it were that easy to change feelings and behavior, this member would not have been sitting in my office pleading for help." Instead of reprimanding or criticizing, the bishop told the member, "I don't know a lot about these issues, but I want to learn. You will have to help me just as I will try to help you. One thing I know for sure is that Jesus Christ is the solution to every problem. I'm glad you are in the Church, glad you are in my office, and glad that you are trying to draw closer to Him."

In the weeks that followed, the bishop did quite a bit of reading on the topic. He spoke with friends who were professional counselors and with others who had experienced same-sex attraction but had found peace and resolution in their efforts to live the gospel. These experiences helped the bishop see that homosexual thoughts, feelings, and behavior can often serve as a window through which to address other deep, important issues.

Comparing same-sex attraction to a tree, one friend encouraged the bishop to deal with the roots and not just the leaves. The bishop said, "I learned to stop focusing so much on changing the member's behavior and to focus more on the member himself. In our times together, we didn't speak about his past mistakes as much as we spoke about his feelings of not belonging, his shame, his loneliness, the perceived judgments of others, and his goals for the future."

Slowly, the bishop's perspective expanded. At first he wanted only behavioral compliance; he wanted the struggling member to live up to Church standards. Now he wanted this member to feel wanted and valued in the Church. He wanted him to feel truly needed, not just welcome. The bishop explained, "I made a conscious effort to recognize and cultivate the good and the positive qualities in this man rather than just focusing on what I perceived to be negative and broken. As I did, I saw how much he had to offer others in our LDS community. Of course, the man's behavior mattered. The very fact that he was willing to speak to me in the first place was evidence that he wanted desperately to find peace in living the gospel. But I wouldn't have been helping him by making him feel devalued, shamed, and even disposable."

Over time, both the bishop and the member began to feel a powerful sense of mission. They saw not only the big picture but also that they both had vital parts to play in it.

My Expanded Answer

Perhaps the next time I am asked, "Am I gay?" I will not stop with saying, "You are a child of God." Instead, I will say, "No matter your past, your current difficulties, or your fears about the future, you are a child of God with the potential to become as He is. You have a Redeemer who makes that statement believable and possible. You have an important role to play in His kingdom, and you have all the love you will ever need to keep going."

"Arise, and Walk"

Robbie Pierce

Robbie Pierce was raised in California's Napa Valley. He is a theater major at Utah Valley University. He loves to write poetry and plays, explore nature, and learn about everything he encounters. The oldest of several siblings, Robbie loves his family. He served a mission in Osorno, Chile. He believes that people are the greatest of all God's creations, and he loves to make them laugh, think, and prosper.

I'm gay. That thought first entered my mind one day when I was thirteen. I was walking to gym class behind a boy and looking at the muscles in his legs and having mildly lustful thoughts when suddenly, unbidden, there it was: *I'm gay.*

The crisis here was one of identity. I couldn't be gay. I was a good Mormon kid. Mormons aren't gay; in fact, we're completely against that sort of thing. But there it was, put into words and therefore real. The notion both terrified and excited me. This was something I'd have to deal with. Instead, I let the thought come to me again: *I'm gay.* Same effect. *I'm gay! I'm gay! I'm gay!* Repeated about seven hundred times. After a while, I wasn't conscious of the individual repetitions—I was panicking. But in my head, each repetition sounded more significant and the letters a little more capital. Something I had not asked for was happening to me. I began retrospectively to arrange my memories of my life to make them fit in with this new idea. *I'm gay!* I thought. *There was that one time when I was nine and there was that lifeguard at the pool, and he could do flips, and I thought he was so cool. Maybe that's where it started.*

While it's true that I was experiencing homosexual attraction at age thirteen, I was losing my sense of identity through those repetitions in my mind. The more I thought, *I'm gay,* the more *that* became all I thought about myself. This wasn't where my life was supposed to go. I'd pictured myself ending up so differently. Indeed, this was the beginning of what would turn out to be the major struggle of my life.

I'd heard stories about gays, of course. I knew what one was. I'd heard the asperity in my parents' voices as they talked about gays with whom they'd gone to high school or with whom they worked. The family attitude toward homosexuality was that it was a sin, without much further thought on the subject. At dinner in a restaurant shortly after my own self-discovery, one brother tauntingly called another "gay," and Mom slammed her fists on the table. The bang and the clinking of silverware and glasses made every head turn toward her as she seethed, "None of my children would ever be evil enough to be gay."

And yet, "gay" was the most accurate adjective I had for myself. I didn't feel evil. But do evil people ever feel evil? How could I have become that person? Thus began a period of secret, desperate prayer: "Please make me not gay. Please make me not gay. Please make me not gay." That lasted for years. I grieved and denied and got angry and bargained. Boy, did I ever bargain! "If you make me not gay, I will never masturbate for the rest of my life. If I ever think lustful thoughts about a boy, you can send me to hell when I die. I promise that was my very last lustful thought ever." Needless to say, my attempts at bargaining were unsuccessful.

What I didn't realize is that every utterance of "please make me not gay" contained an implicit subtext: "I'm gay." My mantra all over again! Even my prayers served to reaffirm my problem, and Heavenly Father never saw fit to remove that particular thorn. Some have taken God's refusal to miraculously part them from their homosexual feelings as He parted the Red Sea as a sign of His nonexistence, His lack of interest in them personally, or His affirmation of homosexual relationships. I saw it as more of a puzzle.

Maybe I wasn't asking in the right way or at the right time. More likely there was some other commandment I was neglecting upon which showers of heterosexual attractions from heaven were contingent: "Have I paid my tithing and read my scriptures and avoided caffeine and gossip and traveling on the water and having my sideburns longer than missionary regulation? Heck yes, I have! Oh, but dang it, I'm still using substitution swear words. I have to fix that so I can be straight!" This method of "fixing what I can and letting the Lord take care of the rest" did not work any better than the bargaining had.

Realistically, I was never as righteous as I've portrayed here. I mean, I did keep my sideburns short and all of that, but my desires were not all about developing normal attractions and returning to the celestial kingdom. Part of me, like Lot's wife, really wanted just one glimpse of the depravity before it all burned. "What good is abstinence from a sin one has never committed and with which one has zero experience?" I reasoned. "How much more will I have proved myself by gaining a true knowledge of evil before turning away from it?"

Actually, I was just a lonely, confused, often hormone-driven, and tragically curious teenager. I would allow lustful thoughts to consume my attention for only a certain fraction of my day as a sort of self-indulgent self-compromise. I had a library card, and I read everything I could on the subject of homosexuality. I became obsessed.

Of course, there were many other challenges in my life at the time. When seen against the backdrop of my life then, my confused sexual state seemed inevitable. I was, almost comically, a complete outcast at school. To help with the mental picture: my parents, with unparalleled foresight and frugality, had saved bags full of clothing for various ages from the time I was born in the early eighties. Every year before school started, we'd get the big black clothing slugs out of the back of the closet and see if anything fit us. For this reason I was walking around my middle school in the early nineties wearing brown corduroy bellbottoms and a purple tie-dyed shirt. My classmates were not kind. I was in a new city and didn't really have any friends. I spent my lunch period walking around by myself, entering the bathroom every few minutes and just waiting in a stall so I could look, to the imagined observer, as though I had somewhere to go. I knew that I was a goofy, funny kid who would be able to make friends if I could just get someone to stop making fun of me long enough to get to know me.

My home life was even worse. The happy home I'd known for the first ten years of my life became an unsafe place. Dad was a registered nurse at a local hospital but got fired for suspicion of having stolen drugs. Shortly thereafter, he announced that he was leaving our family for the mistress he'd met on a business trip. He took all of our Christmas money and left us on the brink of financial and emotional ruin—he even took the dog. Mom went crazy—understandably. She returned to work and school full time, would come home stressed to a messy house, and would often unleash her anger on us through violence.

In the midst of all that chaos, when I was thirteen I was molested at Scout camp by one of the camp directors. I became sexualized at that early age, and everything I dealt with for the next five years or so seemed to be sexual in my mind. I found it almost impossible to let friends casually touch me, not because I hated it but because I enjoyed it and felt guilty for doing so. I became a broken person, and I couldn't understand how I had let my life and my idyllic childhood get away from me. I hated that adult feelings were forced upon me when I was still a child and still trying to just enjoy playing outside without thinking about sex.

That's where I was in my life the day I found myself lusting after a boy. The word *gay* seemed useful to me. For the first time I had a label that seemed to explain what was different about me. While I hated the label, I was glad that I had found one at all, and I embraced it. I lived in a state of flux, fear, confusion, and deception for the next several years. I made mistakes. I beat myself up about them. As my high school days wound down, however, I found that somewhere along the way I had learned to break out of my shell. Outwardly, things seemed to be going well for me. I had friends and was graduating and getting ready for a mission. But inside, I felt that I was getting further and further away from being the person I truly desired to be.

When I was seventeen and had graduated from high school, I made a typically stupid teenager decision that would have ramifications for the rest of my life. This story is essential for anyone who wishes to truly understand the source of my faith and my reasons for remaining faithful to the Church despite powers that would try to pull me away.

I was with two of my best friends. We drove up to Lake Berryessa, to the rock that's a good diving point. It's next to a bridge, so parking is up at the top of the rock, with the lake about fifty feet below. My friends climbed about halfway down the rock and jumped from there. I stood at the top, looking down at them as they teased me and called me "woman" for my reluctance to jump. That was all the goading I needed, and I jumped. Now, bear in mind that I had no idea what I was doing. I yelled for the first half of my descent, but then I had to take another breath and saw that I was still falling. The surface of the lake rushed up toward me like pavement, and I lost my head. I started to run in midair, much like Wile E. Coyote. The running made me overrotate, and I struck the glassy surface of the lake in approximately a sitting position—which hurt really, really bad.

It felt as though my entire lower body had been dropped into a blender—on fire. I surfaced briefly and was able to hear my friends' laughter and to sputter, "I can't swim!" I literally could not move my legs, and I began to sink. I saw the light growing dim overhead, and then I felt my friends' hands grab my arms as they pulled me back to the air. As soon as I could breathe, the screaming began. The added gravity of getting out of the water proved too painful through several attempts, so I clung to the side of the rock, screaming for what seemed like an hour as shock set in and I realized I couldn't move my legs. Eventually, my friends could think of no other solution than to put one of my arms around each of their shoulders and carry me back up the rock and set me on the road. They pulled the car around, loaded me up, and drove me the forty-five minutes back to civilization. They were about to take me straight to the hospital, but I had another plan.

During all those years, I'd continued to go to church. I had no reason not to go. I liked church, and I liked the friends I had there, and to be honest, I had a bit of a crush on one of the boys from my ward. I'd never gained my own testimony, but I was open to it. I wasn't sure what my place in the Church was. I had some very good leaders who were well informed of the Church's stance on homosexuality. They had answered our questions in the priests quorum about the distinction between homosexual attraction and homosexual sex. I knew I belonged in the Church, even if I didn't know exactly how. So now, with the prospect of having permanently injured myself, I thought I saw a way to fix the problem of my questions about my religion and the problem of my broken body.

I'd test God.

So I had my friends take me to the house of one of the elders in the ward, and he quickly called Mom as well as an additional elder to assist in giving me a blessing. The blessing was short enough, but I was in so much pain that I only remember one key phrase: "You've injured your body, and now it's time to start healing."

No duh, I thought, in my nineties vernacular. You don't get blessings to find out that you're supposed to heal on your own. I wanted a miracle. Instead, I was in the backseat of the car, crying out in agony at every turn and bump, and on to the hospital. The news I received there was heartening. The doctors took X-rays of my back and told me everything was fine. The paralysis in my legs was temporary and normal after a trauma, they told me. The bump I could feel on my back was just scoliosis. They sent me home in a wheelchair and said to just check in regularly with our family doctor.

I quickly regained movement in my lower body, and then over the course of the next eight months, I slowly regained feeling to the point that eventually only my toes were numb. The pain, however, never got much better after the first week. I was never able to sit up straight. I'd bring pillows with me to church and spread out on the pews. I couldn't walk more than half a block without needing to lie down for a break. One day I got a new doctor, and she recognized that something was wrong. She referred me to an orthopedic surgeon, who looked at my back, looked at the X-rays, and then took a Sharpie and circled the bump that had been explained as scoliosis. "This bump isn't even on these X-rays," he cried. "Someone please X-ray this boy's back."

They X-rayed my spine and found that one of my vertebrae was fractured. Pretty badly, in fact. The doctor then told me that I'd never walk without pain. He also told me that had the break been discovered within the first week, they would have been able to operate and fix it, but now it would mean rebreaking the bone, which was too risky. Furthermore, the doctor in the emergency room had made mistakes in his diagnosis. Plenty of signs pointed to the fact that I'd had a spinal injury, and the ER doctor's failure to X-ray my entire spinal column was inexcusable. The orthopedic surgeon said he hated lawyers, but I had a real case and should hire one.

This was devastating news. All the way home, I reflected on the things I would not be able to do. I wouldn't be able to run and jump and play and backpack anymore. I wouldn't be able to serve a mission. I wouldn't be able to carry my bride across the threshold of a new home, should a bride ever enter my life. The thought that I'd never heal was the second crushing blow of this catastrophe.

Here's where this story becomes pertinent to the subject of my same-sex attraction. Faced with the real prospect of never recovering from this injury, I went to another family friend and requested a second blessing. He laid his hands on my head for several minutes and cried. But that's all he did. He didn't say anything. Finally, he simply stated that he didn't know what I was supposed to hear, but that whatever it was, I'd already been told it in my previous blessing. He said I needed to think of it in spiritual terms instead of temporal terms.

"You've injured your body, and now it's time to start healing." That's all I remembered. But in spiritual terms, I was being told, "You've injured your body, and now it's time to repent."

So I started down two paths. The first was legal. I hired a lawyer and presented him with my case. The other was spiritual. I began to read my scriptures every night—to *really* read them, with the desire to find something in them. I discovered a verse one night in Mark that read, "Therefore I say unto you, What things soever ye desire, when ye pray, believe that ye receive them, and ye shall have them" (Mark 11:24).

What things soever I desired! Could it be? Those words struck my soul. I had prayed for many things in the past but more out of desperation than out of a true understanding of my relationship to my God. And the one thing I desired more than anything? It was to know that Heavenly Father loved me and that I could be forgiven. That was the thing I'd never believed. I had thought that I was broken beyond repair. My main desire was no longer to "turn straight" or to be able to walk without pain. It was just to have my sins taken away and be counted worthy of my Heavenly Father's blessings. Until I found that passage of scripture, I hadn't believed that to be possible. But I'd take the Savior at His word—I'd believe.

The next night I prayed, and this was no nourish-and-strengthen-our-bodies prayer. I pleaded with God that night that I could be forgiven. I apologized for having to unload those sins onto Christ. I had always believed that God had the power to forgive me, but what I had doubted was His willingness to do so in my particular case. After all, my sins seemed worse than others' sins, simply because they were the ones we were never allowed to talk about. I doubted that I could be forgiven for all my lustful thoughts and for the way I'd privately acted them out. But my desire was great, and that night I had a spiritual revolution. As I humbled myself to the point of asking God to forgive me and help me, my whole body was overcome with the effervescent burning of the Holy Ghost. I came out of that experience with a profound love of my Savior and a deep awe for His willingness to forgive me and to give me the grace and strength I required to make better decisions.

Meanwhile, the lawyer had good news. We could settle out of court for ten million dollars. Ten million. I thought of all the good I could do with that much money. I could buy my mother a house. I could pay for college and for all my brothers to serve missions. All I needed to do was sign some paperwork, and the lawyer would get the process started.

I agreed to do so but decided first to pray and fast. I'd just recently discovered the joy that comes from being close to the Lord, and I was riding that spiritual high. That Saturday night I began a fast, and on Sunday I went to church seeking confirmation for my decision to accept the money. In Sunday School we had a lesson about forgiveness. *Not too specific, there,* I reasoned. Then in priests quorum the teacher wrote on the chalkboard, "Lawsuits and how they've never helped anybody." You see, our instructor had forgotten to prepare a lesson, and so he was winging it. I'm not suggesting that lawsuits are in any way against the teachings of the gospel. But I recognized this as a clear answer to my prayer and as a test of my faith. Really, what choice did I have?

I called the lawyer and let him know that I'd decided to drop the charges. He was pretty angry. So were many members of my family. But I felt confident that I was making the right decision.

The following Saturday I awoke to a curious sensation. I was pain free. I could scarcely believe it. I hopped out of bed and tested things out. I could move. I went outside and began to walk. I walked all around town. I got a smoothie and a haircut. As the sun was setting that evening, I returned home, having walked at least fifteen miles and having bared my soul in praises to my God that whole way. I was free.

We're all aware of the line between righteousness and sin. Sometimes we come pretty near that line, and that's normal, I suppose. But what I learned through my experience is that it isn't just a line drawn in the sand; it's the edge of a cliff. I had jumped over that line and fallen down—down until I was drowning, losing sight of the light. The Savior had saved me from drowning in deep water, just as He had saved His friend and disciple Peter (see Matthew 14:25–32). He had carried me back and set me on the rock, back onto the road where I could begin my healing. And that's the way life is. We fall. He picks us up. We learn, and we do better.

The healing of my back is usually what impresses people about my story. But I recognize that the greatest gift I received was the grace of God to be able to be considered worthy of His blessings. I feel that the following story in the Gospel of Matthew captures the heart of my story:

"And, behold, they brought to him a man sick of the palsy, lying on a bed: and Jesus seeing their faith said unto the sick of the palsy; Son, be of good cheer; thy sins be forgiven thee. And, behold, certain of the scribes said within themselves, This man blasphemeth.

"And Jesus knowing their thoughts said, Wherefore think ye evil in your hearts? For whether is easier, to say, Thy sins be forgiven thee; or to say, Arise, and walk? But that ye may know that the Son of man hath power on earth to forgive sins, (then saith he to the sick of the palsy,) Arise, take up thy bed, and go unto thine house.

"And he arose, and departed to his house. But when the multitudes saw it, they marvelled, and glorified God, which had given such power unto men" (Matthew 9:2–8).

Just as the sick man in this story was blessed by the faith of his friends, I too feel that I have been blessed by the faith of those around me, including leaders, family members, and friends. But I also recognize the responsibility that the man had to be a witness of the Lord's power to heal and to forgive.

The Lord has blessed me with the ability to walk not only physically but also spiritually in the light along the strait and narrow path. Same-sex attraction is just another trial in my life, and the process of overcoming trials is what's helping me to be more like a loving God. I count myself blessed to have the gospel in my life. Had I not known about the option of forgiveness, I might have held on to anger and never been able to be healed and forgiven. That knowledge, I feel, is what has set me apart from my brothers and sisters who have faltered and wandered from the straight course of the gospel (see Alma 37:33–35). I strive to remember the blessings I am given every day. Someday I hope to be fully worthy of them. I hope to tell my story and live my life in such a way that others will learn of the power and love God has for each of us as His children.

The Lord has blessed me in many other ways, and I've been able to find resolution to many of the problems that plagued my youth. The lessons I learned about forgiveness and letting go of pain were able to spill over into my relationships with my parents and even helped me to let go of the hatred I felt toward the man who molested me. Dad was able to get off drugs and make peace with our family before he died. Mom wrote me a heartfelt letter while I was on my mission, asking for forgiveness for whatever abuse had occurred in our home. She now has a beautiful eight-year-old daughter with her new husband, and that adorable little sister of mine is growing up in a stable LDS home we didn't have when I was a child. Mom is also my main advocate when it comes to dealing with same-sex attraction and remaining faithful to my covenants.

And we're all so poor. Poor and happy. I may not have ten million dollars, but I would have paid that much just for the ability to walk and serve my mission and see the Lord work His miracles in the lives of so many other people.

That's one of the most important things I learned: that the Lord will often require of us a sacrifice that seems huge, but He will then bless us with something even bigger. He has asked certain things of us, and sometimes those requirements seem unfathomably large. When I gave up ten million dollars, I was blessed with the ability to walk. And so I choose to have faith that by obeying the Lord's commandments and foregoing a same-sex relationship, greater, unforeseeable blessings await.

Amid all the miraculous blessings that stemmed from my healing, the Lord has still not seen fit to remove my same-sex attraction. But it doesn't really matter. My faith in our Savior is not contingent upon His removing my homosexual attractions, nor upon the removal of any of my other trials. I will believe in Him and obey Him because I know He loves me, and I trust that if it is ever in my best interest not to struggle with these trials, He will remove them. I fully believe that when I've passed from this life, I will look back on my struggle with my homosexual desires as the single most powerful impetus for developing into a more Christlike being. We all have temptations and weaknesses, and

I believe we'll be judged on the way we handle our trials, not on the number or magnitude or type of trials they are.

More than identifying myself as "gay" or "straight" or "Mormon" or anything else, I am a child of God. That's my new mantra. I am a child of God, and He loves me, and He has provided a Savior who has paid the price of my sins, whatever they may be. I am still attracted to men, but thanks to the grace of God, that doesn't control or have un-due influence in my life anymore. I know that my sins can be forgiven and that I can walk beside the Savior and that He will show me how to walk back to His presence someday.

Becoming

Sarrah Reynolds

During their nine years of marriage, Sarrah Reynolds (pseudonym) and her husband have lived in several western states. With their four young children, they are finally undergoing the experiences of first-time homeownership, both good and bad. Sarrah stays busy balancing her husband, kids, and house projects; serving her ward, friends, and family; and seeking for continued personal growth. She loves being a mom, enjoying the outdoors, training for and competing in triathlons, and playing her guitar.

I believe that there is a time and place for each of us to share our personal stories to allow the Lord to spiritually influence the lives of others. I also feel that there is a time and place for the real names and faces behind the experience of same-sex attraction (SSA) to likewise be shared. I don't feel that this is the time or place for me, and, thus, all names have been changed within this narrative. My deepest desire is to share my story with the purest intent of bringing a hope in Christ to others dealing with any challenge of life, including the trial of faith.

It was the first day of the fall soccer season in my sophomore year of college. I had been training all summer so that I wouldn't repeat my freshman mistake of coming in unfit. We all dreaded the timed three-mile run and the hour of fitness training that followed. I wasn't afraid, though. I had prepared and I was ready.

We were off, and before I knew it, I was on my final lap. It had been a difficult run, and there were times when I didn't think I could push through the pain, but it was almost over. I found a way to demand one last ounce of energy from my tired body. As I came around the final turn, I picked up my pace to ensure I would make it under the required time. I could see the finish line only one hundred yards away. Then everything went black.

I was fading in and out. New faces and voices were swirling around me every time I opened my eyes. I was passing through every emotion possible. I couldn't get control of myself. *What is happening?* I cried silently.

Finally, I had enough sense to understand that I was in the emergency room. It only took moments to realize that my situation was dire. I knew I was going to die. If they didn't act fast and if my body didn't respond, I was going to die! Fear overwhelmed me! The thought of dying at this point in my life was torture. I knew what the scriptures said about those who die in their sins (see 2 Nephi 9:38; Alma 11:37; Alma 12:16). I knew I had to change. *But how can I change something I don't understand?* I thought to myself. Then everything went black again.

Only one year earlier I had graduated from high school and was living my dream. I was playing Division 1 soccer on a full-ride scholarship in sunny California. Life was good. I came from a good Latter-day Saint family. You know, lots of kids, loving parents, and, with few exceptions, a healthy environment. I had never struggled with much. I hadn't had a hard time obeying my parents or choosing the right. From the time I was young, I had had enough faith-promoting experiences to solidify my testimony that God lives, Jesus Christ is my Savior, and the Book of Mormon is the word of God.

For the first time in my life, I was living far away from home. I knew who I was, where I came from, and where I was going. I felt that I was ready to share my testimony with the world, and there was nothing that could bring me down. But that was when Satan struck hard and fast!

I have always been the type of person who makes friends quickly and easily. I have also always longed for a deep, meaningful friendship. This pattern held true during my first months in California. Though I made friends with many people, none of these friendships seemed to fill that gaping hole hidden deep inside me that longed for something more than the superficial. I guarded this hole carefully so that no one could see I was hurting.

Relationships in the past (male and female) left me feeling alone, unfulfilled, disappointed, and hurt. I had always wanted someone who was there just for me. For as long as I could remember, I longed for someone to hold me. I anticipated a relationship in which I could be myself wholly and share myself completely. Now that I was in college, the cycle of unfulfilling relationships continued. My few failed attempts at a more-than-friends situation merely reinforced my conclusion that boys weren't interested in me. I was always the kind of girl that boys wanted to hang out with but not the kind of girl they wanted to date. I was subconsciously searching for someone to fill the void.

All too often I watched as a female friend would cry over the latest disenchantment with her boyfriend. More curious than my lack of interest in having that kind of drama was my strange desire to want to save her from those mistreatments. I wanted to be the one to console her, to show her how amazing she was and how she should be treated. Sometimes my jealousy over her other relationship was overwhelming and incredibly obvious. Many times I became possessive, overbearing, and obsessive in such friendships. I had great difficulty maintaining close female relationships, and it seemed unlikely that I could attain a close male relationship.

I had been taught the importance of temple marriage and seeking to become one with your spouse. I had committed myself to those goals at a young age. Regardless, I had always had difficulty engaging emotionally and physically with men. I figured that when "the one" came along, none of these things would be a problem because he would see past everything on the surface and realize how amazing I truly was. I just assumed that the emptiness I felt would one day magically be filled by my future husband. That was when I met *her.*

Brenda and I were attached at the hip from the beginning. Our relationship was easy and comfortable; I felt so free when I was with her. I never wanted to be apart. It was so natural to open up to her and let her in. Her response to my smothering was reciprocation. As I let down my defenses, I allowed the emptiness to be filled with her. It was like an unstoppable vacuum effect as I was sucked into her emotional abyss and she into mine.

So many times when I was younger, I questioned my attractions. I had thoughts and feelings that I never shared because I thought everyone would think I was weird. At sleepovers I wanted to play with my friends' hair or cuddle while we chatted. Even though everyone else did the same thing and then huddled in the same bed to sleep, I never joined them, fearing that I might accidently make contact with someone. Every time I got emotionally close to a girl, I began to yearn for physical closeness as well. Once, when I was eleven, I was having an emotional moment with my closest friend. I was lying in her lap crying and pouring my heart out. She reached over and placed her hand on mine. It was electrifying! I couldn't believe the amount of love and compassion I felt in that one small gesture. Though I needed this touch, it evoked feelings that frightened me. As a result of childhood sexual abuse and exposure to pornography, I had sexualized all physical touch. This caused me to completely avoid the touch that I needed and longed for, no matter how innocent. I became oversensitive to what others might think.

All the yearning for physical closeness that had once beset me was swallowed in an instant with one hug from Brenda. The comfort of being in her arms or holding her in mine was indescribable. Finally, I found a place that felt safe, consoling, and reassuring. With no walls to protect my emotions, I was able to connect with her on the deepest level and then cement it by connecting physically as well. It didn't take long for our physical relationship to catapult into forbidden behavior. Each moment I found myself pushing the envelope just a little further. What started out as normal, innocent interconnecting quickly turned into sinful physical behavior.

Although I knew what we were doing was wrong, in nearly every way it felt right. My actions were in direct conflict with my undeniable testimony of the gospel of Jesus Christ. I was struggling with my ambivalence. I desired the closeness we shared, but I was repulsed by the sin in which I was secretly living. I felt guilty, shameful, and unworthy. I wanted to stop, but it seemed impossible to let her go. She had come to mean everything to me, and my love for her was so entrenched that I felt I couldn't do anything that might cause her pain.

After much distress, I decided to go to the bishop and confess. In my naiveté, I decided I would stop any inappropriate activity and then hurry through my repentance. Although it was humiliating, the process seemed simple enough. To my despair, the months that followed were filled with a cycle of falling, repenting, and falling over and over again. I finally stopped going to the bishop because I knew I would just fall again. One journal entry reads, "Slowly my prayers ceased to be sincere, and gradually I stopped saying them altogether. I didn't feel worthy to talk to my Father in Heaven. Soon after that, I stopped reading my scriptures. I knew that all I would read about was how much I needed to repent. I wasn't able to feel the Spirit, and all of the blessings I had taken for granted were now taken from my life." My soul was aching to find relief from a burden I could bear no longer.

After a summer of anguish and procrastination, I returned to California for another fall semester. It was in this desperate, sorrowful, spiritless state that I arrived at that fateful soccer practice. When I opened my eyes and found myself alone in a hospital bed, I could see everything so clearly. The Lord had spared my life, offering me the opportunity to give it back to Him. I was ready to "give away all my sins" to know Him (Alma 22:18), no matter the cost. My knowledge of how to enable His saving grace may have been lacking, but my testimony of the saving power of the Atonement of Jesus Christ was ever burning. I knew that what seemed impossible to me was not impossible for the Lord. In that moment I committed in my heart to change. Thus began my journey of becoming.

Shortly after being released from the hospital with my new resolve to change, the Lord granted me my first blessing for choosing to follow Him in faith. Until the previous year, I had lived my entire life worthy of the man who would take me to the temple. Never had I doubted that I would find him. But, like a cruel joke, he showed up during the most confusing, depressing, and difficult time of my life. I thought, *The one time I feel I am not worthy of any gospel blessings, cue Kyle.*

As I was struggling to rewrite the boundaries of my relationship with Brenda, I felt something powerful about the way Kyle lifted me spiritually. From our first car ride home we established a relationship based on trust and open communication. The Lord was prompting me to let Kyle in. I moved forward in faith, not because I thought a guy was "the answer" but because I recognized him as a gift from God. I did not see the wisdom in the Lord's timing, but this taught me what it means to learn "precept upon precept" (2 Nephi 28:30).

Although I had taken this small step, a boyfriend only added to my juggling act of a heavy school load, the thick of my soccer season, and a girlfriend I couldn't seem to let go of. My life subconsciously split in two. I can only describe it in terms of Jekyll and Hyde. During the day, I was immersing myself in the scriptures, church, institute, and gospel-centered literature. I was earnestly working to turn my heart to God. At night, I would hide away in the shadows with Brenda. Over and over I would return to the place that was comfortable and effortless. I felt shame and guilt and hate toward this part of me. "Why can't I stop falling?" I cried. My soul was being torn apart as I attempted the impossibility of serving two masters.

I needed help, hope, and answers that showed me *how* to change. Somehow, during those few grueling months of trying to follow the Savior but still living a double life, my knowledge and testimony of the Atonement increased. My efforts, though far from perfect, had given me the concrete knowledge that it was possible, that I *could* do it. Now I needed to know *how* to do it.

Not by chance, I was given a book that absolutely changed my life. I went home for winter break and was physically sick about my situation. I was fasting, praying, and begging the Lord to lead me to the next step. After work one evening, I sat alone, determined to finish Erin Eldridge's book *Born That Way?* When I closed the book, I had a distinct impression: "Tell Jenny." My jaw dropped, and I shook my head at myself. *There's no way can I tell anyone about all this!* I thought. Not even my best friend from high school. I got in my car and headed home in a blizzard. I arrived, got out, and found I was standing on Jenny's front lawn. Without a doubt, I knew the next step.

Telling Jenny was a difficult test of faith for me because I had never told anyone about these deep personal thoughts. I especially didn't want to divulge the details of my current predicament. It was a long night and a long conversation. She accepted me with open arms and tear-filled eyes. Again, the Lord was generous in pouring out His blessings upon me when I showed my faith and willingness to heed His promptings.

I found many gospel-centered answers in *Born That Way?* The most shattering of them was the idea that I had to sever all ties with Brenda. In my heart I knew it was vitally necessary for my salvation, but in my mind it seemed so unreachable and distant. When I realized that I had been putting something ahead of God, I understood that the ultimatum was not deciding between her and Kyle; rather, the choice was between my relationship with Brenda and my relationship with God. In a very real way, I felt connected to Abraham's struggle when he was asked to sacrifice his son Isaac and that story's parallel to the Atonement. The long process of letting Brenda go taught me about the sacrifice required to show sincere faith. Although it would take me years to make a complete severance, my faith increased as I experimented upon the word (see Alma 32:27). Each step seemed small, and some were even backward, but I had to allow myself room to repent of my mistakes and to rejoice in my successes.

Pushing Brenda out of my life reopened the previous void I had felt before. Only now it was like a tender wound that would eventually become abscessed if filled with external, temporary things. I needed to fill this painful void with Christ before I could truly be one with Kyle. I knew I couldn't give myself to someone unreservedly if I didn't feel whole. As I found the way to cast my burden on the Lord, I was able to come to that wonderful, amazing, indescribable place of feeling whole. I was at peace, and I didn't want to leave the comfort of that haven. Notwithstanding, I knew that the Lord had more for me to do and more for me to become.

At this point, Brenda moved to a new city. My relationship with Kyle was able to progress to a new level now that I was finally unhindered by my double life. It took a *mere* five months of dating exclusively for me to be ready for our first kiss. Together we read a talk by Elder Dallin H. Oaks called "The Challenge to Become,"[4] and we discussed the difference between testimony and conversion. A testimony is something you have; converted is something you become. This became the foundation for our relationship. I was given a glimpse of my true potential and what I could ultimately become with Kyle if we allowed Christ to fill the space between. That first kiss was a token of my commitment to this challenge to become.

Our relationship continued to reach new heights, but eventually we plateaued. After a year of his love and patience, I knew I was at a crossroads. It was time to tell him the whole truth. Here again was a trial of my faith. I wasn't afraid that telling him might scare him off; I was afraid because I knew he would stay. I knew his commitment to us and his deep understanding of the Atonement. The Lord had blessed me with a few trusted friends who encouraged and supported me at this sensitive time. I diligently sought the Lord's help and invited Kyle to fast with me so both our hearts would be prepared. When I finally lifted my eyes from the floor after telling him, I learned a great deal about humility and the pure love of Christ. Though it was a shock, my struggle with SSA didn't change the way he felt about our relationship and me. He entreated me to allow him to carry this burden with me.

When the Lord told me that the next step was the temple, I had many reservations. I couldn't see the wisdom in making temple covenants in my fragile state. I felt I was still too weak to put myself in a position where I could so seriously endanger my salvation. In hindsight, the Lord's plan is completely evident to me. He knew that I needed the power that could come only by receiving my endowment. I began to understand that the temple is not *for* perfect people; it is *to perfect* people.

The Lord also knew the protection that would be provided by a temple marriage and a faithful husband. My faith was severely tested as I resisted the Lord's undeniable directive to marry Kyle without delay. I have three older sisters, and I saw three times what it is *supposed* to be like when you are getting married. I knew it wasn't that way for me. I *loved* Kyle deeply, but I was not *in love* with him. I was so scared that I wouldn't be able to handle things after marriage. I was afraid of how I might react to him emotionally and especially sexually. The image of being intimate with him frightened me, and the thought of being deeply and emotionally connected to him seemed unfeasible. I was so concerned that if I didn't find fulfillment with him I might turn elsewhere. Taking this step of marriage was the greatest leap of faith yet.

The first year of marriage was in many ways a struggle for me. I was unable to separate the things that were normal "newly married" struggles from the things that were tied to my SSA. Thoughts of divorce were frequent but out of the question. I refused to let Kyle in emotionally, and I was struggling with our sexual intimacy. I realized I had not yet completely let go of Brenda. I was unfairly comparing the two relationships and not allowing my relationship with Kyle to develop in its own way. I found myself turning to her emotionally but justifying it because of our geographic distance. I convinced myself that seeing her occasionally would be fine, but all my justifications led me to failure. I couldn't be with her and resist the temptation to sin. My heart ached as I fell again.

All the shame and guilt returned, and I struggled to take steps to resolve the issue. My motivation came the exact moment the Lord told me that it was time to enter motherhood. My heart was broken because I knew I couldn't be the kind of mother I wanted to be until I was whole again and Kyle and I were one. I also knew the many risks and repercussions required to regain my proper standing with God. I thought I had experienced some low points in the past, but this was the lowest of them all. I had betrayed the trust of my devoted husband, relinquished my promised blessings from heaven, and resisted the enabling power of the Atonement. I knew of the pain I would go through as I humbly accepted God's invitation to repent and come unto Him once more (see D&C 18:11). I knew I would have to beg Kyle's forgiveness. I knew I was at the mercy of God's servants to determine my standing in the Church. And I submitted to the reality that divorce and excommunication were possible consequences. I again resolved to change my heart no matter the cost.

We sat on the edge of the bed in an aching silence as my shattering news permeated his reality. In that moment I experienced the most profound lessons of humility, forgiveness, and unfaltering love as my eternal companion reached out and held me in his arms with tear-filled eyes and a broken heart. With him on my side, I was ready to endure the consequences, whatever they might be, as determined by the proper priesthood authorities.

I can vividly replay that tender meeting with my bishop. Immediately after I had finished speaking, I watched as he bowed his head in silence to seek guidance from the Lord. I could feel His presence and knew that I was an active participant during that sacred communication. My bishop responded with justified rebuke, appropriate sensitivity, and merciful compassion. My faith in the divine authority of men who stand as judges in Israel was cemented that day. After subsequent meetings with my bishop and stake president—and much humility, hard work, and time—I was on my final path of repentance. I finally understood the significance of the scriptural injunction to first confess your sins and then forsake them (see D&C 58:43), not the other way around.

From the moment I turned my burden over to Christ, I found the strength and courage I needed to do what seemed impossible. I experienced His overwhelming desire to help me in my struggle. As I endeavored to live righteously, He blessed me in the exact way I needed, although many times I couldn't see His wisdom beforehand. My faith was tried again and again as I was asked to do more, sacrifice more, and become more. I experienced firsthand that faith always precedes the miracle (see Ether 12:6).

It has been years since that last meeting. Today I am surrounded by a support system of a husband, select family members, several close friends, and priesthood leaders who sustain and uplift me. With their encouragement, my Savior, and my faith, I know I can triumph over any trial I may face in this life.

The miracle I now enjoy daily is an incredible relationship with Kyle that fulfills me in every way. I am absolutely in love with him. Even more, I have the blessings of the temple and an eternal family. I am filled with peace, joy, and happiness that are more powerful than any unwanted attraction I may experience. Each time I sing "Nephi's Courage" with my children, I am echoing his testimony that the Lord won't give me a trial I can't overcome.

I now understand that trials are personal and unique, and through them, the Lord refines our faith. During my most trying years, I watched people I love prove themselves through their personal trials of faith: I stood alongside a dear friend as she entered the temple after overcoming a life of drugs, alcohol, and sexual promiscuity; my heart ached for a sister as she buried her precious twin girls; I wept with my best friend after she watched her mother die in her arms; I gained greater empathy for my mother in her battle against severe depression. I continue to observe in awe as my father unfailingly stands by her side.

Their examples strengthened me and taught me that my struggle with SSA is just one trial among many. I know that my friend may miss her mother for the rest of her life, and I may have occasional attractions for the rest of mine. But over time, and with a hope in the resurrection, our feelings will change and fade. I know that through the Atonement and the Spirit's continual guidance, Christ is able to transform my feelings completely if that is His will. But if not, I will continue faithful and, with my husband, become all that He intends.

The Gift of Hope

Kirk Reidman

Kirk Reidman (pseudonym) is single and lives in the southwestern United States. He owns and operates a multimedia production company and enjoys photography, travel, and reading. He has twenty-five nieces and nephews and currently serves in the Church as a stake executive secretary and a home teacher.

The old box made cracking noises as I lifted the lid. *Another pile of history to sort,* I thought as I lifted a stack of drawings I had made as a child. The crayon colors had not faded on one of the drawings: a simple portrait of my family. We all stood in a row, holding hands. With a blue sky above, I had drawn images of my mom, dad, two brothers, and a sister. In my four-year-old depiction of myself, there is no clue to the adventures that were ahead for my family and me. There was no way to guess that in fourteen years I would have two more sisters and two more brothers.

I gently laid that picture aside and continued looking through photos and report cards. Then I found another drawing. This one looked like it had been done in Primary. It was named "My Family" and showed me standing in front of a large, spired temple with a wife and a few children. I suppose, in my naive innocence, that I believed that going to the temple was like going to a "church" store where you picked out a wife and took home a few kids to start. I stared at the drawing, trying to imagine the simple view of life that I held as I drew that picture. Nowhere in my child's mind was there any concept of same-gender attraction or the unique challenges that would someday become such a prominent part of my life.

My mind was carried away to the thoughts of how life-changing these feelings of same-gender attraction had been for me. Like aching muscles, they were invisible to the world, but real to me. Since I became aware of their existence, they have changed every part of my life. Because of prejudice and social awkwardness, I have never felt it necessary to share my experience openly. However, with sadness I have heard of many souls challenged with these feelings who have turned away from the Church, claiming that they are unwelcome. I have heard of many souls who have spent their lives looking outside of the Church of Jesus Christ for answers to the most important of life's questions—often looking for answers in worldly excitement, pleasure, and acceptance.

In my fifty-one years of life on this planet, I have learned this: the best the world can offer is shallow and superficial compared to the grandeur and intensity of peace and hope offered by the gospel of Jesus Christ. So I end my silence by telling you the story of how I gained this gift of hope.

I am now and have always been an active member of the Church. I have deep pioneer blood, dating back to John and Luke Johnson, who were friends of the Prophet Joseph Smith and are mentioned in the Doctrine and Covenants. I say that not because heritage should bring privileges, but because it brought into my life generations of strong belief that God was an active part of our lives and would always provide the answers to life's questions and problems. So at a young age, when I became aware that my attractions where not aligned as I had expected them to be, I asked the Lord to help me as I went on my quest for a "cure."

As a teenager, I had a simplistic belief that there had to be a quick and easy solution for same-gender attraction and that God would guide me right to it. I remember going to the dusty old city library many afternoons after school. I needed to find out if there were scientific methods to cure my ailment, and the library seemed the best place to start.

On my first visit, I entered and stood near the door like a soldier about to enter a dangerous battlefield. I had to be quick and act as though I knew what I was doing to avoid getting help from the vigilant librarian, who seemed to silently appear out of nowhere. The last thing I needed at that tender age was for her to find me and peer at the subject card I held in my hand. I had this awful fear that if she did, she might sternly announce in a voice that could be heard by the entire library, "The books on homosexuality are in abnormal psychology, bottom row, aisle 13." Then she might whisk her finger out to point at the far side of the room in disgust.

No way, I thought. I didn't want any help for the kind of investigation I was starting.

I invented two escape plans in case the librarian or anyone else ever saw my secret topic. First, I would tell her that I was trying to look up "Homo sapiens." Alphabetically, the two words were close enough to make that a believable explanation. Second, before I went to the book section, I always retrieved a copy of the Scouting magazine *Boy's Life* to cover up what I was really reading. Sure there were dangers, but to me the research results were as important as gold.

As fear-inducing as it was to find the books, I was not ready for what I would find in the large and heavy psychology books. After pages of incomprehensible jargon, I was disappointed to find conflicting statistics and inconclusive findings. But even that was preferable to the wide-eyed horror that I felt as I read in other books of electroshock, mind retraining, and experimental surgeries. (Remember, this was the 1970s.) These books should have been marked with reader warning labels. Once, after reading about some of these test therapies, I almost destroyed my stealth cover by slamming shut a large psychology journal and muttering too loudly, "That's crazy! The cure sounds worse than the disease!" After months of this research, I dejectedly concluded that there were no easy cures, no trusted therapies, and no magic pills.

I turned my search for answers to the Church and the scriptures. I grasped quietly and firmly to the belief that with my obedience to gospel principles the attractions would shift into alignment and I would live a perfect life—or something like that.

Within a few years I was called to serve a mission. I worked hard and obediently responded to every leadership position and assignment I was given. On one occasion, the mission president wrote to me and asked me to serve in a quiet but necessary way. He asked me to be the companion of an elder who was on the tipping point of quitting his mission and returning home. He did not like any of his companions, and he did not like the people. He had an attitude that infected people faster than a cold virus. The mission president's plea to me was this: "Please save him; I have done everything I can for him." I was patient and kind, and the Lord used me to help Him turn the heart of this elder.

Later the mission president wrote and told me that I had earned a great blessing because of my service. I realize now that I was convincing myself of an incorrect spiritual principle. I really believed that, with enough of these blessing *points,* I could trade them in for a remission of my socially awkward challenge. But over time my attractions did not budge and, discouraged, I felt that I must have failed in faith or obedience.

When I returned home, I attended college, dated a lot, and served as an elders quorum president, a Sunday School teacher, and a ward mission leader. The thought that stayed riveted in my brain was *Serve as perfectly as you can, and your attractions will align themselves when you have served well.* I found that being perfect is more than a full-time job! Friends and roommates joked that I was making them look bad by serving as much as I did. More than once I was the object of the saying "All work and no play make Jack a dull boy." I didn't dare share my wretched secret with anyone or my desperate conviction that obedience might be my only chance to gain freedom from this perceived awful monster of same-gender attraction. Again, I blamed myself when my attractions didn't change. I blasted myself for not working hard enough.

In my mid-thirties, I met a talented young woman in my singles ward. We became good friends. It was my first dating relationship in which I remember feeling comfortable with just being myself. For months I quietly pondered this question: "Is it possible that I could be successful in a marriage to this woman?" I concluded that the answer to that question might depend on how my girlfriend would respond if I shared my deep, dark secret with her.

One December evening, I timidly shared with her my difficulties with same-gender attraction. I was prepared for the worst but hoping for the best. She was gracious and kind in her acceptance and assured me that it would not harm any relationship we might have in the future. With my confidence in high gear, we became engaged and then married. Marriage was awkward in many ways because my attractions did not shift. Again I had blindly believed that obedience would cause my attractions to change. They didn't. I tried to be a good husband. My wife tried to be a good spouse. For a number of reasons—my feelings of same-gender attraction being only one of many—our marriage ended after three years.

I felt that my divorce was the second big failure of my life. The first was not being perfect enough to be healed from same-gender attraction. How crushed and disappointed I felt. Boy, was I going to get a thrashing when I showed up in the spirit world someday! I could hear the lectures already—but none of them was as bad as my *self*-inflicted arrest, trial, and conviction.

The jolting disappointments of life had awakened me to the realization that I had been handling life's problems by my own power. I had not been using the energy and power of Christ's Atonement that had been all around me. I was like a crazy man who builds a sailboat. Not wanting to depend on the wind, he installs a large fan on the back to push the sails. The fan is powered by a windmill on the front of the boat. The physics of that plan were as ludicrous and faulty as my spiritual plan to save myself by obedience. I began to realize that I was in the hospital of life, reading medical journals and planning a self-operation rather than calling upon the only true Physician—the only one with power to save and redeem me. I began to rebuild my life on the Savior's foundation.

My prayers got a spiritual overhaul. Rather than blindly offering a checklist of righteous wishes, I began to reflect somberly on the Lord's plan for my life. I slowly learned to quit giving the Lord childish directions on how and when to bless me. Instead, I learned to submit myself with more childlike faith to the Lord's will. The real power of the Atonement started to make sense as I realized that the Lord was gradually changing my heart. He was softening it and molding it into something more usable to Him.

Years have passed, and in place of my own self-inflicted punishment, the Lord, in His mercy, has granted me a stay of execution. Some of the greatest lessons from the Lord have come as I have been called to serve, including twice as a seminary teacher and once as a counselor in a bishopric. Through service and study I have come to know the Lord's love and the peace of His Spirit. The Master Builder has entered my life and made more out of it than I ever thought possible.

Even though the Lord allowed me to live in peace and happiness, I did not cease with my request for healing. I continued to pray for the attractions that would lead to a healthy marriage. I asked for a family. I actively prayed for it. I told the Lord that I didn't care if it happened in this life or the next but that I was eager for the blessing. Besides asking to be healed, I also asked to understand why this challenge was given to me. I suppose that, because of my asking, the Lord gave me two glimpses behind the eternal door at which I was knocking.

The first glimpse happened late on a Sunday afternoon after church. I had decided to tell my bishop about my challenge and seek a blessing. I had no wrongdoing to confess, but I had wondered for a while if my attractions would ever change in this life and if there was something further that I should do. I wanted advice and counsel from the bishop. I waited to speak to him after the three-hour meeting block. I didn't want to be rushed, so I waited until everyone else had left the building. I didn't have to wait too long. It was fast Sunday, late afternoon, so I imagine the congregation was drawn home quickly by the thoughts of a steaming hot dinner. Within ten minutes, the halls were vacant.

Each time I had previously shared my challenge with a bishop, I had felt nervous. This time was no different. As the clerks were finishing their work and leaving, the bishop invited me into his office with a big smile. He made it easy for me to share the vulnerable things of my heart. He listened, he counseled, and he understood. He had great insights. He had comforting words. Then, as the profound silence of the building settled over us, he offered to give me a priesthood blessing. I eagerly accepted his invitation.

As the words of the blessing entered my ears, a vision opened to my mind—my eyes began to see, even though they were closed. In my mind, I could clearly see the bishop with his hands on my head, and I could see myself seated with my eyes closed. It was as if I were viewing the scene through the lens of a camera that was floating upward. The ceiling became invisible as the scene widened and moved away from us.

I could see, surrounding a hole in the ceiling that was about seven feet wide, a balcony supported by short white columns. Standing side by side around the edges of the railing were about fifteen people dressed in white looking down on the bishop and me. They were young people, men and women, in their twenties or thirties. They were looking down, so I could not see their faces. As the scene expanded and moved back, I could see a second balcony above the first, but it was wider with about thirty people looking down. Then a third balcony became visible above the second, and it was filled with about fifty or sixty people. In total there were about one hundred people, all gathered and looking down at the blessing I was receiving. All of this time I could hear and comprehend every word of the blessing. What a remarkable experience this was to witness this scene while I sat with my eyes closed under the hands of my bishop.

I had the distinct impression that the people watching from the balconies were not there by assignment; they were there voluntarily. Somehow they knew my challenge, and they knew my struggles. Somehow I knew that they wanted me to know that they were offering their support. *They loved me.* What a comforting thought. Maybe I wasn't going to get a huge thrashing when I showed up in the spirit world after all. Maybe I have some friends there who are not ashamed that I have this unpopular challenge.

As the blessing ended, the view of the balconies and friends faded away. Before I left the bishop's office, he hugged me and told me he loved and respected me. I left and walked slowly down the darkened hall and out the building into the evening twilight, still feeling electric from the experience of the blessing. I got into my car, sank into the seat, and remained motionless for several minutes as I pondered what had happened. Returning from my thoughts, I dug out some paper. I wrote the things I saw and heard, hoping that I could preserve a small ember of the spiritual glow that had filled me.

I have returned often in my memory to recall the feeling of love and comfort that was given to me that evening. I went to the bishop's office with a simple question. I left with so much more. It was as if I had asked for a simple drink of water and the Lord had given me a river in return. The river is still there when I take the time to revisit it. As I have reflected on that blessing and personal experience, I realize that my question—"Will I be healed in this life?"—was not directly answered. However, that question now seemed irrelevant in the eternal view that was shown to me. The personal knowledge that I am loved and accepted was and continues to be manna for my hungry soul. This experience and the next I will share are sacred to me. I do not share them lightly. However, I felt then as I do now that these experiences were intended for more than my own personal benefit. I knew the time would come that, under the right circumstances, I should share them with others who would be blessed and lifted by hearing them.

The second sacred experience happened a few years later while I was serving in the bishopric of that same ward. I have always felt that Friday and Saturday nights are some of the most challenging times of the week. On those occasions, it seems that the world makes noise just to remind me that I am single. On one particular Friday night, my defense was to plan a great Saturday, starting with an endowment session in the Oakland California Temple. As I was saying my prayers that evening, I asked the Lord if He could help me know when I would be healed. Maybe, I thought, the Lord could help me to have an impression while I served in the temple.

I suppose that the Lord might have been eager to give me an answer because the answer came before I could get to the temple the next day. The answer came in a dream that night that is still vivid and memorable to me. It is a source of hope. In the dream I was in a large banquet hall. Music, food, and laughter seemed to float all around me. The hall was filled with friends and family who all had spouses, but I was alone. Each friend or family member would stop and ask, "Where is your wife?" I am so used to that question, both in and out of dreams, that my response was a polite smile. If only they knew my challenge and how much I wanted a spouse. I continued walking through the crowd. Then I walked along one of the walls and spotted a large oak door. It looked out of place to me, and yet it seemed to be inviting me to enter.

As I shut the door behind me, I could see a pathway leading to rolling green hills of grass. About fifty feet down the pathway were two women talking together. The closer of the two suddenly turned and looked at me. She smiled and immediately started walking toward me. I was spellbound. She was beautiful. I instantly knew that I was seeing my wife. Her features were clear enough and memorable enough that I will recognize her when I meet her someday. I quickly ran down the path to her.

I embraced her like a long-lost friend. I don't know how, but we seemed to know each other very well. After a moment I looked, and just over her shoulder I spotted two little girls off in the distance playing on the grass. One was about four years old, and the other was about two. The older girl stood up and pointed at us, saying, "Look, it's Mom and Dad." I was seeing my wife and my daughters. I was home. I cried.

I woke, sitting directly up from sleep. It was so vivid and clear. Since that day, I have played the dream over in my head thousands of times. What a great source of hope. Whenever I hear the topic of hope discussed, because of that dream I know what hope is. A curious thing happened to me the following day as I left the temple. As I walked along the temple grounds on the way to my car, I was suddenly aware that my attractions had shifted slightly. I don't know if I can describe it more accurately because it was an immediate awareness that something significant had changed in a small way. That magical, mystical mechanism that controls physical attractions had moved. After all my years of trying to force it or maneuver it, suddenly it had moved. I also knew that it was nothing I had done; rather, it was the Lord's work. It was as if the Lord was saying to me, "Here is the answer to your prayer. Last night I showed you that you will be married. You will have children. The blessings of eternity can be yours. Remember that I, and only I, can truly heal you. Today I have shown you a small degree of what I will do."

A few months after the dream, I was visiting with my younger sister. She is close to me and very righteous. I related the dream to her. When I started describing my wife to her, she said, "Stop. Let me continue the description." She then went on to list details of my wife's appearance. She was completely correct. I was surprised. I asked her how she knew. She responded, "I saw her in a dream also. I also had the impression that I was seeing your wife."

As I write these words, I am filled with a great desire that you, the reader, will accept these experiences in the same way I have tried to present them. They are sacred to me. I hope they will be for you also.

As I glance down at the faded drawing I made of a future family, I realize that my childhood faith was not childish. Because of God's grace and some spiritual work, my childhood faith is joined by hope. My actions are now driven by the sure hope that there is another side of the veil and that I will have the marriage and family I have prayed for. This gift of hope is the sacred gift I now leave for you. Please accept my imperfect but sincere attempt to share it with you. May you seek for and find the sure hope that you also have friends and supporters on the other side of the veil. If you don't have a spouse and family now, may you have sure knowledge, as I have, that the Lord will bless you and provide for you. May you receive this gift of hope.

A Mighty Change of Heart

Rich Wyler

Rich Wyler lives with his new wife and their newly combined family in central Virginia. He was married to Marie (Massey) from 1988 until her death in 2006, and together they had a daughter and a son. He married Janet (Leavens) in the Washington DC Temple in 2010. Rich is the founder and director of People Can Change, a nonprofit organization that provides seminars and other support to help men of all faiths resolve unwanted homosexual attractions and recommit to living chaste lives. As a certified life coach, he works with individual clients from all over the world to make positive changes in their lives.

Walking into the high council room for my disciplinary council was the single most frightening, most shameful event of my life. I had spent years trying to hide my homosexual struggle from the Church and everyone around me—except my wife, Marie, who was patient, long-suffering, loving, confused, hurt, and angry. I had confided in her about my homosexual temptations before we ever became engaged, and I had been amazed and relieved at how she had responded with deep and abiding love. But now, nine years into our marriage, with my struggle seeming only to increase over the years, her patience was running out as my life seemed to be spiraling downward.

It had taken four months of intensive counseling sessions with a therapist to prepare myself to confess my hidden homosexual behavior to my bishop. I knew I couldn't simply confess and expect my bishop to just offer help and guidance privately, with no real consequences, as he would with lesser sins. I couldn't expect him to ignore my betrayal of marriage vows and priesthood and temple covenants and take no disciplinary action against me. It didn't work that way. Going to my bishop meant that I would have to be prepared to face a disciplinary council, and I knew that most likely I would be excommunicated. Any disciplinary action would naturally require that I confess (again) to my wife. Could our marriage withstand yet another revelation of my betrayal?

It wasn't just fear of these consequences that had kept me from confessing. I also had an enormous fear of revealing my deeply private struggle with unwanted homosexuality, first to the bishop and then to fifteen other priesthood leaders in a disciplinary council. The idea was more terrifying than I could imagine. I deeply distrusted that men could be compassionate toward other men—or at least toward me. My history led me to believe that men would ridicule me and be cruelly dismissive of my pain. Given these issues, a confession and disciplinary council seemed especially torturous.

Another issue that had kept me from confessing earlier was my utter lack of hope for meaningful transformation. From the Church, I knew that my behavior was forbidden, but all I had heard or read led me to believe that the best I could hope for was a lifetime of painful, white-knuckled resistance to temptation. Nothing I had heard led me to hope that these unwanted feelings would ever actually dissipate. From the world, I heard that I was born gay, that meaningful change was impossible, and that the only responsible thing for me to do was to leave my wife and children, find a more liberal church (or discard religion altogether), and embrace life as an openly gay man. It seemed like a choice between two versions of hell, each as undesirable as the other.

All of this finally began to change when I found Evergreen, an LDS ministry to people who want to live the gospel fully and faithfully, despite having same-sex attractions. Evergreen led me to a therapist, David Matheson, who not only specialized in helping people resolve homosexual problems but who also happened to be a member of the Church.

With David, I found hope. He openly admitted that he too had once struggled with same-sex attractions, but through counseling, living the gospel, and personal growth, he had resolved them and no longer felt homosexual feelings. He was the first real-live human being I had ever met who claimed to have experienced such a transformation, and for the first time in my life, I grabbed on to the hope that I too could experience similar change.

Four months after starting my work with David, I was prepared to face my deepest fears and face the consequences of my actions. With great trepidation, I met with my bishop and made a full confession. He responded with kindness but at the same time seemed stunned and overwhelmed by my situation. He told me that because I was a Melchizedek Priesthood holder, he would have to speak to the stake president about how to proceed. I said I understood but asked the bishop to please not identify me by name to the stake president until he and I had spoken again. He agreed.

Within a day the bishop called me back and said the stake president wanted to see me. My bishop had already given my name to the stake president, breaking his promise to me. This played further into my fear and distrust of men.

Things moved swiftly. Within two weeks I was facing twelve high councilors, the stake presidency, and a stake clerk, with my bishop at my side—seventeen men hearing the deepest sins, lies, and betrayals of my life. I was filled with remorse and shame, but I was also near-panic at confessing a nearly lifelong homosexual struggle to seventeen men who, I told myself, couldn't possibly have the slightest comprehension of, or compassion for, what I was going through.

After a thorough hearing, the council's decision was excommunication. I fled the room, never having felt such rejection in my life but, at the same time, knowing I had brought it upon myself. I spent much of the rest of that August day with my wife, Marie, in the countryside. She was loving, kind, and reassuring. In hindsight, I see that although she felt great compassion and sadness for me, she perhaps had never felt so proud of me either. I saw something else in her eyes too: a bright glimmer of hope that maybe we would make it after all.

Repenting and Rebuilding

Going to church after my excommunication was harder than ever. I fixated on who knew and who didn't, what they knew, and what they were thinking of me. Although no one really treated me any differently, I assumed the worst. I understood that certain ward leaders needed to know that I had been excommunicated, but I was angry, hurt, and afraid when I found out that my bishop had told them it was for homosexual behavior. *Why did they need to know that?* I wondered. My fear and distrust continued to grow.

Somehow I felt safer with the first counselor in the bishopric, even though I didn't really know him well. He seemed genuinely kind and concerned and interested in me. One day, in what must have been a moment of inspiration, I asked him if I could work with him rather than with the bishop. I would still have official interviews with the bishop when I needed to, but as far as ongoing counseling and support—well, the bishop just reminded me too much of my emotionally aloof father, and that created too much distrust in me. The first counselor, Brother Onken, didn't seem surprised by my request, and he said he would talk to the bishop about it.

My bishop seemed pleased and even a little relieved by the suggestion, admitting to me that he really wasn't sure how to help me. He said he would assign the first counselor to be my family's home teacher, and Brother Onken's ongoing support of me would be in that capacity. Sometime later, Brother Onken—who by then I knew as Martin—disclosed to me that he had been prepared for my inquiry by a spiritual prompting he had received that he would be called to somehow support me in my repentance process.

Martin was a godsend. Over the year and a half that I was out of the Church, he supported and mentored me in myriad ways. We often spoke on the phone several times a week, and we met informally at my home or over lunch or breakfast every week or so. He didn't have any prior experience with the issue of homosexuality, but he knew a lot about spirituality. He understood emotional pain and that it could lead someone into self-destructive paths. He understood repentance and the Atonement. Perhaps most important to me at that time, he believed in me and saw me as inherently good, despite everything I had done. He believed in the "mighty change" of heart spoken of in the scriptures

(Mosiah 5:2; Alma 5:14), and he trusted implicitly that I was in the midst of just such a change. He believed in me when I couldn't believe in myself.

Martin journeyed vicariously with me as I worked with my therapist. He walked with me on my journey to uncover and address the unmet needs and life hurts that had caused me to seek connection with men in such unhealthy ways. Martin became a big brother to me. My relationship with him was a healing balm, like the relationship I had always wanted with my father but had never had. His authentic interest in me and the time he spent with me helped me to begin letting down my defenses against men. I learned that I could, in fact, have platonic, brotherly friendships that would meet a deep need in me for masculine love.

At one point I approached my elders quorum president, a compassionate, spiritual, and athletic man, and asked him to teach me to play basketball. At thirty-five years old, I still carried deep peer wounds from sports in my youth—one significant source of my fear of men and all things masculine. I thought if a man could compassionately help me get reasonably comfortable on a basketball court, those self-doubts and self-criticisms brought on by years of teenage ridicule would begin to heal. And they did. To his credit, my elders quorum president met with me every Saturday morning at our chapel for several weeks, patiently coaching me on the basics of basketball, without ever grilling me about why this was so important to me or what it had to do with my spiritual reconciliation.

To increase my accountability and build my support system, I began participating in a weekly twelve-step group in my community for people struggling with sexual temptations. I consider the twelve steps to really be a repentance program, with their emphasis on reliance on God, confession, humility, rigorous honesty, surrender of our temptations to God's far greater power, and yielding our own will to the divine will. The meetings and readings, with their emphasis on spiritual surrender, accountability, and moral chastity, complemented my church attendance and scripture reading as I worked diligently to turn my will and indeed my whole life over to God. The meetings also gave me more than a dozen accountability partners—other men walking similar roads—whom I could call in a moment of weakness or just any time I needed encouragement or to feel an authentic connection with a brother.

My therapist also referred me to a men's organization whose purpose was to teach men to live lives of integrity, brotherly connection, and devotion to a personal life mission. I started attending weekly and found there a brotherhood and authenticity beyond anything I'd ever known.

Through all of this I felt a deep transformation taking place. I was bonding with men in ways I never had before in my life. I was letting down my defenses and learning to trust men. I was increasingly meeting my authentic need for same-sex connection and intimacy in healthy, platonic ways, and as I did, my temptation to connect with men sexually was becoming less desperate, less frequent, and less intense. My homosexual behavior was receding further into my past.

In all those years of struggle, I had never even realized that I had such a great unmet need for healthy, platonic, brotherly connection with other men. I had tried so many times to stop the sinful behavior. But without the godly substitute—the pure love of Christ, true brotherhood, and the charity spoken of in scripture—I had always fallen back to the cheap imitations of intimacy that ultimately caused even more pain.

This time it was different. As I experienced authentic brotherhood more and more, I was learning to live in accordance with God's will in a way that brought more peace, joy, and fulfillment than I had ever known. Not only was my behavior changing, but my desires were changing as well, coming more and more in line with God's will.

My relationship with Marie grew closer, more tender, and more trusting. Her compassion, her readiness to forgive, and her constant belief in my goodness and in me were and are a source of awe to me. At one point, I sat Marie down and acknowledged all the ways I had hurt her over the years, and I asked her forgiveness for each one. It was a tearful moment of renewal in our marriage.

A year and a half after my excommunication, I wrestled with God in prayer for hours one Christmas night, begging for His forgiveness. I walked away from that prayer with a peaceful assurance that I could be forgiven and a conviction that I was ready for my disciplinary council to reconvene. It was time.

The reconvening council felt completely different from the disciplinary council as I reported with gratitude and humility the "mighty change" that God had worked in my life. I faced this same council of seventeen men with my head held high and with gratitude in my heart. A week later, I was rebaptized in a simple, beautiful witness of the power of the Atonement to effect change and restore to wholeness.

About that time Martin testified to me that he felt certain, through a witness of the Spirit, that God had a great work for me to do in His kingdom and that my repentance was necessary not only for my own salvation but also to prepare me to serve the Lord in the future.

An Instrument in the Hands of God

In the scriptures, one powerful indication of a repentant heart is the desire to share the good news of the gospel and to help bring others out of darkness and into light. The Lord Jesus Christ told Simon Peter, "When thou art converted, strengthen thy brethren" (Luke 22:32). My scriptural heroes include the Apostle Paul, Alma the Elder, Alma the Younger, and the four sons of Mosiah—all of whom turned from grave sins and dedicated the remaining years of their lives to devout missionary service to repair the damage they had done.

The further I turned from my past sins, the more driven I felt to share my testimony of change with others. In 2000, a year and a half after my rebaptism, I felt strongly that I wanted to share a message of hope with others who were at a place in life where I had been for so long—struggling with unwanted same-sex attractions with little hope that those feelings could be diminished or eliminated. By networking with therapists, authors, and Christian ministry leaders, I found and interviewed a dozen men who, like me, had experienced remarkable transition away from homosexual desires. I started a new website to share their real-life stories with the world. Their testimonies of the reality of change now reach tens of thousands of website visitors every year.

I gave the website the simple, direct name People Can Change to tap into what I believe is a self-evident truth that humans have the inherent agency and ability to change their lives in meaningful ways if they want to. But, privately, the name also has a deeper meaning to me. I closely associate the word *change* in this context with the principle of repentance, especially the mighty change of heart spoken of in the Book of Mormon: "The Spirit of the Lord Omnipotent . . . has wrought a mighty change in us, or in our hearts, that we have no more disposition to do evil, but to do good continually" (Mosiah 5:2).

Still, I felt called to do more. Because therapy to help men and women with unwanted homosexuality is so controversial within the mental health professions in the United States, relatively few counselors are willing to specialize in this area or have significant skill or knowledge in helping people overcome unwanted homosexuality. Most people seeking help don't know where to turn, and many flounder for years, as I had, believing that there is no hope. I thought of Bill W. and Bob S., the founders of Alcoholics Anonymous, who created their own self-help group when the mental health professions had given up on the idea that a drunk could ever recover. Because of their work, AA, with its twelve steps, has become the most successful self-help program the world has ever known.

I was also motivated by the scriptural injunction that "men should be anxiously engaged in a good cause, and do many things of their own free will, and bring to pass much righteousness" (D&C 58:27). Why wait for someone else to do something to meet the need?

My dream was to create a self-help model for men who didn't necessarily have access to specialized therapy. In 2002, building on everything I had learned in my own journey, I organized a peer-led weekend program of instruction and emotional and spiritual renewal. Starved for this kind of support and information, twenty-three men came from twelve states for that first weekend program in 2002, which we called "Journey into Manhood."

It became the first of many. My former therapist, David Matheson, joined me in refining and further developing the weekend program, and in the ensuing years, we have offered it dozens of times across the United States and in England. As a result, I've been privileged to witness firsthand profound changes in the lives of many hundreds of men. I see over and over again that as they grow in their sense of innate masculinity and in platonic brotherhood with other men, their sexualized attractions to men greatly diminish and their capacity and desire to relate romantically to women increase.

Although we intentionally make the weekend program not overtly religious so that it is welcoming to men of all faiths or no faith, essential to our approach is the spiritual principle of "surrender"—or as scripture would describe it, "yielding [our] hearts unto God" (Helaman 3:35). Humbly aligning thoughts, feelings, behaviors, and goals with the will of God in all things is essential to experiencing the fulness of joy promised in scripture.

As I think of the tremendous impact I have had the privilege of making on the lives of so many, I catch a glimpse of the prophet Alma's exuberance when, upon glorying in the Lord's work and in the missionary success of the sons of Mosiah among the Lamanites, he said, "I do not glory of myself, but I glory in that which the Lord hath commanded me; yea, and this is my glory, that perhaps I may be an instrument in the hands of God to bring some soul to repentance; and this is my joy" (Alma 29:9).

But my joy in doing this work was severely challenged in 2005 when my employer, an openly gay man, discovered that I was running People Can Change and its Journey into Manhood program as a volunteer effort in my private life. Deeply offended by my volunteer work, he promptly dismissed me from my job despite the rave performance reviews I had received for years. I was stunned. I feared for my ability to provide for my family and especially to provide health care for my wife, who by then had been diagnosed with terminal breast cancer.

It was a tumultuous time, and yet even in that awful turmoil, the Lord evidenced His tender mercies. I was able to spend most of the last year and a half of Marie's life at home with her, laughing with her and enjoying her company when she felt well, caring for and tending to her when she was failing. I was able to spend more time with our two children, who needed extra attention and support at such a difficult time. Ward members brought meals, helped with household chores, and even built a wheelchair ramp when Marie lost the ability to walk. Severance benefits and freelance work kept the money flowing and health insurance active. No, the Lord had not forgotten us.

Of course nothing could fully prepare me for losing the one woman who had loved me so completely and unconditionally. She died over Thanksgiving weekend 2006 at the age of forty-six in the nineteenth year of our marriage. Even in that terrible loss, I thank God that He prolonged her life for as many years as He did and that He sustained her in such a way that she was largely pain-free for most of that time. I thank my Heavenly Father that Marie did not pass away until after He had brought about in me the mighty change of heart that enabled me to remain completely faithful to her during the second half of our marriage, to have the covenants associated with our temple sealing renewed, and to become the husband she always deserved. Our earthly marriage ended at the high point of our relationship: completely in love, completely trusting, and mutually devoted to serving the Lord.

Through all of this, it became increasingly evident that the answer for this stage of my life was for me to permanently leave my corporate career. Instead, I decided to make a living building up the nonprofit organization I had founded and working full time from home coaching individual clients by phone who were seeking to resolve unwanted same-sex attractions. In this way, not only was I living more fully the life mission to which I felt called by God, but I was also blessed to remain at home with Marie in the last months of her life and be a work-at-home dad to my daughter and son after they had lost their mother.

Truly, my life and trials are a testimony of the Lord's promises:

"All things wherewith you have been afflicted shall work together for your good, and to my name's glory" (D&C 98:3).

"And if men come unto me I will show unto them their weakness. I give unto men weakness that they may be humble; and my grace is sufficient for all men that humble themselves before me; for if they humble themselves before me, and have faith in me, then will I make weak things become strong unto them" (Ether 12:27).

Chapter 2

A Gift of Love:
Perspectives for Parents

M. Catherine Thomas

*He doeth not anything save it be for the benefit
of the world; for he loveth the world, even that he layeth down
his own life that he may draw all men unto him.*

—2 Nephi 26:24

The precious child born into our home who later comes struggling with a revelation of his or her* same-gender attraction is a gift. At the outset, this revelation may feel like anything but a gift. But even though fear and guilt and shame engulf us and hopes and expectations fade, the revelation is not only a blessing but also likely belongs to our personal path. In recognizing these circumstances as a gift, a parent can be led to see the hand of the Lord in all that is transpiring.

In the first hours and days after the revelation of his child's troubles, a parent may grieve and mourn. In his confusion he may say and do unhelpful things. But he can learn, and as he does, his awareness will expand, as will his heart. The realization can come that what has surfaced is a provocation to a purer love and a call to step up spiritually on several fronts.

---

*To avoid the awkwardness of indicating male and female, I will primarily use the masculine form in this chapter.

Relief from traumatic situations comes when we can put the problem into a new context and then find appropriate action. In this chapter we will explore (1) how to cast new light on this situation so as to detect the benefit hidden in it and (2) how to put the greatest good into it.

This chapter will not address all the concerns of the parent whose child confronts same-gender attraction. Nor will it give all the how-to's. Its main purpose is to help the parent shift from a state of anxiety to a sense of being able to deal spiritually and profitably with the situation, to find comfort and hope.

The first glimmers of hope appear with the realization that heaven is involved. Three perspectives can help us come to this awareness: the perspective that enables us to see heaven open behind us, revealing the preparations of the premortal past; the perspective that allows us to see heaven revealing itself in our troubled present; and that which opens our eyes to the infinite vision before us.

I. The Heavens Behind: A Customized Curriculum

And we know that all things work together for good
to them that love God, to them who are called according to his
purpose. For whom he did foreknow, he also did [foreordain]
to be conformed to the image of his Son (Romans 8:28–29).

It seems that all circumstances and events that appear in this world were planned for in the world before. Nothing happens without the Lord's intention to provide the challenges and experiences necessary to exalt His children. And all the challenges we agreed to there were to be consecrated to our gain here (see 2 Nephi 2:2) whether we grasped what it was we were to do or not.

As we can feel the *immediacy* of the unfolding plan in the labyrinths of our own life, we can experience a feeling not of defeat but of empowerment. Elder Neal A. Maxwell provides the context for the circumstances of our lives: "I believe with all my heart that because God loves us there are some particularized challenges that he will deliver to each of us. He will customize the curriculum for each of us in order to teach us the things we most need to know. He will set before us in life what we need, not always what we like. And this will require us to accept with all our hearts . . . the truth that there is divine design in each of our lives and that you have a rendezvous to keep."[1]

Premortal Preparations

We understood this distant rendezvous even as we made our preparations in the premortal world, but we must have looked forward with sober anticipation at what lay between our final destiny and us. And even though we agreed to go through the challenges that lay before us, we might have preferred to avoid them. Nevertheless, we chose to come because of a common perspective we shared with our Savior. President Joseph F. Smith recalls our feelings:

"Had we not known before we came the necessity of our coming, the importance of obtaining tabernacles, the glory to be achieved in posterity, the grand object to be attained by being tried and tested—weighed in the balance, in the exercise of the divine attributes, god-like powers and free agency with which we are endowed; whereby, after descending below all things, Christ-like, we might ascend above all things, and become like our Father, Mother and Elder Brother, Almighty and Eternal!—we never would have come; that is, if we could have stayed away.

"I believe that our Savior is the ever-living example to all flesh in all these things. He no doubt possessed a foreknowledge of all the vicissitudes through which he would have to pass in the mortal tabernacle, when the foundations of this earth were laid, 'when the morning stars sang together, and all the sons of God shouted for joy.' . . .

"And yet, to accomplish the ultimatum of his previous existence, and consummate the grand and glorious object of his being, and the salvation of his infinite brotherhood, he had to come and take upon him flesh. He is our example. . . . If Christ knew beforehand, so did we."[2]

We knew what would be, and we chose it. Elder Maxwell

comments on the reason we chose these trials and their purpose: "For all we now know, the seeming limitations may have been an agreed-upon spur to achievement—a developmental equivalent of a 'thorn in the flesh.'"[3]

So we each came into this present world with a set of particular predispositions that would form part of our customized curriculum. Apparently specific weaknesses or predispositions were chosen as catalysts for godly growth, as stated in Ether 12:27: "I give unto men weakness that they may be humble; and my grace is sufficient . . . ; I make weak things become strong unto them." In this context, we can accept that our child may have brought with him to this life a predisposition for same-gender attraction, a tendency that could serve as the impetus he would need "to accomplish the ultimatum of his previous existence, and consummate the grand and glorious object of his being." Likewise, we as parents can accept that we too agreed to shepherd this child for the same reasons.

Considering the detailed nature of the premortal plan, it is not by random chance that this child was born into our family. Elder Bruce R. McConkie teaches how detailed the premortal plan was: "All men are the spirit children of the Eternal Father; all dwelt in his presence, awaiting the day of their mortal probation; all have come or will come to earth at an appointed time, in a specified place, to live among a designated people. In all of this there is no chance. A divine providence rules over the nations and governs in the affairs of men. Birth and death and mortal kinship are the Lord's doings. He alone determines where and when and among what people his spirit children shall undergo their mortal probation."[4]

Our children come into specific lineages that reflect premortal invitations and assignments into the great premortal house of Israel. This child, present now in our family, brings something of the *elect* in him as well as special preparations received in the premortal world (see D&C 138:56). That is, this child was placed on purpose in our lineage and in our family, and being of Israel, he comes with powerful possibilities.

Concerning those who may wander for a time because of ignorance and confusion over their feelings, Elder Orson F. Whitney asks, "Who are these . . . wayward sons and daughters? They are children of the Covenant, heirs to the promises, and have received, if baptized, the gift of the Holy Ghost, which makes manifest the things of God. Could all that go for naught?"[5] Specifically, foreordinations and powers were conferred on these children before they were born into this world: "All Israel, according to the doctrine of foreordination, have it in their power to gain exaltation; to be like the Son of God, having gained his image; . . . to be participators with their fathers in the covenant that God made with them; and to be inheritors, to the full, of the ancient promises. Implicit in all this is the fact that they are foreordained to be baptized, to join the Church, to receive the priesthood, to enter the ordinance of celestial marriage, and to be sealed up unto eternal life."[6]

These doctrines help us realize that whatever those inner mortal predispositions may be, the Lord has provided the way by which they can be managed and transcended through premortal preparations and the broad-spectrum powers of the Atonement, which can save anyone "afflicted in any manner" (3 Nephi 17:9).

The Lord declared in the midst of the premortal intelligences, "And we will prove them herewith, to see if they will do all things whatsoever the Lord their God shall command them" (Abraham 3:25). Elder George Q. Cannon describes the penetrating purposes of the Lord's testing and what our response to Him must be in order to fulfill the objectives of the mortal probation: "Whatever fate may threaten us, there is but one course for men [and women] of God to take, that is, to keep inviolate the holy covenants they have made in the presence of God and angels. For the remainder, whether it be life or death, freedom or imprisonment, prosperity or adversity, we must trust in God. We may say, however, if any man or woman expects to enter into the Celestial Kingdom of our God without making sacrifices and without being tested to the very utmost, they have not understood the Gospel. If there is a weak spot in our nature, or if there is a fiber that can be made to quiver or to shrink, we may rest assured that it will be tested.

Our own weaknesses will be brought fully to light, and in seeking for help the strength of our God will also be made manifest to us."[7]

There may be times that we think we cannot stand what we are faced with, that the universe is unfair, that our child's burden and our burden are unfair. But Elder Richard G. Scott reassures us: "He would have you suffer no consequence, no challenge, endure no burden that is superfluous to your good."[8]

II. Heaven in the Midst of Our Troubled Present

My son, peace be unto thy soul. . . . Let thy bowels . . .
be full of charity . . . then shall thy confidence wax strong in the
presence of God. . . . The Holy Ghost shall be thy constant
companion (D&C 121:7, 45–46).

Perhaps peace has fled, but it can return. And even though the tests are real, the dangers great, and the stakes high, we can find deeper bases for contentment in our lives, even in stressful circumstances and even while the Lord does not allow us to circumvent a trial. Elder Jeffrey R. Holland speaks in the context of Liberty Jail to our fragile faith:

"You can have sacred, revelatory, profoundly instructive experiences with the Lord in *any* situation you are in. Indeed, you can have sacred, revelatory, profoundly instructive experiences with the Lord *in the most miserable experiences of your life*—in the worst settings, while enduring the most painful injustices, when facing the most insurmountable odds and oppositions you have ever faced. . . . *Every* experience can become a *redemptive* experience if we remain bonded to our Father in Heaven through it. . . .

"Whenever these moments of our extremity come, we must not succumb to the fear that God has abandoned us or that He does not hear our prayers. He *does* hear us. He *does* see us. He *does* love us. When we are in dire circumstances and want to cry, 'Where art Thou?' it is imperative that we remember He is right there with us—where He has always been! We must continue to believe, continue to have faith, continue to pray and plead with heaven, even if we feel for a time our prayers are not heard and that God has somehow gone away."⁹

We can come to know that it is, after all, a safe universe, in that everything is in the Lord's hands, and that it is He that sets the latitudes and limitations to what can happen. When the Lord comforted the Prophet Joseph Smith, He taught him that even the worst trials would give him experience and be for his good. We learn, as Joseph did, that there is often no profitable way around the tutorial, only through it.

Though we may be tempted to pray that the Lord will take this problem from us or from our loved one, Elder Maxwell suggests a different approach. There is an "eternal ecology," he says, in which we are all interconnected in a "process of becoming": "In the eternal ecology of things we must pray, therefore, not that things be taken from us, but that God's will be accomplished through us. What, therefore, may seem now to be mere unconnected pieces of tile will someday, when we look back, take form and pattern, and we will realize that God was making a mosaic. For there is in each of our lives this kind of divine design, this pattern, this purpose that is in the process of becoming, which is continually before the Lord but which for us, looking forward, is sometimes perplexing."¹⁰

So, settling down, we look at the situation we have with our child and ask what the Lord would accomplish through us. The answer to that question will mark the sanctifying path before us. Still, we may feel distracted by the question "When will this trial end?" Elder Holland answers, "When what has to be has been and when what lessons to be learned have been learned."¹¹

Changes in this challenge will surely come but perhaps not on our schedule. Some will find full transformation in this life, and some will not. But we keep this reason for hope—that a human being, like all life, is a fluid process, not a fixed, rigid system, and is susceptible to continual change and forward movement—more than we might imagine. Instead of wanting to circumvent it, we can come to love what the Lord has given us to do. And to the parent who feels weary of it, to the child who feels tempted to yield to the world's solutions, Elder Holland says emotionally, "Hope on, and wait and let me walk with you, and we'll be faithful, be clean, and we'll get to the end of this."[12]

Now let us look at what some of the lessons might be.

Taking Care of Ourselves

The way to peace comes in taking care of ourselves and then taking care of our child, insofar as we can. We will consider here what the parent can do to cultivate peace and clarity so as not to become blinded by fear, guilt, shame, pride, and bitterness.

But let us review first the nature of the human being, the child of God, so that we can have fresh in our mind some of the resources that have been planted in us from before the foundations of the world.

Being created as we were out of the stuff of "truth and light" (D&C 93:28; see also 23–27), we possess at our core not only goodness but also the small flame of a steady joy, which is always present. It is the nature of man that when he is in a state of repentance, this joy is more accessible and can be experienced more clearly, such as with the people of King Benjamin: "They were filled with joy, having received a remission of their sins, and having peace of conscience" (Mosiah 4:3). Often, when our joy is obscured, we do not know what it is we need to repent of in order to feel better. Sometimes what we need to repent of is troublesome thoughts and negative emotions of the mind like resistance, irritation, resentment, willfulness, condemnation, and despair. These feelings may be undefined in our minds; they may be nebulous and anxious, creating a heaviness we can hardly parse out, clouding faith and clarity, and blocking relief.[13]

I use a simple little technique that is effective for me.[14] I remind myself that getting distance from uncomfortable thinking can take the sting out of it. I look at these anxious thoughts as though they were my little children, and in my mind's eye I gather them to my side. I befriend them and am kind to them, but I am clear that they are only occupying some space in my mind and do not represent a durable reality. I recognize that they have some element of falseness in them. As I gather them gently to my side, I find in their wake a comfortable, empty space; I can rest in that. Here in the inner peace of this present moment, perhaps there is even a little light, and—if I am attentive— that steady joy at my core. And though they may try to swallow me up again, I enjoy this emotional distance. I feel that this is a truer state than the troubled one. Yes, I can leave so much more to the Lord than I thought—I just don't have to keep stewing, trying to work it all out myself. And I find that being gentle with my own troublesome thoughts soothes me, helps me be my deeper self, so as to be gentle also with others. In this space I can feel some new options.

So our initial response to the situation may range from stressful feelings of what it will mean to our child to what it may mean to us, and it is likely a mixture of the two. But troubled feelings, even though they feel clingy, are fluid; they only float over the eternal in us, and we know from experience that they can shift and leave us in a more comfortable place, helping us to be open to new solutions.

Possible Approaches to Distress

Anxiety: Human beings have a tendency to be addicted to disturbance and to resist peace. In recognizing that, we can care for ourselves by disarming the temptation, and it is a real temptation, to cooperate with the adversary in fanning the flames of torment and amplifying anxiety around the bare situation. As these emotions fill the mind, they block the reassurance and guidance that are seeking access to our spirit. Elder Holland counsels: "The Spirit has a near impossible task to get through to a heart that is filled with hate or anger or vengeance or self-pity. Those are all antithetical to the Spirit of the Lord. On the other hand, the Spirit finds instant access to a heart striving to be charitable and forgiving, long-suffering and kind—principles of true discipleship. What a testimony that if we strive to remain faithful, the triumph of a Christian life can never be vanquished, no matter how grim the circumstance might be."[15]

Elder Maxwell penetrates to the root cause of exaggerated emotions: "In most emotional escalations with which I am familiar, if one goes to the very center of them, there is ego asserting itself relentlessly.

The only cure for rampant ego is humility, and this is why circumstances often bring to us a kind of compelled or forced humility—so that we may recover our equilibrium."[16]

Guilt in Parenting: In caring for ourselves, we can gently replace the guilty fear that we might be the cause of our child's same-gender attraction. We did not cause it.[17] But at the same time we can see how several factors—nature (biologically influenced temperament and sensitivity) and nurture (family, parenting, and social dynamics) and premortal arrangements—likely worked together to produce this current situation. We can, therefore, take some responsibility (which is not the same thing as blame or guilt) in order to see how we can address the situation for the benefit of all. We should set aside our fear of finding ourselves lacking as parents and begin to recognize the ways in which we may not have met some of our child's needs.

In this process of self-examination, we reflect on what it has been like to be parents. A few years back, being new parents, we operated with the tools we had when this child was born to us. We likely did the best we could, but which of us was fully mature or spiritually developed when our first baby came? We were in some ways still children ourselves. I looked at the beautiful baby in the bassinette in the hospital and wasn't sure how to go about picking her up. We had to grow with our children, and we made mistakes as we dealt with our own confusions and conflicts. Of course, our parents had done the same with us, and we inherited some of their confusions; then we in turn passed some of this baggage on to our children.

Even though this transgenerational situation operates by divine design, the turning of pain and confusion into loving peace may require something like surgery, which is best done with penetrating honesty, with as little guilt as possible, and with a willingness to make some old weaknesses into strengths. Elder Scott acknowledges the pain of remodeling and the trust needed in the Lord's plan:

"Just when all seems to be going right, challenges often come in multiple doses applied simultaneously. When those trials are not consequences of your disobedience, they are evidence that the Lord feels you are prepared to grow more (see Proverbs 3:11–12). He therefore gives you experiences that stimulate growth, understanding, and compassion which polish you for your everlasting benefit. To get you from where you are to where He wants you to be requires a lot of stretching, and that generally entails discomfort and pain. . . .

"This life is an experience in profound trust—trust in Jesus Christ, trust in His teachings, trust in our capacity as led by the Holy Spirit to obey those teachings for happiness now and for a purposeful, supremely happy eternal existence. To trust means to obey willingly without knowing the end from the beginning (see Proverbs 3:5–7). To produce fruit, your trust in the Lord must be more powerful and enduring than your confidence in your own personal feelings and experience."[18]

Fear of Others' Judgments: For all our fear for our child, perhaps one of the things that hurt is our fear of what others will think. Those of us who have managed a satisfying image of our family will find this situation a particular trial. But this trial is also a blessing because it points out the spiritual path ahead. Sooner or later, each of us finds that the Lord will go after our ego issues until He has disengaged us from the need for the good opinion of others. He does this so that we may learn to keep our eye single to His glory and purposes (as in D&C 88:67—that "your whole bodies shall be filled with light"). Getting rid of this fear belongs in a discussion on self-care because we often do not realize that all actions that we have undertaken in order to "look good" will necessarily end in some sort of pain. Most of us are slow to disentangle our ego ends from purer ones. Therefore, the Lord will provoke us to let go of defensiveness, self-righteousness, self-protection, and self-justification, which will have inevitably caused a certain spiritual superficiality. These act as blinders as our struggling child comes to us. We don't really see *him,* his face, his confusion, the struggle that has brought him to us, or his need for our love and support. Getting beyond what this situation means for us, by turning with full intent to the Lord, will help us lay hold on a purer love.

A Purer Love: Love, a well-worn topic, nevertheless causes us some confusion, and most of us realize we have a distance to go in order to experience the love the scriptures describe. We're apt to think that those we love owe us something in the way of compliance or gratitude. This sense of entitlement is not related to the love that we are here specifically to cultivate. Dr. M. Scott Peck's familiar definition of love is worth revisiting here: "I define love thus: The will to extend one's self for the purpose of nurturing one's own or another's spiritual growth."[19] That is, love is less of a feeling and more of an activity and investment, involving effort and possibly courage.

Dr. David Hawkins extends the definition of love to describe a state of being: "[Pure love] is unconditional, unchanging, and permanent. It doesn't fluctuate—its source isn't dependent on external factors. Loving is a state of being. It's a forgiving, nurturing, and supportive way of relating to the world. Love isn't intellectual and doesn't proceed from the mind; Love emanates from the heart. It has the capacity to lift others and accomplish great feats because of its purity of motive. . . . As Love becomes more and more unconditional, it begins to be experienced as inner Joy. This isn't the sudden joy of a pleasurable turn of events; it's a constant accompaniment to all activities. Joy arises from within each moment of existence, rather than from any other source."[20]

Our loved one may not do what we want him to, but we can find fulfillment in doing that which love bids us do, letting the consequences be what they must be for now. Love is a choice as to how we are going to encounter the world around us—until all our works are the works of love. As Mormon says, "Whoso is found possessed of [charity or pure love] at the last day, it shall be well with him" (Moroni 7:47).

Dependent Happiness: Love and self-care also have to do with learning to accept that our own happiness is not dependent on our child's happiness or decisions. We can wake up from the illusion that our sense of fulfillment is dependent on what another does; we can reexamine the idea that "when they're unhappy, I'm unhappy." It helps to see that it is not kind to require happiness of another. One reason is that when he knows you're too anxious about him, he will have to worry not only about his own problem but about you too. He's not in our life to make us happy.

On reflection, we realize that we don't want our child to live for us; rather, we want to learn just to be with him, to listen to him, to look at his face, to understand him, and to feel without all the fears and judgments and guilt in order to sense what the situation is saying to us or asking of us. The past cannot be changed, but it can be reconfigured with forgiveness; and to focus on what can be done now begins to open the channels of healing for all concerned and prepares us to be able to endure the purifying fire of heavenly love.

As we cultivate compassion, it helps to become conscious of the struggle that likely led to your child's revelation. As he became aware that his feelings weren't like those of most of the people he cares about, and as he may have considered taking steps to choose a same-gender partner (or may have already done so), he felt conflict over what this would mean for him and for you. Fearing that he would lose your love, he likely needed courage to share with you what may have been years of struggle within him. Our job is not to control or manipulate his feelings or behavior but to do the work of love.

To be clear, however, loving and supporting do not mean condoning; the law of chastity is the same for all the Lord's children. Nevertheless, Elder Marlin K. Jensen counsels regarding whatever decision our child may make: "We understand this is a condition that some people are dealing with and that even if it needs changing or even if it needs controlling, that can't be done without our support, our love, our empathy, our interest in them as people."[21]

Fulfillment: Self-care has to do with stepping back, clearing a space in the mind, and cultivating sanity and dispassion because the issue of same-gender attraction can take over one's thinking, in parent and child, and become the lens through which one looks at all of life. But this too is unnecessary. Parent and child can realize that fulfillment in life is a cluster of things, a holistic creation. As Elder Lance B. Wickman explains, our highly sexualized society complicates finding fulfillment aside from gender orientation, but this complication can be side-stepped: "We live in a society which is so saturated with sexuality that it perhaps is more troublesome now, because of that fact, for a person to look beyond their gender orientation to other aspects of who they are. I think I would say to your son or anyone that was so afflicted to strive to expand your horizons beyond simply gender orientation. Find fulfillment in the many other facets of your character and your personality and your nature that extend beyond that. There's no denial that one's gender orientation is certainly a core characteristic of any person, but it's not the only one."[22]

People with same-gender attraction are often talented, sensitive people. Finding fulfillment in discovering what they were placed on earth to do in order to express their talents and make a unique contribution can become a transcending source of fulfillment.

Instead of confronting life with a feeling of deprivation, we will see that many compensations present themselves to parent and child as we look at ways to make life rich and meaningful. While we do what we can for our child, we can give ourselves permission to enjoy the most simple pleasures of life. As we loosen knots in mind and body, we can make our own contentment. It is simply true that both parent and child can find deeply felt compensations, reassurances, and satisfying happiness, even in trying circumstances, as Elder Scott describes:

"I testify that when the Lord closes one important door in your life, He shows His continuing love and compassion by opening many other compensating doors through your exercise of faith. He will place in your path packets of spiritual sunlight to brighten your way. They often come after the trial has been the greatest, as evidence of the compassion and love of an all-knowing Father. They point the way to greater happiness, more understanding, and strengthen your determination to accept and be obedient to His will. . . . True enduring happiness with the accompanying strength, courage, and capacity to overcome the most challenging difficulties comes from a life centered in Jesus Christ. Obedience to His teachings provides a sure foundation upon which to build. That takes effort. There is no guarantee of overnight results, but there is absolute assurance that, in the Lord's time, solutions will come, peace will prevail, and emptiness will be filled."

He advises us to avoid the trap of falling into total absorption in the problems that appear: "Don't let the workings of adversity totally absorb your life. Try to understand what you can. Act where you are able; then let the matter rest with the Lord for a period while you give to others in worthy ways before you take on appropriate concern again."

Elder Scott reassures us that the steady joy that flickers below the accumulated sorrows of this life can be felt: "Please learn that as you wrestle with a challenge and feel sadness because of it, you can simultaneously have peace and rejoicing. Yes, pain, disappointment, frustration, and anguish can be temporary scenes played out on the stage of life. Behind them there can be a background of peace and the positive assurance that a loving Father will keep His promises. You can qualify for those promises by a determination to accept His will, by understanding the plan of happiness, by receiving all of the ordinances, and by keeping the covenants made to assure their fulfillment."[23]

New and unexpected doors can open, and new solutions can present themselves, making life an exciting adventure. Miracles can appear at any time.

Caring for the Child

Continuing self-care, as we look to our child, we may find it possible to identify some ways in which we have unwittingly made life more difficult for our child; and then we may consider offering a detailed apology. This is self-care as well as child care because our spirit knows when we have not measured up in a relationship; to heal ourselves, we have to come clean in the relationship. During this apology we will not mention the child's failings, only our own. We will humbly ask forgiveness and ask how we can be more helpful. We will listen undefensively, as dispassionately as we can. Healing communication can then begin.[24] Then, in addition to much listening, we may be able to share with our child, as time goes on, some points of view that can reassure both our child and us.

Shame and Guilt: Our child will likely be suffering from shame and feelings of unworthiness, even if he has not chosen to express his same-gender attraction sexually. He may have felt directly or indirectly the negativity, sometimes amounting to hatred and vitriol, being poured out, even by some members of the Church, on people dealing with same-gender attraction. His feelings of shame will interfere with his ability to draw close to the Lord for comfort.

Following are responses that two people have had as they have confronted both shame and guilt over their same-gender feelings and the issue of sex. A young LDS woman in her thirties who has just begun coming to terms, after a fifteen-year struggle, with her feelings of attraction for other women, and is wondering what this means for her, wrote me the following about her perception that, at their inception, same-gender feelings do not seem intrinsically sexual.

"It's not about sex. Other people think that those who might be/are gay are struggling with immoral thoughts/feelings and behaviors. But what you will hear across the board is that the first feeling is that 'I am different.' As other teenagers or young adults start to explore with giddiness their crushes and dreamy thoughts of an ideal future, those with same-gender attraction start to try to figure out what is wrong with them. I think THIS is the battlefront.

"They begin to feel shame over their nonsexualized attraction to the same gender, where heterosexuals are encouraged in that attraction, understood, given boundaries to work within, etc. Ultimately, heterosexuals can find legitimate physical/sexual expression for that attraction, but many same-gender-attracted people freeze in that shame—never drifting to immoral thoughts/feelings/behavior, but having no route, or reroute, for that part of themselves—and begin to internalize this struggle."

Another LDS young man who deals with this challenge wrote similarly:

"The shame is a huge problem. . . . I had similar feelings of being 'different' when I was younger, and while I occasionally fantasized about being physically close with other boys, I don't recall it ever feeling sexual until well into high school—and even then I was so afraid of those feelings that I never allowed myself to acknowledge them. More often than not, I just wanted to feel close to other guys, or I would allow myself to overfocus on qualities in them I felt I lacked, and wanted, in myself.

"I remember once wanting to give my best friend a hug when I saw him, and he looked at me funny and asked if I was gay. That was in fourth grade, I think. All I knew about 'gay' was that it was bad, and the shame I felt in that moment led me to tenaciously avoid any behaviors that might be perceived that way. I disowned a lot of parts of my personality, and it's only been in my adulthood that I've been learning to reclaim, reintegrate those parts, and learn to love men in the deep and intimate and healthy ways I only ever wanted anyway."

Caring for your child would include helping him to let go of shame for the feelings themselves and reassuring him of the Lord's love. Many people who experience same-gender attraction find that, despite the fact that they are dealing with a set of deeply disconcerting feelings, they can exist in a loving relationship with the Lord in the same system of faith, repentance, and having the Holy Ghost that anyone else can. In this way they are able to embrace a sense of worthiness that allows them to move forward spiritually as they manage these feelings within the bounds the Lord has set.

Elder Holland wrote on making the distinction between feelings and behavior: "While same-gender attraction is real, there must be no physical [sexual or romantic] expression of this attraction. The desire for physical gratification does not authorize immorality by anyone. Such feelings can be powerful, but they are never so strong as to deprive anyone of the freedom to choose worthy conduct. In saying this, let me make it clear that attractions alone, troublesome as they may be, do not make one unworthy."[25]

Labeling: People tend to behave according to the way they see themselves. Help him to take care with the labels he puts on himself.

Lift your child's sights to a vision of who he really is. Elder Dallin H. Oaks offers this counsel to a parent about what he might say to his child:

"You're my son. You will always be my son, and I'll always be there to help you. . . .

"Homosexuality . . . is not a noun that describes a condition. It's an adjective that describes feelings or behavior. I encourage you, as you struggle with these challenges, not to think of yourself as a 'something' or 'another,' except that you're a member of The Church of Jesus Christ of Latter-day Saints and you're my son, and that you're struggling with challenges. . . .

"You've described a particular kind of challenge that is very vexing. It is common in our society and it has also become politicized. But it's only one of a host of challenges men and women have to struggle with, and I just encourage you to seek the help of the Savior to resist temptation and to refrain from behavior that would cause you to have to repent or to have your Church membership called into question."[26]

From a Pure Fountain: Perhaps same-gender feelings can fit into a broader understanding of love. We acknowledge that human beings are capable of a wide spectrum of affinities and attractions—yin and yang, femaleness and maleness. Both these seeming opposites occur in each person in unique proportions and, as a result, some people are drawn with strong affinities to their own gender. The scriptures offer a few examples of how powerful the bonds of same-gender love can be without any sexual ingredient. David, for instance, expresses his feelings for Jonathan, who has just died: "I am distressed for thee, my brother Jonathan: very pleasant [Hebrew: beautiful, sweet, delightful, lovely] hast thou been unto me: thy love to me was wonderful, passing the love of women" (2 Samuel 1:26).

As another example, Brigham Young's last words were reported to be "Joseph, Joseph, Joseph." Perhaps we can expand in our minds the bounds of acceptable love and help our child see that the feelings may arise initially out of that which was originally good and pure.

Because we live in a hypersexualized society, and nearly everything is sexualized, deep feeling for the same gender is either proscribed as morally suspect or, at the other extreme, is recruited into sexual activity. But in other periods, even in the history of the United States, this bifurcation did not exist. One historian, for example, remarks on nonsexual relationships between same genders in the years before the Civil War in which ideals of spiritual friendship became incorporated into Christian and American traditions. General expressions of love or nonsexual intimacy between two men or two women were considered perfectly normal. "'Women hugged, kissed, slept with, and proclaimed love for other women,' and 'men did the same with other men'" without anyone considering this behavior aberrant. If these relationships became sexual, then moralists considered the behavior wrong.[27]

I'm suggesting that, for many, the problem may not be the original same-gender feelings themselves but the lack of acceptance of those feelings in their pure form and then the sexualizing of them, both of which cause their distortion.

What if the feelings themselves could be completely accepted without their sexual expression? Might they be less distorted, less sexualized? One young man writes, "As I've worked through my own stuff, I've felt my feelings had to do with sexualizing an emotional need in male peer relationships." But as he continued working, he found that there were, underneath the more superficial sexual attraction for other men, "underlying streams of what was good and healthy and right. To try to shut off the feelings altogether is as spiritually and emotionally damaging as indulging in their sexual expression. The challenge is the level of discernment it takes to separate healthy from unhealthy, truth from error, light from darkness. I've had to learn to become a skilled deconstructionist simply for the sake of spiritual and emotional survival. So, as families and as a Church, the more we can cultivate and encourage expression of the 'real thing'—love in its purest and most satisfying forms—the less we'll lose members who will seek to find it somewhere else, and likely in counterfeits. Similarly, the more we encourage people to stay in the bushes, so to speak (as did Lucifer, who told Adam and Eve to hide from the Lord), and simply give them nothing more than a bunch of behavioral 'don'ts,' the more we are going to lose them as they seek for something—anything—that *resembles* the real thing."

The child's feelings of being "different" might tend to isolate him and make him distrustful of close attachments, even in a nonsexual way. But often, close attachments are what he needs most. One therapist remarks about not being afraid of deep feelings for others but finding and walking the line of integrity, not only for her own welfare but also for that of others in her life:

"We have such rich and deep connections with people, with one another, truly deep loving intimacy. So how to keep that door open, how to keep that heartfelt life there, but not be seduced by the power and attraction of that intimacy? Because it is in that deep intimacy, of course, that sexual attraction and energy can arise and emerge. So how to maintain an integrity in that intimacy, and be true to our feelings of love for one another, and not fall into that well of sexual misconduct? . . . I have many boundaries and ethics that I apply in those situations, particularly through my psychotherapy training."

She implies that we not "superficialize" our relationships just because we are afraid, but that we stay open to all life and to all the satisfying richness available in connection with the beauty of the people and nature around us. She says, "May all beings venerate life as a state of deep spiritual intimacy. Here in the fields: just those young green fronds making their way out of the earth. This is so . . . beautiful."[28]

Might it be helpful to reassure our loved one that the feelings of love for those of his own gender arise out of his primeval loving nature and do not in themselves represent unworthiness or cause for shame but are, rather, a sign of his ability to love and to connect deeply with others? Feelings and expressions of pure love and intimacy, including those for our own gender, are a beautiful and important part of all our most valued relationships, and in that eternal world, such feelings and expressions of love were not subject to the distortions so present in this fallen world. Neither will they be after this life if one pursues here that higher love in chastity and self-restraint. It seems that this world tends to sexualize that which was not originally sexual. In any event, Elder Holland, among others, reassures us that these feelings will be resolved into their proper place in the world to come.[29]

Shaping a Life: As people dealing with same-gender attraction look at traditional lifestyles, they may not see where they fit in. One young man wrote me: "All of the talks at BYU on dating and marriage, including some in which we were told that if we weren't dating 'X' number of times per week we weren't magnifying our priesthood, left me feeling especially depressed, broken, and like I was failing God and everyone else around me. It wasn't until I had a very powerful spiritual witness—in association with Isaiah 56:3–4, actually—that all I needed to do was my best to nurture my relationship with the Lord and to cultivate and follow the Spirit in my life (and whether I married in this life or the next, I was completely accepted of the Lord) that I felt so much of that burden of shame and guilt and depression and failure lift. The love I felt was overwhelming and taught me what my central focus should be. Prior to that, the cultural box I was being shoved into was spiritually and emotionally suffocating."

Another young man, who chose to serve a mission even while dealing with the challenge of same-gender attraction, describes how he had been mentally and emotionally stuck in choosing the gospel way over the world's way until he found that he didn't have to live a traditional life and that, indeed, stereotypes can be ignored:

"I understood, finally, that I was an individual on my own path and that it was impossible to know where that would take me. I did have to make choices along the way, but I wasn't limited by those stereotypes in my head. And the only thing I had to commit to was the gospel of Jesus Christ. The important distinction was between LDS culture, which isn't necessarily true, and the fulness of the gospel, which is. When I realized that my path might not look like everyone else's and that it was really just between the Lord and me, I felt a new confidence. I handed that map over to the Savior and let him navigate—I jumped into the driver's seat. . . . If we truly trust the Lord, we don't need to fear the unknown vistas that await us. We can listen to the Spirit and the compass of our hearts and look forward to that day . . . when we realize we have happened onto an answer and that it was the Lord who brought us there. But until then, there's no reason we shouldn't roll down the windows and breathe deeply, even if we're not sure exactly where we are. It's okay, the Lord does."[30]

Boundaries: At some point parents are faced with situations in which they wonder what boundary lines might be appropriate because their love for their child versus their sense of right and wrong can create conflict in their minds. Such situations might include whether to attend a marriage or commitment ceremony, or what role a potential partner might play within the family. Elder Oaks was asked: "At what point does showing that love cross the line into inadvertently endorsing behavior? If the son says, 'Well, if you love me, can I bring my partner to our home to visit? Can we come for holidays?' How do you balance that against, for example, concern for other children in the home?"

Can a parent's love cross a line and inadvertently endorse homosexual practice? Elder Oaks responded: "That's a decision that needs to be made individually by the person responsible, calling upon the Lord for inspiration. I can imagine that in most circumstances the parents would say, 'Please don't do that. Don't put us into that position.' Surely if there are children in the home who would be influenced by this example, the answer would likely be that. There would also be other factors that would make that the likely answer. . . . There are so many different circumstances, it's impossible to give one answer that fits all."

Elder Wickman emphasizes a parent's need to avoid the pitfall of defending a child's homosexual lifestyle: "I think it's important as a parent to avoid a potential trap arising out of one's anguish over this situation. I refer to a shift from defending the Lord's way to defending the errant child's lifestyle, both with him and with others. It really is true the Lord's way is to love the sinner while condemning the sin. That is to say we continue to open our homes and our hearts and our arms to our children, but that need not be with approval of their lifestyle. Neither does it mean we need to be constantly telling them that their lifestyle is inappropriate. An even bigger error is now to become defensive of the child because that neither helps the child nor helps the parent. That course of action, which experience teaches, is almost certainly to lead both away from the Lord's way."[31]

One mother remarks that she has said to her son: "'I love you and respect your feelings, and I know you will respect mine. Because you were reared in the Church, you know what my standards are.' He is fine with that because he prides himself on being an honest person."

Elder Oaks mentioned that different circumstances may require different responses. After fasting and prayer, one set of parents in a home where there were no younger children chose to let the child and his long-term partner make the decision as to whether they would share a bedroom in the family home. The key seems to be Elder Oaks's statement: "That's a decision that needs to be made individually by the person responsible, calling upon the Lord for inspiration."[32]

III. Heaven before You—the Long View

Know thou, my son, that all these things shall
give thee experience, and shall be for thy good. . . . Therefore,
hold on thy way (D&C 122:7, 9).

As parents we have a personal ministry that extends beyond this life. It's a long journey we've undertaken with these children. This is comforting doctrine. The Brethren have taught that if we cannot get them in this life, we will be able to work with them in the next and bring them a good way along the path in our work as undershepherds. We have this reassurance: "These [the saints who had passed to the spirit world] the Lord taught, and gave them power to come forth, after his resurrection from the dead, to enter into his Father's kingdom, . . . and continue thenceforth their labor as had been promised by the Lord, and be partakers of all blessings which were held in reserve for them that love him" (D&C 138:51–52).

And we have this assurance: "The dead who repent will be re-deemed, through obedience to the ordinances of the house of God, and after they have paid the penalty of their transgressions, and are washed clean, shall receive a reward according to their works, for they are heirs of salvation" (D&C 138:58–59). Here we add the Prophet Joseph's statement: "There is never a time when the spirit is too old to approach God. All are within the reach of pardoning mercy, who have not committed the unpardonable sin."[33] This statement spans the stages of man's progression, showing that after this life the spirit is still susceptible to sanctifying.

In this same vein, let us look at the words of Elder Whitney, familiar to many but deserving revisiting here: "Don't give them up. Don't cast them off. . . . They were his before they were yours—long before he entrusted them to your care; and you cannot begin to love them as he loves them. They have but strayed in ignorance from the Path of Right, and God is merciful to ignorance. Only the fulness of knowledge brings the fulness of accountability. Our Heavenly Father is far more merciful, infinitely more charitable, than even the best of his servants, and the Everlasting Gospel is mightier in power to save than our narrow finite minds can comprehend.

"The Prophet Joseph Smith declared—and he never taught more comforting doctrine—that the eternal sealings of faithful parents and the divine promises made to them for valiant service in the Cause of Truth, would save not only themselves, but likewise their posterity. Though some of the sheep may wander, the eye of the Shepherd is upon them, and sooner or later they will feel the tentacles of Divine Providence reaching out after them and drawing them back to the fold. Either in this life or the life to come, they will return. They will have to pay their debt to justice; they will suffer for their sins; and may tread a thorny path; but if it leads them at last, like the penitent Prodigal, to a loving and forgiving father's heart and home, the painful experience will not have been in vain. Pray for your careless and disobedient children; hold on to them with your faith. Hope on, trust on, till you see the salvation of God."[34]

Being undershepherds suggests that, even though we do not have absolute power to save our children, we can serve as powerful catalysts in that process. The power we do have rests in our own obedience.

The Savior Himself knew that His saving influence depended on His own personal preparations. In His great Intercessory Prayer, He said, "And for their sakes I sanctify myself, that they also might be sanctified through the truth" (John 17:19). That points the way for us. To sanctify oneself is a work of pure love.

If we wish to obtain the power to bless, we have to find credence with the Lord through getting increasingly serious with Him. Each of us can do that, inspired by Mormon's editorial note: "There was not any man who could do a miracle in the name of Jesus save he were cleansed every whit from his iniquity" (3 Nephi 8:1); or by the Lord's words: "And if ye are purified and cleansed from all sin, ye shall ask whatsoever you will in the name of Jesus and it shall be done. But know this, it shall be given you what you shall ask" (D&C 50:29–30).

We learn from these scriptures that the Lord requires us to move out of the thought-world of the natural man and into that faith-expanded dimension where blessings can be drawn down on the heads of loved ones. We learn that we have to become clean to receive certain privileges from God. For example, we learn to seek and retain a remission of sins, and we keep a current temple recommend, magnify Church callings, incorporate the teachings of the Book of Mormon and other scriptures into our life, fast, learn to pray without ceasing, and descend into the layers of our soul, ever refining it. Each of us can do these things, but they take thought, time, love, and reorganization. Then life takes on a richness and expansive quality that we may not have suspected possible.

As to the power of our temple covenants, the Brethren teach that parents' temple marriage and faithfulness to their covenants wield an influence in the destiny of their children. Elder Boyd K. Packer, for example, states, "We cannot overemphasize the value of temple marriage, the binding ties of the sealing ordinance, and the standards of worthiness required of them. When parents keep the covenants they have made at the altar of the temple, their children will be forever bound to them." He also cites President Brigham Young: "'I care not where those children go, they are bound up to their parents by an everlasting tie, and no power of earth or hell can separate them from their parents in eternity; they will return again to the fountain from whence they sprang.'"[35]

Our own spiritual efforts can stabilize us and keep despair at bay, even when our children do not follow the path we so desire for them. President Lorenzo Snow adds his witness and promise:

"You that are mourning about your children straying away will have your sons and your daughters. If you succeed in passing through these trials and afflictions and receive a resurrection, you will, by the power of the Priesthood, work and labor, as the Son of God has, until you get all your sons and daughters in the path of exaltation and glory. This is just as sure as that the sun rose this morning over yonder mountains. Therefore, mourn not because all your sons and daughters do not follow in the path that you have marked out to them, or give heed to your counsels. Inasmuch as we succeed in securing eternal glory, and stand as saviors, and as kings and priests to our God, we will save our posterity. . . .

"God will have His own way in His own time, and He will accomplish His purposes in the salvation of His sons and daughters. . . . God bless you, brethren and sisters. *Do not be discouraged* is the word I wish to pass to you; but remember that righteousness and joy in the Holy Ghost is what you and I have the privilege of possessing at all times."[36]

In view of all the insight, comfort, and resources available to us, perhaps things are proceeding along as they must for now, while we walk our path the best we can, our consciousness expanding in a more comprehensive love. Let us live each day for the sake of life and goodness and love, trusting that the Lord will lead us along; in this simplicity we can find a larger, more comforting reality.

"Therefore, dearly beloved brethren, let us cheerfully do all things that lie in our power; and then may we stand still, with the utmost assurance, to see the salvation of God, and for his arm to be revealed" (D&C 123:17).

"Trust in the Lord"

Tony Clarke

Tony Clarke (pseudonym) was born and raised in Utah, where he resides with his wife, Vickie. They have been blessed with a large family. Tony earned a bachelor's degree from the University of Utah and a master's degree from Brigham Young University. His favorite calling in the Church is teaching. He enjoys backpacking with his children, playing with his grandchildren, and going on road trips with his wife. For over a decade, he has been associated with men and women who experience same-gender attraction and their families. All names have been changed within this narrative.

"What's the matter?" I cautiously asked.

Vickie was fighting to hold back the tears as muffled sobs shook her body.

The flight to Los Angeles had lifted off the ground a few minutes earlier. This was to have been a restful and relaxing opportunity to spend time with our new son-in-law's family and friends. Unable to speak, Vickie slowly handed me a letter from our son Alan. I began reading: "Dear Mom and Dad, I don't want to hurt you, but I must tell you something about myself. I'm gay. Please don't blame yourselves. I love you!!! This is something I have known for . . ."

Tears made it impossible to read further. Just four months earlier we'd been through a soul-stretching family challenge when one of our daughters announced that she and her boyfriend were getting married, but not in the temple. Her announcement broke our hearts because, in our family, it was understood that every child was to be married in the temple. There were many days of tears and introspection as we had frantically prepared for her wedding.

We were concerned about what others would think, but as family and friends found out about the impending marriage, they responded with love and support. The teachings of the gospel gave us understanding and hope, the Spirit brought peace to our souls, and the bishop provided counsel and encouragement. To our surprise, all our physical, emotional, and spiritual needs were quickly met.

After the wedding, as Vickie and I prepared to visit our new son-in-law's extended family, we felt good about our situation. We'd been through a trying experience, but with the Lord's help we had come out stronger. The family was still together, and our daughter and son-in-law were actively preparing for their temple sealing.

But with Alan's announcement we faced a family situation we'd never imagined was possible. Even after we had landed and happily embraced members of our son-in-law's family, I couldn't forget the words: "Dear Mom and Dad, . . . I'm gay!"

That night Vickie and I tried to make sense of our feelings. We verbalized questions that had haunted us throughout the day, criticized our parenting skills, and wondered what was next. We fell asleep crying, blaming ourselves, and fearing the future.

Although we enjoyed our vacation, meeting Alan when we returned home was never far from our thoughts. And while I imagined countless scenarios when greeting Alan at the airport, I couldn't figure out if he needed to be hugged or told to leave the home. As I shared my concerns with Vickie, she thoughtfully replied: "He is our son. We love him and Christ loves him. We need to love him the way Christ loves him." I agreed, even as I struggled to make sense of my feelings.

Upon our return, the children greeted us at the airport with smiles and a "Welcome Home" sign. I looked for Alan and found him standing behind the others, probably as scared and apprehensive as I was. Greeting the children with hugs and kisses, I worked my way toward my son, finally taking him in my arms and whispering softly that I loved him.

Alone

Alan's coming out shifted a huge burden from his shoulders onto ours. We now carried an enormous secret and had no one to share it with. Later we began to realize that as awful as our feelings were, Alan had been struggling with far more intense feelings for years. Our pain was nothing compared to the suffering he had endured in silence and isolation.

Alan came out only after he was certain that God had deserted him. Several members of his extended family quickly rallied around him. They accepted him completely and encouraged us to love and support him in the new lifestyle he had embraced. When we responded that we did love him but that we could never support the choice to live a gay lifestyle, they patiently explained that Alan and his actions were inseparable. They reminded us that despite our weekly family home evening lessons and our dinnertime gospel discussions, Alan was gay. They presented us with two options: reject our lifelong religious faith and love Alan and his new lifestyle, or reject our son and cling to our outdated, intolerant religious beliefs. We couldn't think of either option without crying.

Because Alan had visited with our bishop several times after his mission, Vickie and I felt we could approach him for help. But while he sympathized with our plight, he didn't have any answers. We both felt uncomfortable approaching other family members or neighbors for counsel or support. Suddenly, all the people and beliefs that had strengthened us through our challenges a few months earlier were no longer available. We felt overwhelmed and absolutely alone.

Trust in God

Shortly after Alan's announcement, Vickie and I had made a commitment to trust in God and to live as close to the Spirit as possible. We prayed, studied the scriptures, fasted, and attended our church meetings. We continued to feel that there was something we could do or say that would help Alan come back to us. As we attended the temple, we received the direction we sought, but it was not for Alan—it was for us. While we were in the celestial room, the Spirit taught me that I had the agency to make changes in my life, but only Alan could choose what he would do with his life. I also felt a strong desire to meet as a family and receive a blessing from my sons and sons-in-law. In the past I would have set up the meeting with no thought of how it would affect others. But the Spirit inspired me to first visit with Alan. He was supportive of the idea, asking only that we delay the gathering for several weeks so he could share his feelings with each of his brothers and sisters. I was amazed at the courage he showed as he visited with his siblings.

We gathered on a beautiful Sunday evening. All of our children, including the spouses of our married children, were present except for one son who was on a mission. Several members of the extended family who were supportive of Alan's new lifestyle also attended, which bothered me. Only later did I realize how much their presence and support meant to Alan.

After an opening prayer I received a priesthood blessing from my sons and sons-in-law. As they laid their lands on my head and my oldest son pronounced a blessing, I was overcome with the feeling that God was aware of what was happening in that small room. Vickie and several other members of the family also received blessings.

During the ensuing discussion, conflicting opinions about Alan's circumstances were voiced. Several family members stated that Alan was born gay and that we each needed to love, accept, and support him. Listening to them, I worried that I was homophobic to the point that I would never be able to fully love or accept my son.

Several of Alan's sisters, with tears in their eyes, expressed their love for him. They didn't care how he got to where he was; they loved him without reservation. Throughout the evening, the Spirit witnessed that God was aware of us and would bless us according to our righteousness.

Finding a Support Group

Eventually I stumbled onto a support group for families and friends of gays and lesbians. I attended the first meeting with such fear and trepidation that I couldn't admit I was there because my own son was gay. I justified my presence by saying I wanted to learn how I could help a gay acquaintance. Despite my dishonesty, I was impressed with the honesty and sincerity of others as they talked about their challenges and their love for children and spouses who experience same-sex attraction. (This was the first time I'd heard that term.) As they bore testimony of Jesus Christ and expressed gratitude for His Atonement, the Spirit warmed my soul.

I was especially interested in the comments of one man who talked about the attractions he'd felt toward other men since he'd been sexually abused as a child. With his wife sitting beside him, he talked about how good he felt since leaving a gay lifestyle and returning to Church activity. As we mingled after the meeting, I questioned him extensively. He patiently answered my questions and suggested several books I could read.

I continued to go to the support group, finally being honest about my own son's attractions. As I asked questions and read, I slowly became more aware of the complex issues and strong feelings surrounding homosexuality.

Was I to Blame?

One of the first things I read was that in some cases an absent or weak father was a possible factor contributing to homosexual attractions. I was devastated. If someone had told me I was a lousy basketball player or an awful handyman around the home, I would have immediately agreed. But to be labeled a bad father cut to the very core of how I perceived myself. I loved God, I loved my wife, and I loved my children. And although I'd often struggled to maintain a healthy balance between my work, Church callings, and my family, I couldn't admit that I'd let anyone down. Forced to examine myself more closely, I began to see many shortcomings. A particularly damning failure was that I'd often interacted with my children as just a group of people, not as individuals with unique talents, interests, and needs.

After he came out, Alan helped me see this shortcoming. As we were talking one day, he said, "Dad, you always had time to play basketball with my brothers, but you never had time to sit down and play the piano with me." I realized he was half right; I had, in fact, never sat down and played the piano with him. But it wasn't a time issue; it never crossed my mind that Alan, who could play complex classical music from memory, would want me to sit next to him and plunk out a tune with two fingers. After many years, I've begun to understand why Alan would want me to play the piano with him. How I wish we could both go back ten or twelve years and play a simple piano duet together.

My First Conference

Through the support group for families and friends, I became aware of an annual conference sponsored by Evergreen International (a nonprofit organization that provides support for individuals who experience same-sex attraction and desire to live in accordance with the doctrines and teachings of the Church). I attended the conference reluctantly, afraid that I might meet someone I knew. In the opening session, tears filled my eyes as I listened to stories and testimonies from several individuals with feelings of same-sex attraction. I was impressed by their faith in Jesus Christ and their dependence on Him for help in living the gospel.

As I entered the first workshop, my worst fear was realized as I came face to face with a good friend and neighbor. After welcoming me with open arms and helping me to feel at ease, he explained that he'd previously lived a gay lifestyle for years. I was speechless. This was a man who had sat next to me at church and in the temple and who had often visited our family. After talking with him, I realized he would have been a great help to Vickie and me when Alan came out. At the conference I also met a close business associate who experienced same-sex attraction. Happily married and the father of several children, he bore a strong testimony of the power of the Atonement to change lives and heal relationships.

That day the Spirit bore a powerful witness to me that it is only through the Atonement of Jesus Christ that any person can be made whole. I began to understand that faith in Jesus Christ is the only sure foundation for men and women who experience same-sex attraction and for their families and friends. For the first time since Alan came out, I felt free of guilt and full of hope.

Always Remember Him

After the conference, I again felt that there were positive ways in which I could help Alan. (How soon I'd forgotten the lesson learned about agency in the temple.) While I realized that I couldn't do much by myself, I felt that with the Lord's help nothing was impossible.

I recommitted myself to living the gospel with exactness. Although I never consciously bargained with the Lord, subconsciously I had, in fact, made a deal. I promised I would live my life as righteously as possible, and in return God would change Alan's heart. The change didn't have to be big, only enough for Alan to believe what I believed.

I studied the scriptures, prayed, fasted, attended my meetings, magnified my calling, and served others. I tried to not only live the letter of the law but also to bring all my actions into line with the spiritual requirements of discipleship. Alan was never far from my thoughts or the prayers of my heart. Yet I saw no change in him as he moved forward in his new lifestyle. I wondered where I was failing, and I began to wonder where God was. Each day became darker and harder to face as I struggled with feelings of depression and discouragement. I continued to plead for strength and direction, but for the first time in my life the Spirit seemed far away and answers did not come.

Late one night, after an especially depressing day, I was preparing a Sunday School lesson on the Savior's visit to the Nephites. The scriptures record that Christ lovingly taught and blessed the people. He instituted the sacrament, personally breaking and blessing the bread. After commanding His disciples to give it to the multitude, He taught, "And this shall ye do *in remembrance* of my body, which I have shown unto you. And it shall be a testimony unto the Father that ye do *always remember me*. And if ye do *always remember me* ye shall have my Spirit to be with you" (3 Nephi 18:7; emphasis added).

As I read the verse, the Spirit whispered that I had forgotten Jesus Christ. During the previous several months, I had constantly thought about my son but had seldom remembered *the* Son. I made a commitment to change.

As I awoke the next morning, my first thoughts were again of my son. But remembering the experience from the night before, I immediately began reciting a scripture I'd memorized in seminary: "Trust in the Lord with all thine heart; and lean not unto thine own understanding. In all thy ways acknowledge him, and he shall direct thy paths" (Proverbs 3:5–6). The Spirit whispered to me that if I would trust in the Lord, He would direct me.

While I showered, thoughts of Alan again entered my mind. I began to sing aloud, "I know that my Redeemer lives. What comfort this sweet sentence gives!"[37] For the first time in weeks, I truly felt comforted. Throughout the day, each time I began to think of my son, I would sing a hymn, recite a scripture, picture Christ in my mind, or say a prayer. That night, as I went to bed, I felt the peace and comfort that I'd been missing.

I learned again that God will not infringe on Alan's agency. As a child of God, he was free to make his own choices. And, while I could use my agency to change my life, I had no right or power to change my son's life. I also learned that I don't dictate the terms of my relationship with God. As painful as the fourteen months had been since Alan's announcement, I was growing in gospel experience and understanding faster than at any previous time in my life.

A Partner

Over the years, Vickie and I had enjoyed associating with our younger children's friends and our older children's dates as they visited our home. It was always easy to tell who was a friend and who was a date. But with Alan it became harder to separate his friends from his dates, and we seldom had the courage to ask who was who. While we were impressed with the friends he brought home after he came out, we weren't prepared for his announcement that he'd be living with one of them. Vickie and I had met this friend several weeks before.

With our feelings so tender that even a small wave could capsize our emotional boat, this announcement was like a tsunami. Vickie and I weren't sure that we wanted Alan's partner in our home. Even though he seemed like a good person, we worried about the influence this man could have on the younger children. And what if Alan and his partner did things in our home that we didn't want them to do?

We succeeded in making a mountain out of a molehill, but the love we felt for Alan held constant. We did want to associate with our son. We wanted him to feel our love and the love of his brothers and sisters. And if the only way Alan would come to our home was with his partner, then they were both welcome. Whenever Alan and his partner were in the home, their behavior was impeccable. We saw them often—at Sunday dinners, birthday celebrations, holiday activities, picnics, and for no reason at all. We felt blessed to have both of them associate with the family, and we came to love his partner as one of our own children. Then, after nine months, Alan and his partner separated.

Another Support Group

For several years an acquaintance had encouraged me to attend a support group for parents of gay and lesbian children. Still looking for answers, I agreed to go with him. Most of those in attendance were LDS, and, like the first support group I had attended, they began their meeting with a song and a prayer.

That night there was a presentation on the legal efforts to gain equal rights for gay, lesbian, bisexual, and transgender individuals. There was wild applause as the speaker reviewed each court decision that expanded gay rights. He emphasized the need for parents to become advocates for their gay and lesbian children and to pressure Church leaders to change.

After the presentation I visited with a number of those in attendance. As we talked, each person emphasized that he or she was an active member of the Church and believed it was true. Each person also expressed a concern that the prophet and other Church leaders didn't understand the larger issues associated with homosexuality and the individual struggles of gay members. One mother pointed out that

President Gordon B. Hinckley had admitted that he didn't know what caused homosexuality. She felt it was not acceptable to deny gays and lesbians full rights in the Church if the prophet himself didn't know what caused a person's sexual orientation. I sensed that those in attendance loved their children and wanted them to be happy. And although I didn't feel the Spirit at the meeting, there was compelling logic to their arguments.

Over the next few days I struggled with what I'd heard and felt. I knew that I loved my son as much as those people loved their children. How should I show that love? They wanted their children to be happy, just as I wanted Alan to be happy. How could I help him find happiness? They believed the Church was true and that the prophet taught the truth on every subject except homosexuality. Should I believe as they did? I began to worry that the prophet and the Church were wrong on this one issue.

As I pondered and prayed, the Spirit directed my thoughts. I knew that I couldn't compartmentalize my faith in the teachings of the prophet; I either followed every word the prophet spoke or none at all. I was concerned that if I didn't believe what the prophet taught about homosexuality today, tomorrow I might choose not to believe what he taught about another issue. I would essentially be saying that I knew better than God or His prophet what was right and what was wrong. That sounded like pride. In the end, I made the choice to follow the prophet.

Core Beliefs

As Vickie and I have struggled over the years to love Alan and stay true to the gospel, we've identified several core beliefs that have helped us stay on a true course.

Faith in Jesus Christ: Faith in Jesus Christ and obedience to His teachings is the foundation on which all our beliefs and actions regarding same-sex attraction have been based. Although some people teach that love is the most important response to a child with same-sex attraction, the fourth article of faith states that the first principle of the gospel is "faith in the Lord Jesus Christ."

Love is essential, but Christ taught that we show our love through obedience to all the commandments. He instructed His followers, "If ye love me, keep my commandments" (John 14:15; see also John 14:21, 23). Abraham loved his son Isaac and must have struggled when God commanded him to offer Isaac as a sacrifice. Abraham chose to be obedient to God, not because he didn't love Isaac but because of his faith in Jesus Christ. In Hebrews we read, "By faith [in Jesus Christ] Abraham, when he was tried, offered up Isaac . . . accounting that God was able to raise him up, even from the dead" (Hebrews 11:17, 19). Because of the faith of Abraham, the scriptures say, he and his posterity will be blessed throughout eternity.

Vickie and I believe in Jesus Christ and in the power of the Atonement. We also believe that if we, like Abraham, are true to our faith in Jesus Christ, our posterity will be blessed eternally.

Follow the Prophet: After Alan came out, Vickie and I encountered many voices that claimed to speak the truth regarding same-sex attraction. There were voices that claimed men were born gay and deserved the same rights, including marriage, as every other person. There were voices from members of the Church who felt the Church was true but that the prophet was wrong regarding same-sex attraction. Finally, there was the loving voice of the prophet, teaching that all of us, including those who experience same-sex attraction, are sons and daughters of God and that we are to love, comfort, and sustain each other. His steady voice reminded us of God's standard of moral behavior and taught us of the sacred nature of marriage and family in God's eternal plan.

We've chosen to follow the prophet. We believe that as God's watchman (see D&C 101:44–57; 124:61), he stands on higher ground and can see dangers others can't. We'll follow him, even if he doesn't have specific answers to every question.

Christlike Love: When Alan came out, Vickie and I were encouraged to love him unconditionally. But no one taught us how to love unconditionally; nor were we able to find the term in the scriptures. Over the years we've come to understand that unconditional love is generally defined by the person who expects to receive the love. For example, when my teenage son said he needed a shiny red sports car, he suggested that the best way for me to show my love was to give him what he desired. When I didn't give him the car, he accused me of hating him. But to give a person everything he wants or to enable every behavior is unhealthy and can be dangerous. (See Russell M. Nelson's talk on "Divine Love." [38])

Christlike love, or charity, is defined in the scriptures (see Moroni 7:45–48; 1 Corinthians 13:1–13). Christlike love is always pure and perfect and will never harm the giver or receiver. It honors agency while never enabling unrighteous behavior. A disobedient or unrighteous person can never possess Christlike love because it is a gift bestowed by God upon those "who are true followers of his Son, Jesus Christ" (Moroni 7:48).

Since Alan came out, Vickie and I have tried to maintain a Christlike relationship with him. To the best of our ability, we've respected his beliefs and have shown him in word and deed that we love him as Christ would. But just as we have no right to control his actions, he has no right to define how we love him. We recognize that he has his agency to accept or reject our love.

Conclusion

We believe it is possible to love God and love a family member who feels same-sex attraction and chooses to act upon his feelings. We are only one of many families who consistently strive to maintain a healthy balance. For us, the key has been to exercise faith in Jesus Christ and to demonstrate our faith by word and action in every facet of life.

As a family and as individuals, we've made mistakes, but Alan knows we love him. He and I enjoy literature and have recommended favorite books for each other to read. Several times Alan and I have taken time off work and attended an international piano competition held near our home. I am currently taking piano lessons from Alan, who is a patient, encouraging, and understanding teacher for someone who learns slowly.

Over the years I've attempted to associate with and understand men who experience same-sex attraction. Alan once asked if I did this in an effort to bring about change in his life. I replied that initially I was motivated by a desire to help him but that I'd come to realize that only he could make the decisions that affect his life. I told him that I'd come to love, respect, and appreciate him even more because of what I'd learned from others with similar attractions.

Vickie and I cry as we think of the difficulties, fears, and loneliness Alan has had to face over the years. Daily we pray for him and his brothers and sisters. And daily we feel God's blessings and are grateful for His interest and involvement in our family. We're thankful for a prophet we can look to for counsel and direction. We're especially grateful for Jesus Christ and for the blessings of the Atonement in our lives.

"As I Have Loved You"

Antoinette Cocco

Antoinette Cocco is a happily single thirty-four-year-old living in Southern California. She feels blessed to be surrounded by family and friends and enjoys teaching young people at church and in her employment as a teacher. Her two favorite places are the temple and the beach. She has served in the Church as a Relief Society president, Sunday School teacher, and temple ordinance worker. Her hobbies include reading, playing beach volleyball, and stand-up paddle surfing. All names have been changed within this narrative.

A few years ago I found a white towel in my mom's temple suitcase. I recognized the towel from my college basketball days; it had my jersey number on it. I realized that my mom had carried this towel to the temple for many years. I thought of how her heart must have ached for me and the lifestyle I had chosen. I thought of the courage and faith she had demonstrated by serving in her callings while I was finding my way. I thought of the numerous prayers that she had offered on my behalf. As I reflected on these things, I was overwhelmed with deep feelings of love and gratitude for a righteous mother who trusted in the Lord and never gave up on me. I hope that my personal experiences will inspire parents to follow the Savior's example as they strive to love and support their children who experience same-sex attraction.

When people ask me, "What made you decide to come back to church?" I usually give the simple reply: "My mom prayed for me." Obviously, other factors influenced my decision to abandon a lesbian lifestyle and return to full activity in the Church of Jesus Christ, but none was more powerful than my mother's love. By following the Savior's example and striving to live His teachings, my mother helped me overcome the tremendous challenges I faced. My mother sought the Lord through prayer and scripture study, she attended the temple, she respected my agency, she never judged or criticized me, and she kept the door open for me to return home. All of these things are examples of charity—a Christlike love that never fails but endures forever, which He bestows on those who are His true followers (see Moroni 7:45–48).

I was two years sober from drugs and alcohol when I began dating Maya. I was focused on my sobriety, and she was focused on her studies. My parents liked Maya when they met her. My mom was more concerned about me associating with drug addicts than lesbians because she feared I would relapse. She didn't realize that Satan had a backup plan to keep me in his grasp. Just as I was gaining freedom from my obsession to use drugs, I began to act out on my feelings of same-sex attraction, and I fell deep into a lifestyle that didn't offer me true happiness. Satan played on my vulnerability of being newly sober and tempted me until I gave in.

Maya and I spent a lot of time together, and my parents began to notice. Eventually I told my dad that she was my girlfriend. He cried and told me that he loved me, and he promised not to tell my mom. I couldn't bring myself to tell my mom I was romantically involved with a woman. I didn't want to cause her any more grief. She was already worried about my recovery from drug and alcohol addiction, and her marriage was falling apart. During these trying times, my mother could have withdrawn from her Church responsibilities. Instead, she lost herself in service. She faithfully served as Relief Society president in our ward. She selflessly served as an ordinance worker in the temple. She loyally served her parents by regularly visiting and caring for them in their senior years. In the midst of her personal trials, my mother forgot about herself and reached out to others. As a result, she experienced joy in her heart, and the Spirit of the Lord came into her life abundantly.

My parents decided to move to Los Angeles because my mom wanted to be near her parents and siblings. I chose not to go with them because I didn't want to leave San Diego, and I especially didn't want to leave Maya. We had developed an unhealthy emotional attachment, and we were too insecure to let each other go. So, although we had dated only for a few months, Maya and I agreed to be roommates. We moved in with a lesbian woman named Sara. She was a single mom with six cats, and she smoked in the house. She would disappear for days at a time, and I soon discovered that she was a drug addict. Although she didn't use drugs in the house, she used them everywhere else. Maya became extremely busy with her graduate program and eventually stopped coming home at night. I ended up spending a lot of time babysitting the cats. It wasn't long before I began to feel depressed about my living situation and my relationship with Maya.

One day when I was feeling particularly sorry for myself, I received a phone call from my mom. She was coming down to San Diego to attend the temple and she wanted to visit me. Initially, I was excited. Then the panic set in. My mom was a clean freak. She had zero tolerance for dirt and clutter. How was she going to respond to the stench of cigarettes and kitty litter? What if she asked me why there was only one bed? What would she think of my roommates? What would she think of me? I knew my mom would be out of her comfort zone, so I removed the pictures of Maya and me hugging and kissing and I put the ashtrays outside. I cleaned the house as well as I could, and I hoped for the best.

All of my worries and concerns disappeared shortly after my mom arrived. In the spirit of the Savior's teachings, she refrained from judgment and criticism. She showed me that our relationship was valuable and she would never reject me. She took advantage of the precious time we had together. We ate dinner, we talked, we laughed, and we prayed together. Like the Savior, she loved the sinner and not the sin. She even slept in the same bed I shared with Maya. That weekend, I felt my Savior's love through my mom's actions.

In contrast to the uplifting influence of my mother, Maya became more irritating and bitter each day. We were both dissatisfied with our relationship. I began to feel empty and alone, but I knew I could turn to Heavenly Father for comfort. Very early in my life, my mother instilled in me the importance of prayer. As a young girl I used to yell for her when I was getting ready for school. When I wouldn't get a response, I would open her bedroom door to find her kneeling in prayer. As I watched my mom pray, it was obvious that she believed someone was listening intently. So even though I wasn't active in the Church, I prayed daily.

Heavenly Father answered my prayers regarding my relationship with Maya the day I found her apology note that ended our relationship. I was sad yet relieved. I finally felt free from the codependent patterns I was struggling to break. I hit my knees and offered a prayer of thanks. I called my mom and told her that Maya was moving out. She offered an immediate and unconditional invitation to come home. I graciously refused her offer with the excuse that I wanted to attend San Diego State University. Actually, I was too scared to leave San Diego. I had a strong recovery support group, and I felt comfortable in the gay and lesbian community of which I was a part. I needed to be away from my family so I could fully experience, guilt free, the lifestyle that seemed so natural to me. I loved my family, but I didn't want to be pressured or even nudged to attend church. I had replaced Church meetings with my twelve-step meetings.

After my stressful relationship with Maya, I looked forward to being single and focusing on personal growth. I craved physical affection, but I didn't want to settle for meaningless flings. I felt good about the progress I was making spiritually and academically. I used exercise to curb my appetite for physical pleasure, but my strategy backfired the day I met Lisa leaving the gym. I recognized her from school, and I knew she was a lesbian. I was surprised at how eager I was to get to know her. Lisa and I clicked right away. She was easy to get along with and fun to be around. It didn't take long before we decided to date exclusively.

I remember when I met her family. Lisa introduced me as her girlfriend. At first I felt weird showing her affection in front of them. After a few visits, I didn't think twice about it. Her parents and siblings were wonderful to me. I thought of my own family and wished they would accept our relationship the way Lisa's family so easily did.

Longing for acceptance from my family, I mustered enough courage to open up to my older brother, who already knew almost everything about me. Growing up, he was the man of the house because my dad was always traveling with the military. My brother honored his responsibilities in the priesthood and set a righteous example. Like my mother, he never judged or criticized me. I was nervous about telling him the truth, but I was optimistic about his reaction. I hoped that he would approve of my lifestyle and wish me the best in my relationship with Lisa.

I'll never forget that phone conversation. When I told my brother that I was a lesbian, he didn't say anything for a long time. When he finally spoke, I could hardly recognize his voice. It was a deep, trembling voice, and it gave me goose bumps all over. First he told me that he loved me. Then he told me that I could never be truly happy in the lifestyle I had chosen. He told me that he didn't want to get to the other side of the veil and have me come up to him and ask, "Why didn't you tell me?" His words seemed harsh to me, and I was crushed. In a defensive tone I asked him to explain how I *could* be truly happy. He chose not to expand on his comments; he told me that I wouldn't understand his explanation because I didn't share his perspective. Although my brother didn't respond the way I had hoped, our relationship didn't change and he still loved me. We talked on a regular basis, but he never mentioned the topic of my sexual orientation.

Lisa and I spent as much time together as possible. It was refreshing to be with someone who trusted me and allowed me to be myself. I grew to love her as a friend, a sister, and a mate. We moved in together and received frequent help from both her parents and mine. My mom sent me money when I was short on rent, took me grocery shopping when she came to visit, and loaned me her car when I crashed my own. Sometimes I felt torn between my mom and Lisa. I wanted to please my mom by going back to church, but I knew I wasn't willing to give up my relationship with Lisa. I have since learned that my parents made those sacrifices for me for no other reason than that they loved me.

My mom worried about me a great deal, but she didn't let my choices consume her life. She prayed to Heavenly Father for peace. He assured her that she would be blessed for her personal righteousness. He told her not to feel guilty about the choices I was making. My brother was also a great source of strength to my mom. He reminded her that I knew right from wrong. My mom respected my agency because she understood that I needed to grow and learn by making choices, even if I had to suffer. It was difficult for my mom to watch me struggle, but she knew that there was hope. She found comfort in the scriptures as she read about parents with wayward children. She held onto promises made to those parents who teach their children correct principles. She studied the teachings of the Savior so she would know what steps to take to help me. My mom did not let my choices weaken her faith.

Lisa and I dated for more than a year, and I wanted us to continue to move forward and achieve our goals. We both expressed our desires for building careers, getting married, and having children. I loved her immensely, but I was frustrated that we didn't have the physical ability to get pregnant. We discussed the options of a donor or adoption. That is when the Spirit began to prick me. During one of our conversations about raising children, I mentioned to Lisa that I wanted my kids to attend the Mormon church. She wasn't thrilled with the idea, but I had a strong feeling that it was important for my children to be raised in the gospel. The Spirit was helping me remember the valuable lessons and truths I had learned as a child. I reflected on the countless hours my mom spent teaching my brother and me about Jesus Christ and His gospel.

The topics of marriage and children didn't come up again until my brother got engaged. Lisa hadn't met my brother, but she knew we shared a special relationship. I wanted her to travel to Hawaii with me for the wedding, but we couldn't afford for us both to go. I watched my brother on his wedding day, and I had never seen him so happy. I stood outside the temple during the sealing ceremony, and I thought about the conversation we had had when I told him about my lifestyle. I sensed that his definition of true happiness had something to do with being in the temple. I didn't want to think about the temple because I couldn't take Lisa there.

After my brother's wedding, the Spirit would not leave me alone. I received the impression that something needed to change in my life. I asked Heavenly Father to help me make changes in every area of my life except in my relationship with Lisa. I knew that Heavenly Father was aware of my feelings for her, and I expressed gratitude that He had allowed her to be in my life. I didn't understand why I was feeling that I was going to lose her.

Mother's Day was approaching and that looming feeling lingered. As usual, I went to an LDS bookstore to find a gift for my mom. I found a gift right away, but my plan to be in and out quickly was ruined. The Spirit prompted me to ask an employee if the store carried a certain book about same-sex attraction (SSA). A few months previous, I had been there shopping for my mom's birthday. I had noticed a book about same-sex attraction [*Born That Way?*] but ignored it because I didn't want to know what the Church had to say about SSA. I hadn't even given that book a second thought until the words were out of my mouth. I realized that I only had a few dollars left after I bought my mom's gift, but the employee told me that the book was on the clearance rack, marked down to $2.99. In that moment my mind flashed through the numberless attempts the Lord had made to invite me to turn to Him. How could I refuse Him again?

Later that day I sat in the car and started reading the book while my clothes were drying at the Laundromat. I was shocked to discover that the author was a female member of the Church who had struggled with same-sex attraction. I thought the book had been written by a Church leader or a psychologist, and I expected to feel guilty and ashamed because I wasn't keeping the commandments. Instead, I felt hope and empathy as I read about this woman's journey. I was amazed at the similarities in our personal stories. The Spirit bore witness to me that I could experience true happiness if I followed Christ and did whatever He required of me.

I knew that I needed to have a serious talk with Heavenly Father. I was afraid to ask Him what I needed to do about my relationship with Lisa. I had never prayed with a willingness to act on the answer He would give, but I exercised a small amount of faith that evening as I promised Heavenly Father that I would do whatever He wanted me to do. The moment I opened my heart to receive an answer, the Spirit washed over me and I literally crumpled to the floor. The answer was so clear and powerful; there was no way that I could misunderstand it. Heavenly Father told me that I needed to surrender Lisa to Him. He would take care of her. I needed to follow my Savior. He promised me that it would be worth it. He didn't give me any other details, but I trusted Him.

I knew I had to act promptly on my answer, so I immediately opened the yellow pages to find the closest LDS ward and bishop. I don't remember many details of my first meeting with Bishop Miller. I can recall, however, that from the moment he shut the door, I felt the Spirit so strongly that I was bawling before I even sat down. I started by telling him that I wanted to come back to church. After sharing with him the shortest version of my life story, I was overwhelmed with peace and calmness. He looked me in the eyes and in a gentle voice told me that my Heavenly Father loves me. He gave me a sincere hug and invited me to church.

I wanted to attend church that Sunday, but I had previously committed to attending a gay and lesbian festival in Long Beach. As I walked around the festival, I saw everything with a new perspective. People were laughing, dancing, and celebrating their love for each other. They appeared to be happy, but I knew it wasn't *real* happiness. I began to understand that my brother was right. I realized that his words about true happiness seemed harsh to me because they were the truth. I couldn't believe that I had been so blind. On the way home from the festival, Heavenly Father gave me the strength to tell Lisa that I was going back to church. Somehow she knew that this would disrupt our relationship in a major way.

When I told my family I was going back to church, they rejoiced. My brother cried and my mom could hardly speak. I attended church the next Sunday, committed to keeping every Sabbath day holy. This was one of the first spiritual goals I had set with Bishop Miller. I could sense that he was in tune with the Spirit, and I trusted him. He never rushed me in my repentance process, and he guided me gently back onto a path of righteous living. The Lord's blessings were abundant on my first day back. He had prepared a number of people to meet me. I met Emily, who was privately struggling to overcome the challenge of same-sex attraction. We became great friends, and we encouraged each other to stay close to the Lord. I also met two sister missionaries, who came to my apartment every week for two months. They taught the discussions to Lisa, and in the process, my testimony grew stronger. I never wanted them to leave because the Spirit that attended them reminded me of home.

Another goal I set was to keep the law of chastity. I needed Bishop Miller to give me a specific definition of sexual relations. It was painful for me to establish those sexual boundaries because physical intimacy was a huge part of my relationship with Lisa. I remember calling my mom and crying to her about how much I loved Lisa and how it wasn't fair that she had to suffer. My mom listened with compassion and understanding. She prayed for Lisa to feel the love of the Lord.

I called my family every Sunday to tell them what I had learned at church and what I had done throughout the week. I had so many exciting stories to share because the Lord was performing miracles in my life every day. I was able to quit smoking by fasting and praying. When my cravings were almost unbearable, I called my mom and told her that I wanted to give up. She sent me a huge bag of candy and encouraged me to have faith.

That Christmas, while I was visiting my parents, I had an unmistakable impression that I needed to move home. My mom must have thought she was dreaming when I woke her with the news, because she almost fell off her recliner. She was trying not to show her excitement, but it was obvious that she wanted me to return home. After telling Lisa that I was moving to Los Angeles to live with my parents, we made arrangements for me to pay rent and sleep on the couch for the three days a week that I had classes in San Diego.

Moving to Los Angeles was frightening, but I knew it was the right thing to do. I needed to be in a new environment where people didn't know me as Lisa's girlfriend. It took me a while to get used to my new singles ward. Bishop Brown wasn't as gentle as Bishop Miller; he was brutally honest with me. While it was hard at first, I grew to appreciate his tough-love approach. He knew my spiritual goals, and he pushed me to reach them. He challenged me to become worthy to partake of the sacrament, receive my patriarchal blessing, and receive my temple endowment.

In anticipation of once again being worthy to partake of the sacrament, I grew closer to the Lord than I had been at any other time in my life. I experienced the miracle of the Atonement every Sunday during the administration of the bread and water. Most of the time I was too emotional to sing the sacrament hymn, but I paid close attention to the words that spoke of my Savior. I listened to the sacrament prayers, and I longed to have the Spirit of Christ with me. I felt intense sorrow as I visualized my Savior suffering for me. As I pleaded for forgiveness, I felt His merciful arms wrap around me, and I experienced the sanctifying power of His love.

As I matured in the gospel, the Lord required more of me. When I was worthy to partake of the sacrament, I was called to be a teacher in Relief Society. A few months later, Bishop Brown told me it was time to attend temple preparation class. I remembered the things my mom had taught me about the sacred nature of the temple. She had explained that it is a place of holiness where families are sealed for eternity. She stressed the importance of living a clean and pure life so I could be worthy to go there one day. Participating in the cleansing process of the sacrament was an important step in coming closer to the day I would, in fact, enter the temple.

After I spent sixteen grueling months of taking what seemed to be tiny steps toward the temple, the last step proved to be the easiest of all. Bishop Brown said he would not sign my temple recommend until I found another couch to sleep on during the week. At that moment I realized that I was finally willing to cut all ties with Lisa. The Lord's blessing was immediate as my friend Emily and her husband opened their home, and their couch, to me.

Naturally, my mom was my escort the day I received my endowment. The Lord had blessed my life through her faith and obedience. Her capacity to follow the Lord's directive to love as He loves is what ultimately drew me back to Him. The Lord fulfilled His promise to her that I would again walk in truth because she had taught me correct principles. In the celestial room, I watched my mother rejoice with Bishop Miller, Bishop Brown, and many of the Saints whom she had faithfully served while I was struggling to find my own true happiness.

In the years since that time I have felt privileged to follow my mother's example of service as I have been given callings such as temple ordinance worker and Relief Society president. My feelings and attractions have not disappeared, although they are less frequent, and I find the strength to manage my feelings when I think of the sisters I serve. My greatest fear since receiving my endowment is that I might do something that would result in having my recommend taken away.

I am pained at the disappointment and sadness that a relapse might cause those I serve. Nevertheless, I have confidence that they, like my mother and my Savior, would never give up on me no matter the challenges I might face. My mother's love and example will always be constant and sure.

I know that while I'm faithfully honoring my covenants, my mother no longer carries a white towel to the temple. Instead, she enters with me at her side.

Love Is Always the Answer

Kathleen Marsden

Although of Utah pioneer heritage, Kathleen Marsden and her husband raised their four children in Alberta, Canada. After retiring from education, they returned to Utah, where they continue to teach, study the gospel, travel, and love to watch their thirteen grandchildren grow. Kathleen has previously served in the Church as a Relief Society president and seminary teacher.

Heavenly Father blessed my husband and me with four beautiful children—two girls and two boys. When our older son, TJ, was twenty-seven, he told me that he had been struggling with same-gender attraction. He was attending graduate school at Brigham Young University at the time, and as we were talking on the phone one day, he told me that he had been going to counseling. As he told me why, my immediate reaction was disbelief, but devastation and an all-consuming pain soon took over. I was sure I was dreaming someone else's nightmare. My mind raced with questions: How could *we* have a gay son? To our knowledge, he had been never abused. (I had previously thought this was the main cause of homosexuality.) His home life hadn't been perfect, but it had been normal, and his parents and siblings all loved each other. We loved the Lord and strived to keep His commandments. TJ had never given us any trouble. He had gone on a mission and served honorably. Things like this only happened to other people, didn't they?

Coming to Terms

That was nine years ago. As I reflect back on the phone call that forever changed our lives, even in positive ways, I now marvel that I was able to find peace in a relatively short period of time (though at the time it seemed like an eternity), even though the process wasn't easy. I would frankly describe the first year as *hellish*. I didn't think I could ever learn to come to terms with what felt at the time like such a horrible situation.

My first priority was to tell my husband so we could help TJ in his efforts to stay close to the Lord and the Church, but I dreaded telling him. As difficult as it was for me to hear that our son was attracted to men, I was sure my husband would be deeply hurt and would not want to talk about it at length. He would keep his pain to himself and simply press on with life, loving TJ all the while. And that is exactly what happened. When my husband came home from work the day of TJ's phone call, I told him I had something terrible to tell him. I ushered him into the bedroom, where, sobbing into my pillow, I blurted out the crushing news.

In the following days we talked about TJ's childhood behavior and acknowledged that there had been clues. Our two boys were born only nineteen months apart, and they looked very much alike. But as they grew, it became increasingly obvious they were different in the way they played and in the interests they developed. TJ was such a tenderhearted child. He was always kind to his sisters and little brother. Like his siblings, he was obedient and brought such joy to us. As he grew, he never displayed the mannerisms society would stereotypically label as gay, but there seemed to be other signs. My husband asked me once when TJ was about fourteen if I thought he might be gay. I told him I had entertained the idea, but it just didn't seem possible given the preconceived ideas I had at the time about people who were same-gender attracted. The thought crossed my mind again when, after he had been home from his mission for some time, he still hadn't begun to date seriously even though he was in his mid-twenties. He had many female friends and admirers, but he never seemed interested.

The initial steps in my journey to peace were trying to find someone or something to blame. First it was my fault, and then it became my husband's. I read and devoured every word I could find that Church leaders and other Latter-day Saints had written on the subject of homosexuality. Everything I read seemed to indicate that we should be careful about placing blame for the agony our boy was experiencing. Amidst his own anguish, he tried to assure me that nobody had ever abused him or mistreated him in ways he felt contributed to his attraction. During the following months, he often commented that he would rather be burdened with anything but this particular trial, occasionally even alluding to thoughts of wanting to end his life. As a younger man, he thought if he was good enough the feelings would go away. I cried incessantly. It broke my heart to think that he had suffered in silence for so many years.

Sharing the Burden

Through the resources I was able to find, I soon realized we were not the only LDS parents who were going through this. My son repeatedly told me I would be shocked to know how common same-gender attraction is among Latter-day Saints. Knowing this made me feel like I wasn't alone, although I had absolutely nobody to talk to who really understood what I was going through. I didn't feel I could tell even my closest friends, thinking they wouldn't comprehend what we were experiencing. It turned out I was wrong, but I didn't know that at the time. Strangely, as time passed, I felt comfortable discussing this with my coworkers, none of whom were LDS. But I worried about judgment from other Church members.

Thankfully, TJ had confided to his bishop about his attractions months before he told me, so he'd at least had *some* support. This kind and wonderful leader had drawn our son close to him, even calling him to be his executive secretary. Despite the bishop's efforts, however, I became increasingly worried, almost holding my breath as to whether TJ would ultimately choose to remain chaste and live faithful to the standards of the Church. Prior to our learning of his attractions, he had broken up with a girlfriend we hoped he would marry. His mission companions, friends, and younger siblings, he said, were getting married, yet here he was still single, feeling increasingly hopeless and lonely.

Though many miles apart, we talked often. I tried to give him pep talks whenever I could. We reflected on the promises in his patriarchal blessing and the great rewards that were in store if he remained faithful. I thought if he kept himself on track with the Church he could win the battle. Whether or not he could ever fully overcome his attraction to men, I believed he could *control* his attractions if he drew near to the Savior. If he was able to accomplish that, I felt I could deal with the situation.

For a short time it was all about *me*. I felt that my peace and happiness were contingent upon his choices and were possible only if he stayed on the path of righteousness. Although his burden was heavy, we could all remain happy if he maintained a temple-worthy lifestyle. Admittedly, it was heartbreaking to watch him struggle, keeping the inner turmoil to himself as he outwardly showed friends an easygoing and fun-filled facade.

Preparing for Changes

As I sensed TJ slowly becoming more bitter, I began to fear he wouldn't maintain his activity in the Church much longer. I wondered to myself how I would handle things if he decided to act on his feelings. His counselor had taught him that he should never say he was "gay" unless he acted on his attractions—he experienced same-gender attraction, but he was not "gay."

I tried to convince myself that nothing had really changed for the worse in our family as long as the rest of us strived to keep the commandments. I still believe that was true, but watching a loved one struggle the way TJ did certainly affected my sense of peace and contentment. Reality began to settle in as he confided that he had put himself in a couple of situations where he became involved with other men. I tried to prepare myself for the possibility that he was heading in the direction of living an openly gay lifestyle, even though he said he had confessed those indiscretions to the bishop. How could I ever cross the bridge of accepting that I had an openly gay son?

After much meditation, prayer, soul-searching, and discussion with family members, I remembered truths I had known long before this difficulty had consumed my life: my peace and happiness were not dependent on TJ's choices. I still loved him as much as I knew the Lord did. I reinforced my own relationship with the Savior and tried to act as I felt He would in our situation. My sadness came from contemplating how this might affect TJ's eternal destiny should he change his lifestyle so completely.

Once more I began studying the scriptures with that question in mind. I read books and talks on the subject of children who strayed. I pondered and prayed, and soon my heart began to acknowledge that my son's life was in heaven's hands, that our Eternal Father loved and was mindful of him, regardless of how he was living. I tried my best to endure with faith as I watched his slow, downward spiral, but I often found myself in tears as I pondered the reality of what was happening.

Finding a Partner

When TJ finished his master's degree and moved to the East Coast to begin further study, our other son was nearing the end of his medical school training in New York City, where he lived with his family. We visited our sons a few times while they were living back East. The younger one could sense that TJ was distancing himself from activity in the Church. I felt strongly that he was reaching a crossroad. In the spring of 2003, we stood in Times Square and said good-bye to TJ after an enjoyable visit. As he turned and headed for Grand Central Station, I looked at my husband and said, "We've lost him."

In hindsight, I see that attitude as hopeless, but at the time I felt that all I could do for the rest of my life was merely *endure,* possibly not having a close relationship with him ever again. I had no idea where his choices might lead him. While my studies had convinced my head what was right for me to believe and do, my heart hadn't had the time or experience to comply—and the time I spent in tears increased.

Within another month, TJ had found a job in his profession and moved to New York City as well. He reported to us that he had secured a great apartment on the upper west side of Manhattan and he would be living with a roommate who was about his age. Something in me knew that this young man was more than a roommate, although TJ wasn't immediately forthcoming with that information. Finally, I e-mailed him one day from my office and bluntly told him I was aware of the nature of their relationship. I even spat out the words: "So now you're gay." Many of my words were pointed and harsh—insensitive, to say the least. I rationalized that my attitude was a justifiable reaction to the grave and drastic change to his life. After all, he couldn't expect me to be happy with his decision.

Fortunately, he responded with patience and a heartfelt explanation. He told me how he was so tired of being alone, and he wanted someone to share his life with. He saw no future with a woman. He saw no future in the Church. He and his partner wanted a normal, quiet home life like most couples. He was tired of lying, he was weary of sneaking around, and so on. As he explained himself, I was deeply touched and tormented at the same time.

A new set of questions bombarded my mind and soul: If this is a serious relationship (and he assured me it was), how do I handle this as his mother? I believe and support the standards of the Church, and I don't believe in same-sex marriage. My testimony of the restored gospel of Jesus Christ is sound, so I can't encourage or support this relationship without them thinking I accept it, can I? Where do I draw the line between accepting my son and setting standards in our home? What about the rest of my family? Now my other children will have to face the responsibility of teaching their children to love their uncle while not affirming that part of his life. How can that be done? Is this fair to small children, not to mention teenagers? Would our loving acceptance of TJ and his partner as individuals encourage sinful behavior in them or in our other children and grandchildren?

My heart and mind were in conflict as these questions and many others racked my soul for a long time. As with many events and happenings in the course of life, the experiences that followed answered my heart's questions one by one. I learned that I sometimes need to just feel my way one step at a time, keeping my foundation solid through prayer and holding tight to that iron rod. Mortality will provide the experiences necessary to grow and to learn what must be done.

Meeting the Partner

After TJ moved in with his partner, I had nearly a year to discuss those questions with the family before we all met him. None of us wanted to alienate any member of the family. That meant we would have to at least tolerate our son's partner. Doctrinally, I knew TJ was accountable for his choices; he had made sacred covenants in the temple and held the Melchizedek Priesthood. His partner had been raised Catholic but had long since disassociated himself from Catholicism. He was not responsible in the same way TJ was for his actions. Once again, my head told me that, but my heart had not yet had opportunity to contribute to my decision regarding how to relate to this man in my son's life.

When we finally met him, it was initially uncomfortable for the entire family. I'm certain it was for him as well. But it wasn't long before we could talk easily and actually enjoy each other's company—and they seemed happy and very much a normal couple in every way except for the obvious. TJ's partner was affable, intelligent, friendly, kind, and spiritual. The family agreed that he was a great guy, and TJ seemed happier than he had been for many years.

Incidentally, another family member also has a son who experiences same-gender attraction, although his son is much younger than mine. His wife has been a wisdom-filled resource for me. It was a blessing to have them to talk with and seek support from. As I was slowly coming to terms with TJ's relationship with his partner, the wife said to me, "When I discovered that my only responsibility is to love my son and not to judge him or try to change him, I started to feel real happiness again." She explained to her son that he was aware of her beliefs and values, that she didn't need to remind him—and that her love for him would never change, regardless of his choices. Her advice impressed me and helped me to start finally regaining a sense of peace about the situation.

Following her example, I told my son how much I loved him and that I would always love him. I reassured him of the Lord's love. Telling him I loved him was nothing new, but I was also clear with him regarding my support for the Church, including its doctrinal teachings regarding homosexual conduct. I love both TJ and his partner with all of my heart and at the same time feel loyalty to the Lord and his appointed prophets and apostles. At one point, as I was seeking spiritual guidance in my search for peace, I had a clear impression from the Spirit that the Church's responsibility is to maintain moral standards and true principles and to outline appropriate behavior for members; the family's responsibility, in addition to affirming those standards and principles, is to make the depth of the Lord's love real to one another, regardless of how each family member lives those standards and principles.

Reconciling Love and Loyalty

I believe that Heavenly Father provided family life so every person has someplace where they are loved and accepted, a place where they feel protected and where they can get the support they need to progress along life's path. I wish to be understood regarding what I believe concerning the Church's role. I believe the gospel teaches us to love everyone, which includes those whose lives are not fully aligned with revealed truth—which is all of us! There is a difference between the Church as an organization and the people within that organization. The Church is the vehicle the Lord established in order to proclaim truth, to help perfect its members, and to redeem those who have gone before. Upholding standards of truth is paramount. Right and wrong are clear and must be defended unflinchingly. Members should be able to defend and adhere to truth in addition to following the Savior's command to love everyone.

My dilemma between loving my son and his partner and loving the gospel was gradually resolved: I love the gospel and the Church of Jesus Christ, and I love TJ and his partner. For me, it eventually became that simple. I learned not to experience those truths as mutually exclusive. I need not choose between my son and the gospel. The Church does not need to alter its teachings because I love these young men. For me, it isn't a choice of being faithful to one or to the other; I have heart enough for the gospel and for TJ, and to spare.

Once I finally confided to a close friend that TJ was gay, she was supportive and understanding. She wondered if Latter-day Saint men and women who experience same-gender attraction feel like square pegs trying to fit into round holes where the Church is concerned. I told her I had no expectation that the Church would ever alter its standards of right and wrong. I have never felt anguish over the Church's teachings regarding homosexual conduct. I know without question that Heavenly Father knew that my son would experience these feelings and that I would take on the challenge and blessing of being his mom, for I believe that His foreknowledge prepared me in the premortal world for this experience.

There are times when I still have conflicted feelings. It's difficult to articulate to myself, let alone to anyone else, how I can feel such a deep sense of peace given my spiritual beliefs and TJ's choices. Considering the stereotypical alternative of the wild and promiscuous gay lifestyle, I'm thankful that my son is in a committed relationship. I love and embrace each of them as special young men whom the Lord knows and loves. I believe the situation is as good as it possibly could be, given that TJ is choosing not to live Church teachings regarding sexual chastity.

Recently, we have talked about the need to maintain some kind of spiritual connection even though he has distanced himself from the Church. My hope is that he will someday find his way back, but I must live in the here and now and make the best of where we are today.

Sometimes I dream of the two of them feeling comfortable attending Church meetings together, even if they are not partaking of the sacrament or participating in full fellowship. At least they would have opportunities to be spiritually nourished and receive the friendship and fellowship of Saints who will love them where they are. My hope is that eventually the majority of Latter-day Saints will understand that feelings of same-gender attraction are not inherently evil, that wonderful children of Heavenly Father experience conflict between their sexual attractions and the plan of salvation, and that love and compassion should not be withheld even from those who are not currently living in accord with the gospel plan.

Conclusion

I've learned to love TJ's partner like my own child and have accepted him as part of our family. Our general comfort level increases each time the entire family gathers together. We appreciate the respect TJ and his partner demonstrate for the values and beliefs of our family with regard to the kinds of affection they share during family gatherings. They have been together several years now, and I'm finally to the point of feeling content with the situation, knowing that the Lord's mercy and justice will prevail and trusting that He will judge TJ's heart with divine wisdom and mercy.

I have discovered along the way that love is always the answer. I feel so much more compassion and understanding for others than I felt prior to learning about my son's situation. Ultimate judgment never belongs to me. Above all, I have come to know my Savior just a little bit more than I did before TJ came out. Giving the burden to the Lord has meant everything. My gratitude for the Atonement has been strengthened deeply, and I am humbled daily just to know that all of us have hope now and beyond the grave.

Life is good. Peace prevails. I am blessed immeasurably as this journey unfolds. These days I still shed plenty of tears, but they are tears of joy and thankfulness—the joy I feel when my entire family gathers together.

Chapter 3

"Come unto Me": Exploring the Heart of Christian Discipleship

Wendy Ulrich

With His oft-repeated phrase, "Come unto me," Christ invites us close. He invites us to know Him, trust Him, and follow Him, and to join the community of Saints He will warmly embrace on His return. Christ extends these invitations to all, including, of course, those who experience same-gender attraction.

In contrast to Christ's inviting bid for closeness, our experience in this world often fosters distance. Alienation seems to be our common lot in mortality, and our physical, mental, or spiritual differences can accentuate our feelings of alienation from ourselves, others, and God. When we feel judged and found wanting; when we are ill, injured, or abused; when we struggle with the weaknesses inherent to mortality; or when we simply feel our individuality as a burden instead of a gift, our feelings of alienation may increase. We may long for relief and restoration to the state of well-being we once enjoyed or that we imagine others enjoy. Yet even the most faithful do not universally find a "cure" for either alienation or the maladies that evoke it.

Some of the factors hypothesized to contribute to same-gender attraction are apparently more amenable to change than others, but even people who are determined to reengineer their attractions do not always accomplish all the transformations they seek.[1] But whether we find resolution for all that ails us, Christ promises us healing. Healing is not dependent on cure. Healing includes broadening our identity, solidifying meaningful relationships, and strengthening faith. Healing transforms disappointment and difficulty into resilience and compassion. Healing means finding a place for our trials as well as our triumphs in the story of our life and in the story of Zion, even if the plot line differs from the one we once imagined.

Christ's redeeming sacrifice is aptly named the Atonement, the *at-one-ment,* for it draws us into healing circles, bridging the distances created by pain, affliction, temptation, sickness, weakness, loss, and even sin (see Alma 7:11–13). Regardless of the category of our personal challenge, Christ invites us to come to Him and be "at one."

As a psychologist, I have counseled people wrestling with many kinds of mortal challenges. As a human being, I have experienced at least a taste and sometimes a long-standing diet of many of these challenges. I have wrestled with my own psyche, with my most important relationships, and with God. Perhaps for this reason the Old Testament story of Jacob speaks to me—Jacob, who wrestled with an angel for the blessings God had promised him, just when he appeared to be in danger of losing them all (see Genesis 32). Jacob's name was changed to Israel, a paradoxical name that can either mean "one who struggles or perseveres with God" or "one with whom God prevails." We are the children of Israel when we care enough to struggle and persevere with God until He prevails with us. His promised blessings are not dependent on our ability to find a remedy; they depend only on our ability to find the Lord.

Christian discipleship is the process of finding and following Christ through faith and repentance. This process ensures healing and growth, joy in this life, and eternal life in the world to come. Let's consider six aspects of coming to Jesus as our personal Savior.

Faith

All Christian discipleship begins with faith in Christ. Faith is more than acknowledgement of Christ's existence or sovereignty. Faith includes heartfelt trust that Christ's version of what is real and reliable is superior to all others. It includes trust that what He reveals is sufficient to guide, save, and exalt us, even if it does not answer all our questions or solve all our difficulties. It includes trust that He knows us and loves us individually, perfectly.

You probably learned the basics of faith early in your Church experience. Whether in Primary, youth conferences, or the missionary discussions, you learned that you are the offspring of a Heavenly Father who loves you, knows you, and has prepared a plan for your growth and learning. Hopefully, your early experiences with the Spirit built your confidence in God and the Church, even amid questions and self-doubts. If you are like me, you assumed that as you grew up in the gospel you would conquer your doubts, overcome your weaknesses, and find a secure, comfortable place in the Church. But as we tackle college, return from missions, begin work, consider long-term relationship commitments, or in other ways face the challenges of adulthood, we may also realize that our temptations and trials, personalities and predispositions, doubts and difficulties are not all magically resolved.

As we sense that we are in for a long haul, we may wonder if we are headed down the right road or if we have the stamina for the journey ahead. God can be frustratingly silent about our concerns, and we may wonder if He can be trusted. The Church can be frustratingly vocal about its teachings and standards, and we may wonder if it really speaks to us. We can be frustratingly feeble against our temptations or challenges, and we may wonder if we have it in us to keep trying.

Christ calls out to us from a position of deep, personal experience with our mortal suffering, a cup from which He drank fully. His words to the ancients echo to us as well: "Arise and *come forth unto me,* that ye may thrust your hands into my side, and also that ye may feel the prints of the nails in my hands and in my feet, that ye may know that I am the God of Israel, and the God of the whole earth, and have been slain for the sins of the world" (3 Nephi 11:14; emphasis added).

Christ asks us to know Him as One who was willingly and mortally wounded—One who fully joined us in our vulnerable human condition. His compassion for our wounds, defeats, trials, and sacrifices is deeply personal. But He also asks us to know that His wounds healed, that He rose again and returned to His Father, and that He then came back for us. He is the God of Israel and the God of the whole earth. He has commissioned prophets to testify of His life, Resurrection, and Atonement and to teach us of His plan.

Those who experience same-gender attraction have many decisions to make regarding belief in God: "Is homosexual behavior really counter to God's law?" "Why do people have same-gender attractions if God doesn't want them to act on them?" "Does the Church really speak for God in these matters?" "If I am faithful and obedient, then why doesn't God take these feelings away?" "How can I be happy and fulfilled if I forfeit the opportunity for a complete, loving relationship with someone I am attracted to, or if I sideline such a big part of who I am?"

These are important questions. We can look at them from many angles. Faith invites us to trust the voice of the Spirit, a particular challenge if trusting that voice would require us to change our mind, our heart, or our behavior. The first children of Adam and Eve faced such challenges as Adam and Eve taught them to trust God, His plan, and the promised Atonement of Christ, while Satan came and told them to "believe it not; and they believed it not, and they loved Satan more than God. And men began from that time forth to be carnal, sensual, and devilish" (Moses 5:13). We are faced with such choices every day. Whom will we believe? Whom will we trust? Of course, Satan seldom reveals his hand when he casts doubt on our belief in God. Few of us will follow Satan or mere mortals or our own logic over God's wisdom if we are not first convinced that we are reasonable, right, maybe even inspired.

Ultimately, I think faith in God means two things. First it means that we hold fast to the things we believed to be true when we were most confident that the Spirit was with us. That confidence is grounded in humbly studying the scriptures, following the counsel of prophets, and engaging in sincere prayer. It is grounded in serious reflection about our personal vulnerabilities to deception in spiritual matters because of inexperience or vested interests. It is grounded in acceptance that God's version of what is real and reliable will not always line up with current human understanding.

Second, faith in God means that we act in accordance with our covenants, even when we don't feel like it or doubts arise or the way is not easy. Despite our misgivings about our ability to endure hunger and frustration day after day, we determine to trust God to give us "today's bread today,"[2] sufficient for our needs in this moment. We recognize that with His help and the support of others, we can get through our trials one day at a time. That, in fact, is all we have to do. We also recognize that however unique the challenge of same-gender attraction, every disciple has a cross to bear for Jesus. This is the nature of Christian discipleship.

Faith in Christ is a spiritual gift, a learned capacity, and a personal choice we make again and again. Each of us has the opportunity to learn by the confirmation of the Holy Ghost whether there is a God, whether The Church of Jesus Christ of Latter-day Saints is His Church, and whether we personally have hope in Christ of returning to Him. These things, once felt by the Spirit to be true, are our surest guide in life. Choosing to trust them is the most important decision we make.

Repentance

Once the seed of faith is planted, God's most urgent message to us is to repent, which means to change our minds, turn away from sin, and turn back toward God. "Now this is the commandment: Repent, all ye ends of the earth, and *come unto me* and be baptized in my name, that ye may be sanctified by the reception of the Holy Ghost, that ye may stand spotless before me at the last day" (3 Nephi 27:20; emphasis added).

The scriptures speak often of repentance, which implies recognizing that we have been in error and turning our hearts back to God. Repentance includes renouncing sin and changing our behavior. We all sin, and we all need to repent. Satan is the author of sin, and sin is a dangerous state, one we want to get out of as quickly as possible because it stops our progress and leads to misery, whether sooner or later. We sin when we rebel against God, disobey His commandments, or participate in being deceived by the adversary. Sin includes violating one of the Ten Commandments, doing things that would keep us out of the temple, or disobeying a clear commandment given through scripture, modern prophets, or personal revelation. Modern prophets have consistently stated that consenting to sexual relations outside of a God-sanctioned marriage is a serious sin and that any homosexual relations constitute serious sin.[3]

Another serious sin associated with both heterosexuality and homosexuality is lust. Although not as serious as sexual behavior, lust prevents the Spirit from being with us, undermines our confidence with God, and often leads to more serious sin. However, lust should not be confused with either attraction or sexual arousal, neither of which is sinful in itself. Let's look at the differences.

In the broadest and healthiest sense, attraction, which can include romantic attraction, suggests interest in another as a whole person, with respect for the person's values, goodness, talents, intelligence, and character, and with compassion for the person's sorrows, weaknesses, and flaws. Attraction can be the basis of friendship, romantic desire, or deep love.

Attraction can also be based primarily in physical or emotional characteristics of another person that we long to have in ourselves, or that feel familiar. Attraction can lead to either meaningful connection or misplaced intensity and confusion, depending on how we channel it.

Similarly, sexual arousal in itself is neither good nor bad but is simply a part of being human. Arousal can occur in a variety of situations, not always in our control. We can choose to enhance it and indulge it or to ignore it, distract ourselves from it, or redirect its energy. What we choose to do with attraction or arousal can be appropriate and Spirit enhancing or inappropriate and sin enhancing.

In contrast to attraction and arousal, which are neutral, lust is always defined scripturally as sin. It involves seeking and focusing on sexual images and intensifying and indulging in sexual desires that are not lawful. Lust involves reducing ourselves or others to sexual objects.

Lust is a choice to focus our attention on *sex*-uality, not *person*-ality. Lustful thoughts and feelings are fostered by pornographic images and films, passionate descriptions in novels or lyrics, and physical contact with someone other than our spouse that deliberately promotes sexual arousal. The sin of lust requires repentance.

Repentance for a disciple of Christ begins with changing our mind about the nature of our thoughts and actions. Repentance includes choosing to see (rather than ignore) how our choices hurt others or us, or distance us from God. We acknowledge to God that our choices have been wrong, though we may have previously believed they were justified. With repentance we turn back toward God. Repentance includes changing our mind, heart, and behavior; apologizing or confessing to those we have offended or harmed; making restitution; and rebuilding trust through honesty and continued right choices. In the case of a serious sin such as sex outside of marriage, we also confess to our bishop or branch president and submit to his counsel. This is the process of repentance.

Repentance is not the backup plan for those who fall short of perfection—repentance is the only plan because none of us has any hope of forgiveness or wholeness on our own merit. When we repent, we can rely completely on the Atonement of Jesus Christ to satisfy the debts we incur through sin, and God promises us complete forgiveness. As we repent and rely upon the merits of Christ to make up for our own lack of merit, we can stand blameless before God. We are "at one" with Him again. This promise is absolutely sure.

Humility

In addition to repentance for sin, a vital aspect of Christian discipleship is humility in the face of our weakness. Weakness is not the same as sin. In fact, the Book of Mormon indicates that God, not Satan, gives us weakness, which includes all our natural limitations as humans. God prescribes a specific course of action for weakness—a course somewhat different from repentance. He said to Moroni, who was concerned about his weakness in writing: "If men *come unto me* I will show unto them their weakness. I give unto men weakness that they may be humble; and my grace is sufficient for all men that humble themselves before me; for if they humble themselves before me, and have faith in me, then will I make weak things become strong unto them" (Ether 12:27; emphasis added). So in the face of sin we are to repent and obtain forgiveness, but in the face of weakness we are to humble ourselves, come to Christ, and obtain grace. Let's consider how these processes differ.

Weakness is part of the mortal condition God sent us here to learn from. Weakness includes all the ways we are ignorant, foolish, inexperienced, and frail. In our weakness, we are subject to physical and mental illness, to temptation, and to emotions like anger, shame, anxiety, and depression. Weakness may include our poor judgment calls, our doubts and uncertainties, and problems we experience after being abused or traumatized. It includes our predispositions to laziness, greed, fatigue, or addiction. Weakness means there are real limits to our endurance, skill, wisdom, patience, and self-discipline.

Potential vulnerabilities associated with same-gender attraction might be classified as weakness. While Satan is the author of sin, God gives us weakness, in that God placed us in mortality, giving us bodies, minds, and hearts that are subject to limitations, temptations, injuries, hungers, and suffering.

As humans we tend to confuse sin and weakness. Out of self-justification or self-deceit, we may assume we are weak when in fact we are sinful—a problem because then we don't repent and obtain forgiveness. We may also assume we are sinful when in fact we are weak—a problem because then we can become discouraged, hopeless, and ashamed.

In a given situation we may be both sinful and weak. We need to distinguish sin that requires immediate repentance from weakness that requires patient effort, learning, and growth. What is sin to me may be weakness in you, and what is weakness for me today may become sin if I refuse God's counsel and help. For example, drinking alcohol is for us a sin, but poor coping skills or depression that underlie the drinking may result from mortal weakness. A Church member who drinks may need to both repent of drinking and related sins of rebellion or self-deception and then humbly and persistently work on weaknesses of addiction, stress intolerance, and depression. We can completely change our mind (repent) about violating God's commandment to avoid alcohol but still need time to tackle the weakness of addiction. Prayer, scripture study, counsel with others, and reflection can help us distinguish our sin from our weakness.

Homosexual behavior is a sin requiring repentance and behavior change, while vulnerabilities associated with same-gender attraction might be seen as weaknesses that we can humbly learn to manage. As we do so, with God's help, weakness can become a source of great strength, learning, growth, and even peace. We are not doomed to white-knuckle resistance to temptation for the rest of our lives, even if we may need it for a time while we build other resources. Managing weakness includes working to understand what makes us vulnerable and what our truest needs are. It includes developing skills to manage our stress, gain support from healthy relationships, engage in meaningful work, find opportunities for creativity and service, and consistently nurture our spirituality.

When we have sinned, God calls us to repent and then promises us forgiveness; when we face weakness, God calls us to humility and then promises us grace. The LDS Bible Dictionary defines *grace* as divine help made possible by the Atonement of Christ. It says that grace is an enabling power that strengthens us to "do good works that [we] otherwise would not be able to maintain" on our own. As Ether 12:27 states, we qualify for grace by humility, which means being teachable, meek, and patient. With humility we recognize we can't do everything. We seek out tutors and helpers, we practice, and we keep trying when we fail. We take the necessary risks to improve, building on what we do right as well as learning from our errors.

When Moses was called as a prophet, he worried greatly about his weakness, and he wrestled with God about his poor speaking ability, lack of leadership stature, and fear of Pharaoh and the children of Israel. For each of these weaknesses God graciously promised help, answers, even miracles. But when Moses then told the Lord to go find someone else for the job because he was too weak, God became angry at Moses for claiming weakness when he was actually rebelling against a call from the Lord. Moses repented of his sin and tackled his weakness, setting an example for us on both counts. God is patient with our weakness, and we are to be patient with one another's weakness and with our own.

Christ not only atoned for our sins but also succors us in our weakness. Alma describes seven categories of experience Christ would atone for on our behalf. One of these categories is sin, which He took upon Himself "that he might blot out [our] transgressions according to the power of his deliverance." In addition, Christ took upon Himself our "pains and afflictions and temptations of every kind . . . sicknesses . . . death . . . and . . . infirmities." He took upon Him these mortal weaknesses "that his bowels may be filled with mercy, according to the flesh, that he may know according to the flesh how to succor [comfort and help] his people according to their infirmities" (Alma 7:11–13).

The pains, afflictions, temptations, infirmities, family dynamics, and physiology associated with same-gender attraction are not something we need to repent of but something we need to be humble about—that is, learn from, learn about, and plead with God for comfort and grace (help, strength, and enabling power) to manage. As we humble ourselves and call upon God, He will strengthen us to bear our burdens and grow from our difficulties. He will make weak things become strong unto us. He may not change us any more than He changed Moroni's ability to write when he complained about this weakness. But He can ensure that our weakness does not stop us from completing our personal mortal mission or finding happiness and peace. We may not gain the approval of the world by trusting God's grace, but we can obtain the constant companionship of the Holy Ghost, the friendship of Jesus Christ, and the approbation of our Father.

What does humility look like in action? Humility does not mean shame, humiliation, groveling, or self-hatred but is their antithesis.

Humility means we are meek, teachable, and open. With humility we approach our weakness as we might approach learning to play the piano, learning a sport, or learning medicine. We study the subject, talk to people who have more experience than we, gain insight, practice coping, and create routines and structures that support our efforts. We work on reducing errors and learning from them. We work even harder on developing our skills, strengths, and gifts. We prioritize, recognizing that we cannot do everything at once. As with sin, we may hurt others through weaknesses such as susceptibility to temptation or strong emotion or because of our limitations or ignorance. When we do, we feel deep regret, sincerely apologize, and try to make restitution. We take necessary risks in order to improve and grow. We avoid unnecessary risks that would undermine our strength or subject us to temptation. We use humor, pacing, balance, and the support of other people to cope with our weaknesses. We exercise patience. We pray for God's help, submit to His tutoring, and strive to be people of integrity and character despite our limitations.

Whether or not we eliminate a specific weakness, we will never eliminate all weakness. The resurrection will endow us with physically perfect bodies and Christ's redemption ensures forgiveness if we repent, but we may continue to work on our weakness over eons to come. Humbly working on our weakness is a vital aspect of Christian discipleship. Although we will never overcome all of our weakness in this life, we can fully repent from sin and stand blameless before God through Christ's Atonement. For me, this is cause for great hope.

Sacrifice

In addition to faith, repentance, and humility, Christian discipleship always requires sacrifice. Joseph Smith taught, "A religion that does not require the sacrifice of all things never has the power sufficient to produce the faith necessary unto life and salvation."[4] Sacrifice is not just about giving things up. The roots of the English verb *sacrifice* mean "to make something holy." Sacrifice includes taking something that is precious to us and offering it to God, making it holy because we give it to the Holy One. We do this, trusting that He in turn will give us everything we truly need, making us holy like Him in the process.

Sacrifice is an act of worship and loving devotion that both demonstrates and increases our faith in God as we acknowledge Him as the only life-sustaining power in the universe. The sacrifice God asks of each of us is a broken heart and a contrite spirit, and in turn He promises us sanctification, revelation, and the matchless gifts of the Spirit: "And ye shall offer for a sacrifice unto me a broken heart and a contrite spirit. And whoso *cometh unto me* with a broken heart and a contrite spirit, him will I baptize with fire and with the Holy Ghost" (3 Nephi 19:20; emphasis added).

Beginning with our first parents, God commanded His children to make sacrifices to Him of their flocks and crops—the things that sustained their lives (see Moses 5:4–5). Adam and Eve did not initially understand the meaning of sacrifice. Adam was later told by an angel that it was "a similitude of the sacrifice of the Only Begotten of the Father," and that he should repent, pray, and do all things "in the name of the Son" from that time forward (Moses 5:6–8). The law of Moses formalized these sacrificial offerings as religious rituals. After the time of Christ, His disciples continued to offer their tithes, talents, time, substance, and sometimes even their lives to build His kingdom and acknowledge Him as the Giver of all blessings. The Hebrew concept of sacrifice did not refer to forfeiture or death, however. The Hebrew word for the sacrificial offering, *korban,* comes from the word for *near.* The intent of these offerings was to help us close the rift between God and man resulting from the Fall and from personal sins. The ultimate sacrifice of the Savior bridges this gap, making it possible for us to return—to draw near—to God.

For some who experience same-gender attraction, the sacrifices that may be required to live gospel standards can feel daunting. Placing on the altar God's gifts of sexuality, romantic love, and committed family life is not easy for single men and women, regardless of sexual predisposition. As we commit to put our relationship with God first, He promises to sustain us now and eventually return to us all His promised blessings. When facing the possibility of a life without romantic love, without a committed partnership, without a family of our own, we may wonder why God asks so much of us. I don't pretend to have a complete answer to that question. What I do believe is that sacrifice is a source of faith and power, so no follower of Christ escapes the requirement to sacrifice.

For example, few single people grasp the degree to which their married counterparts may also struggle with sexual frustration, loneliness, identity questions, and disappointment over the course of a marriage. Romantic intensity is a short-term stage of a long-term commitment. No marital partner understands or completes us fully or consistently. Marriage does not exempt us from difficult questions about who we are and what we want. Children are demanding and complicated. While the blessings and opportunities that come with family life outweigh the problems for most people, those who marry shoulder a fair share of sacrifices, losses, and disappointments. Those for whom marriage is not a viable option have not been singled out for a disproportionate share of hardship and heartache—only a different share. Their challenges will be substantial, but life can still be fulfilling, satisfying, purposeful, and joyful as they draw close to God.

Like the ancients offering their flocks and crops, we still put something valuable at jeopardy when we sacrifice. We might sorely need that lamb, that tithing, that extra time on Sunday morning, that distraction from our problems, that shortcut to self-esteem, that hope-inspiring dream, and if not now, some day soon. By making this offering, we declare our dependence on God alone to provide our deepest needs. The same holds when we sacrifice our sexuality, our relationships, or aspects of our self-expression. In all these things we also declare our dependence on God, not on sex, other people, or ourselves to fulfill us in the highest sense. We trust that both in time and in eternity, He will provide full measure, pressed down and running over, to fill our waiting cup of righteous hopes and dreams.

God also put something at risk when He made the sacrifice of His Son to draw His children close to Him. He risked that we would not receive this infinite gift, not allow our hearts to be touched, not repent and trust Him, and not receive His promised forgiveness and grace. In fact, He put at risk what is most precious to Him: us. Even God must trust in the Atonement and its power to draw us to Him by this supreme demonstration of love. He watches tenderly over us, noting whether His sacrifice will bring Him His truest desires.

Paul clarifies that the sacrifice required of disciples of Christ is not a dead animal but our own living body, consecrated to His service. To the Roman Saints, he wrote:

"I beseech you therefore, brethren, by the mercies of God, that ye present your bodies a *living sacrifice,* holy, acceptable unto God, which is your reasonable service. . . . For I say, through the grace given unto me, to every man that is among you, not to think of himself more highly than he ought to think; but to think soberly, according as God hath dealt to every man the measure of faith.

"For as we have many members in one body, and all members have not the same office: So we, being many, are one body in Christ, and every one members one of another. . . ."

He instructs us further: "Let love be without dissimulation. Abhor that which is evil; cleave to that which is good. Be kindly affectioned one to another with brotherly love; in honour preferring one another; . . . rejoicing in hope; patient in tribulation; continuing instant in prayer; distributing to the necessity of saints; given to hospitality.

"Bless them which persecute you: bless, and curse not. Rejoice with them that do rejoice, and weep with them that weep. . . . If it be possible, as much as lieth in you, live peaceably with all men. . . . Be not overcome of evil, but overcome evil with good" (Romans 12:1, 3–5, 9–10, 12–15, 18, 21; emphasis added).

As we follow inspired counsel and make the "living sacrifice" God asks, our trusting faith in God gradually deepens, becoming "sufficient" to claim for us the "life and salvation" Joseph Smith spoke of.

Resilience

Disappointment and difficulty are inevitable parts of life. The gospel offers much to strengthen our resilience after loss, betrayal, or failure. But sometimes the gospel itself seems to contribute to our disappointment or frustration. It invites us to appreciate the importance of family ties and then prohibits same-sex marriage. It encourages us to have faith in Christ's healing power but doesn't guarantee us a cure. It promises us happiness but promotes teachings that we may struggle to make sense of and live. In the face of such difficulties we may wonder if we would be better off to just leave and find our own way. It is one thing to sign up for the Church when doing so reduces our risk of cancer, answers life's questions, gets us involved with good people, and ensures us of eternal life. It is another thing to sign up when we get cancer anyway, life is not making sense, those good people don't accept us, or we are not sure we want to live another day.

During Christ's ministry, many would-be disciples chafed when their expectations of how a Messiah should teach or behave were not met and when His teachings seemed too strange, His paths too difficult. We read:

"Many therefore of his disciples, when they had heard [Christ's teachings], said, This is an hard saying; who can hear it? When Jesus knew in himself that his disciples murmured at it, he said unto them, Doth this offend you? . . . And he said, Therefore said I unto you, that no man can *come unto me,* except it were given unto him of my Father. From that time many of his disciples went back, and walked no more with him" (John 6:60–61, 65–66; emphasis added).

When Christ's teachings or life's demands are hard or offensive, we need special help from the Father to not go back but to continue to walk with the Savior. That help generally comes after—not before—we make the decision to do whatever God requires. We often struggle with this order. We want God to do His part first—to make us happy, cure our ills, bring us love, remove our frustrations, meet our needs—and then we will sign on the dotted line. After all, wouldn't we be suckers to spend all our emotional savings before seeing the merchandise we are purchasing?

Dealing with God is not an economic exchange, governed by the rules of the marketplace. The decision to follow God comes from our deepening conviction that God, unlike our fellow mortals, can always be trusted to do His best for us, free from selfish intent. The decision to follow God is not a bargain we strike but a statement about who we are and an expression of our deepest values, regardless of temporary outcomes. Our covenant relationship with God is not based on short-term economic exchanges (I'll stay as long as I'm happy, as long as I'm fairly compensated for my efforts, as long as it makes obvious sense) but on an emerging trust that God's best is as good as it gets, ever, even when we cannot quite see how. Such a commitment provides direction and sustenance regardless of the vicissitudes of life.

Resilience is both a gift of the Spirit and a skill we can cultivate. Our resilience in the face of confusion or disappointment increases as we remember past spiritual feelings and experiences, take things one day at a time, allow other faithful people to know and love us, learn to soothe and comfort ourselves, and deepen our self-understanding. We take resilience to new levels as we covenant that God will be our God and trust that He will claim us as one of His people—that He will fight our battles and provide for our needs as He did for His covenant people of old.

When we do not fully understand God's teachings, and when we are angry, fearful, or jealous of those who seem to have an easier lot, the Lord turns to us and asks a crucial question, just as he asked the Twelve in the situation described above: "Then said Jesus unto the twelve, Will ye also go away? Then Simon Peter answered him, Lord, to whom shall we go? thou hast the words of eternal life. And we believe and are sure that thou art that Christ, the Son of the living God" (John 6:67–69).

Will we also go away, as many do? When we are frustrated, hurt, and confused, the most natural thing in the world is to place distance between us and whatever or whoever is frustrating us. Christ acknowledges that this is our option. We imagine Him asking us the question as well: "Will ye also go away?" I have contemplated this question many times in moments of frustration, disappointment, or pain when staying close to God or to the Church has felt like a fool's choice. Again and again I find myself remembering, however, that I have found words of life here in the past, that I believe Christ is their author, and that I believe He is still the repository of any lasting good I will come by. It is not always easy to walk with Christ, but there is simply no better place to walk. He has the words of life-giving truth that describe what is real and lead us to God.

Sociality

When Christ invites us close to Him, He also calls us close to others who seek to follow Him. Isaiah writes, "And the ransomed of the Lord shall return, and *come to Zion* with songs and everlasting joy upon their heads: they shall obtain joy and gladness, and sorrow and sighing shall flee away" (Isaiah 35:10; emphasis added).

Zion is a community of Saints who truly seek to follow Christ, becoming of one heart and one mind. This does not mean all are alike in personality, struggles, gifts, or circumstances but that all love the Lord and have covenanted to follow Him. There are "no poor among them" (Moses 7:18), which I take to mean that there is *no one in Zion with nothing to give.* All of our mortal experiences—the character we develop, the compassion we acquire, the discipline we build, the faith we cultivate, the gifts and talents we magnify—help build this Zion community that will greet the Savior when He returns.

Zion needs us, and we need Zion. If we are going to find meaning, purpose, and fulfillment commensurate with what we have sacrificed, we must be fully engaged in the life of the Spirit. Casual participation will not be enough to fill our hunger for connection, meaning, and intense engagement with life. We need the nurturance of regular scripture study during which we invite God to be our study companion. Prayer must become a personal time to imagine God near as we speak with honesty and feeling. We need opportunities for meaningful and engaging work to contribute from our strengths. We need relationships in which to learn essential skills of problem solving, listening, sharing, helping, and giving and receiving support. We benefit from opportunities to interact with people of all ages as we create a family of choice to supplement our family of origin. We need the spiritual university of Zion.

With same-gender attraction, closeness to others can be both longed for and feared. We long for understanding, connection, friendship, and love but also fear misunderstanding, rejection, condemnation, and distance from those whose life experience has not prepared them to relate easily to the diversity of others. While many in the Church will take same-gender attraction in stride, some will not. Judgmental comments, teasing, or simply thoughtless off-hand remarks can sting, making us wonder if we will ever belong. Christ's call to everyone includes a call to make peace with those who offend us or whom we offend. He says:

"Therefore, if ye shall *come unto me,* or shall desire to come unto me, and rememberest that thy brother hath aught against thee—Go thy way unto thy brother, and first be reconciled to thy brother, and then *come unto me* with full purpose of heart, and *I will receive you*" (3 Nephi 12:23–24; emphasis added).

Making peace with others requires maturity, charity, and sometimes a good sense of humor. Just as we hope that others will be patient with and tolerant of our weakness, we have the opportunity to be patient with and tolerant of the weakness of others who are rude or thoughtless. Sometimes our best course is to ignore others' offensive comments, chalking them up to ignorance and immaturity rather than taking them personally. If this becomes too difficult, we can take aside the person who has hurt us, calmly and in a friendly manner ask for the person's help, tell the person what was said that hurt us and why, and invite support. Not everyone will respond positively to such a request, but many will. Honest words, shared in love, help Zion grow.

Joseph Smith prayed that temple covenants would help Zion individuals to "grow up in [God], and receive a fulness of the Holy Ghost, and be organized according to [God's] laws, and be prepared to obtain every needful thing" (D&C 109:15). Without the social marker of marriage to signal that we are now adults, we may feel stuck in a prolonged adolescence unless we make deliberate efforts to "grow up in [God]." The temple has a particular function of initiating us into spiritual adulthood. Participating in wards and branches gives us further opportunity to grow into our adult status. We round out our adult development through

- Finding meaningful work with opportunities for advancement, creativity, and learning
- Maintaining financial independence, including saving, paying tithes and offerings, and investing
- Creating routines and structures for physical self-care, time management, and social interactions
- Creating a home with order, pleasing surroundings, and a spiritual focus
- Nurturing the next generation, such as children, teens, new members, new move-ins, new employees at work, or younger professionals in our field
- Contributing to a civic and church community through service, callings, home or visiting teaching, priesthood service, and offering our gifts and talents to others
- Investing in social networks that include one or two people we talk to almost every day; people whose lives we keep track of and who keep track of us; people we can turn to for emergency help; and people we celebrate and mourn with, plan to do things with, and socialize with spontaneously
- Taking responsibility for our spiritual growth through regular prayer, scripture study, meeting attendance, Church callings and service, and charity for others
- Committing despite difficulties—to the Church, other people, and ourselves.

In all these things God invites us to participate fully as one who is not poor but as someone with much to give. If we are not called to positions of leadership or visibility, there are always opportunities to reach out to less-active members, help in missionary work, volunteer

for ward projects, attend the temple, work on family history, participate in classes and activities, and in other ways offer our talents, perspectives, and energy to build the whole. As we build Zion, Zion will
bless our lives with opportunities to forgive, bounce back, and "grow
up in [God]."

If we have been distant from the Church community or skeptical
about its ability to meet our deepest needs and longings, we are not
alone. In the end I believe our hope will come through strengthening
our faith, not eliminating our doubts. President Ezra Taft Benson once
said, "When obedience ceases to be an irritant and becomes our quest,
in that moment God will endow us with power."[5] We could also say,
"When knowing God ceases to be a casual interest and becomes instead
our greatest longing, in that moment our lives will find direction and
purpose."

As we decide to trust God at all costs, repent, humble ourselves,
sacrifice, grow into spiritual adulthood, and participate in a Zion community, we enjoy blessings that can come through no other vehicle:
the promises of the temple, the sanctifying gift of the Holy Ghost, the
guidance of patriarchal blessings, the support of inspired leaders and
friends, and the personal power that comes through willing obedience
to all of God's commandments. We draw near to God.

I believe that mortality, including our experience with mortal
weakness, is specifically designed to help us know God—intimately,
personally, lastingly. Christ is the Bread of Life, the Living Water, who
alone can satisfy our deepest hungers. As we come to Him in faith, He
promises us a life of full satisfaction, rich meaning, and eternal potential. I believe with all my heart that these promises are real. I believe
them not because I fully understand all of Christ's teachings or commands but because I fully trust Christ as the Author and Finisher of
my faith. His arms reach out to each of us. As ancient prophets have
testified:

"Yea, he saith: *Come unto me* and ye shall partake of the fruit of the
tree of life; yea, ye shall eat and drink of the bread and the waters of life
freely" (Alma 5:34; emphasis added).

"And I rejoice in the day when my mortal shall put on immortality, and shall stand before him; then shall I see his face with pleasure, and he will say unto me: *Come unto me,* ye blessed, there is a place prepared for you in the mansions of my Father. Amen" (Enos 1:27; emphasis added).

Learning the True Gospel: The Transforming Power of the Atonement

T. S. Richards

T. S. Richards (pseudonym) enjoys cooking, literature, traveling, photography, and hiking and camping. He is grateful to be married to his wonderful wife of nineteen years, with whom he shares the blessings of family life.

As a young teen, I spent many nights lying awake, staring out my window into the darkness and trying to understand what was wrong with me. I remember reading in a Scout manual that at a certain age I would suddenly discover that girls were the most wonderful thing in the world. I certainly liked girls and had a lot of friends who were girls, but that special feeling mentioned in the manual seemed to be materializing more clearly in my feelings for other boys instead. Having never wanted these feelings, I constantly prayed that God would take this attraction away and let me feel normal.

Nothing seemed to change, however, and as I got older, my inward despair grew to be almost unbearable. I was certain I was the worst person in the world. Determined that no one would ever know about these feelings, I became driven to deflect any possible attention to what I perceived to be my great failing. As a result, I was obsessed with being a "good boy" so that no one would ever suspect this terrible flaw, working hard to get good grades, win academic contests, and garner other obvious achievements.

Adults unwittingly reinforced my need to be perceived as "perfect" by heaping me with praise and accolades for my accomplishments. The response I perceived from other boys my age was limited to a distant respect, however, and I felt that they never liked me in the same way they seemed to like each other. Other boys seemed a different breed from me and shared a language between them that I couldn't speak. Their interests and activities outside the classroom, no matter how I tried to study or understand them, felt outside my ability to imitate.

My sense that I was different from other boys was pronounced by the time I reached my mid-teens. I was keenly conscious of my attraction by then and deeply anxious about what it might mean for my life. Being a "good boy," I never considered acting on my feelings, and I stuffed them as deep and far away as I could within me. There was little understanding at the time within the Church or society at large about same-gender attraction, and I perceived absolutely no resources for me at that age to support or reassure me in what I was going through. I felt that I could never tell my parents or Church leaders because, in my naiveté, the only possible response I could imagine from them would be shock, disgust, rejection, and undoubtedly excommunication. I didn't have any information to help me understand how the Church might view the difference between having an unbidden feeling and acting on that feeling because there was no dialogue anywhere at that time that provided access to such thinking.

To stave off the anxiety and depressive feelings I had about my same-gender attraction, I continued to work harder at exceptional achievement in the areas I could to make up for feeling so flawed. Perhaps all this effort to be perfect caused me to miss some important spiritual lessons that were probably available in my religious training. Maybe my deer-in-the-headlights fear of failure distracted me from meaningfully understanding the fundamentals of the gospel, such as faith, repentance, hope, charity, and grace. But somehow from the way

I experienced the Church, I understood my spiritual life to be a sort of challenge in which the object was to be perfect by making all the right choices all the time—especially by avoiding the short list of serious sins. My understanding of the Atonement at that time was that it was simply an insurance policy I hoped I would never need. I fully expected that I needed to solve any problems on my own, especially a big mess like same-gender attraction. I could then use the Atonement for a little cleanup as needed after I had perfected myself through willpower and discipline.

Consequently, I didn't ever quite understand how people in testimony meeting could get so teary-eyed about how Heavenly Father loved them or about how grateful they were for Jesus Christ or the Atonement. On a deeply personal level, I simply didn't feel God's love for me. Rather, I felt that the gospel and the plan of salvation obligated me to perform almost impossible tasks and carry horrendous burdens, completely alone, with Jesus a distant figure whom I was somehow supposed to imitate through my independent efforts. I had never even heard of grace except as something that other churches talked about, churches that I thought didn't understand how important our choices and efforts were in achieving salvation.

As the time for my mission approached, I was afraid of what it might mean to live and work so closely with other young men. I was afraid I would feel the same distance and rejection from them that I had felt on our Church basketball team or Scout troop. Even though I had never acted on my attraction, I was afraid that experiencing same-gender attraction at all meant that I wasn't a good enough person to be a missionary. But again, I couldn't tell anyone about my fears because then they would know what a failure I was, and I would be in an even worse position than if I just toughed it out alone.

To my pleasant surprise, when I got my call and entered the Missionary Training Center, I thrived. Like many missionaries, I learned to seek and feel the Spirit with new intensity and my testimony grew considerably. Through many experiences, the presence of the Spirit confirmed to me repeatedly that the gospel was true and that

I was doing the right thing at the right time. When I returned home, I knew the next step was supposed to be marriage. While my attractions to other men were a conscious fact in my mind, I had by this time learned to compartmentalize that aspect of my life and concentrate instead on my other goals and aspirations.

I had always enjoyed the companionship of young women and had dated consistently throughout high school. Now that the stakes were higher, however, I was concerned that I would be unable to find a relationship in which my feelings for the young woman would be strong enough to overcome the implications of my same-gender attraction. Perhaps an even stronger fear was that I would never be able to inspire the love of a young woman in return. Most of my dating in the past had a fun and friendly but platonic cast to it, and I feared that this tendency would continue. I had experienced significant personal and spiritual growth as a missionary, but the mission had not, of course, resolved me of my attraction. Still, I thought that perhaps finding the right marriage partner would somehow erase any remaining concerns, and I would sail off into the sunset of temple-marriage bliss. My understanding of life was heavily influenced by the illusion that once I had served a mission and married in the temple, I would somehow navigate any challenges arising thereafter through some kind of magical spiritual autopilot.

I dated a number of great young women after my mission, and shortly before I graduated from Brigham Young University, I met my future wife. She had it all: spiritual depth, inner and outer beauty, intelligence, accomplishments, similar interests, ambition, and talent. Most of all, I felt a sympathy of spirit within her that allowed me to trust her implicitly and to feel safe and loved. Although I couldn't bring myself to tell her anything about my struggles with same-gender attraction, I felt that everything would work out somehow and I would be able to keep that issue separate and safely away from harming our relationship. After a time, we became engaged and were married in the temple. Shortly thereafter, I began graduate school, and we started our life together.

The first years of our marriage were joyful and rich. My wife was every bit the companion I had imagined her to be, and our love grew and developed, particularly as we started our family. As wonderful as our situation was in those early years, however, the long, silent struggle I had faced for so long alone was taking its toll. The combination of my perfectionism and my imperfect understanding of the Atonement contributed to a serious and growing depression. To ease the pain, I slowly distanced myself—psychologically, intellectually, and most important, emotionally—from God and the Church. While I never stopped Church activity, my testimony gradually became less vibrant, and my sense of spiritual well-being sank.

My cynical approach didn't cure my depression, but it provided some short-term relief for the tensions I had felt for so many years. I felt deeply responsible for my same-gender attraction while also feeling bitterness over the fact that I had never consciously chosen to have it. The fear of being so flawed permeated every aspect of my thinking and gave rise to a tremendous sense of guilt and shame within me, even though I had never acted on these feelings. Instead of really processing these difficult emotions authentically in order to let them go, however, I bottled them up. I found them too frightening and painful to explore and experience fully, which in turn caused them to grow exponentially over time, digging me deeper into the hole of depression.

Around age thirty I stumbled upon gay pornography on the Internet—a relatively new phenomenon at the time. In my weakened spiritual state and with so many unresolved emotional issues eating away at me internally, I soon found it to be a compelling and habit-forming medication for all of my painful feelings. As a result, a potent, downward-spiraling cycle began to form: my basic state of mind was wracked with fear, guilt, anger, and resentment, which led to powerful anxiety, which led me to seek some form of immediate numbing relief, which made me susceptible to the urge for pornography, which ultimately reinforced the fear, guilt, anger, and resentment that drove the whole sequence. As this cycle began to take on a life of its own, the feelings of same-gender attraction I had so carefully sealed away surfaced more consciously and confirmed to my mind that they were real and growing. In my mind, this proved that my life truly was a complete failure.

The summer I was thirty-one years old, I found myself unable to maintain my facade any longer. During that time, my wife awoke one night to find me sobbing in bed next to her, unable to explain my grief. After a time, her mounting alarm led her to urge me to get some counseling to address whatever issues were troubling me. Eventually, I realized that she was right, so I contacted a therapist.

When I met my counselor, I forced myself to explain my attraction issues in the first session. I asked him if he thought I should tell my wife, to which he replied that it was not a matter of "if" but "when." He pointed out that the word *intimate* comes from the Latin *intimus,* which means "innermost." He suggested that if I wanted to have a truly intimate relationship with my wife, I would need to allow her into the innermost places of my heart and trust that she would still love and respect me. He assured me that doing this would be a first step toward bringing my inner and outer life into harmony and would ultimately direct me to the path of healing. I immediately knew he was right, but I was terrified of having to tell my wife something so shocking, particularly because I had hidden it so carefully from everyone for my entire life.

A few nights later I told my wife that I needed to tell her something. After some stalling, somehow I managed to say it, and as I did, I fell into uncontrollable weeping, asking her if she would still love me. The whole experience had a surreal cast to it, something like a car accident in which everything moves in slow motion and your body goes into shock as life as you knew it is torn to pieces in an instant. Despite the difficulty of that moment, she responded with great love and reassurance and listened patiently as I poured out some of the grief I had held inside me for a lifetime.

I was amazed and relieved that my wife still loved me and that she genuinely seemed to accept this new fact about me. Over the ensuing weeks and months, we had many long conversations through which I shared my pent-up feelings and emotions. She tried to convey to me her understanding about the Atonement and the grace of Jesus Christ, which could give me the power to feel whole and loved. I felt that this version of the gospel was like a foreign language to me. At first, it seemed like gibberish that I could learn piecemeal, but at the deepest level, I didn't really understand how it worked. Practically speaking, I couldn't see how to "turn it over to the Lord." My ingrained perfectionism had ruled my life for so long that I couldn't understand how, if I did my part and let go of the burden of trying to save myself, I could trust God to do the rest. Besides, it seemed impossible to know where my part of the equation ended and where God's began.

With the encouragement of my therapist, I chose to tell a select group of individuals close to me about this issue. He urged me to be discerning and deliberate about whom I told, and that I should choose people I trusted who could be long-term confidants and supporters. Without exception, these individuals lovingly accepted what I had to share with them. They were quick to demonstrate that this knowledge changed nothing of their regard for me and that they were sorry I felt that I had to carry this burden alone for so long. With some trepidation, I went to my bishop to discuss my challenges; like the others, he responded with compassion and support. It was a great relief not to experience the rejection that for my entire life I had believed would come if anyone knew. This feeling of acceptance from my wife and from others was the beginning of overcoming much pain.

After a few months things seemed to be going better, and I stopped therapy. However, the relief I had felt at first gave way to the reality that there was still much work to do in repairing my psyche and learning new ways of viewing myself in relation to the Church and the gospel. I found that the depression I had hoped would be attenuated still remained after my initial efforts to share this burden with my wife and others. In addition, my difficulties with avoiding pornography continued despite many attempts to stop through willpower and self-discipline. The repeated failures sent me into deeper self-loathing.

Eventually, I knew I needed to return to therapy, and, after a few false starts, I found a counselor who worked well for me. This time I stayed in weekly sessions for several years to begin the long, slow process of rebuilding my emotional and spiritual life. I had always believed that the main point of therapy for me would be to understand the reasons behind my same-gender attraction and that maybe through that understanding it would go away. What I found instead was that deeper emotional issues were really driving my depression. I gradually came to understand that for years I had relied on patterns of perfectionist behavior as a form of medication for my fears of not being good enough.

A crucial change in perspective came when a friend introduced me to the concepts of mindfulness and meditation as tools for healing and serenity. The writings of Vietnamese Buddhist monk Thich Nhat Hanh in particular inspired me to reconsider how I viewed myself as well as how I viewed my religious foundations. Hanh urges people to go back to the religious tradition they know and, with insights gained through meditative mindfulness, to rediscover the spiritual jewels that were always there. As I did this, I learned how to quiet my mind enough to gain access to new realms of emotional and spiritual insight. As a result, I was able to slow down and look deeply into the destructive habits of mind that I had blindly persisted in for so many years—habits that had prevented me from understanding the true message of the gospel.

As I looked more carefully than I ever had before, calmly, and without my habitual self-rejection, I was able to see underlying patterns of thinking and motivation that had not served me well. Without judgment or anxiety, I simply began to let them go, layer by layer, like so much extra clothing on a warm day. Through this process I became aware of the fear that drove my suffering—in particular, the fear of being separate, small, inadequate. Ultimately, I understood that I was afraid that I am less than what I really am: a son of God with infinite potential, the object of His work and His glory. I finally realized that my divine nature as a child of God meant that I could let go of striving for others' approval to be enough. As this knowledge began to work in me, I found comfort in the Apostle Paul's teaching to the Roman Saints: "For ye have not received the spirit of bondage again to fear; but ye have received the Spirit of adoption, whereby we cry, Abba, Father.

The Spirit itself beareth witness with our spirit, that we are the children of God" (Romans 8:15–16).

Most important, my new approach allowed me to begin to see the root of our Christian faith clearly for the first time: the Atonement of Jesus Christ and the grace, hope, charity, and compassion that radiate from it. For the first time in my life, I really knew that if I was armed with a sure knowledge of God's incredible love for me as expressed through the life and sacrifice of Jesus Christ, I could then partner with Him to identify and turn lovingly toward my most profound fears in order to calm and diminish them. I saw not only that the gospel is true but also what the true gospel is: transformation in and through Christ and His Atonement.

As long-standing spiritual deficits became replenished and old fears faded away, I no longer felt the medicating need for pornography, and I was able to let it go. The presence of the Holy Ghost increased dramatically in my life as I began to change, which encouraged greater assurance and peace in my heart, which encouraged greater righteousness, which in turn increased the presence of the Spirit—an upward-spiraling cycle opposite to the negative cycle I had experienced before.

As these changes occurred, I eventually knew deep within me that same-gender attraction in and of itself did not matter. Even if the attraction remained to a degree, I recognized that I would not be defined in the end by what tempted me but rather by how well I embraced the power of the Atonement to cope with all my struggles and weaknesses. I understood that coming to the knowledge of our human weakness is necessary for all of us, regardless of our temptations or the nature of our mistakes. Though I had felt alone in my struggle for so many years, I realized that I am not alone in needing the Atonement but in fact share that need with all of God's children. Once I realized I was not "worse" than others for experiencing same-gender attraction, I felt my depression lift more quickly and permanently than ever before.

What my struggle with same-gender attraction has taught me is that we all must experience the great change the scriptures call being "born again." The Atonement, which transforms the separating power of the judgment of justice to the reuniting power of mercy, makes being born again possible. As I have felt the influence of the grace of the Atonement, I've found that my deepest inner desires are being transformed; my fear has started to give way to charity and compassion, and my sense of separation from God and from my fellow beings has progressed toward connectedness as I understand the deeper reality of my identity and potential as a son of God. This message is clearly given in Mosiah 27:25–26:

"And the Lord said unto me: Marvel not that all mankind, yea, men and women, all nations, kindreds, tongues and people, must be born again; yea, born of God, changed from their carnal and fallen state, to a state of righteousness, being redeemed of God, becoming his sons and daughters; and thus they become new creatures; and unless they do this, they can in nowise inherit the kingdom of God."

This great miracle I have experienced came when I finally understood what I was not capable of doing by myself. It came when I recognized and admitted: "There is no way out of this problem. I cannot possibly be enough or do enough to overcome it. Only a miracle can help me." God knew that this miracle would be necessary, and He provided it through the Atonement of his Son. My access to that miracle comes when I let go of my own will in favor of God's will. In doing so, I am simply letting go of fear sustained by numerous deceptions and misapprehensions of how things really are. Letting go of that fear has allowed me the peace that only comes from feeling the Savior's love through the presence of the Holy Ghost in my heart. With the help of the Spirit, I am able to reconcile my fragmented understanding and consequent behavior with an increasingly whole perception of spiritual truth and to change in ways that would be impossible on my own.

One of my first therapists years ago suggested that I would someday be grateful for my experience with same-gender attraction. That idea seemed impossible—even insulting—to me at the time. I could not imagine then how such painful experiences could possibly ever feel useful. But I now understand that all of my difficult life experiences are a blessing if I allow them to help me know my need for the Savior and to encourage me to come unto Him. The lessons I have learned from this struggle have brought me invaluable insights into compassion, patience, mercy, and forgiveness—attributes that I am now better able to incorporate into my relationships with others.

The reassurance and support of concerned loved ones, most particularly my remarkable wife, have shown me the living embodiment of the Savior's injunction to love in beautiful and tender ways. Same-gender attraction has brought me to a path that has led me to turn more fully to our Savior with a broken heart, which is our ultimate reason for entering mortality. For this, I am grateful.

Being My True Self

Tyler Moore

Tyler Moore calls the Rocky Mountains home. He feels it a blessing to have been raised by strong parents who taught by example the importance of being open, honest, and willing. Tyler met his wife while earning his associate's degree. Additionally, he holds a bachelor's degree from Brigham Young University and has also completed graduate school. Tyler is blessed by the joy and strength his wife and children bring to his life.

"We are wont to condemn self-love; but what we really mean to condemn is contrary to self-love. It is that mixture of selfishness and self-hate that permanently pursues us, that prevents us from loving others, and that prohibits us from losing ourselves."

—PAUL VALÉRY[6]

"It's not about the sex," I said. I was sitting on the sofa in our living room. My wife and Matt (name changed), my one Latter-day Saint friend who knew what was going on in our home, could not seem to understand this concept.

"Come on, it really is just about the sex," said Matt as my wife nodded in full agreement with him. At this point we had been discussing the matter for quite some time, and my patience was short.

"Last I checked, neither of you have dealt with this issue, so unless you have been hiding your own same-sex attraction," I said, "I really do not think you are in a position to lecture me on what this is *really* about!"

At this point I was through. I was through before this conversation, in fact, and had already made my decision: I wanted a divorce. I was going to leave my wife and help raise my children on weekday visitations, weekends, and every other holiday weekend. It is what I *had* to do—to be "real" and "true to myself."

My wife and I were sealed in the temple during the summer of 2003. It was a beautiful day and a wonderful ceremony, and I was confident that taking this step would cure my homosexuality entirely. Not that I had considered myself gay prior to marriage—in fact, I had considered myself anything but. I had made some poor choices in high school, choices that precluded me from serving a mission, but I had gone through the five Rs of repentance, received some counseling, and was good to go with my life. The next life step then was to get married. Marriage would be the final nail in the coffin to put this whole issue to rest.

I was dead wrong.

I was faithful to my wife for the first year of our marriage as far as not acting out with another man. But it was in our first year of marriage that pornography and its constant companion, masturbation, became an issue again. Sure enough, my indulgence in pornography and masturbation soon became insufficient to satisfy me, and I started chatting online. Soon chatting became insufficient, and I started meeting people offline in person. It was almost immediately after that that

I began to sexually act out with other men in complete violation of my covenants with both God and my wife.

In the beginning I acted out sexually about once every six to nine months. After each time I acted out sexually with another man, the pendulum would swing back to the side of righteousness, and I would purge my computer of all pornography, throw out anything that might trigger me, read my scriptures more intensely than ever before, pray harder, and vow "never again," which is what I swore the time before and the time before that and so on. And it would work—for a month, maybe two. Then pornography and company would creep back in. Then I would start tearing myself down with negative thinking: since I couldn't get over my addiction to pornography and masturbation, why not act out even further if I was going to hell anyway? Why should I fight so hard when I am inevitably going to fail? After being in that frame of mind long enough, I would eventually act out again. Each time this cycle repeated itself, it would gain momentum.

Our marriage after the first year wasn't what we had imagined or wanted, which was not surprising given the pressure I was placing on myself and the double life I was living. I was attending Brigham Young University, so we went to the university counseling center, hoping for change. A funny thing about counseling is that it can only really be effective if the participant is honest. I was honest enough to admit I was sexually attracted to men, but I was not honest enough to admit I had already acted out. The counseling intern we saw was pleasant and helped enable me to talk to my wife about what I was facing, but his approach did not allow me the space I needed to make real progress. Each session he would ask me on a scale of 1 to 100 how gay I felt. With my wife present, how could I do anything but drop the number every week?

After we had gone to counseling a few months, the intern asked if we had considered starting a family. We had thought about it, so he recommended going forward with it. And so we did. My wife was pregnant within two months, and once we told him that we had a baby on the way, he seemed to figuratively stamp my file "cured" and sent us on our way. I remember leaving the clinic thinking, *I really do not think that this has been resolved, but they would know better than me.* So I dismissed my hesitations and moved on.

Nine months later my wife and I became the proud parents of a beautiful little girl. I immediately saw the wisdom of the BYU clinician—I was cured! It had worked! Marriage was not the answer, but becoming a father was! I didn't feel the least bit of temptation to act out, and I had no desire for pornography or masturbation. I could think clearly, and it was wonderful! This state lasted for about six months, and then slowly but surely the stresses of life began to wax, and the novelty of fatherhood began to wane. Once again the old pattern resumed—pornography, masturbation, chat rooms, acting out sexually with other men.

Somewhere in all of that I graduated from BYU and we moved out of state so I could attend graduate school. At first this novelty boosted my resolution more than ever to change my ways. This was a new state and a new me; I was going to address this issue once and for all. That lasted about two months. Long hours at the library, the stress of getting through readings, preparing for classes, and studying for exams was added to my already full plate of living two lives, one of which required a picture-perfect husband and father who did his Church calling faithfully, while the other required a large piece of time devoted to finding my next fix of male connection.

I was soon acting out more and more frequently. If I had spent as much time studying as I had looking at pornography and cruising, I would likely have been a 4.0 student! I had received a scholarship for my first year of studies, but because of my addictions, I lost it after that first year. More important, my addictions nearly cost me things infinitely more valuable—my relationship with my wife, my ability to effectively father my children, and, ultimately, my salvation.

During the first month of the second year of my program, my wife lived with her parents because she was in the last month of her second pregnancy and needed more help than I could provide at the time as a student. I returned for the birth of our son, remained through the hospital stay, and then flew back to where we were living. While we were separated, I ached to have my family with me. Yet at the same time, I traveled ever further down that dark path I was choosing. I started staying overnight with some of the men I was connecting with. It was then that I started to realize it really wasn't about the sex. The real satisfaction came just from being with a man—essentially in being wanted and accepted as a man by another man.

Over the next two months the inner conflict grew such that for the first time I seriously contemplated ending my life. Two main fears, however, kept me from it. First, who would take care of my wife and kids? And the second, what if I failed? If that happened, I could end up in a vegetative state. In the midst of contemplating the potential ramifications of suicide, my mom called with the timing and intuition that only a parent could have. Although I resolved not to say anything to her when I answered the phone, it was barely twenty minutes later that I started sobbing as we spoke. I didn't tell her about all my acting out, but I did share all the feelings I'd been struggling with for so long.

As I started opening up and being fully honest with others and myself, I went slowly at first. I told my mom it was okay for her to tell my sister if she needed an outlet. Then, sometime later, I told my dad, who took it so well that I wondered if he even understood what I was saying. I sought out and reconnected with an undergrad friend who had left the Church and was living his life as an openly gay man. He had much concern and empathy for me, and he consistently provided me with affection and with messages that told me I was doing the right thing in leaving the Church and my family. To this day I vividly recall him telling me that I had to be true to myself.

After all that, I told my wife that I needed to start seeing a counselor again and then told her why, mentioning only my continued struggle with same-sex attraction. Naturally, she was hurt. It wasn't until a few weeks later, after having just come home from confessing everything to our bishop, that I finally told her about the extent of my past behavior. She was devastated.

Over the next few months, my wife and I went back and forth as to what we should do. This is when I told her and Matt that it was not about the sex. Finally, she and our children went to live with her parents in our home state. It was intended to be a temporary separation, but in my mind it was a step toward ending our marriage. I flew back to Utah sometime later for a family event—and to tell my wife that I wanted a divorce. But I was never able to get the words out. I returned to school alone, depressed, and in the gall of bitterness. I was racked with the pains of a damned soul.

At the end of that week, out of desperation, I signed up for an online discussion group sponsored by North Star, an organization that supports LDS men and women who experience same-sex attraction and desire to live faithful to Church values and standards. I posted to the group and stated in full honesty where I was in life. At that point I had nothing to lose. Within an hour I began receiving responses of love and concern, encouragement and support. I immediately began to feel a sense of community and connection that, until that point, I had only felt in seedy chat rooms and other unhealthy locales. After some additional personal and sacred experiences, I began to feel a shift in my perception. The next night I broke up with a guy I'd been seeing for the previous couple of months, which was incredibly painful to do. The following morning I called my wife and told her I wanted to save our marriage and to keep our family together. I was also rigorously honest with her about what I had been doing while she was away, and that was even more painful. Somehow she found the strength to leave her parents and return to our apartment, and we began reassembling the shards of our shattered relationship.

I needed to repent of many transgressions. I had started a dialogue with my bishop and stake president months earlier, but no formal disciplinary action occurred until after my wife returned to our home. Within two weeks after her arrival, I faced the stake high council and was disfellowshipped from the Church. The experience strengthened my testimony because I went in with shame and anguish but left knowing of my Eternal Father's love for me. The love I felt from the men in that room was the pure love of Christ, and it buoyed my heart. After they made their decision, each of them pulled me into a warm embrace, the majority of them with tears in their eyes. While of course I felt a great deal of remorse for my actions, I no longer felt the shame I had previously felt.

A year later, I faced the high council again and was welcomed with open arms again into full fellowship. How fortunate I was to have such a wonderful group of men who not only loved the Lord but also loved me as I believe the Lord would have had He been physically present. The timing of all this was surely divinely orchestrated. Before my change of heart, I only wanted to see the high council so I could be excommunicated and move on with my life as an openly gay man. In my mind, being excommunicated would justify my leaving the Church—it would have felt like the proof I wanted that I had no place in the Church. I am so grateful for a stake president who listened to the Spirit and kept delaying the council, giving the Lord time to soften my heart and prepare me for repentance.

Through that year of disfellowshipment, and with the support of my loving bishop and stake president, I began to rebuild my testimony and my relationship with the Savior. I also had the help of an incredible counselor at LDS Family Services, whom I had started seeing shortly after opening up to my mother. He did what all good guides do: he gave me information for each of the paths I saw before me and pointed out paths I did not realize were there; then he gave me plenty of time and space to make my own decisions.

Ultimately, it has been through the Spirit and the Atonement of Jesus Christ that I have begun to experience real peace. It has been my Savior who has brought healing and restored my hope. Through it all I have been extremely blessed to have an incredible support system as well. My amazing wife, my parents, my sister, my in-laws, and some truly remarkable friends who are like brothers have all been in my corner. They have loved me despite my weaknesses.

One of the most fundamental things I have learned through all of this is the essential character of needs. Needs are called needs rather than wants for a reason. When we have a valid need, it cannot be suppressed, ignored, or denied indefinitely. Each time I acted out or engaged in homosexual behavior, I was trying to meet a need. For me, that need is acceptance, support, and love from men. It's something I never had, or at least felt that I never had, and I didn't know how to meet this valid need—which all men have—in healthy, authentic ways. Therefore, I sexualized it and sought that connection in shallow ways that pacified but never satiated.

Today I actively seek and strengthen healthy connections I've made with brothers, some who experience same-sex attraction and some who don't, and I do it in a transparent way to ensure that these healthy relationships don't become dangerous opportunities to regress.

One of the difficulties I experienced for so many years in the LDS community was a feeling of extreme isolation and loneliness. I had no relationships in which I felt I could honestly and openly speak about my attractions without facing judgment. I felt so inherently evil that I thought my fellow Saints, had they really known my feelings, would have rejected me outright. So, desperate for love and acceptance and a sense of belonging, I felt that the only people who would understand me when I finally started talking about my feelings were those in the very community I had previously always tried to avoid! Those in the gay and lesbian communities were the only ones I felt I could turn to. And those I encountered were extremely welcoming, offering me a great deal of kindness, support, and affirmation. I know that they meant well and have good hearts. Fortunately, as I started to have a change of heart, I was blessed to have a community of family members and other Latter-day Saints who offered me far more love and connection than anything I had experienced in the gay and lesbian community. Not all are so fortunate. Indeed, the community that ultimately shows the most love will be the one that wins the hearts of the men and women dealing with this issue.

During the years I was acting out, particularly during the time I saw divorce as the only viable option, I could see only one source of connection with other men. I believed the only way to meet my legitimate need for male connection and same-gender emotional intimacy was to have a romantic or sexual relationship with another man. Anything that kept me from meeting that need was a threat. I look back now and can clearly see that my goal was not sex for the sake of sex. Instead, it was sex for the sake of some sort of connection. As my stress rose, so did my need for support and connection with other men. It simply wasn't about the sex. I've since learned how to get that healthy connection from multiple places: friends, coworkers, and even the elders quorum. The community I yearned for was right in front of me, but I couldn't discover it until I dared to be authentic.

As scary as increased honesty and openness have been, it has felt great not to have to carry the load by myself. So great, in fact, that I actually started to have some feelings of really liking myself, something previously totally foreign to me. Initially, I associated those feelings of self-acceptance with finally accepting that I was gay, but I've realized over time this was naïve. I now know that the reason I started liking myself is because I was being honest and appropriately authentic, and I felt support and love from others in that authenticity.

At the beginning of this journey, I thought I would have to tell everyone I was gay in order to be authentic. I was wrong on two counts. First of all, I simply don't choose that label for myself; the common understanding of that word doesn't define me or resonate with how I desire to live my life. Am I attracted to other guys? You bet! But I'm not acting out sexually on those desires, and I fully support the Lord's prophets and apostles in their teaching regarding the sanctity of heterosexual marriage and the sexual intimacy that must be reserved exclusively for that union. Second, I do not have to discuss my attractions with everyone I get emotionally close to. It's part of who I am but certainly not the essence of who I am.

I've learned that what so many in what is commonly referred to as the lesbian, gay, bisexual, and transgender (LGBT) community told me is absolutely correct. I do need to be "true to myself." My true self, my first and foremost identity, is a *brave son of God*. From this identity I gain the ability to be a husband, a father, a son, a brother, a friend, and a student—*all* secondary to my primary identity. Because I am a son of God, I can lay my weaknesses and sins at the feet of my Lord and Savior, Jesus Christ. As I have allowed Him to take my heart of stone and replace it with a heart of flesh, He has made true peace possible.

Being able to see my true self is a testament to the power of prayer. I know it has been through the fasting and prayers of many that I am where I am today. For so many years I prayed to have this challenge taken from me, but my prayers have changed to asking that I have the faith and strength to learn what I need to learn from the path I am on and to have the courage to press forward with faith that all will be well. I pray that I may be able to keep my perspective in seeing my true value as a son of God. He continues to respond to those petitions with the answers I need, line upon line.

Prayer alone, however, was not enough to bring about and maintain a change in my perspective. The change in my perspective has also come through meeting my needs for connection and intimacy with other men in healthy ways. One of the most important parts of fulfilling my needs has been to know that I belong among men. I do not consider myself effeminate, but for most of my life I didn't feel masculine either. In fact, I had drawn a circle around what it was to be masculine to protect myself from it. In my old definition, masculinity entailed all the stereotypes I saw as so pervasive in our larger culture. It was irresponsible and selfish. It was sports, hunting, and cards, none of which interested me. Masculinity was not creative; it was static. By drawing the perimeter there, I locked myself out of what I defined to be masculine.

Today I have healthy ways to meet my need for love and acceptance from other men, and this has allowed me to genuinely feel that I belong. And feeling that I belong has led to a substantial decrease in my feelings of same-sex attraction. The answers haven't been easy to find, but through trying many different approaches, I know what works for me. One thing I felt I needed to do was broaden my ideological circle of what it is to be a man: as a husband and a father, I am a man; as a priesthood holder and a brother, I am a man. I know I am a man because I am a son of God. These are the real pillars of my true self.

Another thing I needed to do was explore some of the things I had associated with my old definition of masculinity. There were things I always wanted to do that I had allowed my fears to prevent me from attempting. From my new perspective of confidence, I wanted to push through those fears and insecurities. For instance, sports—football in particular—have always been quite daunting to me. I know that playing sports doesn't make people straight, but I wanted to confront my fear and see what it was all about. So I signed up to play with a team during my university's intramural season, and much to my surprise, I didn't die! I'm sure I looked goofy out there because I had only a vague idea of what I was doing, but the world did not end as a result of my fumbles. The majority of the guys I was playing with were glad to offer constructive pointers and help me improve. I walked away slightly embarrassed but thrilled that I had faced my fear. I didn't let fear stop me from trying something and being my true self, even if that person is less than talented in football.

Through all of these experiences, I have uncovered the foundation of the identity of my true self. My path to this point has been varied, to say the least. At first I had no idea who I was. I went through the motions of who I thought I was supposed to be, which was what I thought was expected of me. I believed I had to be a perfect Mormon in order to be happy. That line of thinking led to unhappiness. Then I started being honest about my biggest secrets. With that openness came a level of self-acceptance, which I originally viewed as evidence that my happiness was to be found in a homosexual relationship. Many voices at that time were telling me that I had to be "true to myself," which to them meant leaving the Church, my wife, and my family.

Thankfully, the Spirit changed my perception in a way that allowed me to see my true self. For me, *this* is the change that is *always* possible. It is real, and it has changed so much about me. It was change from the inside out, not the reverse. It was more than just finding healthy male relationships or simply learning sports. It was something deeper

I needed, deeper even than sex or sexual identity: it was finally finding a way to accept myself as worthwhile and to know I was worth loving.

It's not about the sex; it's about the needs. I can return to old habits to get my needs met in a fleeting way, or I can choose to meet them in healthy, lasting, and far richer ways. Ways that are within the bounds the Lord has set. Ways that allow me to have a fulfilling relationship with my dear wife. Ways that strengthen my resolve to be a good father for my children. As my true self, a brave son of God, I choose the latter.

"This Will Be for Your Growth": A Wife's Journey to Self-Discovery and Healing

Rhonda Moses

Rhonda Moses was born and raised in Spokane, Washington, where she still resides today. She served a mission for the Church in 1992 and 1993 in the Texas Houston East Mission. She is a full-time mom, part-time massage practitioner, facilitator of personal growth at women's and couples' retreats, and a full-time student pursuing a degree in counseling. Rhonda and Barry are the parents of three beautiful children.

In 1990, at the age of nineteen, I went away to Brigham Young University, and my life changed forever. My parents divorced after twenty-eight years of marriage, and the missionary I had waited to marry came home and fell in love with someone else. I sank into a deep depression and began to question all the teachings of my youth. I had no idea what to do.

One evening, through my sobs, I poured out my heart in prayer, asking if eternal marriage and true love really exist. In that moment I had one of the most powerful spiritual experiences of my life. In my mind's eye, I saw myself in the temple kneeling across the holy altar from a beautiful man with dark hair, dark eyes, and an amazing smile. I had never seen this man before, but in that moment I knew he would become my husband. The Spirit was unmistakable: I would have my eternal marriage. Shortly after this experience, the Spirit also instructed me to prepare for a mission.

I came home that summer with renewed faith, and I began studying the Book of Mormon, seeking gospel knowledge, and preparing to teach others. During that same time my friends told me about a young man who was also preparing for a mission. They said we would make a perfect match. I really had no interest in meeting anyone new at that time, but they insisted and arranged for us to meet.

When we met, he looked so familiar, but we each made a bad first impression. A few weeks later, however, we had the chance to meet again, and within minutes we were talking and laughing as if we had known each other for years. In that moment I knew he was the one the Spirit had shown me. I went home and wrote in my journal that I had met the man I was going to marry.

After our second meeting, Barry and I saw each other every day. We had a wonderful relationship, and yet he seemed so different from anyone I had dated before. I was falling more and more in love with him, and I knew he was growing closer to me, but I felt that something was missing. He never tried to kiss me, and I was frustrated and couldn't understand why he didn't like me the way other guys did. Yet he cared for me and was becoming my best friend. Sometimes I thought he was just so focused on preparing for a mission that he wanted nothing to stand in the way of his goal, but on a deeper level I knew there was something more.

One evening, we attended a Church dance and decided to go for a walk. It was then that he told me he did not feel attraction for women but for men instead. Suddenly, it all made sense, and now I understood why something felt different. I must have seen the world through rose-colored glasses, for I simply trusted that he would still become my eternal companion and everything would turn out right.

We continued to prepare for our missions. We attended every possible fireside and Church education event. Barry was one of the most spiritual young men I had ever dated or even known. We read scriptures together and listened to uplifting music. Barry's great commitment and dedication to the gospel inspired me. We grew closer as a couple and closer to the Lord. It was a wonderful year!

In the summer of 1991, Barry received his mission call to Guatemala. He was the only member of the Church in his family, so my mom and I took him to the Missionary Training Center. I cried as I left through one door and he left through the other, and yet I felt so excited for him because I knew he was giving his time to the Lord. Shortly thereafter, I received my call to serve in the Texas Houston East Mission.

We wrote the entire time, sharing our experiences and testimonies with one another. During the first months of his mission, he shared a dream confirming that we were supposed to marry. Our love for one another grew stronger and stronger that first year; we were filled with the love of our Father in Heaven, and we loved the people we served. But during the second year, sadness entered his letters. Some missionaries reach their year mark and feel happy to have only one year left, but Barry felt the opposite. He couldn't believe it was already half over. He loved his mission and never wanted it to end. He felt a sense of belonging and truly loved the people he served. His feelings of same gender-attraction had decreased greatly, and he felt the Spirit more than ever. He never wanted to lose the Spirit. When it came time for him to return home, he sobbed and sobbed. Leaving his mission felt like a kind of death to him.

We both came home the summer of 1993 and felt awkward for the first few days. We had to get reacquainted, but it didn't take long before we were once again inseparable. Barry proposed on Christmas Day, and I accepted gladly. We set a date for a spring wedding, but a couple of weeks after his proposal, Barry's father died of a sudden heart attack. This took a lot out of my sweetheart. Barry loved his father greatly, but there had been a great deal of pain in their relationship due to his father's past alcohol abuse, and now there could never be the close relationship Barry longed for with his dad. We moved the wedding date to summer.

On June 16, 1994, we were married for time and all eternity in the Portland Oregon Temple. It felt as though hundreds of celestial beings filled the room to celebrate our commitment to one another on that beautiful day. I had never experienced anything quite like it either before or since. Many in attendance at our sealing felt the spiritual presence as well. It was a perfect day.

At first, things were wonderful. We were typical, happy newlyweds, and to our great surprise and happiness, Barry found that he enjoyed being with me sexually. He thought he had been cured of his feelings of same-gender attraction. We were very happy.

Unfortunately, our happiness did not last. I got pregnant within a couple of months and with that, issues from my own childhood came back to haunt me. Every time Barry touched me, I felt dirty and unworthy. I withdrew from him and left him feeling frustrated and confused. Our first child was born. He was a beautiful baby boy, but for the first five months of his life, our precious new baby screamed and screamed. We took him to doctors and gave him medicine, but nothing helped. The constant pressure of a screaming baby and unresolved issues drove a wedge through our marriage. We struggled to be gentle and patient with each other and the baby, but we both felt nowhere near adequate for such a responsibility.

During that stressful time, Barry became distant, depressed, and angry. He withdrew and isolated himself for hours on the computer. Life continued and the stress only got worse. Within a relatively short time, we bought our first home, got pregnant with our second child, and took in three foster children. We did have good days and we did try to follow the Spirit, but more and more Barry felt trapped in the marriage and in our crazy life of bills, children, and insanity. Suddenly, I realized that my best friend had become the source of my greatest pain. I was lonely, hurt, and angry. I blamed him for all of our struggles. I thought life would be happy again if only he would change or make better choices or be a better person. The list went on and on, and the more I blamed, the more he distanced himself. It was a vicious cycle.

Over time, all his hurt and pain turned to anger. He was angry at me, angry at God, angry at the Church, and angry at life. He felt deceived by priesthood leaders who said his feelings of same-gender attraction would go away after marriage. He felt lonely. He felt that if God truly loved him, He would ease his pain.

Sunday became the darkest day of the week in our home. Every time we came home from meetings, we fought about the Church. He still attended and even held callings, but in his heart he did not want to go anymore. One summer day in 2001, I was sitting in Relief Society meeting when the Spirit whispered to me that Barry would not come back to church for some time. As I walked down the hall after class, I could see in his eyes the confirmation of what I had felt a few moments before. We went home, and he proceeded to tell me he was not going back. I told him I already knew. We decided that we should tell the children, but before doing so, Barry went for a walk, and I fell to my knees with a pain in my heart that felt as if I were going to die. I cried and cried, begging God to stop this from happening. I felt sick with disbelief.

Then once again the Spirit spoke to me, but instead of giving me comfort, the Spirit said, "This will be for your growth." I couldn't believe it. How could this be for my growth? How could anything good come from something I perceived to be so terrible?

The following months were very difficult for me. I stopped reading my scriptures and even praying. I still attended church for the sake of my children, but my heart was broken and I was numb. I had no joy and no hope, and I was angry at God for bringing us together and for expecting me to learn something from this hell. I believed I was a victim. I felt that I had been the righteous one, and I felt betrayed by my husband and by our Father in Heaven.

During this dark time, I awoke one morning reminded of an experience. Years before, I had attended a workshop during which the participants faced an imaginary scenario where only a small number of the group would survive. The participants had to choose who would live and who would die. The group chose me as one of the survivors. As I reflected on this event, the Spirit told me, "They chose that you live, and you have chosen death." It was the biggest wake-up call I had ever had. I turned my heart toward God again. I had no money for counseling, so within a couple of weeks, I started a support group for women that met twice a month in my home. I was the only woman in my situation, but the group was open to all women who just needed a safe place to share their feelings without judgment and to set personal goals. Each time we met, we shared our successes and failures with our goals, and we accepted accountability. It started as a small group of three women, but it grew over time.

I also took baby steps of faith by listening to modern-day prophets and apostles and taking to heart lessons on forgiveness and love. I received multiple priesthood blessings reminding me of the great love our Heavenly Father has for my husband and me.

I was moving forward in my life, but another blow came the summer of 2002 when Barry decided to have his name removed from Church records. The day he planned to submit his letter, I avoided him by taking the kids to the park. Once again my heart was filled with fear, pain, anger, and judgment. I called him from the park, and he asked me to go with him to take his letter to our bishop. I took the kids to my brother's house and met Barry at the stake center.

The bishop met us at the door, smiling and whistling a happy tune. I couldn't believe it! He knew the reason for our visit. How could he smile? How could he possibly be happy on such a day? He accepted Barry's letter graciously. Barry just sat in his office and cried and then asked for a blessing. The bishop gave him a beautiful blessing. He also gave me a blessing, reminding me once again to love my husband as our Father in Heaven loved him. The bishop told us time and time again that this was a good day and a new beginning. I had known our bishop almost all my life, and I knew he was a good man of God, but I couldn't believe what he was saying. Once again I turned to anger and feelings of victimhood. How could our Father in Heaven promise my husband so many great things when he was turning his back on Him?

But a funny thing happened after Barry had his name taken off the Church records; we actually stopped fighting on Sunday and experienced more peace in our home. The Church became my faith and only mine. Barry felt no more connection to the Church and accepted that I took the kids. Our marriage was in a strange place. We were becoming friends again, but we didn't know if we would stay together. We still blamed each other for much of our misery and felt unsure about the future. Barry said he was not sure he could ever be truly happy being married to a woman.

We decided to see a marriage counselor. One night while attending a counseling session, we said some cruel things, and it was like a dam of emotion broke. I lost it and started screaming at Barry to just leave. I screamed and sobbed and screamed some more while the counselor sat speechless and stunned. He let me scream, and when I was finally done, we left. I was so shaken. I could not drive. I could not think. I was numb.

After some time I drove to the temple. It was beautiful, all lit up. I sat in the car and poured out my heart in prayer to God. I begged Him to rip the bandage from our marriage. Something needed to change in a big way, and it needed to change now. I believe I had finally reached a point where I allowed God to clean my life on a deep level. The events that followed my plea were frightening and painful, but God had His hand in all things.

Over the next few weeks our world began to unravel at a terrible pace. Barry became very emotional and unpredictable. He fell into uncontrollable crying spells, mixed with unexpected fits of rage and talk of suicide. It seemed as if he had become disconnected from all reality.

Finally he crashed and was admitted to a hospital. After his release from the hospital, we separated. Barry's personality changed dramatically as he tried to find his place in the world. Before these events, Barry had worked for many years to stay sober, but for about three months after our separation, he went on a series of drinking binges. He also had relationships with several men.

My brother Steve told me to leave Barry and that he would take care of my family. Despite all the pain and hopelessness I felt up to this point, I said, "God promised me that we would make it."

Steve said, "Yes, but Barry has his free agency."

"But God promised *me*," I insisted. "I don't know how it all works, but God promised it would all work out. He knows Barry, and nothing Barry does can surprise God." By the end of this conversation, I was shaking, but I felt more hopeful than ever. I knew we would not divorce.

Even though we were still separated, we connected every day. We prayed like never before, both individually and as a couple. We felt broken and heavy but closer than ever. Sometimes we fought, but we talked about everything. All our walls had fallen down. We were the most real we had ever been. We came to realize that we choose our own misery; no one else is responsible.

During this time my brother Mike went to visit Barry. He said, "My greatest wish is for you to choose what really brings you the most joy. If marriage to my sister brings you the greatest joy, then go back to her and your family. But if a man brings you the greatest joy, then choose, but don't stand in the middle." His words surprised Barry. He expected judgment, but there was only love. Barry says this was a turning point for him.

Another turning point came when a friend told me about Evergreen International, an organization for members of the Church who experience feelings of same-gender attraction and for their loved ones. For the first time in our marriage, we fasted and prayed together as a couple to decide if we should attend Evergreen's annual conference less than two weeks away. We both received a confirmation and attended. The conference was good, but most important for us, we made new friends and discovered that we were not alone. We had walked through hell, but we were now on a path of healing.

After seven months away, Barry came home. He did not come home because he felt an obligation or because someone had told him it was the right thing to do. He came home because he chose to. He chose our family. He chose our marriage. One of our greatest gifts from our Father in Heaven is the right to choose for ourselves. I've learned there is power in choice.

It hasn't always been easy since that terrible summer many years ago, but we have learned so much along the way. I know God lives and loves us. He is aware of each one of us.

Barry and I are stronger than ever. He is still not a member of the Church, but we pray together, and he supports our children and me in our faith. He attends every baptism and talk in Primary. We pray as a family every night and work on being kind to each other and to ourselves. We want to be more like our Savior and allow the Spirit to dwell in our home.

Barry has found a great source of spiritual support through his Native American traditions. He had spent so many years in pain, thinking that God did not love him, that no matter what he did he could not be worthy of this great love. He has now come to know that God loves him. For this knowledge I am so thankful.

I have also become a stronger person. My women's group evolved into an annual personal-growth women's retreat, where I have the opportunity to serve and love women of different faiths, cultures, personal histories, and ages. My experiences have made me more compassionate, less judgmental, and more hopeful about who they are and the lives they live.

I am also pursuing my degree in marriage and family counseling, which I have wanted to do for a long time but now feel so much more prepared for because of my own journey through pain, personal growth, and joy.

I would never want to feel the pain again from all that we have gone through, but I would not take any of it back. Everything serves a greater purpose. I can teach my children and others about our Father in Heaven and the great compassion He has for His children. I have tasted His love. As all who walk through the refiner's fire, I have been blessed and I am grateful.

A Sacred Gift

Blake Smith

Blake Smith was born into the Church, served a mission, graduated from Brigham Young University, and earned an MBA. He works in the health care industry doing contracts and finance. He has served in many Church callings and is currently the elders quorum president in his ward. He is married to his soulmate. Loving an active lifestyle, he has hiked the highest peaks in seven states and white-water-rafted class four rapids. He also loves kickboxing and spending time with friends and family.

I take heart in the prophetic promise that our weaknesses are gifts from God: "And if men come unto me I will show unto them their weakness. I give unto men weakness that they may be humble; and my grace is sufficient for all men that humble themselves before me; for if they humble themselves before me, and have faith in me, then will I make weak things become strong unto them" (Ether 12:27).

When I was thirteen years old, I remember a specific moment of being overwhelmed with budding thoughts and feelings that I did not choose or want. They seemed so wrong. I wanted to be a husband and father, to marry in the temple, and to be an honorable and faithful priesthood holder. At that moment I vowed I would never act inappropriately on those very powerful attractions I had toward other boys. As a thirteen-year-old, I would never have referred to the difficulties I experienced as a gift. Growth in the gospel of Jesus Christ and increased maturity, however, have helped me to see that this has been one of the most important gifts that I was given by a loving Heavenly Father.

For much of my life, my attraction felt comparable to the hunger experienced at about hour twenty-three of a twenty-four-hour fast, but the hunger was present twenty-four hours a day, seven days a week. I struggled all day containing my thoughts just to dream about my attraction at night. But I knew I could never give in because of my belief that in doing so, I might jeopardize eternal life with God.

What I did to try to resist temptation was no way to live. I lived much of my youth and young adulthood in social isolation. I had few friends, and the loneliness I felt was often staggering, perhaps even compounding the feelings I had. Also, I was always afraid of being found out. It didn't help that I was a skinny, scrawny kid with a high voice and zits, which made me a target for bullying. The beatings and teasing I endured were often unbearable. I would stay home from school for days at a time because of the way I was treated. On one occasion, I was beaten up by three guys throwing out homophobic slurs. When the assistant principal was told about it, he was heard to say, "He's just a queer anyway." I have almost no happy memories of my youth.

Pleasing people became a pattern that I developed in my efforts to fit in and have friends—and, frankly, to not get beaten up. I would do just about anything to get people to like me. It took many years and considerable intervention from the Holy Spirit to break what became a pretty destructive pattern.

During most of my youth and young adulthood, my attractions to men seemed to be a constant companion. I sought help from therapists and Church leaders and followed all of the counsel I was given, but nothing I did resulted in any long-term relief. Many times, including even some pretty serious depressive periods when I considered suicide, I felt so weary that I couldn't go on.

When I turned twenty I served a full-time mission, all the while hoping that, because of my faithful service, the Lord would take away my attractions to other men. I bartered continually with the Lord, believing that if I gave above and beyond what was asked, it was His job to "cure" me of my feelings. I felt that I beat the Lord over the head with my works, demanding that He bless me with my desired cure. I have since learned that bartering with the Lord and demanding that He give me what I want, no matter how seemingly righteous the desire, is the opposite of the humble surrender I now believe He desires of us. I worked hard as a missionary and experienced considerable success, but my struggle with same-gender attraction did not go away.

After my mission I started seeing a therapist who helped me so much that I genuinely thought my attraction to men was a thing of the past. For a time, there was an almost complete elimination of same-gender desires. During that time I married in the temple and began a family. For the first few years of marriage, there were only one or two days when I experienced fleeting attractions that felt mostly like remembrances of something past.

The biggest mistake I made in my life was not to tell my wife about the struggle. My thought at the time was that I was cured, so there didn't seem to be much to tell. It wasn't long before my life seemed to fall apart. For months, nothing seemed to go right. It was the darkest period of my life. During that time I read the entire standard works in less than six months and attended the temple weekly. I was almost obsessively faithful in my Church callings and prayed fervently for resolution to my difficulties and my reemerging feelings of same-gender attraction that, after a few years of reprieve, returned in an increasingly powerful way. Once again I started bartering with the Lord, demanding that He give me what I wanted because of everything that I, in my mind, was doing for Him.

One very lonely night, I seriously contemplated suicide. I got through the crisis but moved into a mode where my goal was to feel nothing. Feeling nothing was better than feeling pain and a constant hunger to feel loved by another man. The three years that followed were characterized by feelings of numbness. I ceased opening the scriptures, praying, or attending the temple. My Church attendance was spotty, and my fear of being found out kept me isolated and alone. No one benefited from my irregular church attendance, especially me. I began frequenting local gay hangouts, looking for someone to love. Thankfully nothing ever happened.

During that time, my job was going well. I was definitely an up-and-coming person in the organization. My supervisor told me that he was going to give me a promotion that meant more money, but it also meant I would have to travel. I saw this as an opportunity to live a double life. I could live one way at home, but when I was on the road I could finally satisfy my renewed constant craving for same-sex connection.

One afternoon as I was leaving work, my boss asked me to stay late so he could take me around and show me what I would be doing when I got the promotion. It was mine for sure. I looked forward to my future opportunities to live a double life and to act on the powerful cravings that had plagued me for so long.

On my next day off, I was home alone and I had some time to myself. Like Enos, in that moment my soul began to hunger (see Enos 1:4). I hadn't opened the scriptures for years, but that day I felt a strong desire to read them. I picked up my triple combination and as the pages fell open, a passage of scripture jumped off the page: "And now behold, I ask of you, my brethren of the church, have ye spiritually been born of God? Have ye received his image in your countenances? Have ye experienced this mighty change in your hearts?" (Alma 5:14).

My answer to that question was a resounding *no*. I fell on my knees and began to pray for the first time in years. I poured out my heart to Heavenly Father and asked Him to bless me with this "mighty change of heart." I questioned Him, wondering how He could love someone who was as repulsive as I perceived myself to be. I didn't feel anything great and miraculous right away, but there was something about that moment that changed me. I felt different. The Apostle Paul taught that when we are in Christ, we are new creatures (see 2 Corinthians 5:17). I continued to struggle with same-gender attraction and was still a mess, but the difference was that I became the Lord's mess, and my heart and desires had been transformed. I indeed felt like a new creature.

As a result of my spiritual experience, I began to learn what it meant to rely totally on Him. From that point forward I began to pray and read the scriptures in a completely new way. The lesson for me was that *what* we do is less important than *why* we do what we do. In the past I had worked hard, demanding that the Lord bless me the way that

I wanted to be blessed. What the Lord cares about is the motivation— love of God and of our neighbors—that gives us a righteous desire to serve. I stopped believing that my works would bring me anything, and I stopped trying to earn eternal life. I began passionately to serve my Savior, who had already redeemed me through His blood, and to rely wholly upon His merit. I quit "reading the scriptures" and began feasting upon the words of Christ—I felt that I was reading them for the first time. I quit "saying my prayers" and began conversing with my loving Heavenly Father, who changed my heart and offered me the gift of eternal life through the atoning sacrifice of His Son.

Soon after experiencing my "mighty change of heart," I thought about the impending promotion and my former plans to lead a double life. Being aware of how weak I was in my still-growing relationship with Christ, I was concerned about my ability to resist temptations. I prayed and asked the Lord that I not get the promotion if I was not strong enough to resist the temptation. And that is what He did. The interview for the job, which had previously been a mere formality, re- sulted in someone else getting the promotion. I was humbly grateful that Heavenly Father knew my strengths and weaknesses and took care of me.

During that time, few resources were available in my community to help individuals with unwanted same-gender attraction. At some point I stumbled onto an organization called Homosexuals Anonymous, which used a modification of the Alcoholics Anonymous twelve-step program, and I began attending their meetings in a local evangelical Christian church. When they found out I was a Latter-day Saint, they made it clear to me that I wasn't welcome. One of the attendees said he wouldn't attend if a Mormon was present. I decided not to return. The rejection was hurtful, but they did provide me with information about the program. I worked the steps on my own as best I could. I grew closer to the Savior as a result of the experience but was still not able to talk to anyone but the Lord about my struggle. Fear of being found out continued to be in the forefront of my mind.

I worked hard in my job with a strong desire to be successful.

Because of the pressures of work and the challenges of daily living, the physical and emotional weariness began to take their toll. One Sunday someone who had recently made a homophobic statement in my presence had just been called to be our bishop. I was disappointed and hurt. Not only did I feel isolated, but I also felt that I now had a bishop who would find me disgusting if he knew my deepest struggle. I had misjudged him, however, without knowing that the Lord had prepared him to help me transform my life.

The next Sunday the bishop came up to me after church and shook my hand. He asked me how things were going, and I responded with a disingenuous "Okay." He was sincerely trying to help, but I wasn't willing to let him in. "Just okay?" he responded. I lied and told him that everything was fine.

A few weeks later, I was asked to speak in church by a counselor in the bishopric. Preparation for the talk brought me peace and helped me to become more grounded, but I still wasn't doing well. After sacrament meeting the bishop came up to me to shake my hand and thank me for my talk, adding, "You and I need to talk—tonight." I reluctantly agreed to the appointment.

We met at the appointed time and spent a couple of minutes with social niceties as I avoided opening up to him. He suddenly stopped talking and looked right into me. For a moment I was speechless. His earlier homophobic statement and my memories of the years of mistreatment flooded through me. He continued to stare into me, his eyes piercing mine. I broke the silence: "If at any time you can't handle this conversation, please be man enough to say so. There is no law that says we have to talk about this." He gave me a puzzled look, raising his left eyebrow, and then responded, "Okay?"

We spent the next three hours talking. I told him about my struggle with same-gender attraction and everything I had done to try to overcome it. The hurt of mistreatment and loneliness I had experienced over the years poured out. He said little, listening intently and occasionally asking excellent questions for clarification. At the end of our conversation he came over and held me in his arms as tears streamed down my face. That was the first time in my life I remember ever *really* feeling loved and accepted by another person just for who I was at that moment.

He and I spent many hours together over the next couple of years. There was nothing magical about what we did, but the results were miraculous. There was a lot of sharing and accountability. Sometimes we would go to lunch together and talk about things that normal people talk about over lunch. Other times we would play racquetball with little talking. He regularly included me in activities that he had with other friends and their families, treating me as a friend and an equal. Every meeting in his office began and ended with a prayer. I could also always count on a warm fatherly embrace as I was leaving.

It's interesting for me to recall how upset I was when he was called as our bishop, particularly since he turned out to be the single most important person in my life other than the Savior. Because of my relationship with him, my feelings of attraction to men went from something that consumed every moment of my life to something that felt again to be little more than a distant memory. While I do experience minor fluctuations in my attractions, I no longer experience anything close to the powerful craving that characterized my life before the time I spent with that bishop.

I do not see that bishop as often as I did in the past. When I do get to see him—this brother who was an instrument in the hands of God to bring me a great deal of healing—I am reminded of everything good that I have become because he was there to walk with me in my journey. I remember how overwhelming my feelings of same-gender attraction used to be and how little of an issue they have since become. My heart is filled with gratitude and love for him and what he was willing to do for me.

The prophet Moroni referred to our weaknesses as gifts meant to humble and strengthen us if we turn our hearts to God in faith (see Ether 12:27). That is how I view my experience with same-gender attraction. In a way it has become something I embrace. I feel gratitude for the blessings I have received because I have faced this challenge. My relationship with Deity has grown to be a deep and rich part of my life. Aid from the Spirit has become common, though never commonplace. Because of all I've learned as the Lord has transformed my weakness into strength, I have come to view this experience as one of my greatest blessings, and I often give thanks for the many other blessings that have come into my life through it.

I wish I could say that life has been "happily ever after" since that time, but that isn't the case. My spiritual resolve has continued to be tested in ways I didn't anticipate. In return, however, the Lord has continued to bless me spiritually in ways that were beyond my imagination. I learned that no matter what we face in this life, if we will turn to Him, He will be there for us. He may not give us what we want, but He will give us gifts beyond our ability to imagine.

I faced a major test when my marriage ended. Many rumors circulated about me during that time, some that included reference to my same-gender attractions. During the ensuing weeks and months, I walked into church each Sunday knowing that I was the subject of gossip. I could hear people talking about me as I walked down the halls. Some people refused to shake hands with me even as I extended my hand to them. Once, when I was teaching a Sunday School class of high school-aged students, a few of them walked out and told the bishop that they wouldn't stay in a class with me as their teacher. The bishop, who was very supportive of me, firmly told them to go back to class.

During that time I had some loving and supportive friends and Church leaders, besides my bishop, who looked out for me. In one of my meetings with my bishop, he suggested that if I would move to the other side of town, the gossip would stop. I asked him if moving would be an admission of guilt. He agreed that it could be seen that way. That admission was not one I was willing to make. Even if I did struggle with same-gender attraction, and even if I had at times struggled severely with temptation, I had remained faithful to the commitment I had made as a thirteen-year-old youth not to act on my attractions.

As is true to my character, I became weary again. I seemed to take all week rebuilding my spirit from the way that I was treated on Sunday so I could have the strength to return to church the next week. I seriously considered ceasing church attendance completely because it hurt so much to be there. Having just about solidified my decision, I planned a hike in a national park near my home. As I got up in the morning to drive to the trailhead, the only CD I took to listen to was "Consider the Lilies," by the Mormon Tabernacle Choir. As I listened to the beautiful hymns of Christ presented by that magnificent choir and orchestra, the Holy Spirit enveloped my soul. I felt immersed in peace and joy, giving me the strength to continue attending my Church meetings.

During this period of my life, many of my prayers were discussions with Heavenly Father about getting people to stop doing things to hurt me. In answer to those prayers, however, the Spirit reminded me that the Council in Heaven was over the gift of agency and that Heavenly Father honors that sacred gift. If we live by faith when other people are not living as they should, we will be blessed for our efforts in sacred and soul-expanding ways. Some of the most beautiful revelations received by the Prophet Joseph Smith came when he was on the receiving end of other people's unrighteous use of their agency. Similarly, some of the most sacred and spiritual experiences of my life occurred when other people misused their agency against me.

In addition, I learned that the only thing of value I have that no one can take from me is my faith in the Lord Jesus Christ. We can lose our jobs, family, friends, support system, and all of our worldly goods in the blink of an eye. Because the only thing I have that no one can take from me is my faith in Jesus Christ, the nurturing of my faith is the thing that deserves the single most effort in my life.

What I learn from Moroni's teaching in Ether 12:36–37 is that I am to concern myself only with what the Savior thinks of me, not what others think of me. I am to just get up every day and be faithful to Him. When I'm faithful, acknowledge my weakness, and surrender it to Him, then, and only then, am I made strong and able to return to live with our Heavenly Father.

Consistent with the Lord's promise that on the other side of faithful endurance are marvelous blessings, my life has dramatically improved the past few years. After I had been single for about a year and a half, I started a new job. I met a woman who had exceptional leadership skills. I was constantly impressed with her abilities to deal with difficult situations. She was a strong, solid, intelligent, hardworking woman, and I wanted to learn from her. After we had worked a few years as colleagues, she informed me that she would be getting a divorce.

We became good friends and spent time hanging out as she went through a difficult period. Then, just after her divorce was finalized, she had some spiritual experiences that led her to the Church and gave me the opportunity to baptize her. Soon afterward our relationship changed, and we started dating. Two years later we were married. Determined not to make the same mistake twice, however, I told her of my past struggle with same-gender attraction before we even began dating. She has loved me for who I am from the very beginning.

I think often about the reason for the differences between my two marriages. The difference is like that of midnight and noonday. When I married the first time, my personal and spiritual maturity was that of a man who built his house upon the sand. I was critical of Church leaders for just about any reason I could find. And although my feelings of same-gender attraction had decreased significantly before I entered into my first marriage, I didn't have the grasp of the gospel I do now, and my heart wasn't in the right place.

When entering into my second marriage, I had become a man who was building my house upon the rock of Christ. My wife treats me with love and respect, and I strive to do the same with her. We both desire to serve the Lord and be faithful members of His Church. We have family and friends in our home often, and we are humbled by the support system we have in our LDS community. I used to feel guilty about how easy my second marriage is. When people tell me how difficult marriage is and how much they have to work at it, I feel that much more grateful for the beauty of my current relationship. It's remarkably happy and easy.

The Savior has blessed me abundantly for my efforts to live faithful to Him in the face of adversity. Many opportunities to serve the Church and community have come my way. Relationships with people who were once hostile have become loving and mutually supportive. My once-troubled life is now characterized by peace and joy. I've been sealed in the temple to a wonderful and beautiful woman.

As stated earlier, the only thing I have that no one can take from me is my faith in Jesus Christ. My faith, therefore, is the most important thing I have. I am also grateful for my testimony of the restored gospel, which has been such an anchor in my life. And I am grateful for my testimony of the programs of the Church that are designed to help people who struggle with life's difficulties to come unto Christ and be transformed in Him. I look forward to the day when I will stand with my Savior at His coming. I am unexpectedly grateful for the challenge that at one point I hated, that brought me only heartache and pain, but that has ultimately proven to be one of my greatest blessings. My struggle with same-gender attraction has blessed me with spiritual insights I don't think I would have gained any other way. For that, I count it as a most sacred gift.

Chapter 4

A Church for All, a Gospel of Inclusion

Camille Fronk Olson

At baptism, members of The Church of Jesus Christ of Latter-day Saints make a covenant with God that, with the help of His Spirit and the enabling power of the Atonement of Jesus Christ, they will "bear one another's burdens, that they may be light; . . . mourn with those that mourn; . . . and comfort those that stand in need of comfort" (Mosiah 18:8–9).

Various circumstances, however, challenge our promise to honor that covenant. For example, fellow members whose personalities clash with ours, whose outward performance of the commandments appears either flawed or flawless in comparison to our own, or whose weaknesses or unique trials are publicly known are frequently those who stretch our resolve to welcome and befriend all those who belong to "the body of Christ" (1 Corinthians 12:27). Likewise, those whose difficulties are completely foreign to our own life's experiences often frighten us into withdrawing our compassion and friendship. For example, in our efforts to honor and protect divinely sanctioned marriage between a man and a woman, we may be tempted to cling to an ungrounded social theology that perceives same-gender attraction as an unforgiveable sin. This overzealous and mistaken tenet presents an opportunity to reconsider the teachings and doctrines of Christ.

I have friends and acquaintances who are homosexual or who experience same-gender attraction, but I do not pretend to understand the breadth of their difficulties and concerns. Such a void, however, does not interfere with the quality of friendship and learning from each other that is possible. This chapter will therefore consider the gospel of inclusion in a general sense while considering homosexual attraction as a specific example. It will discuss various challenges facing Latter-day Saints in creating a community where all of those desirous to take upon them the name of Jesus Christ will feel welcomed and loved. It will also acknowledge those who are at times excluded and offended by Church members yet remain faithful within the gospel net. Finally, this chapter will suggest specific ways we may, in reality, bear one another's burdens rather than merely talk about doing so, and it will suggest some of the remarkable gifts the Lord has given us to succeed.

Challenges to Keep the Covenant

In our efforts to create an environment that shows reverence to the Savior, we may inadvertently send a message that only the respectable, the *sinless,* and the elegant are worthy to come unto Christ. The natural product of such a message is a new definition of righteousness, one that is outwardly recognizable to a casual observer. That revised definition automatically excludes those whose mortal struggles are obvious, who battle emotional demons, or who appear different from the rest of the community. A sobering observation that the Book of Mormon prophet Moroni noted about us in the latter days is that "ye do love money, and your substance, and your fine apparel, and the adorning of your churches, more than ye love the poor and the needy, the sick and the afflicted" (Mormon 8:37). Would Christ be offended to have the outcasts, the unclean, and those who are battling temptation join the *respectable* believers in worship services? I don't think so.

President Boyd K. Packer told of a poignant experience in which he witnessed the pain of exclusion. He and another General Authority were attending a sacrament meeting in Cuzco, Peru. The door to the room used for the meeting led immediately to the street outside and was opened to allow ventilation for the capacity crowd.

"While Brother Tuttle was speaking, a little boy appeared in the doorway," President Packer related. "He was perhaps six or seven years old. His only clothing was a tattered shirt which almost reached his knees. He was dirty and undernourished, with all the characteristics of a street orphan. Perhaps he entered the room to get warm, but then he saw the bread on the sacrament table."

As the ragged boy slowly inched his way toward the sacrament table, one of the women in the congregation noticed him. "Without saying a word, with only a movement of her head," President Packer remembered, "she clearly communicated the message, 'out.'" After a slight hesitation, the boy turned around and ran back into the dark street. "My heart wept for him. Undoubtedly the sister felt justified because this was a special meeting, with General Authorities present, and this was a dirty little boy who wasn't going to learn anything." Somehow the misconception that the "unclean" diminish the reverence and sacredness of our meetings had taken root in some of the members. The lost, the fallen, the outcast, however, are precisely those whom Jesus invites to come to Him.

The little boy returned to the doorway; he had seen bread—literally the bread of life for him. Again, he quietly approached the sacrament table. Just before he reached the row where the woman was seated, President Packer succeeded in catching his eye. "I held out my open arms. He came to me, and I picked him up to hold him." He then had the boy sit in Elder Tuttle's chair "in order to teach the members an important principle." The principle was that "dirty little boys and girls, in tatters, are not offensive to me, nor are their brave parents repugnant to me because they are ours."[1]

Phillip Yancey, an esteemed Christian writer, recognized the propensity in those who profess discipleship with the Savior to ostracize people whose lives don't fit their definition of being "worthy." Contrasting today's practice with that at the time of Christ, he observed:

"The more unsavory the characters, the more at ease they seemed to feel around Jesus. . . . Why don't sinners *like* being around us? . . .

"Somehow we have created a community of respectability in the church. . . . The down-and-out, who flocked to Jesus when he lived on earth, no longer feel welcome. How did Jesus, the only perfect person in history, manage to attract the notoriously imperfect? And what keeps us from following in his steps today?"[2]

Choosing to be blind to their own sins, some scribes and Pharisees at the time of Christ criticized the Savior for associating with sinners. To these self-righteous leaders, Jesus responded, "They that are whole have no need of the physician, but they that are sick: I came not to call the righteous, but sinners to repentance" (Mark 2:17; see also Matthew 9:12; Luke 5:31). Christ's true followers know they have shortcomings, but they also know that the true Physician heals them. Furthermore, He does not require that they be whole before they come to Him; such a law would exclude all. That realization softens their hearts toward others who struggle with life in a fallen world in different ways than they do.

Aren't We All Beggars?

Truthfully speaking, we are all still works in progress. Qualification for temple recommends and Church callings does not signify that we are free from temptation and shortcomings. So where do we derive the idea that some challenges or temptations make us *unworthy* to serve or belong?

Some time ago, my ward's gospel doctrine class was engaged in a discussion about the "designs of Satan" in the latter-days. A man who was visiting our ward that day raised his hand to comment. He emphatically told of the most "devilish" design he had observed—devilish, he explained, because it was so subtle in its trap. He related that the evil thing was placed right by the checkout stand in the grocery store and looked quite innocent to the casual shopper. When the man finally identified the wicked design as bottled, caffeinated water, I felt a comic relief ripple through the class. I remember thinking, *If that's the worst Satan can do, I think I'm pretty safe!*

Later in the discussion the man again commented, this time revealing his previous problem with substance addiction. Immediately I felt pangs of remorse for thinking the man was foolish. I began to appreciate what made caffeinated water so devilish to him. For someone who had struggled with addiction, any substance that was habit-forming could become the catalyst that whirled him back into its captive hold. I then thought of how easy it would be to mock and even play tricks on such a vulnerable man without ever realizing how tenuous his condition was. That day the visitor helped me to be more sensitive to others' weaknesses and less quick to judge. I do not have to experience substance addiction or same-gender attraction to empathize with those who face such challenges; my own struggles with other temptations foster feelings of understanding, respect, and love for courageous believers who do not let their weaknesses define them or their Church participation.

In one of the most life-changing sermons of all time, King Benjamin directed a people who were "diligent in keeping the commandments" to a remarkably new level of humility and reverence. After Benjamin's inspired witness of the Redeemer, his people "viewed themselves in their own carnal state, even less than the dust of the earth," rather than taking pride in their obedience. Crying for the Savior's mercy through the Atonement, they fell to the ground and pled to God for forgiveness and purified hearts (Mosiah 1:11; 4:1–2). In their humble state of rebirth, King Benjamin taught them how they would naturally act toward others when they retained this reverence for God and dependence on Him. He instructed, "Ye yourselves will succor those that stand in need of your succor; . . . and ye will not suffer that the beggar putteth up his petition to you in vain, and turn him out to perish. . . . For behold, are we not all beggars?" (Mosiah 4:11, 16, 19).

The prophet Nephi explicitly taught that we are rejecting the Savior's commands and proffered power when we exclude others from association in the household of faith. In several verses that focus on the Savior's generous and free salvation, Nephi wrote:

"Behold, doth he cry unto any, saying: Depart from me? Behold, I say unto you, Nay; but he saith: Come unto me all ye ends of the earth, buy milk and honey, without money and without price. Behold, hath he commanded any that they should depart out of the synagogues, or out of the houses of worship? Behold, I say unto you, Nay. Hath he commanded any that they should not partake of his salvation? Behold I say unto you, Nay; but he hath given it free for all men. . . .

"Behold, hath the Lord commanded any that they should not partake of his goodness? Behold I say unto you, Nay; but all men are privileged the one like unto the other, and none are forbidden. . . . He denieth none that come unto him, black and white, bond and free, male and female; and he remembereth the heathen; and all are alike unto God, both Jew and Gentile" (2 Nephi 26:25–28, 33).

By extension, does the Lord deny fellowship or salvation to those among us dealing with same-gender attraction? I say unto you, Nay, for all are alike unto God. By sincerely acknowledging our fallen natures and admitting that we have not come this far in life without "relying wholly upon the merits of him who is mighty to save," we are filled with God's love for others (2 Nephi 31:19–20). Our covenant with God to succor those who stand in need of succor is finally doable. We are divinely enabled to see others as the Lord sees them.

Positive Examples

Miraculous healing and strengthened communities that become places of refuge emerge when we honor the covenant. Our patience with others increases, and we avoid making assumptions and judging unkindly. Consider some examples:

A ward family rallied around a less-active member who was fighting a smoking problem but who wanted to return to church. The three-hour meeting block posed a problem for the man because his addiction necessitated a cigarette break. Rather than have him reduce his attendance to only one meeting, individual ward members took turns accompanying him to the Church parking lot for a needed break. The members' thoughtfulness and humility facilitated the man's return to Sunday meetings, to the Church, and to the Lord. In turn, the ward members were strengthened in their covenant with the Lord to "bear one another's burdens, that they may be light" (Mosiah 18:8) and in their blessing of being filled with the pure love of Christ.

In another branch of the Church in a different part of the country, members sustained a new member of their branch presidency. The new counselor created a potential challenge for them because it was widely known that he had AIDS, acquired through homosexual activity. With a vibrant testimony of Jesus Christ and the restored gospel, the man had repented of his former lifestyle and served faithfully in the Church before this calling. His sexual orientation had not changed, but his devotion to the Savior had deepened, which then altered his actions.

Exemplifying true disciples of the Savior, the members grew to love and support their new priesthood leader. They saw multiple Christlike qualities in him that engendered respect and deeper faith. Sensitive to his concerns with same-gender attraction, they were careful not to lay additional burdens on him by reducing him to that single characteristic or through unkind speech. When his disease finally left him bedridden, members took turns staying with him to comfort and assist. With the man's death imminent, they recognized in him an important means by which they had become a united and loving community of Saints. Through his example of selfless service as a Church leader, the members saw the power of the Redeemer in all of their lives: the Savior's forgiveness is real and His healing balm is limitless.

The Book of Mormon provides a parallel example of inclusion and acceptance of the Savior's Atonement for all who come unto Him. At a time of widespread apostasy and persecution against the believers, Alma the Elder was weighed down by concern for many Church members who found that the Lord's requirements were too hard. In response to his prayers, God instructed Alma that he should forgive all those who heard His voice, confessed their sins, and repented in the sincerity of their hearts.

In addition, God commanded Alma that individual church members were to accept the Lord's forgiveness for others and sincerely welcome them back to the community of believers. "And ye shall also forgive one another your trespasses," God explained to Alma, "for verily I say unto you, he that forgiveth not his neighbor's trespasses when he says that he repents, the same hath brought himself under condemnation" (Mosiah 26:31).

In a remarkable example of obeying these instructions, the Nephite believers chose as their political leader a man who was, in their recent collective memory, a ring leader among the unbelievers and "a very wicked and an idolatrous man," whose clear objective was to destroy the Church (Mosiah 27:8, 10). Although all his crimes are not specified, Alma the Younger was known for being "a great hinderment" to the church, "stealing away the hearts of the people; causing much dissension . . . ; giving a chance for the enemy of God to exercise his power over them" (Mosiah 27:9)—all the while reflecting no concern for the consequences of his influence. One wonders how many loved ones of the believers followed Alma's flattering words and disobedient example to abandon their devotion to God indefinitely.

And yet, when Alma the Younger heard God's voice, he turned away from his destructive agenda and sincerely repented before the Lord. Faithful followers of God selected him to be their first chief judge and sustained him as their spiritual leader after the death of Alma the Elder. Their actions testified that they believed the Lord's command to "forgive one another your trespasses" because they chose to forget Alma's wicked past and trusted the power of the Atonement in his new birth.

During an interview with a young man who had expressed concerns over same-gender attraction, Elder Jeffrey R. Holland taught the principle of inclusion under the banner of the Atonement. "If your life is in harmony with the commandments," he counseled the young man, "then you are worthy to serve in the Church, enjoy the full fellowship with the members, attend the temple, and receive all the blessings of the Savior's Atonement." Clearly, same-gender attraction in and of itself is not a reason to exclude a member of the Church from a calling, including one in priesthood leadership.

Next, Elder Holland cautioned the young man, "You serve yourself poorly when you identify yourself primarily by your sexual feelings. That isn't your only characteristic, so don't give it disproportionate attention. You are first and foremost a son of God, and He loves you."

Finally, adding his witness to the declaration of President Boyd K. Packer, Elder Holland promised the young man and all those who have similar concerns over sexual orientation, "We *do not* reject you. . . . We *cannot* reject you, for you are the sons and daughters of God. We *will not* reject you, because we love you."[3]

In every story where a true community of Saints is evident, we rejoice to see the pure love of Christ, the baptismal covenant in practice, and the beauty of the inclusive gospel of Jesus Christ, whether or not someone chooses to repent. Even as the Savior associated with many sinners in various stages of change, so we as His disciples can be less judgmental about others' sins and more focused on showing compassion and fellowship. In every positive example of supporting the Church as a safe place for all those who desire to come unto Him, we want to belong to that community and become an active participant. By contrast, whenever we replace our trust in the Lord with the approval of the world and feed our insecurities with denigrating others, we abandon our brothers and sisters who suffer. By such misplaced trust, we also fail the Lord.

When We Are Offended

Not all examples, therefore, are positive. Most likely, each one of us has felt the sting of exclusion at one time or another when we were among those who covenant to be our brothers and sisters. Subtle—or not so subtle—messages are sometimes sent to indicate that we are not quite worthy to be fully accepted among the faithful.

Perhaps because of the central importance of marriage and family to the restored gospel of Jesus Christ, personal circumstances that strain at our definition of "eternal families" are particularly vulnerable to censor, judgment, and exclusion in our communities. When we label a fellow member, the assigned moniker often reduces the person to that single characteristic. Anything that the labeled member does that is praiseworthy may subsequently be explained away to retain the *veracity* of the label. Consider the following examples: She is divorced. He has never married and isn't interested in marriage. They have rebellious kids. Her husband isn't active in the Church. Their daughter isn't marrying in the temple. He is a returned missionary with same-gender attraction. Their son doesn't want to serve a mission. She has a career but not a family. Although each statement may be true, not one of these individuals is denied the healing and enabling balm of the Atonement. Is there ever a *perfect* or an *ideal* family in everyone's estimation? In reality, there is not. So why do we put that yoke on each other's neck that neither we nor our parents are able to bear? (see Acts 15:10).

Some of the most faith-promoting and most tragic examples emerge from reactions to thoughtless, uninformed, or fearful judgments about various family situations by Church members. The blow is especially poignant when the offender is a priesthood leader. In such cases the member falsely judged must be grounded in a testimony of Christ and His doctrine to weather the storm of misunderstanding and rejection that often follows. What can we learn from the abiding faith of the presumed outcasts?

Elder John H. Groberg of the Seventy related a poignant example that offers a revealing response. Because of the direct relevance to this topic, I cite here Elder Groberg's full account:

"In the early 1900s, a young father and his family joined the Church in Hawaii. He was enthused about his newfound religion, and after two years of membership both he and his eldest son held the priesthood. They prospered and enjoyed the fellowship of the little branch. They anxiously looked forward to being sealed as a family for eternity in the temple soon to be completed in Laie.

"Then, as so often happens, a test crossed their path. One of their daughters became ill with an unknown disease and was taken away to a strange hospital. People in Hawaii were understandably wary of unknown diseases, as such diseases had wrought so much havoc there.

"The concerned family went to church the next Sunday, looking forward to the strength and understanding they would receive from their fellow members. It was a small branch. This young father and his son very often took the responsibility for blessing and passing the sacrament. This was one such Sunday. They reverently broke the bread while the congregation sang the sacrament hymn. When the hymn was finished, the young father began to kneel to offer the sacrament prayer. Suddenly the branch president, realizing who was at the sacred table, sprang to his feet. He pointed his finger and cried, 'Stop. You can't touch the sacrament. Your daughter has an unknown disease. Leave immediately while someone else fixes new sacrament bread. We can't have you here. Go.' . . .

"The stunned father slowly stood up. He searchingly looked at the branch president, then at the congregation. Then, sensing the depth of anxiety and embarrassment from all, he motioned to his family and they quietly filed out of the chapel.

"Not a word was said as, with faces to the ground, they moved along the dusty trail to their small home. The young son noticed the firmness in his father's clenched fists and the tenseness of his set jaw. When they entered their home they all sat in a circle, and the father said, 'We will be silent until I am ready to speak.' All sorts of thoughts went through the mind of this young boy. He envisioned his father coming up with many novel ways of getting revenge. Would they kill the branch president's pigs, or burn his house, or join another church? He could hardly wait to see what would happen.

"Five minutes, ten minutes, fifteen minutes—not a sound. He glanced at his father. His eyes were closed, his mouth was set, his fingers clenched, but no sound. Twenty minutes, twenty-five minutes—still nothing. Then he noticed a slight relaxing of his father's hands, a small tremor on his father's lips, then a barely perceptible sob. He looked at his father—tears were trickling down his cheeks from closed eyes. Soon he noticed his mother was crying also, then one child, then another, and soon the whole family.

"Finally, the father opened his eyes, cleared his throat, and announced, 'I am now ready to speak. Listen carefully.' He slowly turned to his wife and said, meaningfully, 'I love you.' Then turning to each child, he told them individually, 'I love you. I love all of you and I want us to be together, forever, as a family. And the only way that can be is for all of us to be good members of The Church of Jesus Christ of Latter-day Saints and be sealed by His holy priesthood in the temple. This is not the branch president's church. It is the Church of Jesus Christ. We will not let any man or any amount of hurt or embarrassment or pride keep us from being together forever. Next Sunday we will go back to church. We will stay by ourselves until our daughter's sickness is known, but we will go back.' . . .

"The daughter's health problem was resolved; the family did go to the temple when it was completed. The children did remain faithful and were likewise sealed to their own families in the temple as time went on. Today over 100 souls in this family are active members of the Church and call their father, grandfather, and great-grandfather blessed because he kept his eyes on eternity."[4]

We have innumerable examples of such resilient Saints today. After spending eighteen years outside of the Church, an acquaintance was re-admitted several years ago. He has a profound testimony of Christ and His Atonement, but at times he becomes discouraged and feels slighted by others in the Church. After brief musings about leaving the Church, he realizes how pride and self-pity have begun to control his life and he returns to the Lord with a deeper desire to be acceptable to Him, independent of the way others may respond toward him.

My friend explained his secret for returning kindness and love toward those who may not be particularly compassionate to him. "I know the Savior has suffered much for me, and I beg Him sometimes to let me carry some of the load. At these times the Lord and I are so close I can almost feel Him touching me. When we reach that level of intimacy with the Master, when His approval means more than anything else in our lives, we will live beyond such trivial things [as being slighted by fellow members]. . . .

"Please know the Savior and His Atonement mean everything to me," he wrote, "and I so love Him that it is very hard to want to stay here and not be able to fall before Him and bathe His nail-scarred feet with my unworthy tears. I am no longer comfortable referring to the Savior as my 'older brother' since I experienced His Atonement in a way few people do. Now He is my Savior and Redeemer."

The primary and most compelling reason that members of the Church remain steadfast and immovable in their covenants with God, despite circumstances when they feel excluded from the community of Saints, is their faith in Jesus Christ and trust in His infinite Atonement. They have come to rely on the incomparable peace and comfort that comes through the Holy Spirit.

Like the Apostle Peter, misjudged believers hear the "hard saying" that drives so many of Jesus' disciples to walk "no more with Him," yet they unflinchingly report, "Lord, to whom shall we go? thou hast the words of eternal life. And we believe and are sure that thou art that Christ, the Son of the living God" (John 6:60, 66, 68–69).

The Inclusion Responsibility for the General Church Membership

The resurrected Savior gave a different commandment to the Nephite multitude than to their priesthood leaders in His teachings about preserving the sanctity of their worship services. Similar to a vigilant shepherd, a priesthood leader's directives include guarding against predators and any other destructive forces that could harm or weaken the flock. To the general membership, the Lord directed, "Ye shall meet together oft; and ye shall not forbid any man from coming unto you when ye shall meet together, but suffer them that they may come unto you and forbid them not; but ye shall pray for them, and shall not cast them out." Reminding the Nephite multitude that He had not excluded any of them, notwithstanding their weaknesses, the Lord underscored their need to reach out to others, for "whosoever breaketh this commandment suffereth himself to be led into temptation" (3 Nephi 18:22–23, 25).

Oftentimes it is through the example of the believers that those living with temptation and those who are lost first discover the love of God. If they don't feel a reason to hope and the power of charity around them, they will likely go elsewhere in search of the closest substitute. As members of the Church, we have a tremendous obligation and opportunity not to quench the Spirit when those who are searching for a reason to hope interact with us. In many ways we live our baptismal covenant to bear one another's burdens, comfort those who stand in need of comfort, and stand as a witness for God by welcoming all those who sincerely seek the Lord's grace. Being led and inspired by that same Spirit, we can say and do specific things that will lead our friends to feel for themselves the incomparable love of Christ.

In all of our efforts to help others discover the Savior's perfect love, we can first remember that the enabling power to succeed comes only through Jesus Christ. Because of His selfless sacrifice, we can receive His desired *at-one-ment* with the Father and Him. This divine unity is not compulsory conformity. Forced compliance is Satan's mode of operation. Jesus told Peter that Satan's desire was to "sift the children of the kingdom as wheat" (JST, Luke 22:31). Sifting forces a substance to conform to a predetermined shape and isolates each unit with cookie-cutter uniformity. God's plan encourages the uniqueness of each of His children and their potential to offer viable contributions to His work.

As recipients of His various gifts, each of us can thereby enlist to labor in His vineyard to bring others to Him. We can lose any preconceived expectation that the "body of Christ" is made up of people just like us, and we can recognize the unique contributions that other members bring to the Church. The Apostle Paul taught the necessity of "those members of the body, which seem to be more feeble." He suggested placing "more abundant honour" on the members of the body "which we think to be less honourable. . . . That there should be no schism in the body: but that the members should have the same care one for another" (1 Corinthians 12:22–25).

Through his metaphor, we can see the beauty of divine unity and complementary gifts in the Church of Jesus Christ. The truth is that we *need* those whose challenges are different from ours; we *need* the

God-given gifts that those with same-gender attraction can offer us to bring us closer to the Lord. Collectively, we are the temple of God; we are not complete without all being "fitly framed" on the foundation of Christ (Ephesians 2:21).

Furthermore, we can bear one another's burdens by publicly and verbally supporting those who struggle with various challenges in mortality. Quiet service is always needed, but sometimes public expression of support is particularly meaningful to those who worry that their personal trials and temptations exceed the reach of God's love and therefore they may not be *worthy* to participate in the Church. We can compassionately correct those who ignorantly label a fellow Saint as "unsalvageable," and we can refuse to gossip about or categorize others in the community because of gender orientation, marital status, size of family, childlessness, and so forth. This is particularly true in our casual comments around others whose personal struggles are not publicly known. Without intending to be cruel, we can cut off a person's hope in Christ by a thoughtless attempt at humor or an uninformed judgment. Continually remembering that we do not know who among us may be struggling, we can openly communicate ways to strengthen one another and reflect the Lord's pure love wherever we go—and do it without being condescending or self-righteous.

For example, a few years ago, an acquaintance of mine felt the reassuring embrace of such compassion when no one else in a discussion group knew of his own challenge with same-gender attraction. In a unique and remarkable opportunity, he and a select few other members of the Church were invited to discuss various topics and questions with a member of the Quorum of the Twelve. In the course of the discussion, the topic of same-gender attraction arose along with questions about how to best support those among us who face it. When one of the members of the small group made a joking comment about gay people in general, the Apostle kindly but sternly rebuked him, telling all in that small group that such a comment is never appropriate or funny. That day my friend was offered much-needed safety within the Church. These words from the Lord's representative continue to sustain him in his discipleship and reinforce the reality that the Church of Jesus Christ does indeed embrace a gospel of inclusion.

Next we can find ways to expand the circle of our *family* to include those who come to church alone. Every one of us who has been single or without immediate family in the Church knows the discomfort of finding a seat in sacrament meeting. The invisible but very real fences that surround each family pew can be daunting. We can be overt in our gestures of inclusion to communicate that every family is strengthened and blessed by additional members.

Additionally, we can remember our own times of feeling that we didn't fit in and thereby try to understand another's potential pain. Empathy—and not pity—for those whose family situations present added challenges will go far to invite the love of the Lord. Compassion also helps us lose our fears for circumstances that we may not understand. Association and empathy with those whose weaknesses are publicly known do not mean approval or dismissal of their challenges. The Savior certainly understood that and was unfazed when *the righteous ones* criticized Him for associating with *sinners.*

Finally, we can remember and reverence the purposes for the doctrines, covenants, and ordinances of the restored gospel while halting the perpetuation of destructive and unfounded social theologies that suggest that those struggling with certain challenges are not "worthy" to participate. Every truth included in the gospel focuses on the Savior and His sacrifice. We can therefore avoid placing nonexistent barriers around the truly *infinite* Atonement.

The Unifying Power of the Sacrament Service

Our worship services revolve around the renewal of our covenants with the Lord. The blessing and administration of the sacrament is a noteworthy reminder and promise of divine power to help us succeed in bearing one another's burdens and comforting those who need comfort. Elder Henry B. Eyring explained: "The sacramental prayer can remind us every week of how the gift of unity will come through obedience to the laws and ordinances of the gospel of Jesus Christ. When we keep our covenants to take His name upon us, to remember Him always, and to keep all His commandments, we will receive the companionship of His Spirit. That will soften our hearts and unite us."[5]

The Apostle Paul taught the Corinthian Saints: "The cup of blessing which we bless, is it not the communion of the blood of Christ? The bread which we break, is it not the communion of the body of Christ? For we being many are one bread, and one body: for we are all partakers of that one bread. . . . Ye cannot drink the cup of the Lord, and the cup of devils: ye cannot be partakers of the Lord's table, and of the table of devils" (1 Corinthians 10:16–17, 21).

Symbolism within the ordinance of the sacrament of the Lord's Supper is to remind us that we can become one. For example, we partake of the broken bread from one loaf; in an earlier era, all drank the sacramental water from one container. In one voice we sing a hymn of praise in gratitude to our Savior for His atoning sacrifice and our shared dependence on Him. Consider words such as these to sacrament hymns that reinforce our individual and collective blessings through the Savior's grace:

"No creature is so lowly, No sinner so depraved,
But feels thy presence holy, And thru thy love is saved."[6]

The sacramental emblems are presented to us individually, but we receive them as one body. We make the same promises to the Lord, and each of us receives the same divine promise in return. No one is distinguished above another; we each accept the same requirements, and we all are promised the presence of the Holy Spirit to help us to succeed.

Becoming the Pure in Heart

Among the Savior's beatitudes is the blessing that the "pure in heart . . . shall see God" (Matthew 5:8; 3 Nephi 12:8). Filled with the Spirit and the sole desire to do and be what God wants them to become, the pure in heart see God wherever they look. He is in all that He created, including each of us, the struggling souls who come to be nourished by the good word of Christ. Empowered to keep their baptismal promise to "always remember Him" and to "comfort those that stand in need of comfort" (Mosiah 18:9), the pure in heart see God's imprint and potential on all He creates.

Immediately before entering the Garden of Gethsemane and His ultimate suffering for the sins and inadequacies of the world, Jesus fervently prayed to His Father on our behalf. Making reference to His apostles and those who "shall believe on me through their word," the Savior acknowledged our worldly orientation; we are products of a fallen world (John 17:5–6, 20). His prayer was not for the fictitious few who lived lives of continuous humility, perfect obedience to God, and pure love for others; His offering was for the fallen. Prefiguring His magnanimous sacrifice, He acknowledged that we all sin and have need of His enabling power.

The Savior then petitioned His Father, "I pray not that thou shouldest take them out of the world, but that thou shouldest keep them from the evil" (John 17:15). The implication is that He saw value in His followers interacting with those who face different challenges and who develop different perspectives than their own. Through our various encounters with the world, Christ's greatest desire for us was that we become "one; as thou, Father, art in me, and I in thee, that they also may be one in us" (John 17:21).

Will we accept the Lord's petition for us? Will we be among the pure in heart? Will we desire unity with all of our brothers and sisters in the "body of Christ"? Will we actively seek to create a place of safety and rest for the honest seekers after truth? Like the early Nephites and members of the early Christian church, will we join with our priesthood leaders in acknowledging that the Savior's Atonement applies to others besides ourselves? Will we bear witness by our every action and thought that He sacrificed His life for all who have need of the Physician?

God bless us that we will. There are far too many wounded souls who are looking for a safe and healing refuge—and who don't know that such a place can be found among us.

Finding My Home in the
Faith of My Fathers

Steven Frei

Steven Frei was born Easter morning nearly a half century ago.
He met his wife on a blind date, and, twenty-six years and four children
later, he considers himself blessed. Steven grew up on a family farm on the
banks of the Snake River, professes to be a recovering accountant, and
currently works in commercial real estate. His favorite Church calling
is teaching youth in Sunday School. He is an avid BYU fan
unless the Cougars are playing Boise State University.

As I knelt in the small cubicle of the temple's locker room that fall evening following my reinstatement to the Church, I pled, "Father, please forgive me for abandoning you again. Please hold me tight and never let me stray again. Please help me to never again forget who I am or where I belong."

I don't remember how young we were when a neighboring boy and I began exploring each other's bodies. Our early childhood experimentation began innocently enough but became increasingly sexual through our mid-teens. I don't know if these activities led to my same-gender attraction or if predispositions toward homosexuality led to the longevity of our physical relations. Whatever the reason, we continued our physical involvement through my freshman year of high school.

Unlike some who have early childhood same-sex experiences and appear to pass through this phase of life unscathed, I became trapped in it. I did not understand why I lacked the same feelings about the opposite sex that other boys had or why I was drawn physically to boys, but these thoughts were never far from my young mind. By the age of eight, I was already steeped in shame and, thinking I was a disappointment to God, prayed that my younger brother wouldn't turn out to be evil like me. In my deacons quorum and Scout troop, I considered myself inferior to the other boys and was fearful of the rejection I would face if my secret were to be exposed.

Near our farm, the county landfill provided an ample supply of pornography for curious young boys. We would walk or ride our bikes or horses to the dump and haul home dirty magazines. Pornography became a part of my life early on, and I have battled it off and on ever since. On one excursion we found the mother lode. We put it all in a gunnysack and hid it in the basement of a deserted old house on our farm. One of the magazines in the stack was a *Playgirl.* I was captivated by it. My friends said it was disgusting and threw it out. Later, when they were gone, I snuck it back into the pile. I didn't consider myself homosexual or even understand what that meant. All I knew was that I was much more attracted to the male body than the female body.

I loved high school. My friends were athletic and popular. I was a wannabe, never very coordinated and lacking the self-confidence and skills to do well in sports. Even so, I was in student government, worked a job through high school, and was thrilled to be accepted in the popular crowd. My friends had girlfriends and I wanted one too. However, I had no confidence that I could ever have a girlfriend and really only wanted one to fit in with the other guys. I did well academically, was fairly well adjusted, and made it through high school without acting out further on any of my same-sex desires even though I remained conflicted and ashamed of them.

At the end of my senior year, when I received my patriarchal blessing, I was told I would someday serve as a bishop. That weighed on me but helped me to avoid serious sin that might have jeopardized my membership. Before turning nineteen, I fully confessed, repented of my sins, and got ready for my mission. I was not as prepared as I should have been, and I didn't really go for the right reasons. I went because it was expected. It was part of my plan for doing the right thing and setting the stage for the rest of my life. I was confident that serving well would help take away my attractions to men.

I was called to Italy. I loved the Missionary Training Center. It changed my life. The first night there, I knelt and dedicated myself to the Lord for the remainder of my mission. I would be completely obedient and give it my all. I loved my mission. The people were incredible, the food was wonderful, the culture was deep and rich, and my companions were great. My spiritual understanding grew by leaps and bounds. For the most part, it was a time of reprieve from my attractions to other men. The attractions were always there, but I was so focused on my service to the Lord that I didn't think much about them.

But within one week of returning from my mission, I had purchased gay pornography again. I was so disappointed in myself. How could I do this after all I had experienced? For the next year I was engrossed in my addiction. I repented (again), went to Brigham Young University, and began teaching at the MTC—an incredible experience I will always treasure.

The first week of my second semester, I moved into an apartment with an old childhood friend and was promptly set up on a blind date. Although the reason for moving into an apartment was to have a better social life, I was upset and scared. Begrudgingly, I went on the date and, to my surprise, met the love of my life! I loved her the moment I heard her voice from behind the door. She was only nineteen but very mature and classy. Most important, she loved me! We were engaged three months after meeting and married three months later. It was a miracle that events unfolded as they did. I was caught up in the marriage furor with my roommates and was blessed to find my wife.

We didn't kiss for over two months. She thought something was wrong with her. I told her I was just waiting and didn't want things to get out of control. I didn't know why I couldn't get excited about kissing her, but I couldn't, even though I loved her. When I asked Heavenly Father if my decision to marry her was correct, I initially felt nothing. I was determined to get an answer, however, and told Him I had to know and that I felt I deserved a clear answer. I got one—the strongest, most sure answer I have ever received to prayer. I couldn't deny it. God wanted us to be together. It wasn't until later that I fully understood why receiving such a powerful witness was needed and granted.

When school let out in April, she headed home to Colorado, and I went back to Idaho to work and save money for our June wedding. I was scared and didn't write or call much. Notwithstanding my previous spiritual confirmation, I worried that I had made a huge mistake. She came a week before the wedding, and I had a pit in my stomach. I could not understand why I didn't feel the excitement about getting married that others seemed to feel. However, we did marry, and despite all the anxiety I had previously felt, it was truly the happiest day of my life! We were in the temple, both entirely worthy to be there. It was a dream come true. I thought that my cross would now certainly be lifted.

Our marriage was good and our love continued to grow. A year later our first son was born. What an incredible experience! Words cannot express the joy and range of emotions I felt. I was on my way to happily ever after. We had three more children, moved around a bit, finished school, opened my business, and went on with life. For several years, things went along fairly smoothly. I was really trying hard to live a clean life and to make myself worthy to serve wherever the Lord needed me. Several callings came: youth Gospel Doctrine teacher, Scout leader, elders quorum president, bishopric member, high councilor, and temple worker.

I was called into the bishopric just before turning thirty and then called to serve as bishop a few years later. I felt prepared and worthy when I was called and tried to do my best. I loved serving as a bishop. I felt that all I had ever worked for was finally falling into place. I was happily married, had a great family and a good job, was serving in a calling foretold in my patriarchal blessing, and my same-gender attraction seemed at bay. My life was on track.

However, a storm was brooding on the horizon. I was working an extremely high-stress job, running my own business on the side, serving as legal guardian for a dying man, and taking care of my family and my ward. The pressure became too great, and I cracked! When I was so overwhelmed with life, Satan remembered my susceptibility to pornography, sexual immorality, and alcohol that I had created in my youth. While caring for the dying man, I found some pornographic videos in his apartment. I shook as I put a video in the player.

I soon began looking at men in underwear and swimsuits on my computer at work, which led me to pornography. It seemed to provide a needed escape from reality. I felt horrible and prayed for help. I told my wife and the stake president what had happened. At first he wanted to work with me, keeping me in my calling as bishop. He felt that it was something I could put behind me and still serve effectively. So did I. I didn't think it was necessary to tell him what kind of pornography I was viewing. It never even occurred to me. After all, I told myself I wasn't gay, and the fascination with men was just a remnant of my past. I told myself that I was honoring my wife by not looking at women.

Unbeknownst to me, my employer had installed tracking software on the shared network. Another employee told a neighboring stake president what kind of pornography I was viewing, and he called my stake president. After consulting with our area presidency, he released me within the week "for medical reasons" and "for my own benefit." I truly was a depressed mental and emotional wreck, but I couldn't accept the medical release as anything short of complete failure.

I was brokenhearted, devastated. I had tried so hard. The promised calling was sometimes the only thing that had kept me from going over the deep end, from giving into my homosexual desires. I felt deserted. I felt like I was Laban—it was best to throw me away so I didn't destroy the entire ward. I felt that my leaders were probably right in their decision, but I let it destroy me. I felt that I had nothing to live for. I sank further into depression, began to drink heavily, and spiraled down. I was extremely fragile, spiritually and emotionally.

I began to rely on pornography even more to get me through the difficult times. It was a release, a drug. I would drink to take away the pain, not really knowing or admitting what the root of my depression and anxiety was all about. With the loss of the Spirit, I began to doubt and to visit anti-Mormon websites. Over time I totally lost my testimony. I no longer believed in the existence of God, an afterlife, or anything spiritual. Everything that I understood about God and religion I had learned through the lens of Mormonism. With that foundation gone, I no longer felt there was a reason to resist my "natural man" (Mosiah 3:19). I wish I would have had the desire to do good just for the sake of being a good human being or to honor the marital covenants I had made, but I didn't.

One night while out of town and inebriated, I engaged in activities that put my Church membership at risk. I gave in to my carnal desires. I didn't feel any remorse. I didn't feel *anything*. Nothing mattered. There was no life after this, Mormonism was a myth, and I was playing the game. I continued to serve in a Church calling to keep the peace at home. I rationalized that, yes, it was hypocritical, but it was only a game. Despite my disbelief, I didn't try to force it on my wife or family. I continued to read, pray, and attend meetings with them. I knew the Church was good for them, and I did my best to support them in their Church and school activities.

During this period of time, I had made a good friend in the ward who could sense something was happening to me. I guess I wasn't hiding things as well as I had thought. He picked me up one night, and we went for a drive to talk. I finally opened up and told him my darkest secrets. He must have tipped off my wife that something was wrong, because soon afterward she came right out and asked me when the last time was I had sex with anyone besides her. I sat down, took a deep breath, and told her everything. She wept, but, being the wonderful companion she is, she wanted to help me. I confessed to our stake president with my wife by my side. A disciplinary council was held, and I was disfellowshipped from the Church. My self-respect was in shreds, and I was ashamed and embarrassed to tell my children that their father was an alcoholic addicted to pornography. I felt I had failed in my most important roles of husband and father. It would be a few years before I found the strength to tell my children that their father had homosexual desires and had acted upon them.

When I was first disfellowshipped, I felt like a leper, like everyone knew and was watching my every move. I no longer felt that I belonged in the Church, which had once been such an integral part of my life. After a while, I came to accept my status and was even relieved that no one had expectations of me. I didn't have to feel guilty about taking the sacrament—I couldn't; I didn't feel anger or frustration about temple attendance—I couldn't go; I didn't have to worry about a calling—I couldn't have one; I didn't have to participate in meetings—I couldn't; I wouldn't be asked to use the priesthood—I wasn't allowed to. Being disfellowshipped became a comfort zone for me, and when, after six months of praying, reading scriptures, staying clean, and keeping the Word of Wisdom produced no perceived spiritual results, I returned to my old ways without feeling remorse.

Later that summer while we were out of town together, I told my wife that I had returned to my former sins. I was so tired of living a double life that I needed to come clean. For the first time she briefly reacted with anger. She cried, and I could not bear the pain in her eyes. I decided then and there that I would never hurt her like that again. Something had to drastically change—me. I promised her that I would never lie to her again. I then asked her what she would do if I fell again. After all, my track record wasn't all that great. My way of coping with my internalization of everything was to drown it with alcohol or por-nography. They had been my best friends for years.

Her response made all the difference in our marriage and literally saved my life. She hugged me and said, "We will just start over again." She truly understood the meaning of charity and eternal companion-ship, of bearing one another's burdens. How could I ask for more? I now felt confident that I could always be fully honest with her.

Prior to this time we shared much together—but not the heavy burden I bore, not the self-hate, not the insecurities, not the daily temptations I faced. I had told myself she wasn't strong enough to deal with my inner turmoil and that it wasn't fair to share with her my doubts about faith. I had to be strong. I had to hold in all my feelings. I could share them with no one—until the weight of my burden crushed me, and the man I had so carefully constructed broke into tiny pieces.

And now there I lay, all my secrets exposed to the light of day. Surely she would abandon me. Surely she would be repulsed and seek a spouse more worthy of the divine woman she had become. But no! She saw something in me that I could not. She remained true, and, instead of throwing away our marriage, she wanted to strengthen it. How could this be? Why would she do it? She was still young, smart, beautiful, fun, and talented, but she chose me. She not only wanted to be my wife, but she also wanted to be my best friend. Finally broken and humbled, I tore down my facade of a fictitious life of strength. Now I could share everything with her.

When I felt insecure, when I needed a drink, when my homosexual desires rose from attraction to desire to seek out pornography, when financial pressure weighed me down, I turned to her and found peace, friendship, love, strength, and acceptance. My only regret—and hers— was that it took me so long to *truly* let her into my life. I had foolishly thought I had to save her the pain but, ultimately, I had caused her more pain.

With the mandated one-year waiting period approaching, everyone expected that I would be ready and eager to be refellowshipped. The truth was that I had no desire to come back, and because of that, I again found myself standing at a crossroad in my life. I perceived only three choices: (1) I could feign a desire to return, remain living a double life, lie about it, and take my chances that I could pull off the charade; (2) I could tell my wife, loved ones, friends, and leaders that I could not take it anymore, leave them, the Church, and fully embrace a gay identity and lifestyle; or (3) I could try to make my way back to the Lord, try to regain my faith, repent, and try again to live the teachings of the gospel.

To some, the choice may seem obvious. Unfortunately, to me it didn't. I tried to imagine the ramifications of each choice for those I loved most and for me. I ran various scenarios through my mind, trying to rationalize each option. The easiest to rule out was option 1. I was tired of serving two masters, tired of being a hypocrite, tired of living a double life. For my own sake and for the sake of those around me, I vowed to eliminate that choice. The remaining choices directly opposed each other, but at least I would be living an open, honest life. The allure of embracing a homosexual lifestyle was strong. I would finally be able to fill the perceived hole in my core that needed male intimacy.

The third choice was obviously the one my family wanted me to take, but I felt it would be the hardest for me, especially because I no longer believed in God or organized religion. I could not drive by the temple without feeling anger. I viewed the Church and its leaders with contempt. I felt that it was the Church's fault for tearing me apart and threatening to tear my family apart. I resented that, if I wanted to have a significant role in the future of my family, I would have to embrace a church that I had come to despise. I felt that choosing the path leading back to the Church was like trying to talk myself into believing in Santa Claus again.

A month before my scheduled return to the high council, the stake president pulled me out of Sunday School and took me for a drive in his truck. He asked me if I was ready. I told him no. I had no testimony and no desire to obtain one. He expressed his love for me, and I know he was sincere. He promised me that if I wanted to regain my faith, it didn't have to take long. He cited examples of several in the scriptures who had rather rapid changes of heart. He encouraged me to give the Lord an opportunity to enter my heart again.

I spent a lot of time alone trying to decide what to do, because whatever path I chose, I was going to give it my all and never look back. My overwhelming love for my family and my desire to fully participate in their lives finally won the day. Within my family I find my greatest happiness, my greatest joy. I could not bear the thought of distancing myself from them. I was committed to them, and they deserved a righteous husband and father. Some said abandoning church and family and embracing my "natural" and "authentic" self was the best option. Sometimes it was really tempting to at least leave the Church, but I knew I could never abandon my wife and children.

With my decision made to stay with my family and open myself again to believe the gospel, I knew what I was giving up and what I had to do to make the journey home possible. I knew that I had to drastically change my lifestyle to accommodate a sincere search for truth. I had to give up my addictions to alcohol and pornography. I started getting up earlier, while the house was quiet, so I could have time to study, ponder, and search for answers.

I was so far away spiritually that I had to want to want—to desire to desire—to know if God existed, if Christ was my Savior, and if the gospel was true. I had to open my heart and mind enough to consider the possibility that they might indeed exist and that the gospel might be real. As part of my long and humbling process of regaining my faith, I eventually realized that I *could* trust the Spirit's whisperings to my soul. Sometimes the Spirit was the *only* thing I could trust.

The steps were slow and gradual. I first started with God. Prayers were simple and childlike. "God, I don't know if you exist, but if you do, please help me to know." Eventually I did feel at peace with the idea that He does exist. My next step was Jesus Christ. Was He the Son of God? Was He my Savior? Was the Atonement real? Could Buddha or Allah or someone else also lead me back to God? Why did it have to be Jesus? I opened my heart ever so slowly, barely cracking it open. It was as if the Lord were eagerly awaiting, ready to fill my soul with the peace I sought. The answer came quietly, peacefully to my mind. I knew that He was my Savior. No question.

And finally, what of the Church and Joseph Smith? I honestly couldn't get my mind around all my doubts about the Church. I believed in the gospel but not necessarily in the Church. For a time I had to put my doubts and questions on the shelf and concentrate on what I did believe. I did believe in God, Jesus Christ, the gospel, and the Book of Mormon. That was definite progress and would have to suffice for a while. Father was patient with me, and over time my faith in modern prophets and the restored Church returned.

My testimony today is much simpler and yet more solid than ever before. Although I ultimately returned to the faith of my fathers, my testimony is now *mine,* not one inherited, but a sacred gift, heaven-sent to one of Father's humble sons seeking truth.

Not all my concerns were answered that fall evening as I knelt in the temple and poured out my heart to my Heavenly Father. I was back in full fellowship, but weighty questions yet remained. While I now had a testimony of the reality of God and Jesus Christ and of the divine role of the restored Church, was there place for me in Father's plan and within His church as a man who experienced attractions to other men? Was there purpose in all the difficulties I had experienced? Would I ever feel comfortable participating in church, where so many knew my deepest secrets? Would I ever regain the respect of my wife and children? More important, would I ever know if I was truly acceptable before the Lord? How would I know that He loves me when I had such a difficult time loving myself?

The sweet, simple answer that did come in sweeping peace that penetrated my soul with warm reassurance was that I was indeed loved, understood, and accepted by my Father. In a way that I don't fully comprehend, but for which I am grateful, the Atonement of the Savior swept away the shame and pain of my sins. I am no longer troubled with concerns about others' perceptions of me. I am secure with the knowledge of a higher approval.

I know that God lives. I am one of His sons. I am created in His image. I have the same divine parentage, eternal potential, and promised blessings as any other child of God. The purifying and enabling power of the Atonement is extended to me. The blessings afforded through membership in The Church of Jesus Christ of Latter-day Saints belong to me. It is not the church of the Book of Mormon, the church of Joseph Smith, or the church of married heterosexuals. It is the Church of *Jesus Christ,* and He said, "Come unto me, *all* ye that labour and are heavy laden, and I will give you rest" (Matthew 11:28;

emphasis added), and "Learn of me, and listen to my words; walk in the meekness of my Spirit, and you shall have peace in me" (D&C 19:23).

I feel that peace. I know who I am and where I belong. I am home.

A Christ-Centered Gender Identity

John Alden

John Alden (pseudonym) lives in Texas with his wife and three children and currently serves in the Church as a ward executive secretary. He has a job that takes him from home more than he would like. In his free time, he loves playing board games with his kids and watching reruns of detective shows with his wife.

By all public appearances, I am a nauseatingly "typical" Mormon. I am a husband, a father, and a lifelong active member of the Church who was married in the temple. I was born in the covenant to fine parents who have always been strong in their faith, and I received my first spiritual witness of the truthfulness of the Book of Mormon at about seven years old, when I prayed and asked with a child's faith if it was true. Since that day, my testimony has never failed me. I received the Aaronic Priesthood at age twelve and the Melchizedek Priesthood at eighteen, and I entered the Missionary Training Center the very month I turned nineteen.

Later I married a sweet young lady who had written to me, as a friend, throughout my mission. I have a 72-hour kit on a shelf above the minivan, a wheat grinder in the cupboard, and unused cans of powdered milk in the pantry. I vote conservative, avoid consumer debt, and grumble about taxes. I've taught Gospel Doctrine, been a ward missionary, and served in Young Men, Sunday School, and elders quorum presidencies. I have the *right* number of children, the *right* education, the *right* job, the *right* type of home, the *right* type of car, and the *right* calling. I've even lived on the Wasatch Front and received some of my education at Brigham Young University.

But I am *different,* and not in the way you may be thinking: I'm not even remotely attracted to men. I'm different because my first memories are laden with a desperate, oppressive desire to be a girl—a desire that has persisted throughout my life. This condition is variously called gender identity disorder (GID), gender dysphoria, transgenderism, or gender confusion, and a person with this condition may be referred to as transgendered or transsexual. Use of those terms can vary both clinically and popularly, particularly with respect to whether they refer to people who have had so-called sex-reassignment surgery (SRS). I have not had and will not have such a surgery, and I prefer to avoid labels. I will merely say that I feel and have felt a persistent and pressing desire to be female, and I choose a nonsurgical path for coping with that desire.

I want to share my experience for two reasons. First, I hope that other *typical* Mormons will discover that this is more than just fodder for trashy daytime television. This is a *real* issue that *real* people—maybe even one of your own—deal with. Second, I want to share with others who struggle with GID the hope I have gained. I too have felt the terrible dichotomy between faith identity and gender identity. I testify that the two can be reconciled, not by diagnostic manuals or the learning of men but by learning where those feelings fit within God's plan and purposes.

Childhood

Before I grasped even the most basic physiological differences between girls and me, I wanted to be one of *them.* Little girls got to wear pretty dresses and cute little buckle shoes and bows in their hair. They got to play makeup and dress-up and mommy. I wanted all of that. When I was four or five years old, I would sneak into my mother's closet and dress up in her clothes and shoes. I fantasized about having a magic closet that could instantly make me a girl, and then I could wear those things all the time in front of everybody.

Of course, at five years old, I wasn't very sneaky, so my parents knew what I was doing. At first my mother didn't think much of it. Kids dress up all the time. But the fact that I was trying to hide it bothered her. It made her think that *I* thought I was doing something wrong. So eventually my father sat down to talk to me. I cannot credit either of my parents with a perfect understanding of my condition, but they are good, righteous people who love me and want the best for me. So my father's tone was not angry or accusatory. He simply explained, as simply as he could, that boys are not supposed to wear girls' clothes. I think he even said it was a sin. In my youthful trust I accepted that, so I pushed it all as far back in my mind as I could. For years I simply pretended it wasn't there.

Then I became a teenager. Puberty and adolescence are confusing even for a "normal" teenager, so you can imagine how they affected me. As my hormones started to change, I found that the feelings from my childhood returned, but stronger. Even as I found myself more *attracted* to girls, I found myself wanting more and more desperately to *be* one.

This was a dark and difficult time of my life that I do not dwell on. I maintained the proper image of the good kid everybody thought I was, but I felt filthy and full of self-loathing, guilt, and shame. I started dressing up in my mom's clothes again, but now I was more careful because now I *knew* it was wrong. I was never caught, though in hindsight I wish I had been. Carrying that burden alone was terrible, but I was too ashamed to share it with anybody. After a couple of years, I managed, through whatever quantum of will I possessed—and, I believe, much undeserved help from the Spirit—to stop. Again, I learned to suppress my feelings.

Mission and Marriage

For years I resisted the promptings of the Spirit to share my burden. It wasn't until I was in the Missionary Training Center, where the Spirit is overwhelming, that I could no longer resist its promptings. I finally opened up to my branch president—a good, loving man. More than anything, he was sorry that I had unnecessarily carried this burden alone for so long. He assured me that many teenagers feel confusion as they sort out their identities. So that was it, I told myself—just youthful teenage confusion that many people feel. I was sure that everything had been resolved.

I faithfully served the Lord for those two years and returned home feeling honorable and clean. I felt that I was finally the person I wanted to be. I even felt comfortable enough to talk to my parents about what I had put myself through as a teenager. But by this time we were talking about a problem I *used* to have. There was, I was sure, nothing more to worry about.

I started back at school, and in time I was blessed to marry the perfect bride in the temple. I cannot say enough good about my wife. She is kind, faithful, patient, and loving. She is an anchor to my soul and a constant source of good in my life. Ours had been a storybook romance better than any I had ever read, and I knew that all was now well. I felt no need to tell her about my erstwhile feelings. That was all in a distant past.

I remember with vivid horror the moment they all came back, suddenly and aggressively, about six months after our marriage. It was late, and my wife had already gone to bed. I had stayed up to study but was wasting time playing a computer game when I was suddenly seized with an awful, dark panic. All of the former, desperate feelings returned, but they were magnified, darker, and more disturbing. But again, I didn't tell anybody. I spent several more years suffering in silence, hiding in shame as I had done as a youth. Because I was not *acting* on my feelings, I reasoned that there was no need to tell anybody. It was just a private struggle. I would improve, repent, and move on like "normal" people did.

For years, even as I put on a public show that all was well, I was rotting away from the inside. I felt dark and empty. I was miserable being a man, and though I wanted very much to make myself a woman, I was terrified of the repercussions. I hated myself but I loved my wife, and I couldn't bear to lose her. I was scared and lonely, sometimes suicidal.

And still I kept it to myself. But over a very long time, the Spirit again worked to soften my proud heart. Eventually, I realized that I absolutely *could not* do this alone. I needed to get this out, not because it was a sin I had to confess but because I simply needed help. Things were getting worse, not better. I was headed for a catastrophic collision, and this was going to come out somehow. I could choose the terms, or it would choose its own terms.

Enlisting Support

Even after I had decided to open up to my wife, I could never find the right time. There was always some excuse for delay. But finally, shortly after our fifth wedding anniversary, I resolved to just do it. I sat with my wife on our bed and slowly, with tears and averted eyes, told her what I was. She listened to my story in stunned silence and hardly spoke a word for two days. More than anything, I was scared that she was going to just take the children, get on an airplane, and leave forever.

Finally, she wanted to know just one thing. Was I going to someday decide that it was too much, that I could no longer fight it, and run off and have surgery? Was I going to abandon her and the children for a new life as a woman? Even in the depths of my confusion, some things were clear to me. As much as I disliked the fact, I knew, by abundant temporal and spiritual evidence, that I was male. I knew that God had work for me to do as a man. I knew that if I were to *transition,* I would displease God. And I knew that I loved my wife, that I could not envision any life here or in eternity without her. So I promised her, in all sincerity, that I *never would.* However deep my darkness or depression, whatever the toll in pain or misery, on my honor, *I never would.* Angel that she is, she has stayed by my side ever since.

After speaking to my wife, I felt a huge weight lifted off of my shoulders. I was then able to call and talk to my parents and let them know what was going on. They were supportive, as always—especially my dear mother, with whom I have always been close. Sharing my burden with people I could trust lightened it. I was finally on the long, slow road to redemption, a road that I still walk. To be sure, there was still "an effectual struggle to be made" (Mosiah 7:18), but at least I was going in the right direction.

I do not say lightly that my trials were not over. I still struggled. Things came to a head about six months later when work obligations separated me from my wife for a time. She is my anchor and quieting influence. I don't do well without her. So when we had to be separated, I started losing my grip. Feeling desperate, I looked on the Internet to see if I could find others who were like me. What I found was a great many ex-Mormons who declared how happy they were when they left the Church and decided to transition. I found sites with advice on everything from purchasing and padding bras to sizing clothes to doing makeup to rating surgeons. I wallowed in these message boards for a few days. It was exhilarating to find others like me, a *sisterhood* with a common struggle that would surely understand. I wanted so much to be a part of their world, but I could see where this was heading and how unhealthy it was for me.

I finally decided to speak with my bishop. He gave me some good counsel, and then anointing me with oil, he promised me by the Spirit that I would someday be healed. He also advised me that LDS Family Services might be able to help and gave me the name of a counselor. Unfortunately, circumstances delayed the appointment, and we soon completed an out-of-state move.

Once I was back with my wife, I felt better, so I just kept going for a while. But eventually I started feeling overwhelmed again. With my wife's support, I spoke with our new bishop. I explained that I wasn't coming to confess any grave sin but that I was struggling with these feelings. Our bishop was a man of mighty faith, and, though he didn't understand the problem (at first he just thought I was telling him I was gay), he comforted and strengthened me and gave me a blessing. He also referred me to LDS Family Services.

I wish I could say that the good brother I met with at Family Services had all the answers, but he didn't. He didn't even really know what GID was. I found myself having to explain that, no, I'm not attracted to men, and no, I'm not looking at pornography on the Internet. But even with limited clinical insight, he did have some good advice that got me going in the right direction.

One of his suggestions was to get a notebook and start writing. The notebook was not for sharing with anybody, not even with him. It was just for me to write down what I was feeling, to get those feelings out. The things I wrote at first were confused, dark, and depressing. But writing was like poison extracted from a wound. Eventually, I started writing more positive things. Writing my feelings helped me process them and let them out so that I didn't feel like a pressure cooker about to explode.

I followed up my writing with other positive behaviors. Countless priesthood blessings from my father and others have been a source of strength and insight. And in late 2007, still feeling very alone, I again looked to see if I could find an online group—but one that sustained the Church. I couldn't find one, and I felt impressed to start my own blog, which allowed me to set the tone. Soon thereafter I started to find others who were looking for the same thing. Eventually, a few of us started a discussion group under the umbrella of North Star. Our numbers are still few, but the feeling of community is sweet sustenance indeed because we have felt so alone for so long.

An Anchor to the Soul

An important aspect of my journey has been defining my gender role. The foundation for this task is my testimony of Jesus Christ. I testify that we are led by living prophets, who speak for Him. I also testify of the principle of personal revelation. When possible I like to model my behavior after my righteous predecessors. But Elder Richard G. Scott has taught that "today . . . such a course of action is often not available to us. . . . [This] creates a condition where we, of necessity, are more dependent upon the Spirit to guide us through the vicissitudes of life."[7]

Having little scriptural or doctrinal direction dealing specifically with my condition, I have had to build on a foundation of revealed truth and rely on personal revelation to teach me how those foundational truths apply to my situation. One difficulty is that while the Church unequivocally discourages SRS, the spiritual consequences are not always clear. My plea is that when we meet those who have had SRS, our invitations for them to join us in the fellowship of the Saints will be no less fervent. I hope we can see them as children of God and let the Lord and inspired priesthood leaders see to the states of their souls.

I affirm as a foundational truth what the prophets have taught: each person "is a beloved spirit son or daughter of heavenly parents" and that "gender is an essential characteristic of individual premortal, mortal, and eternal identity and purpose."[8] My gender is not something I can alter at will. But it is also not defined by ever-changing societal norms and expectations that would have me watch too much football and behave boorishly to my wife. I relish Elder Jeffrey R. Holland's invitation that if you need guidance regarding your gender identity, "whatever other steps you may need to take to resolve these concerns, come *first* to the gospel of Jesus Christ."[9] The revealed word of God is the touchstone by which I judge my actions and my personal revelations.

"Peace I Leave With You"

As I've seen postoperative transsexuals fervently testify that they have found peace only by accepting and embracing their new gender role, at times I've felt envious. How could I find peace when the only visible path of peace was closed? Over time I learned that I was seeking the wrong kind of peace. In the latter part of his Gospel, John shares some deeply personal final instructions that Jesus gave to His Apostles. There, with majestic certainty, Christ promised: "Peace I leave with you, my peace I give unto you: not as the world giveth, give I unto you. Let not your heart be troubled, neither let it be afraid" (John 14:27). The Apostles were shortly to be persecuted, beaten, betrayed, falsely accused, and slain. James was beheaded; John was exiled and lived to see the Church fall into apostasy; Thomas was purportedly martyred in a foreign land while preaching the gospel; and according to tradition,

Peter, the chief Apostle, was crucified upside down at his own insistence, considering himself unworthy to suffer the same death as the Lord. Was this the Lord's promised peace? It was, in fact.

The world's peace is freedom from strife, the kind that comes, for example, from spending mortality in a comfortable gender role. But freedom from strife was emphatically *not* the Apostles' peace. The peace that the Lord promised them is a more profound peace. It is the peace that comes in the *midst* of strife, not in its absence. It comes from the assurance of the Spirit, granted to those who make and keep sacred covenants, that their lives are pleasing to God. It flows from the Holy Spirit of Promise, which is the promise of eternal life that "the Father sheds forth upon all those who are just and true" (D&C 76:53).

A profound lesson about this peace came at a time when I felt that my faith and my feelings were at interminable odds. I knew vaguely that I could not feel like this forever, that in some post-resurrection life I would surely feel okay with being male, but even that knowledge felt oppressive. It seemed a sort of Orwellian promise that, although I would be eternally imprisoned, I would be happy in my prison. I felt so trapped between my faith and my gender that my thoughts at times turned suicidal. I couldn't continue to live like this.

Then, on what seemed the blackest night of my life, my wife and I quarreled over something unimportant. Feeling sorry for myself, I retreated to the couch to pout alone. There it seemed that demons were raging around me, shouting that I was foolish to keep trying. She didn't care. She hated me as much as I hated myself. What did my promises to her matter if she hated me? *Take up a knife,* they demanded, *and destroy yourself.* Or if not, at least take up a knife and destroy those parts that cause you so much pain. I cried to the Lord for relief and finally fell into an uneasy sleep. Shortly after this I resigned myself to the proposition that it was simply my lot to be miserable in this life. But perhaps, I thought, I could with my mortal misery purchase an eternal complacency.

Immediately, I heard a strong rebuke in my mind: "Men are, that they might have joy" (2 Nephi 2:25). Living the gospel was *not* to be a source of mortal pain. President David O. McKay stated, "The principal reason the Church was organized [is] to make life sweet to-day, to give contentment to the heart today, to bring salvation today. . . . Today is part of eternity."[10] As I have continued to search, I have learned that my peace, both mortal and eternal, will come neither from the feelings being removed, nor from transitioning. Instead, my peace will come from learning that these seemingly incongruous feelings have a divinely appointed purpose in God's plan for me.

Personal Revelation

One evening about three years ago, the Spirit taught me clearly that I *needed* the constant nourishment of at least thirty minutes of daily scripture study, and I was promised specific blessings if I would get it. But it must be complete and consistent—I couldn't miss a single day, ever, and it had to be no less than a full thirty minutes. I have done it every day since, and this consistent, measured spiritual nourishment has been essential to my progress. As I have studied, I have gained precious knowledge "line upon line" (D&C 98:12) and learned things "I never had supposed" (Moses 1:10).[11]

Trivial as it may seem to those who haven't wrestled with this issue, one profound personal revelation has been that I *am* male. Despite all my feelings to the contrary, I know that I am a son of God. I believe that anybody who sincerely questions his or her own true gender identity can come to a similar knowledge one way or the other, though the earnest seeker must be careful not to confuse emotionally invested personal *preference* with personal *revelation*.

That knowledge has been foundational because I could not progress if I were constantly casting about in a gender-ambiguous darkness. Firmly anchored in that knowledge, I have, over time, gained other insights. The Spirit has incrementally unfolded to my view a beautiful model of truth in which my internal feelings interlock perfectly with revealed truth. And I know that what the Lord has done for me, He can do for others. If He can show me how all of my righteous desires can be fulfilled, how every pure yearning of my heart has a place in His plan, and how He can lift me out of confusion by teaching me things "I never had supposed," He can do the same for you.

I hope that others are wiser than I was—that they will find the peace without the years of darkness and depression. I can testify of the sweet fruits of truth and revelation, and I know that God is ever willing to share them with any who earnestly seek. I am no longer envious of SRS. I would not now trade the knowledge I have been given for living as a poor approximation of a woman. And I no longer even want those feelings to go away. They have helped shape my eternal identity and purpose. And though I still have stressful phases of yearning and anxiety, I feel that God has truly turned my weakness into a strength (see Ether 12:27). Some of the most deeply spiritual moments of my life have arisen from my pondering on this subject. What was once the greatest source of despair in my life has now become a fountain of knowledge, blessings, and peace.

"Thy Will Be Done": Living with HIV/AIDS in Faith and Brotherhood

Kenneth Hoover

Kenneth Hoover was born and raised in the Church in the California Bay Area. He served in the Puerto Rico San Juan Mission from 1988 to 1990. He worked many years in telecommunications, eventually as a 911 dispatcher for the California Highway Patrol. Kenneth is very much a family man. Although he is single and has no children, he loves and spends his spare time with his sixteen nieces and nephews. He finds joy and peace in playing the piano and reading.

"No man can serve two masters: for either he will hate
the one, and love the other; or else he will hold to the one,
and despise the other. Ye cannot serve God and mammon."
—MATTHEW 6:24

I have often wondered why we have the experiences we do during our tenure here on earth. How do our trials and tribulations become ours? Is it merely by chance, purely random? Divinely orchestrated? Or do we bring challenges upon ourselves by and through our surroundings and choices?

I have always been a person of faith, and I've always felt especially sensitive to the whisperings of the Spirit, having a keen sense of right and wrong. It's almost been a physical feeling for me. I've learned to seek the Spirit as the guiding force in my life. In addition to this keen sensitivity to the Spirit, I've always had a testimony of the gospel of Jesus Christ. I don't remember ever doubting the truthfulness of the gospel.

As the oldest of five children, I was brought up in a devout Latter-day Saint home. All four of my siblings are strong and active in the Church and are married with families of their own. I knew from a very early age, however, that my struggles in life would be different than those of my sister and three brothers. Along with my deep spiritual intuition was another force that felt just as strong and bidding inside me: my desire to understand my attraction to the same sex. I was told by my mother that at the age of two I was molested by a neighborhood boy. Maybe that had something to do with it, and why I've struggled with a twisted sense of sexuality from as early as I can remember. Almost from the time I became a teenager, I was constantly visiting with an LDS counselor in addition to either my bishop or stake president.

I have often struggled with how natural and easy it seemed to be for my siblings to progress toward healthy heterosexual relationships with eternal marriages and families, while I, on the other hand, have always been so preoccupied with sex and my sexual identity that marriage always seemed like a distant dream. Though I don't have any recollections of my first abuse, I had another sexual encounter with an adult when I was twelve. It was at that time that I was introduced to pornography. From then on, it just seemed as though my whole being was consumed with thoughts of sex. I have now come to understand and see how such experiences can affect healthy sexual development and identity.

When I was fourteen, my father was called to be the bishop of our ward. I'll never forget how overwhelmed and fearful I was with the thought of having to go to my father for repentance. I remember already needing to speak with my bishop prior to my dad's calling. I just sat there shaking my head when our stake president came to our house to extend the call. I allowed it to put a wall between my father and me for a season.

My parents have always been keenly aware of my exploits, and, like any parents who want the best for their children, they thought it would give me much-needed strength and motivation if I had my patriarchal blessing. Perhaps it would give me better insight into my struggles. So when I was sixteen, we set up an appointment with our stake patriarch, and I got my blessing. In addition to other guidance and counsel, there was a warning, one that has been embedded in my mind to this day. I was told that if I was to "fall into the way of sin and evil, the Holy Spirit will withdraw from you and you will wander with the weak, with a lack of hope and faith."

Following that blessing, I was able to get my life in order. I served an honorable full-time mission, but it wasn't long after getting home from my mission that I began to understand and feel the full effect of those words.

Meeting a Partner

When I got home from my mission, life seemed easy. I had established patterns and habits that helped me stay close to the Spirit. I went back to school, started dating, and was even contemplating marriage to a beautiful young lady. I knew, however, that I still struggled with my sexual identity and would likely not be faithful. I have always been upfront and honest with the girls I've dated about my attraction to men. I had expressed to the young lady that I needed to know what the feelings inside me and a gay lifestyle were all about. She agreed to let me go "find out." So we put things on hold but remained in contact.

It wasn't long before I again started indulging in the self-destructive habit of pornography. Within two years after returning from an honorable mission, I was cruising the San Francisco gay nightlife. My frame of mind at the time was that I was just checking out the lifestyle—to get it out of my system, so to speak. During my second weekend going to a gay club, I met a guy named Steven. We were both there with mutual friends. He and I hit it off immediately and talked for hours that first night. He told me how busy he was with his work, and, having just come out of a relationship, he wasn't ready to jump into a new one. Because I saw this phase as only temporary—I was just checking things out and was still keeping in contact with my LDS girlfriend somewhat and wasn't looking for a relationship, either—I told Steven that first night about the Church, my beliefs in the gospel, and my love for my family.

Almost immediately it was apparent that both of us had very strong emotional feelings for each other. I went home with Steven that night, and, though we didn't do anything sexual, the following day was one I'll never forget. I felt such a powerful connection with Steven the previous evening that I made a conscious decision that day that I was going to give a relationship with him a try. I wasn't expecting to *fall* for this guy, but I had. I felt a connection and oneness with him that I had never felt with anyone else. It was clearly a defining moment in that I knew I was now crossing a line in my relationship with Heavenly Father.

I planned to spend that night with Steven, and on the drive over to his place, I had one of the most profound experiences while praying I've ever had. While discussing with Heavenly Father my plans regarding a relationship with Steven, and the choice I was about to make in going to his place, I broke into tears and sobbed as I prayed. I felt the Spirit bear witness to me that it was my decision to embark upon this new lifestyle, but that in doing so, I was forsaking the promises and covenants I had made. I cried as I told Him that I still needed to find out for myself what the gay lifestyle was about. And I went—"into the night," as they say.

My family had an incredibly difficult time with everything. For the first couple of years no one in my family knew about my lifestyle except my parents, and I did most of my talking about it with my mother. After a while, though, my siblings began asking my parents what was up with me. I guess my parents had hoped it would just be a phase, and so they didn't bother telling them because my siblings were all still quite young at the time.

As my relationship with Steven grew and I spent more and more time with him, my involvement with my family lessened. My weekly Sunday visits home became less frequent as I found other things to do on Sunday. My Church activity dwindled as well. Instead of going to young single adult dances, I went dancing at gay clubs in the city. While everything seemed fun and new, it wasn't an easy transformation into my new lifestyle because I continued to feel the pull of the Spirit.

For a time, whenever I would drive over the San Francisco–Oakland Bay Bridge and see the city, I would feel sick to my stomach. I decided, though, that since I was no longer living by the rules I used to, what did it matter if I obeyed *any* of them? Almost immediately I started drinking alcohol and smoking marijuana. I didn't want to feel the physical pangs of the Spirit and of my conscience, and those substances helped numb the pain. My life became a fog. For a long time it almost felt like I needed to get high just to deal with my reality.

Contracting HIV/AIDS

Over the course of the next two years dating Steven, I made lots of changes. But I had no idea how much a person's life could *really* change until the day we found out we had HIV. For those two years we were together almost daily. We had become so close and familiar with each other that I knew almost the moment I saw the lump on the side of his neck that he—and therefore *we*—had the HIV virus. Now, mind you, back in 1994 AIDS was still killing people at an alarming rate. We had known and attended the funeral services of a few people who had already passed away from the disease, so when we received confirmation that we did indeed have it, I felt a sense of panic as I've never felt in all my life.

I first wondered how I was going to tell my parents, and that conversation turned out to be one of the most difficult I've ever had with them. At first they were angry. It took many more conversations and more time spent together before the sting of that conversation diminished. For a long time they just wanted me to leave Steven and come back to the Church. It wasn't until I had a very emotional and passionate talk with my mom that my parents began to understand that I wasn't leaving Steven—especially now that we were sick! That was a turning point for us. It took some time and getting used to, but they did learn to embrace and love him as well.

I was also faced with having to tell the LDS girl who was still somewhat waiting in the wings. We had remained in contact, and she still had hopes that she and I would still be together one day. I remember telling her that I was now HIV positive. I don't think it was until that moment that she realized to what depth I had fallen. She just stared at me with tears in her eyes and said with pain and hurt in her voice: "Damn you, Ken. Damn you!" As painful as that was, I knew that I would not have been faithful to her had I married her earlier.

In the years that followed, Steven and I went into a state of depressed denial and engaged in self-destructive behavior. We started doing any street drug we could just to numb the pain of our reality. It wasn't until 1996, two years after our diagnosis, that we began to take care of ourselves physically. We had initially gone to see a few doctors and tried some of the HIV drugs then available, but they ended up making us more ill, so we stopped and for two years didn't take any more medications.

By spring of 1996 we were both diagnosed with full-blown AIDS. As I was driving to work one morning, I heard a radio advertisement about medical marijuana and about a place in the city that catered to those with terminal illnesses like AIDS. That afternoon, Steven and I found our way over there and, with our letters of diagnosis, we signed up. We began to meet a whole new crowd of gay folk: the sick ones. It was a sobering look into the lives of those who had been ravaged by this disease—and ultimately, by the behaviors that led them there. For the next couple of years we spent a lot of time with this new community we so related with. Over time I began to recognize that the warning in my patriarchal blessing had very much become my reality.

Summer of 1998

The years of being sick and dealing with HIV/AIDS certainly took their toll on us. Though we both have developed opportunistic infections, Steven fared the worst. He was first plagued with peripheral neuropathy—damage to the nerves of the peripheral nervous system—in the fall of 1996 when one of the first HIV medications he took fried all the nerve endings in his legs. He was given every type of pain medication available to try to ease his pain. The combination of the pain and the constant sickness took a terrible toll on his body. By 1998 his body couldn't take it anymore and began to fail. It was a scary time in our lives. We hadn't taken care of ourselves as we could and should have, and options had run out for Steven. He had been on every AIDS drug available. I was mortified. Here was the man I loved with all my heart—the man for whom I had basically given up everything that was ever important to me—and he was dying.

It was then that Steven again asked me about my faith and my beliefs in God and the afterlife. I turned to the only source of truth and comfort I had ever known, and that was my faith in the gospel, the Church, and the priesthood. Steven began studying the scriptures, and my family started playing a bigger role in our lives. Steven had been invited to family dinners on Sundays and began to see and appreciate the interaction I have with my family. He felt the Spirit on many occasions.

My mother was a seminary teacher at the time, and the class was having its year-end fireside. She invited Steven and me to attend. I remember sitting on the back row of the chapel that I grew up in, and there was Steven, my gay partner, sitting next to me. It seems incredible, but it ended up being a very spiritual meeting. The Spirit was strong. I remember turning to Steven and seeing tears in his eyes. I said to him, "Do you feel that?" He said he did. "That's the Holy Ghost," I said, "the Spirit communicating to your spirit. That's how I know the things I do." He was taken aback and impressed by the experience. I too began feeling the warm, gentle whispering of the Spirit to my soul again.

I remember Steven telling my mom as he gave her a hug that he had never felt anything like that before and that he wanted to be baptized. Both my mother and her friend Bobbie who was there said in unison, "We can make that happen!" That night after we had returned to our home, he said to me that he wanted to take the missionary discussions. I could hardly believe what I was hearing. Here was someone I thought I had given all this up for, and he wanted the same thing! I had long given up hope of ever returning to the Church, and now the man I loved wanted to learn more about the things I already knew to be true. It was surreal.

Over the next few weeks two LDS missionaries came into our home to teach the missionary lessons to Steven. I almost had a sense of guilt as I sat and listened to these young men teach and bear their testimonies not only to Steven but to me as well. I had done the same thing not long before in Puerto Rico, teaching the gospel to those who were lost and searching. I began meeting with our bishop and stake president and had many heart-to-heart talks. President Pimentel had always been a good friend. I spent many hours with him discussing my relationship with Steven. I went over every specific thing that could and couldn't be done within the boundaries of gospel teachings in redefining our relationship.

It was a very sad moment, full of tears from both of us, when Steven and I had *the conversation* and discussed that in order for us to move forward in the gospel, we could no longer be sexually intimate with each other. I honestly didn't want to give that up. We slipped a few times, but our resolve was sure. We knew we both wanted to embrace the light and the gospel. We both felt the need of a blessing of comfort and guidance. I asked my dad for a father's blessing. What a beautiful and touching blessing it was. I was told that I was still loved and watched over by my Heavenly Father. I was also promised that if I kept all of the commandments and obeyed my leaders and my parents that my "days would be long upon the earth." I came away from that more determined than ever to get my life in order. Steven had wanted me to give him a blessing, but I wasn't worthy, so he asked President Pimentel for a blessing. He was promised that his disease would become manageable. We were both so overwhelmed with joy at these promises that we decided to do whatever was necessary to get our lives in order so that we could be worthy of such blessings!

As time passed the desire to be sexually intimate faded. It didn't happen overnight by any means. We knew that in order for us to truly turn our lives over to the Savior, we would need to clean up our home, our space, our minds, our attitudes, and our determination—we would need to lift our entire lives to a whole new level. We wanted our home to be a place where the Spirit could reside. We literally got rid of anything and everything that wasn't conducive to the Spirit. We got rid of all the pornography and other worldly symbols that reminded us of our former lifestyle and gay culture. It was a complete transition from one phase of our relationship to another—the beginning of our spiritual journey.

That summer, Steven was ready for baptism. Because of the changes and commitments we both had made, and because I personally had sought repentance, I was able to perform that special ordinance. What a glorious day it was, not only for Steven and me but for our families as well. It was the first time either family had met each other. My Grandfather Hoover officially welcomed Steven into the Hoover family that day. It was a miracle in so many respects. In attendance were many whom I had known prior to my relationship with Steven. It was comforting to have so much support from so many, both those who had no knowledge of my prior relationship with Steven as well as those who did.

"Thy Will Be Done"

Some family members and friends had hoped that by now, thirteen years after Steven's baptism, we would have started dating women and even each be married by now. We both tried the dating scene for a time. Steven and I began associating with some LDS friends whom I had known before. Steven even went to a couple of single adult dances with a couple of the women I used to hang out with. But even as we each seriously explored the possibility of marriage, when it came down to it, the few women we met and went out with stated, more or less, that they weren't ready or willing to become involved in a relationship with someone with a terminal illness. That was quite an eye-opener for both of us. So for the time being, we are roommates who have decided to take care of each other in our sicknesses until the time when one of us is called home. Steven has been my brother, my closest friend, and my confidant for just over nineteen years now.

Some have asked us, "Isn't it hard being close to someone you used to have a sexual relationship with? How can you just ignore that? Isn't it difficult?" My answer to that is that it's been the most basic of gospel teachings that have helped us to stay close to the Lord and on the straight and narrow path: prayer, fasting, feasting upon the Lord's word in the scriptures, patience, persistence, and commitment to covenants. Believe it or not, they truly work! Steven's growth into a spiritual giant certainly hasn't hurt. We are both committed to staying strong in the gospel, remaining close to the Lord, and continuing to grow spiritually. We both attend our Church meetings and the temple regularly. I am one of the organists at the Oakland California Temple. Steven is currently the secretary in the elders quorum in our ward, and I am the pianist for priesthood meeting, as well as the ward organist. I cherish the ability to play the piano and organ. It has been a wonderful and continuous source of comfort and connection with the Spirit.

Our relationship now feels so spiritually good and pure that, for almost thirteen years, neither one of us has desired to distort that purity sexually or romantically. One of the greatest lessons I've learned in the course of the past few years is that sex has nothing to do with the capacity to truly love someone in the way Christ calls us to love. Steven and I love each other as brothers, but sex and sexual attraction no longer play any role in the love and intimacy we share. For me, that's a miracle. Only God could have so transformed my heart, giving "beauty for ashes" (Isaiah 61:3) regarding how I now experience love and sexuality. While I had previously reduced sexuality to little more than bodily function, it has now become something I hold sacred.

Steven and I have been through many life *hells* together. Having come through those experiences, and now having experienced spiritual rebirth and freedom in Jesus Christ, I've learned that to be truly free from our own carnal selves, we must learn the difference between submitting to our own desires and submitting to the will of God. It's simply a choice. When our lives are fully in line with His will, only then can we truly be free. It took me a long time and a hard road to realize those lessons, but I now know that true self-discipline is not confining—it is liberating. For me, there has been nothing more restrictive than unmet potential. Through self-discipline and reliance on the grace of Christ, I've rediscovered my true potential and made it a reality. I am happy, and I have peace. And in that, I am truly free.

Feeding the Flock of God: The Vital Role of Sensitive and Loving Priesthood Leaders

Robert L. Millet

The words of Jehovah echoed through the gathered assembly of spirits in the premortal existence, our first estate: "We [the noble and great ones] will go down, for there is space there, and we will take of these materials, and we will make an earth whereon these may dwell;

"And we will prove them herewith, to see if they will do all things whatsoever the Lord their God shall command them; and they who keep their first estate shall be added upon; and they who keep not their first estate shall not have glory in the same kingdom with those who keep their first estate; and they who keep their second estate shall have glory added upon their heads for ever and ever" (Abraham 3:24–26).

We must have known, at least to some extent, what earth life would be like. We must have been taught that mortality would be filled with thrills and adventures and joys as well as with pain and sorrow and anguish of soul. I do not know how much we understood about the particulars of our earthly existence—including specific opportunities and blessings as well as challenges and burdens that would come our way. We did know, however, that it would all be worth it, that despite thorns and thistles, scratches and bruises, there would be moments of sheer delight, and that even in our darkest days on earth, we would not be left alone. God our Father would send a Savior to earth: the Lord Jehovah, who had, with Michael, our spirit brothers and sisters, and us, fought against Lucifer and his hosts and would fight for us again in our second estate.

Jehovah would come to earth as a helpless infant in the humblest of circumstances; would be known as Jesus of Nazareth; would grow up as every other child and "be like man, almost"[1]; would be taught the law by parents and leaders and, most important, would be taught by his Father and angelic ministrants things that no mortal man or woman could teach Him (see JST, Matthew 3:24–26); would teach the gospel of salvation as One having authority, which He certainly had; would lift and liberate the souls of His people through His teachings and by means of mighty miracles; would offer Himself a ransom for sin for the sons and daughters of Adam and Eve; and would die, be laid in a borrowed tomb, and rise from the dead the third day in glorious immortality as the "firstfruits of them that slept" (1 Corinthians 15:20), thereby making available to every man, woman, and child the immortality of the soul.

We surely learned that even after our Lord and Master had ascended into heaven, we still would not be left alone. Rather, the third member of the Godhead, the Holy Ghost, would be sent to comfort, warn, teach, affirm, cleanse, sanctify, reveal sacred things, and seal. Further, holy prophets would be called to declare the way, and holy scriptures would be preserved in order that we might savor the words of eternal life throughout our brief stay on earth. Life would be sweet. Life would be difficult. Life would be rewarding. Life would be heart-wrenching during certain seasons. Some would wrestle with the agony of broken bodies or damaged minds. Some would be tested most severely by wealth or beauty.[2]

In this chapter I will speak to those in particular who have been called to serve as priesthood leaders. You have general handbooks of the Church and ongoing direction from area and general Church authorities to guide you in your ministry. My message, therefore, is not an official message—not one I was called to write or one I have official authority to present. Rather, what follows are my reflections and recommendations, sentiments from my mind and heart that come as a result of being a bishop twice and serving in four stake presidencies, including as a stake president. I know, as you know now, the feelings of inadequacy that are ever before you, the sober introspection through which you pass on a regular basis, and the depth of your longings to be worthy and to be made capable by our Lord to minister to and bless His precious children.

It is not easy to be human. Life does not always seem fair. Many bear heavy burdens, some of which you and I cannot even comprehend. We cannot be all things to all people, nor can each bishop or stake president know how to deal clinically with such matters as depression and anxiety, eating disorders, addictions, grief and loss, divorce, or same-gender attraction. We can and should read and ask questions and do what we can to better understand some of the pressures and anxieties and disappointments that our people undergo, but I do not believe the Lord expects the common judges of Israel to be expert therapists or trained clinicians. There are those who have in fact been educated and trained in these matters—those who have a proper orientation toward good and evil and an especial sensitivity to Latter-day Saint standards and lifestyle—who can and should assist us in our work with ward and stake members.

On the other hand, what we can do is seek earnestly the inspiration of the Lord, seek for divine discernment and deeper understanding, seek for that wisdom and that Christlike love that will enable us to exercise the patience, judgment, kindness, and spiritual sensitivity that our people need so desperately. In short, we can meet with our people regularly. We can fast and pray with them. We can read and study with them. We can listen to their hearts' longings—spoken and unspoken—and we can monitor their progress and hold out to them the hope that a better day will come and that there really is a light at the end of the dark tunnel. We can "succor the weak, lift up the hands which hang down, and strengthen the feeble knees" (D&C 81:5). We can help to settle their fears, "for perfect love casteth out all fear" (Moroni 8:16; see also 1 John 4:18). In a very real way we are all in this together. Each one of us needs help. We cannot face life's challenges or lift life's burdens on our own. We stand in need of a power above anything earthly; we are desperate for pardoning mercy and redeeming grace. And the startling and soothing message of the prophets is that "all are within the reach of pardoning mercy, who have not committed the unpardonable sin."[3]

Now, let us come to the matter at hand—how we might minister more lovingly and effectively to our brothers and sisters who discover that they feel an attraction for those of the same gender. Perhaps it would be easiest for me to express myself in terms of some lessons I have learned through my own experience of over thirty years as a priesthood leader.

1. Let's begin with the fact that God loves all His children, no matter who they are, where they come from, or what problems they engage day by day. He does not cease loving us when we sin, but rather we become less sensitive to the Spirit and place ourselves thereby in a condition where, until we repent, we cannot feel and enjoy the love of God in our life (see 1 John 2:15; D&C 95:12). The Son still shines, even when we have blocked the light ourselves. Further, the Father and the Son are "not willing that any should perish" (2 Peter 3:9). They "will have all men to be saved, and to come unto the knowledge of the truth" (1 Timothy 2:4). "God is no respecter of persons: but in every nation he that feareth him, and worketh righteousness, is accepted with him" (Acts 10:34–35). Such sublime scriptural passages suggest that God will do everything in His power to save as many of His children as he can, as many as choose to be saved. There is no ceiling on the number of saved beings. We should find comfort in the assurance that every person who comes to this earth has the capacity, through the Atonement and the associated covenants and ordinances of the gospel of Jesus Christ, to one day inherit exaltation in the highest degree of the celestial kingdom.

2. We do not fully understand all the reasons that some of the children of God experience same-gender attraction. Some contend that it is completely a learned behavior. Others insist that it is a purely genetic phenomenon. At this point, God has not revealed, nor has science concluded, why one woman finds herself attracted sexually to another

female or why a man finds himself attracted to another male. And in working with those who have such attractions, I am not sure that it matters one way or the other *why* such anomalies take place. The issue at hand is less "Why did this happen?" than "What can we do to help?"

I would add that in all of the interviews I have conducted with hundreds upon hundreds of Latter-day Saints through the years, none were more rewarding—none so challenging, to be sure—or more of a blessing than those in which I sat opposite individuals struggling with same-gender attraction and pleaded for the insight, the discernment, and, most important, the Christlike love so necessary to this sensitive endeavor. As I witnessed burdens lifted, I was lifted. As I witnessed peace and perspective descend upon them, I was filled with indefinable insights that could have come to me in no other way. And as I beheld the enabling power of the Savior extended to one who truly sought to do right and feel right, I was transformed and strengthened by the experience. My witness of the majestic power of our Mediator was affirmed, as was my assurance of the Fatherhood of God and the brotherhood and sisterhood of His children. We cannot lift another soul to higher ground without ascending that path ourselves.

3. The moral standard of the Church is set forth in the scriptures and through the teachings of living prophets. It is the same for those who wrestle with homosexual feelings as it is for those who wrestle with heterosexual feelings: any and every sexual relationship outside the bonds of marriage between one woman and one man is contrary to the commandments of God and the standards of The Church of Jesus Christ of Latter-day Saints. "Thou shalt not steal; neither commit adultery, . . . nor do anything like unto it" (D&C 59:6). "The world may have its norm," President Spencer W. Kimball taught, but "the Church has a different one. . . . The world may countenance premarital sex experiences, but the Lord and his church condemn in no uncertain terms any and every sex relationship outside of marriage, and even indecent and uncontrolled ones within marriage."[4]

4. There is an important difference between one having homosexual attractions and one acting upon those feelings—a difference

between attitudes and feelings on the one hand and behavior on the other. If those who have same-gender attraction discuss their difficulties with their priesthood leaders and then strive and commit to observe the law of chastity in thought and action, they are living in harmony with the teachings of the Church and are thereby worthy of full participation.

It is important for us all as disciples of Christ to fill our lives with as much light as possible—to search the scriptures regularly, fast and pray consistently, listen to inspiring and uplifting music, discard those activities (movies, music, television sitcoms, perhaps even people) that would in any way restrain or repel the Spirit of God—in short, "chase darkness from among [us]" (D&C 50:25) so that our thoughts may be worthy of the companionship of our Master and His representative, the Holy Ghost. In addition, regular and tender instruction by priesthood leaders can do much to assist those with same-gender attraction to deal properly with unnecessary feelings of unworthiness, shame, and guilt.

On the other hand, those who yield to temptation and are guilty of sexual activity are subject to the disciplinary procedures of the Church. Such activity may take the form of actual sexual contact or participation in the promotion of homosexuality in public gatherings, speeches, literature, marches, and so forth. President Gordon B. Hinckley stated:

"People inquire about our position on those who consider themselves so-called gays and lesbians. My response is that we love them as sons and daughters of God. They may have certain inclinations which are powerful and which may be difficult to control. Most people have inclinations of one kind or another at various times. If they do not act upon these inclinations, then they can go forward as do all other members of the Church. If they violate the law of chastity and the moral standards of the Church, then they are subject to the discipline of the Church, just as others are.

"We want to help these people, to strengthen them, to assist them with their problems and to help them with their difficulties. But we cannot stand idle if they indulge in immoral activity, if they try to uphold and defend and live in a so-called same-sex marriage situation.

To permit such would be to make light of the very serious and sacred foundation of God-sanctioned marriage and its very purpose, the rearing of families."[5]

Priesthood leaders should always strive to love as Jesus loved (see John 13:34), but they are neither bigoted nor homophobic when they counsel members to keep the commandments and when they call upon those in sin to repent. Sensitive priesthood leaders "cannot modify the Lord's message merely to make people feel comfortable. They are too kind to be so cruel."[6]

Further, we must never forget that when a person sits down with his or her priesthood leader and confides a challenge of same-gender attraction, that act almost always is a statement itself, a powerful indication that the person is serious, genuine, and earnest in a desire to keep God's commandments, eager and willing to receive counsel and the needed strength to move forward with his of her life. Such courage is deserving of a priesthood leader who listens with love, truly listens with his mind and heart, sets aside preconceived stereotypes and solutions, and does his best to hear what is being said and perhaps even what is unspoken but deeply felt.

It is risky and always painful for the priesthood leader to jump to judgment before all has been said. For one thing, the man or woman who has come into the office no doubt feels very much alone, with almost no one to speak with. Surely the priesthood leader can demonstrate what is so desperately needed—that the person has a friend in the bishop or stake president, that he or she need not face this obstacle alone. Further, priesthood leaders need to remember that monitoring behavior without giving appropriate attention to the person's genuine feelings, needs, and desires is to deal with but a portion of the problem. Proper behavior matters, but so do thoughts, yearnings, ambitions, and resolutions, all of which need to be discussed and evaluated if our ministry is to extend to the whole person.

5. It is not necessary that a priesthood leader understand completely the complexities of homosexuality in order to minister properly to a member of the Church. I have never embezzled funds from my

employer, but I have worked with people who have. Until the year 2000, I had never experienced severe depression or anxiety, but I had worked closely with many Saints who had. I have never been the victim or the perpetrator of sexual abuse, but I have worked with a number of men and women who have. I have never committed adultery, but I have counseled with and disciplined members of the Church who have. And I have never felt a sexual attraction for a person of the same gender, but I have spent scores of hours listening to, speaking with, counseling, and encouraging those who have. How could I do what I did in each case mentioned above without anger, disgust, judgment, or even bafflement of how someone could do such a thing? Because I had spent a great deal of time on my knees, pleading with an omniscient Lord to grant to me a portion of His Spirit, a portion of His eternal perspective, a portion of His insight and knowledge—all that I might think what I ought to think and feel what I ought to feel toward this son or daughter of God sitting in the chair before me.

6. Because the covenant union of a man and a woman is the divinely ordained pattern, and because "marriage is ordained of God unto man" (D&C 49:15), priesthood leaders are sometimes prone to suggest to those with feelings of same-gender attraction, particularly men, that what they need to do is simply get married to a lovely young woman, have children, and thereby solve the problem. There have been situations where such counsel proved to be wise and to result in lasting change. I have witnessed them. But this is a risk, given an individual's propensity and inclination.

One man, responding to my question regarding how he felt about heterosexual marriage, said in kindness and earnestness: "Bishop, how would you feel if you were wrestling with improper sexual thoughts or desires and your priesthood leader suggested that you simply choose an attractive young man, marry him, adopt children, and the problem would be solved? I feel the same sense of awkwardness, resistance, and even revulsion at your suggestion. Can you understand that my mind-set and worldview are different than yours?" Consequently, President Hinckley has advised that "marriage should not be viewed as a therapeutic step to solve problems such as homosexual inclinations or practices."[7]

We have a growing number of single adults within the Church. Most of them desire to be married, to have children, to fit comfortably into a family-oriented organization. Few choose to be single; most would have it otherwise. They are entitled to feel like a contributing member of the ward or branch, to be called to serve in responsible positions, to be included in social events and spiritual gatherings. The Church, the body of Christ, "hath need of every member" (D&C 84:110), and our ward or branch is not complete without them. Our task is not to single them out (forgive the pun) but rather to bring them in with rejoicing.

7. There is no room in the Lord's Church and kingdom for bigotry, hatred, or hate speech. President Hinckley emphasized in strong words that "our opposition to attempts to legalize same-sex marriage should never be interpreted as justification for hatred, intolerance, or abuse of those who profess homosexual tendencies, either individually or as a group. . . . Our hearts reach out to those who refer to themselves as gays and lesbians. We love and honor them as sons and daughters of God. They are welcome in the Church. It is expected, however, that they follow the same God-given rules of conduct that apply to everyone else, whether single or married."[8]

All members of the Church, no matter their particular cross or difficulty, are entitled to feel more than tolerated, more even than *welcome*. Each of us has a right to feel that we are *needed* by the Lord and His Church. Each member has an assignment to assume, a role to fill, a contribution to make to spreading the everlasting gospel and the ongoing work of the kingdom of God. Those who wrestle with same-gender attraction who have committed to remain chaste and true to their covenants are entitled to enjoy meaningful labor in a Church composed of imperfect beings who are striving to do their best. People want to feel loved and valued, and to the extent that they do, they are more likely to remain active and involved in the Church.

8. Just as priesthood leaders should not cast out those who are

earnestly seeking the kingdom and sincerely striving to live worthy of participation in the ordinances of salvation (see 3 Nephi 18:28–33; D&C 46:3–5), so priesthood leaders should tenderly counsel mothers and fathers, brothers and sisters of those who have same-gender attraction to create a climate at home that is open and welcoming, an environment that makes home a place where the loved one would always want to be. Even those who have chosen to pursue gay or lesbian relationships and have thereby been subject to Church disciplinary measures need love and kindness and understanding now more than ever. While it is poignantly painful for family members to accept the path their loved one has chosen (and they should not be expected to accept that which is wrong), the individual still needs the ongoing love and support of family and friends and priesthood leaders. This will, of course, require an additional revelation or endowment of divine grace, an outpouring of the pure love of Christ (see Moroni 7:48) that empowers us to love, in a measure, as Jesus loves and to minister as He ministers.

9. People may not choose to have same-gender attractions, but they do have the power to choose how they will respond to those attractions. "In addition to the cleansing effect of the Atonement," Elder Dallin H. Oaks stated, "God has given us agency—the power to choose between good (the path of life) and evil (the path of spiritual death and destruction [see 2 Ne. 2:27; Moses 4:3]). Although the conditions of mortality can limit our freedom (such as by restricting our mobility or our power to act on certain options), when we have reached the age or condition of accountability (see Moro. 8:5–12; D&C 68:27; 101:78) no mortal or spiritual power can deprive us of our agency."[9]

10. There is no power greater than the power of the Atonement. While serving as a priesthood leader many years ago, I had occasion to work with a young man who was struggling with same-sex attraction. He had violated his temple covenants but sincerely wanted to change. Church disciplinary measures were taken, and he and I began to work together toward change. He spoke often of how difficult it was for him to be active in the Church, to attend all the activities, and

in general to be a typical Latter-day Saint when he felt so atypical. He committed to avoid inappropriate sexual activity but wrestled with his same-sex attraction. One day he asked me: "If I do the things you have asked me to do—go to Church, read the scriptures, fast and pray, plead for divine help, receive priesthood blessings when necessary, and be chaste—can you assure me that the Lord will take away these desires, these attractions? Can you promise me they will go away?"

As I recall, I said something like this: "I know that the Lord can indeed change you, change your heart, change your orientation. I know that He can do that instantaneously if He chooses to do so. I know that the power of change is in Jesus Christ, and that dramatic and rapid change can take place. I do not know, however, whether the Lord will change you right away. I know this: If you do what you have been asked to do, and if you do it regularly and consistently from now on, God will change you, either here or hereafter. You may be required to deal with these feelings until the day you die. But I can promise you two things—first, these feelings will eventually be transformed; and second, if God does not choose to bring about a major change in your nature in this life, He will strengthen and empower you to deal with the temptations you will face. You don't need to face this on your own."

Elder Oaks has instructed us, "Through the merciful plan of our Father in Heaven, persons who desire to do what is right but through no fault of their own are unable to have an eternal marriage in mortal life will have an opportunity to qualify for eternal life in a period following mortality, if they keep the commandments of God and are true to their baptismal and other covenants."[10]

I shared with my young friend a few scriptures that have special meaning to me. I reminded him that the celestial kingdom is the eternal abode of those who "overcome by faith" (D&C 76:53). I then turned to the Book of Mormon and read Alma's counsel to his faithful son Helaman: "Preach unto them repentance, and faith on the Lord Jesus Christ; teach them to humble themselves and to be meek and lowly in heart; teach them to *withstand every temptation of the devil, with their faith on the Lord Jesus Christ*" (Alma 37:33; emphasis added).

Truly, Christ is our Advocate, the One who knows "the weakness of man and how to succor them who are tempted" (D&C 62:1).

Conclusion

There may be those reading this book who have been subjected to much pain and distress in their lives, to abuse, to neglect, to the agonies of wanting more than anything to live a normal life and to feel normal feelings but who seem unable to do so. I would say that each one of us, whoever we are, wrestles with something. Perhaps it's things like weight or height or complexion or baldness or IQ. Perhaps it's stuff that passes in time like a phase. Perhaps it's the torture of watching helplessly as loved ones choose unwisely and thereby close doors of opportunity and foreclose future privileges for themselves. And then there are the terrible traumas in our life, those occasions when someone we love violates our tender trust and deals a blow that strikes at the center of all we hold dear and all we value about ourselves.

The day is coming when all the awful wrongs of this life will be righted. The God of justice will attend to all evil and rectify all irregularities. Those things that are beyond our power to control will be corrected, either here or hereafter. Many of us may come to enjoy the lifting, liberating powers of the Atonement in this life, and all our losses may be made up before we pass from this sphere of existence. Perhaps some of us will wrestle all our days with our traumas and our trials, for He who orchestrates the events of our lives will surely fix the time of our release. I have a conviction, however, that when we pass through the veil of death, all those impediments and challenges and crosses that were beyond our power to control—abuse, neglect, immoral environment, weighty traditions, private temptations and inclinations that yielded to faith, and so forth—will be torn away like a film, and perfect peace will prevail in our hearts.

We as mortals simply do not have the power to fix everything that is broken. But the Lord Jesus can. Faith in Jesus Christ consists in exercising total trust in Him, demonstrating complete confidence in Him, and maintaining a ready reliance upon His merits, mercy, and grace.

The Prophet Joseph Smith taught a sublimely comforting doctrine when he declared: "All your losses will be made up to you in the resurrection, provided you continue faithful. By the vision of the Almighty I have seen it."[11]

Every limb and joint and hair of the head will be restored to the human body (see Alma 11:43; 40:23). Stability and soundness of mind will be conferred upon those who have been restricted and challenged by mental and emotional difficulties. And all affections, desires, and yearnings for love and wholeness in the family order will be granted to those who fought a good fight, kept the faith, and finished their course (see 2 Timothy 4:7). The struggles and disappointments and loneliness will be replaced by resolution, renewal, and sweet redemption. Our souls will rest.

My Shepherd Will Supply My Need

Shawn McKinnon

Shawn McKinnon (pseudonym) was raised in Boise, Idaho, by an active mother and a less-active father. He served an honorable mission and has since served in the Church as Sunday School president, executive secretary, and Gospel Doctrine teacher. He lives in Utah, where he is a junior high school teacher and athletic coach. He loves mentoring youth and making a meaningful difference in their lives. He also loves sports, good food, and good music.

I love walking onto the hardwood floor in a gym. It brings back fond memories of camaraderie and fun, of hard work and life lessons. I played basketball in high school, and though I wasn't a superstar, I felt a genuine sense of contribution to the team, I learned a lot, and I had a lot of fun playing. I also made some lasting friendships and learned principles that have helped me in many facets of my life. Sometimes I learned more about myself than I was ready for.

At one particular practice during a scrimmage, a teammate decided to get grabby while he was guarding me. I gave him the benefit of the doubt the first time it happened, though knowing this guy, I strongly suspected his hand placement was not accidental. It's not that I suspected he was gay or that he was trying to come on to me. Rather, in my experience, teenage guys can allow their glands to cloud their better judgment and subdue inhibitions to the point of being strangely and even inappropriately physical with each other. This was often the case with this particular teammate, and I figured his behavior was merely that of a hormone-driven, socially awkward young man.

Even so, his actions were inappropriate, and the second time he put his hand where it didn't belong, I spoke up. I told him to stop and called him a name that called into question his sexuality. He laughed and acted as if he didn't know what I was referring to. He also ignored my warning and eventually grabbed at me a third time. This last time I immediately stopped playing and pushed him hard. He stumbled back a few steps and caught his balance. My annoyance had turned to real anger. I threatened to hurt him if he did it again. I made sure to deliver my threat loud enough so that my other teammates could hear it. Our coach looked our way to see what was going on. I acted as if it was no big deal, but I glared at my teammate, assuring him that it *was* a big deal and that I meant what I had said. Whether out of embarrassment or a desire to avoid a more serious reaction from me, my teammate stopped his grabbing and groping and never did it again.

While I was genuinely unhappy about my teammate's behavior, I was also inwardly confused and even intrigued by it. He was athletic, muscular, and fairly handsome, and though I had previously had trouble admitting it to myself, I had been struggling with feelings of attraction to other guys for some time. His actions were completely uninvited, and I was angry that he would disrespect me that way in front of my team. But in my mind, what was far worse was the possibility that others might witness what had happened and perhaps begin to question *my* sexuality. I was fearful that my confusion, feelings, even fantasies would somehow be discovered, and that if they were, my life and reputation would be ruined. I was also keenly aware of the fact that though this guy had grabbed me, *I* was the one with feelings of attraction to other guys.

Vital Support from True Undershepherds

Though I battled inwardly with myself over these thoughts and feelings, I had never shared them with anyone else until I began meeting with a therapist to address some depression and other issues so I could serve a mission. Admitting this weakness to another person would and did make it real, and it was one of the scariest things I have ever done. I had often heard horrible things—even from good members of the Church—said about "homos" or "fags," and I was deeply fearful of rejection. In time my desire to serve a mission helped me muster enough courage to share my struggle, first with an LDS counselor and then with the bishop of my young single adult ward.

My bishop's face showed surprise and great concern as I told him about my attraction to males, but as he spoke to me following my disclosure, I felt his genuine love for me. This helped me feel the Lord's love for me. He said his heart went out to me, and I knew it did. His eyes were soft yet earnest as he spoke reassuring words of my true worth and of the Savior's real power to comfort and heal. I felt that he was truly empathizing with me, feeling some small portion of the pain I was feeling at that moment. This good bishop walked with me as I prepared for a mission. He met with me regularly, supported me in my callings, and treated me as a son as well as a cherished member of the flock he was called to shepherd. I never felt any judgment from him, and he helped me to feel confident that I could always turn to the Lord and to His servants for hope, comfort, answers, and peace.

With the help of both my bishop and an equally loving and supportive stake president (who eventually ordained me an elder), I made good progress in dealing with my feelings of depression and other issues, and eventually I qualified to serve a full-time mission. My dear bishop passed away only weeks into my service in the mission field, but he forever blessed my life with his understanding, his acceptance, and his example of true Christlike love. I can still see his comforting smile in my mind's eye, an image that continues to provide comfort and remind me of what faithful priesthood service really is. I have had many great priesthood leaders since that time who were willing to support me in my struggle to be faithful and to deal effectively and appropriately with my feelings. Sadly, I have also had a few leaders who were less supportive.

After returning from an exceptional mission experience, I again attended a young single adult ward. My same-gender feelings and thoughts, though diminished some, were still present. Because of how positive my previous experience had been, I decided to continue to be open about my struggle with a few trusted friends and with my priesthood leaders. After moving around some, back and forth from college, I eventually attended the same young single adult ward I had attended before my mission. The ward had a new bishop who was also a good and faithful man. In my first interview with him he expressed excitement to meet me and said he was glad to have me in the ward. After I had shared my struggle of same-gender attraction with him, however, he seemed to recoil from me. He was far less understanding and loving to me than most of my previous leaders had been—especially my premission bishop and stake president.

From that interview on I perceived a noticeable level of discomfort when he was around me. He was fairly affectionate and demonstrative with other ward members, but he rarely said more than hello to me. I don't think it was a personality issue, but more that he didn't know how to be with me. It felt as if he didn't trust me and as if he saw me as strange and even as broken. The feeling was a stark contrast to the love and guidance I had previously felt, and it left me wanting to find a new ward. I wondered if I would be allowed to serve or speak, and I didn't feel that my bishop loved or valued me as a ward member. There was no direct affront or condemnation, and he was never harsh or demeaning—just aloof and dismissive. I consider myself to be rather thick-skinned, but feeling ignored and avoided by one whom I looked to for support and guidance really stung—and worse than I would have suspected.

Though I don't feel that this bishop intended to alienate me or hurt my feelings, the consequences of his apparent difficulty dealing with my same-gender feelings had a painful effect on me. Because of my own already-looming insecurity and shame about my struggle, I wondered if my bishop wasn't partially right to feel the way I suspected he felt. Sometimes I didn't like myself very much because of this issue, so I didn't see it as totally unreasonable for others to feel this way about me once they knew my secret. My lacking self-worth aside, I desired the same love and support I had known from other leaders—the love and support that helped me to feel accepted, confident, and valued as a member of the Church. Those feelings of confidence and acceptance had grown dramatically as I served a mission, as had my faith and trust in the Lord. I had felt the love and approval of a visionary mission president, and my testimony still burned brightly in my heart. I certainly wasn't about to leave the Church over my discomfort, but I did unfortunately allow this lack of support to become justification for checking out emotionally and becoming less involved in my ward.

Eventually, I moved away to college and attended a college ward where again I was almost overwhelmed by the love and kindness of my new bishop. This undershepherd of the Lord pulled me close to his side in every way—emotionally, spiritually, and physically. He, through inspiration, called me to serve as the ward executive secretary. He told me of the potential he saw in me and nearly constantly reminded me of it. Once again I felt trusted by both my bishop and the Lord. I loved the opportunity to serve and learn, and I grew a great deal. I came to learn and accept that some priesthood leaders are better prepared to deal with certain issues than others.

I realized that regardless of my priesthood leaders' level of experience or understanding of my challenges, I could always rely on the Savior to comfort and strengthen me. Even so, I'm grateful that the Lord also blesses me on occasion with real-time, hands-on help from faithful leaders and friends who further assist me in my efforts to live the gospel.

Tutored in His Service

Along with powerful examples of love and service from great men, I have also been blessed to learn from experience. The Lord has been patient in teaching me how to deal with my feelings and has taught me powerful lessons when I was ready and willing to learn. I faithfully served a full-time mission in Southern California and had an incredible experience there. The area I served in had a large gay population, including a number of inactive and former members of the Church. It was a profound blessing to serve there. The Lord showed me personally, day after day, interaction after interaction, where the choice to abandon the truths of the gospel and follow a gay lifestyle would lead. I was often keenly aware through promptings of the Spirit that I was being tutored on this issue as I served. In direct ways, the Lord was showing me the consequences of righteousness versus the consequences of sin, and the pain and loneliness that acting on my same-gender attractions could bring.

One of the most powerful examples of this happened on a warm, breezy evening nearly halfway into my mission. My mission companion and I knocked on the door of a member of record in our area. He invited us in and we sat down with him in his living room and listened to his heartbreaking story. He said he had attempted to follow the Lord's plan but eventually had decided to leave the Church until the General Authorities changed their teachings regarding homosexuality. He had received his endowment in the temple, served a full-time mission, and even married in the temple. But eventually he had come to believe he was living a lie and couldn't resist his feelings any longer. He divorced his wife and embraced a gay identity. As I listened, my heart went out to him as I pictured him straying one step at a time from his personal faith and from the gospel path. As he neared the end of what seemed to me a terribly tragic story, I felt a deep desire to help him. I also hoped and prayed that he wasn't also describing *my* future.

As we spoke, I began to feel strong stirrings in my heart. I listened closely as the Spirit whispered that this was an important moment for me in my life. I felt a powerful and distinct impression that I was to learn from this man's circumstances. I decided in that moment with conviction that no matter what kind of attraction I felt, I would live the truth that I had come to know. With personal understanding of his frustration and love in my heart, I invited this man to reconsider and to come back to the Lord's church. I encouraged him to not wait for the Church to alter its teachings regarding homosexual relationships. I looked him in the eye, and, with a heart full of genuine empathy, I said, "Please don't hold your breath. The Lord's standard on this issue will not change." I felt the power of the Spirit confirm the words as I spoke them—and I knew they were for him *and* for me. He politely thanked us for our visit and invited us to leave.

I stepped from this brother's porch, recognizing that the Lord had just blessed me with a clear, direct message. I could choose to live the gospel and be faithful despite my weaknesses, or I could depart from what I knew and miss out on the precious and lasting blessings I was teaching about every day. I knew that this brother was wrong—that the Lord's standard could not and would not change, but that *we* must strive to change and be reconciled to God through Christ's Atonement to *His* standard of righteousness.

A Blessing, Not a Curse

With help and support from true and dear friends, my loving and faithful mother, and inspired and valiant priesthood leaders, I have made real and meaningful progress in dealing effectively with my unwanted attraction toward other males. Though I still struggle and have many ups and downs, I've come to experience this challenge as one of the greatest blessings of my life. Its refining influence on me has been surpassed only by powerful communication from heaven as impressions from the Spirit have whispered to me the truths of eternity. Through many experiences too sacred to mention, the Lord has blessed me to feel that I could never leave Him or His church.

Through my efforts to come to terms with my same-gender attraction, I have developed great compassion for those who struggle with any unwanted difficulties. I'm not sure I could have developed this level of empathy or compassion without having had this particular challenge. Because of my circumstances, I often feel compelled to reach out to others in an attempt to lift and comfort them in their battles of the soul, whatever they might be. As a Melchizedek Priesthood holder, I want to provide direction, comfort, and support to others. I've had opportunities to mentor many young people and have sought to improve their lives by sharing my faith and testimony and by supporting them in making healthy and wise choices. This has included helping a number of young men choose and prepare to serve full-time missions.

Along with developing a much deeper capacity for love, empathy, and compassion, I have also come to more fully understand and appreciate the Atonement of Jesus Christ. The enabling power afforded us because of Christ's sacrifice and suffering has become very real to me. I have frequently been able to access that power when I have most needed it. On occasion I have experienced heartaching loneliness, sadness, and shame. I've shed secret tears, battled numbing depression, and wished and pleaded for another challenge or weakness instead of this one. When I've felt that no one could understand how I was feeling, the Spirit has brought to my remembrance that there is One who *always* understands. I have been comforted, strengthened, and lifted by the Spirit, and provided with peace that "passeth all understanding" (Philippians 4:7). Though this challenge has felt like my handcart to push, pull, and drag across the plains, I find comfort in the thought that I need Abrahamic-like tests to pass through so that at the end of my journey I can feel that I have a place to sit down with the prophets and Saints who have gone before me.

It seems that there is irony involved in these Abrahamic tests. Abraham was asked to sacrifice his son Isaac, through whom the promise of blessings for all of his posterity, all of God's children, was expected to be fulfilled. The early Saints of the Restoration were asked to leave behind a temple that they had given everything to build and to journey hundreds of miles to the west to begin all over again.

I have a weakness that provides some real hurdles in keeping the Lord's commandments to marry in His holy house and to multiply and replenish the earth by having children. Nevertheless, I choose to trust in the Lord and in His promises. If I can't fulfill all of His commandments in this life, though I hope and pray and even sometimes expect that I will, then I know that the Lord will make a way for me to fulfill those commandments in the next life. So each day I strive to live what I believe, to keep my covenants, and to respond to my struggle with same-gender attraction appropriately. I try to learn what the Lord would have me learn and to help those He gives me opportunities to help. I try to remember that where I lack, He can and does make up the difference.

I love the hymn "My Shepherd Will Supply My Need." It speaks peace to my sometimes-weary soul and reminds me that the Lord is with me, even through my weakest moments and most difficult trials. The words fill me with conviction that one day I will return to live with Him and will be "no more a stranger, nor a guest; but like a child at home."[12]

My Journey as a Priesthood Leader

Jerry Harris

Jerry Harris was born and raised in an active LDS family in Independence, Missouri. He moved to California after graduating from BYU and has lived in California for the past thirty years. He is married and has two children and two grandchildren. He has worked for over thirty years as a counselor with LDS Family Services. In the Church he has served as a family ward bishop, a BYU student ward bishop, and a branch president at the MTC; he currently serves as a counselor in a stake presidency. He loves spending time with his wife and his children and grandchildren, traveling, and reading.

As a bishop, I found this difficult. Yes, this was a different story I was hearing. I expected to deal with divorce, with abuse, and with some addictions. Yet homosexuality was very different. There was a part of me that was uncomfortable with it and another part of me that was almost reverenced by it—it seemed so special, so unique.

It was one of my first encounters with this issue many years ago. A young adult sister shared with me her struggle with same-sex attraction which she had been dealing with for many years. For as long as she could remember, she had felt different, not like other girls. She didn't feel feminine. She liked many traditionally masculine activities and had often felt more comfortable in the company of boys. This was the first time she had ever shared these feelings or thoughts with anyone. She was sharing them now because she felt that she was two different people inside and was worried that she was going crazy. She was also worried that she might act on some of the thoughts and fantasies she had had. She wanted to do the right thing, and as her bishop, I wanted to help her accomplish that right thing—whatever that was—but I didn't know much.

So I started to search out as much information as I could—which wasn't much with the information then available—and I located an LDS counselor for her to see. I tried to be the best help for her I could. It was an unsteady beginning, but it was a beginning nonetheless. We met together regularly. Sometimes we would talk directly about SSA issues; most of the time, however, the topics involved her relationship with God, her feelings of guilt, her attempts to get answers to prayers, and her testimony. Sometimes she felt like giving up; sometimes she felt that she was so strange and unique that God didn't have a place for her; sometimes she felt that no one understood her—no one. Yet, through it all she kept forging ahead. A little at a time, she began to feel some love, some acceptance, some understanding. Today she is a valiant servant in the Church—a wife, a mother, a friend. Does she still have some thoughts and feelings of attraction to other women?

According to her, yes, sometimes. Yet they do not keep her from serving, loving, and doing wonderful things in the kingdom.

That was over two decades ago, and since then I have heard many more such stories. They are each unique and uniquely challenging. Other stories include the following (these stories are composites—purposefully not specific so as to guard identities):

- Two young adult women came in with concerns about their physical relationship with each other. They were roommates who had come to be emotionally dependent on each other. The relationship at some point developed to include physical intimacy. They both became uncomfortable with how the relationship had evolved and sought me out as their bishop. They were confused about why and how the relationship had gotten to where it was. They wanted help. They wanted to cultivate a healthy relationship and to repent of their sins.
- A young man had come home early from his mission to a foreign country. He had engaged in some physical intimacy with a nonmember male while on his mission. He said he had had these feelings for several years and had experienced some minor struggles with same-gender attraction before his mission. He was sorry that he had been such a trouble to the Church, yet he wasn't sure he wanted to give up this relationship. He was preparing to return to his mission area to be with his friends there. He didn't think the Lord expected him to deny these feelings for the rest of his life.
- A seventeen-year-old priest shared with me during an interview that he found himself thinking of other boys and becoming aroused when watching them. He wondered if that meant he was gay. He had never acted on these feelings and knew that doing so would be wrong. But he was confused about his feelings and thoughts and felt ashamed of them, wondering if anyone would like him if they knew of his struggle.
- A middle-aged man who had been married for several years

and had children shared with me his story of never telling anyone about his attraction to men. For years he had held it inside. After working through some other issues, we decided it was time to share the struggle with his wife. With the help of a counselor and others, the two of them struggled with their marriage yet were committed to resolving the difficulties and strengthening their marriage and family.

There are many others, but these represent the broad continuum of stories I have experienced in terms of history, age, gender, attitude, perspective, and motivation. Indeed, my experience over the years has taught me that there is not one true homosexual, but rather many quantitatively different shades of homosexual feelings and experiences. No one feels exactly like another, no one has the same background or support, no one has the same response to thoughts, feelings, and behaviors.

Lessons Learned

I have had the opportunity of serving as a bishop in a student ward and in a residential ward, as a branch president at the Missionary Training Center, and now as a member of a stake presidency. I have been a part of many members' struggles, challenges, and questions regarding same-gender attraction in each of these stewardships. My journey as a shepherd in these various struggles has been troublesome at times and yet almost always rewarding. I have progressed from definitely not understanding to thinking I mostly understand to thinking maybe no one completely understands much about same-gender attraction. However, in the midst of all this confusion, there are some rays of insight I have gained though the years.

Each Journey Is Unique

Members often take different directions in their journeys, which are unpredictable and rarely have a smooth trajectory. As with most people's efforts with growth and change, there are times when it seems that they are doing great and feel hopeful about life, only to be followed by a slip or disappointment. Much encouragement is needed along the way. Whether there has been transgression requiring repentance or other issues requiring healing and growth, change and transformation take time and can happen in a variety of ways. Addressing this idea in the context of any number of issues individuals may face, the Church's missionary guidebook *Preach My Gospel* states, "Both repentance and recovery may take time. . . . Even though a person may have some initial success, further emotional healing may be necessary to completely repent and recover."[13]

It often takes a long time to navigate through the rapids to peaceful waters. Thus, this journey is generally not without a mishap or two. It is not uncommon for many members to have a season of sobriety with regards to thoughts, feelings, or behaviors, only to be followed by a wave of disruption. This is often precipitated by other stresses going on in their lives, which lead to wavering on decisions they have made or failing to keep up on the defenses and guards they have laid out for themselves.

For example, I recall a female member who had come to a good place in her journey (no lesbian behaviors and few same-gender thoughts and feelings—the ones she had were of a short duration). Then she inadvertently encountered a former coach at a sporting event. This former coach had been a partner for a time, and the reunion triggered some old feelings and attractions. This good Latter-day Saint struggled with a barrage of strong thoughts and feelings for several weeks. However, through the help of a good friend and a couple of interviews we had together—where I mainly listened—she was able to stay positive, keep perspective, and get going again in the right direction she wanted to maintain. This is not a trip across town—we are moving to a whole new area of the country. It will often take years for certain thoughts and feelings to begin to fade or to change.

Helping Others Identify and Develop Their Own Core Convictions

Another insight was that as a priesthood leader I could often see when certain gospel principles needed attention. That often meant being patient so the members could discover and indentify those principles themselves. This process takes longer, but it is often longer lasting. As a result, members have more commitment to the process of growth and change.

One typical scenario is the distancing of a parent from a child. This often feels like rejection, and I have known several members who felt a huge amount of pain (anger, hurt, guilt, shame) as a result of this distancing by a parent. Certainly with this situation it is reasonable to discuss forgiveness by the member for a parent's behavior. However, I have found that to mention this vital concept or process too soon is to invalidate the member's pain. The pain and hurt need to be validated and accepted before the member can begin the process of forgiveness.

Different Types of Help

I also became aware that there is a plethora of helps, including but not limited to family, friends, Church leaders, counselors, mentors, books and articles, support groups, prayer, scriptures, temple attendance, priesthood blessings, patriarchal blessings, and so forth. I found that I cannot be the sole source of help, support, and guidance. I found during my journey as a priesthood leader that while I do not and could not have all the answers myself, keeping up to date and knowledgeable on same-gender attraction was valuable. Often the individual who is struggling has some good information and is aware of helpful resources, having dealt with this challenge for some time. Finding out what the Lord's prophets and apostles, as well as science, have to say about the topic proved helpful as I've met with those who are struggling. The amount of inaccurate and misleading information available in our society is amazing.

In addition, the role and degree of help I provided varied with each member. I believe one of the key challenges is a balance between spiritual help and professional help. My experience has been that almost all members need both. Some begin with the spiritual and graft in the professional; others begin with the professional and then add the spiritual. Some need a lot of spiritual help and just a little professional help; others need primarily professional help complemented by some spiritual guidance. For either the ecclesiastical leader or professional counselor to assume that the member will not need both would be a mistake.

Examples of questions or concerns the ecclesiastical leader can help with include the following:

- What is my relationship with God?
- Have I sinned too much for forgiveness?
- Does God hate me because of these thoughts and feelings?

For his part, the professional may focus on the following concerns or issues:

- How did I get here?
- What are the antecedents to these thoughts and feelings?
- Are there some faulty beliefs or thoughts I have about others and myself that need changing?
- What can I do to resist temptation?
- How do I best manage my addictive tendencies?

Many concerns, such as abuse, neglect, forgiveness, and shame, may best be served by a coalescence of both ecclesiastical leaders and professionals. Total health and healing almost always take a blending of both spirit and body, the spiritual and the emotional. This often necessitates the assistance of both ecclesiastical and professional support, with the leader and the professional doing their best to complement each other and making consulting with each other a high priority.

Facilitating Greater Openness in the Church

Another discovery I have made is that as I became more comfortable with the issues of homosexuality, members became more comfortable talking with me about it. Members are often afraid of the initial response of their priesthood leaders and of how they will be seen, so doing all I could to invite the perception or feeling that I could talk comfortably and openly about this topic encouraged more men and women to come forward. Treating them the same after finding out this "terrible" (as they often perceive it) information and giving them a hug at the end of the interview seemed to do much to reassure them that they were still loved. They valued the reassurance that they were not flawed individuals, that this journey was doable, and that God and I loved them. Often I would find a way to mention this topic in interviews or lessons or talks as something I have talked with others about. This lessens the taboo that shrouds this topic and opens the way for ward members to feel a little less fearful to come and share their struggle.

Keeping Perspective

In the beginning I felt that I needed to give—and the members wanted—answers and counsel directly regarding same-sex attraction. I soon found, however, that most members struggling with same-sex attraction have equal concerns regarding their relationship with God, the Church, and their family. They question their worth and their acceptance by others. They sometimes question their faith and their testimonies. These are some of the issues that a bishop can help struggling members resolve. They can be helped to have a greater love of God and feel God's love for them. They can come to understand and appreciate the incredible power and infinite nature of the Atonement. I have frequently read the testimony of Alma regarding the breadth, depth, and power of the Savior's Atonement and stressed the "of every kind" aspect of His suffering (Alma 7:11). After the initial visits, most of our discussions centered on relationships that were important to them—relationships with Christ, family, friends, themselves. As these relationships took precedence, they placed many of their same-sex attraction issues in proper perspective.

This broadened perspective was enabling for those struggling with SSA issues and for me as we realized that being *gay* or *lesbian* was most often *not* the identity of these Latter-day Saints—it was a test, a trial, and an opportunity for growth, or as Paul put it, "a thorn in the flesh" (2 Corinthians 12:7). Each of them was a child of God. It was liberating for us as we kept this perspective, and it was helpful to externalize the SSA issues and not see those issues as their identity.

One young man, feeling empowered by this perspective, said to me, "So it's not *me;* it's just *it*—this thing I have inside of me." This insight enabled him to take a much more helpful and healthful perspective on his issues. He began to see them in perspective with all his other traits, gifts, and blessings. He wasn't an *SSA person;* he was simply a person—a man—who experienced attractions to others of his own sex.

We often discussed the aspects of these desires that are natural and healthy and that we should cultivate. Healthy love and intimacy between those of the same sex that is within the bounds the Lord has set is something we should seek to cultivate. The references of the Apostle John to himself as the disciple "whom Jesus loved" (John 13:23) and as "lying on Jesus' breast" (John 13:25) are healthy and desirable expressions of divine love of one man for another.

Divine Love—The Heart of the Gospel

Finally, one of the most vital principles I have learned through working with members dealing with these issues is the importance of love. That may seem simplistic, yet it is vital to the members that they *feel* the love of their priesthood leader, as opposed to *knowing* that the priesthood leader loves them. My own ability to feel and express love has grown tremendously through working with the issue of same-gender attraction. Maybe I loved those struggling with same-gender attraction just as much in the beginning, but perhaps it was the mixture of other feelings (confusion, frustration, apprehension) that made it difficult for me to identify all of my love for them. However, as I discovered that "love casteth out fear" (1 John 4:18) and that truth chases away confusion, I learned to show my love more fully. In fact, if I were asked to name one single action or belief that helped me the most as I worked with Latter-day Saints who experience same-gender attraction, it would be *compassionate understanding.*

I realize that many other issues and influences help; however, without compassionate understanding, it is difficult to get to the other sources of help. The Prophet Joseph Smith stated, "When persons manifest the least kindness and love to me, O what power it has over my mind, while the opposite course has a tendency to harrow up all the harsh feelings and depress the human mind."[14] It is compassion and understanding that lead people along the path of healing and health, that help them hold onto the iron rod, that help them to have hope in the valleys of despair. Priesthood leaders who show that they are not afraid to listen in order to understand and who show compassion all along the journey are doing the most poignant acts to influence, nourish, and serve these members of the Church.

The parable of the good Samaritan is a powerful example of this truth. Priesthood leaders need to be examples of the Samaritan, who was not afraid to stop and minister (even though others would not go near), who openly showed compassion when others would not (he was not afraid of others' perceptions), and who understood the suffering and enlisted others to help. This we can all do.

Conclusion

While not unique to this time and age, doctrinal, societal, and interpersonal struggles with homosexually have reached new heights in this generation and will most certainly continue in the foreseeable future. It is my hope that priesthood leaders (and others) can render needed compassion, guidance, friendship, and understanding to those members who deal with this issue.

In a significant way I have grown and developed and been touched and healed by my relationships with those I have worked with who experience same-sex attraction. Indeed, it has been a blessing in my life to have had the opportunity to work with these wonderful brothers and sisters in the Church. They have taught me much about the expansiveness of the Atonement, the infinite nature of God's love, the tenderness of His mercies, the peace He can provide, and much more.

The Atonement Can Fix That Too!

Kevin Lindley

Kevin Lindley met his wife, Ashley, after returning from the Finland Helsinki Mission in 2006. They live in Idaho Falls, Idaho, where Ashley teaches middle school and Kevin is studying to become a professional therapist. They both love to share the joy they've found in the gospel, whether it be professionally, through their service as foster parents, or simply through loving relationships with friends and family.

When I was a boy, I loved watching John Wayne movies. One of my favorites was *Big Jake.* In the movie, John Wayne's character, Jake McCandles, is trying to rescue his grandson from a band of kidnappers. In one of the last scenes, Jake says to the head kidnapper: "Now you understand this: anything happens, anything at all—your fault, my fault, nobody's fault, it don't matter—I'm going to blow your head off. It's as simple as that."[15]

I've always liked that quote. Jake is determined to save his grandson's life and isn't going to let anyone stand in his way. I had no idea back then just how personal that quote would become to me.

I clearly remember my first crush on a new boy in my fifth-grade class, but I never thought of myself as *gay.* I wasn't that interested in girls, but I told myself that was just because I was waiting until after my mission to get serious about dating. I failed to realize that the fantasies and attractions I had toward men were anything more than a hormonal teenager's sinful sex drive. I had been taught in church that homosexuality was evil and that it was a sin against nature. I don't recall, however, ever being taught that having those attractions wasn't a sin—that the sin was only in acting on those feelings.

I remembered reading in the pamphlet *For the Strength of Youth* that a person with feelings of attraction toward members of the same gender should talk with his parents and priesthood leaders, but how on earth could I tell a priesthood leader or my parents about my attractions? I wanted to serve a mission. I wanted my priesthood leaders to like me. I wanted my parents to love me. I was sure that if anyone knew what a horrible, evil person I was, they would be disgusted with me. I was determined to take the secret of my attractions with me to my grave.

Fast-forward a few years. When I had been home from my mission for about six months, I met a young woman. We started hanging out and became really good friends. I can remember clearly the night we officially started dating. I'm still not sure what possessed me to tell her that I wanted to date her. I wasn't really attracted to her. A few months later we were driving home from her college graduation. We were just talking, and the next thing I knew, we were talking about getting married. We both looked at each other and one of us said, "We really are going to end up getting married, aren't we?"

When I got home, I had a major panic attack, but then as I prayed to Heavenly Father, a peaceful feeling came over me. I knew I didn't understand how everything was going to work, but I knew it would. Six weeks later my wife and I were sealed in the Idaho Falls Idaho Temple. I had worked with the branch president of my singles branch to repent and break habits of pornography and masturbation that were associated with my same-sex attractions, but we never really talked about the attractions themselves. I knew I was worthy to be married. It was a very happy day for both of us. I was pretty convinced that once I had a healthy and appropriate outlet for my sexual energies, everything would be just fine. That day I felt that my difficulties with same-sex attraction were over.

Oh, how wrong I was.

Married life had a way of throwing fuel on the fire. I loved my wife dearly and we rarely had any disagreements, but I began to notice an increase in the intensity of my attractions toward men. Sometimes I couldn't get an attractive coworker off my mind. Other times inappropriate thoughts began to creep into my mind. At first I tried fiercely to resist them. I knew that acting on those feelings was wrong. However, because I was still unaware of the unresolved issues that I now understand to be at the root of my attractions, the feelings and thoughts didn't go away. I eventually gave in to temptation to look at pornography and allowed myself to fantasize about other men. I began to lead a double life. During the day I would be a loving husband, good student, and righteous priesthood holder. At night I would spend hours on the Internet, viewing inappropriate material and communicating with gay men.

One day, about nine months into our marriage, I realized that I was seriously considering leaving my wife and pursuing an openly gay lifestyle. I firmly believe that the Lord was reaching out to me in loving mercy. That realization and the ensuing battle in my mind over what I was going to do constituted one of the most painful moments in my life. I felt that I was on a ledge of a very high cliff. I didn't know how to get back up to safety—if it was even possible or if I even wanted to if I could. Part of me wanted to leap into the unknown below. Despite my efforts to live a good life, the attractions I felt were strong and real. I felt powerless to resist them. And yet something in my soul fought desperately to keep me from jumping. I felt and thought that the war between these two parts of myself was literally destroying the battlefield where it was playing out. My heart was being torn, broken.

I called into work that day and let my boss know I wouldn't make it. I drove up to a hill outside of town and found a quiet, secluded place. There I poured out my soul to my Father, pleading for some kind of help. I knew I couldn't endure much longer. Eventually a peace began to settle over me. Within that peace I found a firm resolve to try to do what I knew to be right.

It took a tremendous effort to confront the shame inside me, but, receiving strength from the Lord, I told my wife about my attractions, my sins, and my desire to make our marriage work. I don't think I knew until that moment just how strong and amazing of a woman I had married. I have never felt anything but love and support from her. Many times I've wished that I'd realized and dealt with my attractions before we got married. I wish I had told her before we were married. Still, I know that the Lord led me to one of His most precious daughters, knowing full well that I could never have made this journey without her.

A few days later I met with my bishop. I had no idea what was going to happen when I told him that I was attracted to men and confessed my sins to him. All I knew was that on that hill on that cool November afternoon, I had felt and known that more than anything I wanted to be right with the Lord. I was willing to do anything that would help. I wasn't at all prepared for the response I got from my inexperienced bishop.

He looked at me lovingly and said, "I don't know much about same-sex attraction, but I've received some material from the Church about it. I will have to go home and study." He then assured me that I was still loved and even worthy to be serving in my calling. He said that as far as he was aware, the attractions weren't a sin. He offered some advice about dealing with my addiction to pornography. He said that there were some spiritual solutions to overcoming sin but that many individuals also needed additional help. He recommended that I see a therapist and attend a therapy group for those seeking to overcome pornography addictions.

Perhaps most important, he told me that there was hope. He closed our appointment by offering to give me a priesthood blessing. I gladly accepted. I can't remember everything that was said in that blessing, but I do clearly remember hearing and feeling the assurance that God loved me. I also remember a specific blessing of patience as I started the process of confronting my attractions—patience with my wife, the Lord, my priesthood leaders, my therapist, and just as important, patience with myself.

My bishop and I continued to meet regularly for a few months. He found articles written by priesthood leaders online and asked me to read them and discuss them with him. He always offered support and love. He genuinely sought to understand what I was going through. I am very grateful to have had such a faithful servant of the Lord to help me as I started my journey down the path to overcoming my trials, because the road was not an easy one. It was very bumpy, and I was certainly not perfect. My faith wavered, and the initial hope I'd had of healing faded when things didn't change as quickly as I would have liked.

One Sunday I was feeling particularly mad at the world, the Church, and at God. I was filled with skepticism and contempt for the speakers in sacrament meeting. I was fairly close to giving up on God and the Church. I remember thinking that if the Lord was really concerned about me, then surely He would inspire the bishop to come talk to me. I waited around the chapel until I saw the bishop leave without even looking my way. I had no desire to go to Sunday School, where I might have to talk to someone, so I found a secluded spot in the building and hoped no one would find me.

I was looking out the window when I sensed someone behind me. I turned around and saw my bishop standing there. He asked me if I was okay. I broke down in tears and shook my head. He asked if I wanted to talk about it. His encouraging words and inspired counsel helped me push through that difficult time.

I will be forever grateful for that bishop and the Christlike love he showed me. I know that he listened to the promptings of the Spirit and followed them. He didn't know how to respond the first time I talked to him. He had no training in dealing with same-sex attraction. All he had and all he needed was a genuine love for a ward member and an unwavering desire to act as the Lord directed. In the face of a distinct lack of training and knowledge, the grace of Jesus Christ endowed him with the ability to do more than he would have been able to on his own. The Atonement compensated for his inadequacies, and in the strength of the Lord, this humble man worked miracles.

Shortly after that we moved. I knew that including my bishop in my journey was important. However, I was hesitant to talk to my new bishop. Despite the fact that I had had a good experience with my previous bishop, I had heard stories. Many individuals with same-sex attraction have had difficult experiences with some of their priesthood leaders. Unfortunately, many priesthood leaders have not received adequate training in addressing the difficulties of same-sex attraction.

Despite these leaders' best efforts, the members they work with may still feel discouraged, misunderstood, or unloved. I've often wondered how a person can find the courage to remain faithful after such experiences. I was going to find that out with my new bishop.

Things were going well, so I justified myself in not going to the bishop right away. I hardly even knew the man, and he had a lot of other ward members to take care of. I was making a lot of progress in overcoming my pornography and masturbation addictions and figured that things could wait until we got to know each other better.

However, I ended up meeting with him sooner than I had planned. The first time I met with my new bishop could have certainly been a more cheerful occasion. I had to schedule an appointment with him one Saturday afternoon to start the repentance process after I had committed some pretty serious sins. I had already talked to my wife. Until that point I have to admit that I still wasn't sure if I was going to stay married and faithful to the Church or if I was going to end up divorced and openly gay. But in that moment the guilt and sorrow I felt for going against God's commandments was overshadowed by the agony I felt at seeing the pain I had caused my wife. I think I realized then just how much I loved her and how much I wanted to be with her for eternity. I knew that I was willing to do whatever it took to reach that goal. I'm grateful that she shared the same commitment. We were unsure how we were going to make it through this trial, but we knew we wanted to make our marriage work.

So, with my pride stripped away and my heart broken, I approached my bishop without any idea of how he would respond or what would happen. All I knew was that whatever it took, I was going to do everything in my power to access the power of the Atonement to make both my soul and my marriage whole again. I was fairly numb as I told my bishop about my attractions and what I had done. I really didn't have any tears to cry, just a burning desire to reconcile myself with God. I could definitely sense my bishop's reaction to my confession. He seemed very uncomfortable with the situation, but I was impressed with how he handled himself. He told me that disciplinary action would most likely be taken but that it was possible to repent. He also offered a blessing, which I again accepted gladly. As with my previous bishop's blessing, I don't remember all of what was said, but I do remember the feeling of hope I felt as I left his house. I knew that the road ahead was not going to be easy but that it was going to be possible. I had a hope that I could find the happiness I was looking for.

My stake president instructed my bishop to hold a disciplinary council on the ward level. The following Thursday I met with the bishopric and was completely honest with them. They assured me that their only desire in holding this council was to do the will of the Lord. I could sense their commitment not only to find out the will of the Lord but also to obey it. I felt their love for my wife and me. I was grateful for her support and love throughout the process. After a period of prayer and deliberation, they called us back into the office and explained that they felt the Lord's will was for me to be disfellowshipped. My bishop kindly explained what that meant and what restrictions it placed on my participation in church.

I remember feeling a sense of peace and hope as I sat there that night. I felt the confirmation from the Holy Ghost that this was indeed the will of the Lord. My bishop explained that disciplinary action was neither a punishment nor a condition of forgiveness. It was an opportunity to reevaluate my life and to recommit myself to the covenants I had made. I clearly remember the hope with which he told us that in one year the disciplinary council would reconvene and that he had every reason to believe I would be ready to be reinstated into full fellowship at that time.

My bishop wanted me to meet with him at least every other week throughout the year, and I was happy to do so. A number of times he said things that didn't sit right with me. However, I could still sense that despite his lack of understanding of exactly what I was going through, he wanted to understand and help me. I had to speak up a few times and explain that I didn't agree with certain statements. Most often that led him to clarify what he meant. As he did so, it turned out that often we were on the same page. A couple of times he listened to me and thanked me for helping him better understand the difficulties that accompany same-sex attraction. A number of times, he lovingly helped me understand certain gospel principles, which altered the way I viewed things.

I remember one time I told him how I had met a couple of men who also experienced same-sex attraction. I expressed how much their support and friendship helped me. He said that he wasn't comfortable with me associating with other men who have the same feelings I do. I knew that I had felt the Spirit with these men. I knew that God had led me to them. I gently responded that it was really important for me to have that support and to feel love from other men in a nonsexual way. I explained that these men were committed to their marriages and to staying morally clean. I told him that we were careful not to put ourselves in positions where we might be tempted. He told me that as long as I was careful and followed the promptings of the Spirit, it probably would be just fine. But he did warn me against spending time with men who were clearly not living the gospel. I agreed whole-heartedly with him. I'm grateful that my bishop listened to me and that he sought to always *do* what was right rather than to always *be* right.

There were a number of occasions when I'm sure that if I had allowed myself to be offended, I could have become bitter. I could have convinced myself that he simply didn't understand what I was going through or that he just didn't like me. I'm grateful the Holy Ghost helped me see that he didn't intend to hurt me. I'm grateful that I had the courage to be honest with him and to tell him when I didn't completely agree with him. That honesty and openness allowed the two of us to work together with the Lord—to "reason together," so to speak (Isaiah 1:18; D&C 50:10)—helping me resist temptation and strengthen my testimony. The things we disagreed about were usually fairly minor, and it helped to remember that.

Things changed one Sunday afternoon. I had resisted the temptation to relapse into my addictions since the disciplinary council, but then I had a lapse and viewed pornography again. Through my work with my therapist, I knew that this was not the end of the world. It was going to take a long time to overcome my pornography addiction. The fact that I continually made progress was more important than immediate perfection. So, when I told my bishop that I had slipped up but that I was going to keep pressing forward and trying to improve, I expected him to nod and offer encouragement.

Instead, he told me that this time he wasn't going to do anything, but that I needed to know if it happened again, he would start the year of my disfellowshipment over again. I was shocked that he felt that my lapse was so serious. I hardly said another word through the whole interview. By the time I got home I was livid. I felt completely misunderstood by my bishop. I knew how difficult it was to overcome an addiction like this and that with the Savior's enabling grace, I was making remarkable progress. I felt the assurance of the Spirit that I was doing well and that the Lord was pleased with my efforts. If my bishop couldn't feel the same way, I wasn't going to be honest with him again. I would simply pretend that everything was going perfectly well. I was committed to living the gospel, but if I made any more mistakes along the way, I wasn't going to tell the bishop. I wasn't going to let what I perceived as his human weakness and lack of understanding about what I was going through get in my way.

My wife could sense my anger, and in her loving wisdom, she suggested I call a friend who also experiences same-sex attraction. He's a bit older than I am and has more experience, so I figured he would be understanding if I vented to him. I called him and told him all about what had happened. I ended my tirade by commenting, "I guess I'm learning that Church leaders really aren't perfect."

My friend wisely replied, "Yes, that's true, but I believe that the Atonement applies to this situation too."

I was speechless; tears welled up in my eyes. I had been so focused on what I perceived to be the mistakes of another that I had forgotten the Savior's promise of comfort regardless of where my pain came from. I quickly thanked him and hung up the phone. I got on my knees and prayed, begging the Lord to bless me through the power of the Atonement. A feeling of peace and comfort immediately came over me.

I felt Heavenly Father's love for me. I knew that despite how I felt after speaking with my bishop, everything was going to be okay. I was able to get to sleep, completely free from frustration and anger.

At my next appointment with my bishop, I was open with him about how our prior conversation made me feel. He offered a sincere apology for any potential misunderstanding. It turned out that his intention was to say that if I lapsed and acted out with another man, the year would have started over. He wasn't as concerned with a single episode of looking at pornography. I'm grateful that my bishop and I were able to resolve the miscommunication. However, that wasn't nearly as important as what had happened earlier. I know that the Atonement compensates for conditions of mortality. Even though I felt that my bishop had handled the situation in a way that was hurtful to me, I was able to feel peace. I know that the Atonement is infinite enough in scope to apply to the humanness of even our priesthood leaders.

As I reflected on that experience, I was reminded of the quote from *Big Jake.* The words were a little different this time, though. I could almost hear the Savior saying, "Now you understand this: anything happens, anything at all—your fault, his fault, nobody's fault, it doesn't matter—I can fix it. It's as simple as that."

Since that time my bishop and I have developed a very close friendship. My disciplinary council was reconvened, and I was reinstated into full fellowship. I am so grateful for the Church disciplinary process. I know that it isn't always administered perfectly, and I feel for those who have had difficult experiences with disciplinary councils. The process isn't easy, and it certainly isn't fun. But it is inspired. That experience provided me with a unique opportunity to be continually reminded every time I couldn't take the sacrament or say a prayer in church that I needed to change my life and to change the way I think. That year was one of the best of my life. I'm not glad that I sinned to the point where it was necessary, but I am grateful for the changes it inspired me to make. My testimony of the gospel has grown, and my commitment to live righteously has increased.

My journey is nowhere near complete. I have come remarkably

far from where I was, but I know I still have a long way to go to become the man I want to be—the man the Lord knows I can be. I have learned that there is no shame in needing a professional therapist to help me better manage my thought patterns and emotions. I am grateful that I was led to a righteous man who had the skills and knowledge he needed in order to help me. I am so grateful for a loving wife who is a source of strength for me. Her encouragement and support enable me to be a better man. I know that I could never have come as far as I have without her. I am grateful for loving friends who lift me when I'm weak. I know that the Lord works though others to bless and help us.

I am grateful for a loving Heavenly Father who allows us to experience trials so that we can grow and become like Him. Most important, I am grateful for the Savior and His infinite Atonement. I know that whatever my journey may hold in store for me, with His strength, grace, and power, I can endure. No matter what happens—my fault, somebody else's fault, nobody's fault—it doesn't matter. The Atonement can fix that too. It's as simple as that.

Chapter 6

Eternal Marriage: Principles, Possibilities, and Promises

Michael Goodman

Few things are as discouraging as being told there is an ideal we should embrace and yet believing we never can reach it, worlds without end. Good people stuck in that situation often react in various ways. For some, the incongruence creates a barrier to acceptance so high that they simply cannot bring themselves to believe in the ideal. Some of those who cannot believe turn away in anger. Others mourn, wishing they could believe. Others not only believe in the ideal but also know that it is real; and yet, feeling that they can never be part of that reality, they are left in despair and without hope. Yet hope is possible and ultimately essential.

Without hope, there is no way to overcome the despair and approach the ideal. Hope is the necessary ingredient that makes the ideal both possible and inevitable. An experience I had while serving as a mission president cemented this truth in my mind. I worked with dozens of missionaries who became so homesick they wanted to go home. Though none went home early, I learned much from helping them through their homesickness. One thing became clear early on. As long as they were hopeless—as long as they believed they would continue to feel gut-wrenching pain—they could not progress. It was almost always essential that they have hope for a better tomorrow to help them make the right choices today. A rare few had such a strong sense of duty and honor to commitment that even without hope their sheer obedience pulled them through. These missionaries, however, were the exceptions.

I believe the need for greater hope is real for many Latter-day Saints who have feelings of same-gender attraction. There must be hope for a bright future. There must be hope that life can be filled with joy and fulfillment. Ultimately, there must be hope that the eternal joys of marriage, family, and all associated intimacies await faithful members who experience same-gender attraction.

From their youth, most Latter-day Saints have been taught the ideal of eternal marriage. Most start out expecting a future marriage filled with the kind of love and intimacy that, as they are taught, give meaning to life. For those with same-gender attraction, however, at some point that dream begins to fade.

In order for the doctrines and principles in this chapter to help, hope must somehow be rekindled. Ideally, there must be faith that all will work out and that life can be filled with joy, purpose, and fulfillment, whether we are married or single. For some, however, hope and faith may seem as impossible as eternal marriage itself. The prophet Alma gave a key that may unlock the door to that hope. He taught, "Even if ye can no more than desire to believe, let this desire work in you, even until ye believe in a manner that ye can give place for a portion of my words" (Alma 32:27).

Hope for Eternal Marriage

Ultimately (eternally), it is not possible to receive a fulness of joy without entering the new and everlasting covenant of marriage (see D&C 131:1–4). This doctrine can seem hard when juxtaposed with the reality that, for a variety of reasons, many of Heavenly Father's children do not marry in this life. Often, through no fault of their own, this central part of the gospel plan isn't realized in mortality for these individuals. Elder Richard G. Scott said, "The Lord knows the intent of your heart. His prophets have stated that you [all of Heavenly Father's children] will have that blessing [eternal marriage] as you consistently live to qualify for it."[1] As we try to understand the doctrine of eternal marriage and develop a hope for it, we must not make the mistake of believing that we have to *wait on marriage* before happiness can begin in this life. Heavenly Father will not deny His faithful children a rich and fulfilling life based on things outside their control. This will be discussed more fully later in the chapter.

As Alma taught, sometimes faith and hope have to start with simple desire. Desire can make hope and faith possible. There are many reasons to desire eternal marriage, both in this life and in the life to come. The Brethren have regularly tried to help members of the Church understand the joy that comes from eternal marriage. President Boyd K. Packer has taught: "In marriage all of the worthy yearnings of the human soul, all that is physical and emotional and spiritual, can be fulfilled. . . . Marriage is meant to be eternal."[2] Yes, marriage, eternal marriage, is worth desiring. As President Spencer W. Kimball taught, "Marriage can be more an exultant ecstasy than the human mind can conceive."[3] Some sincerely try to find this kind of happiness in relationships contrary to the principles of revealed truth. No counterfeit relationship, however, can ever bring the true eternal joy that comes from a righteous eternal marriage.[4]

As the prophets have taught, there is reason to desire and hope for eternal marriage. It is important to understand that this ideal is ultimately within the reach of all of God's children who choose to be faithful to His gospel plan. None, including those who struggle with same-gender attraction, are excluded. The following statement from the pamphlet *God Loveth His Children,* published by the Church, declares this truth:

"While many Latter-day Saints, through individual effort, the exercise of faith, and reliance upon the enabling power of the Atonement, overcome same-gender attraction in mortality, others may not be free of this challenge in this life. However, the perfect plan of our Father in Heaven makes provision for individuals who seek to keep His commandments but who, through no fault of their own, do not have an eternal marriage in mortal life. *As we follow Heavenly Father's plan, our bodies, feelings, and desires will be perfected in the next life so that every one of God's children may find joy in a family consisting of a husband, a wife, and children."* It further states: "All of Heavenly Father's children desire to love and be loved, including many adults who, for a variety of reasons, remain single. God assures His children, including those currently attracted to persons of the same gender, that their righteous desires will eventually be fully satisfied in God's own way and according to His timing."[5]

The possibility of having to wait until the next life to enjoy the full blessings of eternal marriage may seem of little help to those who desire the blessing of intimate companionship right now. But by more thoroughly understanding the doctrine of eternal marriage, we can receive power and help beyond what we might expect. The more we understand the real nature of eternal marriage, the more we desire it. This is true not only for those dealing with same-gender attraction but also for all of Heavenly Father's children, single or married. It is also true that the more we understand the importance of the doctrinal foundations of eternal marriage, the more we are willing to do whatever it takes not to lose the possibility of those blessings in the future. Therefore, with the assurance that all should hope for the promised blessings, let's try to lay a foundation.

Importance of Eternal Marriage

President Packer has taught that "true doctrine, understood, changes attitudes and behavior."[6] There are few areas where understanding true doctrine is more important than in relation to marriage. The very definitions of marriage and family understood by mankind for millennia are no longer considered valid by many. In fact, the leading scholarly journal in the field of marriage and family recently changed its name from *The Journal of Marriage and the Family* to *The Journal of Marriage and Family* to indicate that there is no longer any universally accepted definition of *the* family. However, the institution of marriage is only changeable by man if it is a man-made institution to start with. Even though much of the world believes that marriage is man-made, those with a testimony of the restored gospel of Jesus Christ know otherwise.

Eternal marriage, as the name indicates, has no beginning and will have no end. Marriage on this earth, instituted by God, began with the creation of Adam and Eve. In the first chapter of the Bible, we read of the creation of man and woman (see Genesis 1:26–27). The first recorded commandment given to man and woman was to multiply and replenish the earth (see Genesis 1:28). This commandment presupposes Adam and Eve's marriage. In Genesis 2, after the symbolic account of Adam and Eve's creation, the scripture record declares, "Therefore shall a man leave his father and his mother, and shall cleave unto his wife: and they shall be one flesh" (Genesis 2:24). But this becoming one was more than just a "till death do you part" ritual. President Henry B. Eyring explained:

"The requirement that we be one is not for this life alone. It is to be without end. The first marriage was performed by God in the garden when Adam and Eve were immortal. He placed in men and women from the beginning a desire to be joined together as man and wife forever to dwell in families in a perfect, righteous union."[7] Thus eternal marriage becomes the focal point of the creation of man from the beginning of sacred writ.

There is no shortage of statements by those we sustain as prophets, seers, and revelators pertaining to the divine origin and centrality of marriage and family in the gospel plan. President Joseph Fielding Smith taught that marriage involves "an eternal principle ordained before the foundation of the world and instituted on this earth before death came into it."[8] Elder Bruce R. McConkie taught, "Marriage and the family unit are the central part of the plan of progression and exaltation. All things center in and around the family unit in the eternal perspective."[9] President Brigham Young taught that marriage "lays the foundation for worlds, for angels, and for the Gods; for intelligent beings to be crowned with glory, immortality, and eternal lives. In fact, it is the thread which runs from the beginning to the end of the holy Gospel of Salvation."[10] President Kimball taught that marriage and family are not only central to Heavenly Father's plan but that the "family is the great plan of life as conceived and organized by our Father in Heaven."[11]

These statements and countless similar statements leave little ambiguity as to the importance of marriage in God's plan of happiness. However, though they hint at the reasons behind the centrality of marriage, they do not lay out a doctrinal foundation for it. Even though Church members may understand the significance of a given doctrine due to such overarching statements, they often struggle to find the intersection between knowing that the doctrine is important and finding the motivation and purpose necessary to implement that doctrine in their lives. One example of this phenomenon is the doctrine of chastity. We can quote Alma 39:5 (which teaches that violating the law of chastity is "most abominable above all sins save it be the shedding of innocent blood or denying the Holy Ghost") in an attempt to teach members the seriousness of violating the law of chastity, but often it isn't until they understand the doctrinal foundations of the law that they find the strength and determination to live it. In a similar vein, it is one thing to be able to quote prophetic statements on the importance of marriage and another thing to understand the doctrinal foundations of marriage to the point that the doctrine dictates the path of life we choose to follow.

Doctrinal Foundations of Eternal Marriage

Eternal destiny. President Kimball's statement that family *is* the plan hints at a doctrinal truth that may elude some members of the Church. I believe that if you asked most members what the purpose of life is, they would respond that our purpose is to so live that we can joyfully return to be with God in heaven forever. There is ample scriptural evidence that this answer is right, at least partially (see 2 Nephi 2:25; Matthew 5:3, 10, 12; Mark 10:21; Luke 18:22; Mosiah 2:41; Alma 11:37; Helaman 3:30; D&C 6:37; 20:24; 127:4; Moses 7:21). Sometimes the scriptures refer to this aspect of our eternal destiny as "everlasting life" (John 3:16; 3 Nephi 5:13; D&C 45:5). Although the term *everlasting life* is descriptive of the duration of our eternal destiny, it is less descriptive of the quality. A more descriptive term appears in the Doctrine and Covenants: "If you keep my commandments and endure to the end you shall have eternal life, which gift is the greatest of all the gifts of God" (D&C 14:70). Both concepts, duration and quality, are brought together in Moses 1:39: "Behold, this is my work and my glory—to bring to pass the immortality and eternal life of man." Though living forever is an important part of our destiny, it is important to make a distinction between immortality and eternal life. Satan and all who follow him are immortal inasmuch as they have no end; they will exist forever. However, they certainly won't enjoy eternal life. They will not have resurrected bodies capable of celestial glory and the ability to become as God is.

God is married. We learn from Doctrine and Covenants 19:11 that *eternal* is another name for God. Therefore, eternal life is another way of saying God's life, or the kind of life that God lives. God's work and glory is to bring to pass not only our immortality but also our eternal life. Our eternal destiny is nothing less than becoming as God is now. This doctrine is clearly taught in the famous couplet by Lorenzo Snow: "As man now is, God once was: As God now is, man may be."[12] If our eternal destiny is to become like our Father in Heaven, we need to gain an understanding of who He is and what He is like. How else can we live our life in accordance with His will and nature? As the Prophet Joseph Smith taught, in order for us to have faith in God (not to mention in God's plan), we need to have a correct idea of God's "character, perfections, and attributes."[13]

Obviously, even the entire scriptural canon cannot contain all there is to know about the character, perfection, and attributes of God, so this chapter certainly won't try to detail them all. God's character is made up of all that is beautiful, virtuous, and good in infinite measure. However, there is one aspect of who He is that must be understood above all else in relation to eternal marriage. That truth is that God Himself is a married being.[14]

The very definition of godhood, or exaltation, depends on the union of a man and woman, eternally married. Elder Erastus Snow taught, "There can be no God except he is composed of the man and woman united, and there is not in all the eternities that exist, nor ever will be, a God in any other way."[15] We learn in the Doctrine and Covenants that "in the celestial glory there are three heavens or degrees; And in order to obtain the highest [to be exalted like Heavenly Father], a man must enter into this order of the priesthood [meaning the new and everlasting covenant of marriage]; and if he does not, he cannot obtain it. He may enter into the other, but that is the end of his kingdom; he cannot have an increase" (D&C 131:1–4).

Eternal marriage is necessary for exaltation because there is no such thing as a single god. Doctrine and Covenants 132:19 teaches that those who enter into the new and everlasting covenant of marriage and are faithful to it will "pass by the angels, and the gods, which are set there, to their exaltation and glory in all things, as hath been sealed upon their heads, which glory shall be a fulness and a continuation of the seeds forever and ever."

It is only through the union of man and woman, eternally married, that a "continuation of the seeds forever and ever" is possible. President Harold B. Lee, referencing the hymn "O My Father," explained: "That great hymn 'O My Father' puts it correctly when Eliza R. Snow wrote, 'In the heav'ns are parents single? No, the thought makes reason stare! Truth is reason; truth eternal tells me I've a mother there.' Born of a Heavenly Mother, sired by a Heavenly Father, we knew Him, we were in His house."[16]

God is our father. Though we know few details regarding Heavenly Father's marriage, there can be few things more central to His nature. If you were to ask, "What does God do for a living; what is His life's work?" the answer would have to be that he is a full-time husband and father. All that He does is intended for the welfare and eternal salvation of His children. Elder Dallin H. Oaks taught: "The work of God is to bring to pass the eternal life of His children (see Moses 1:39), and all that this entails in the birth, nurturing, teaching, and sealing of our Heavenly Father's children. Everything else is lower in priority."[17] Elder Dennis E. Simmons explained: "He [God] has already achieved godhood. Now His only objective is to help us—to enable us to return to Him and be like Him and live His kind of life eternally."[18]

This doctrine is at the foundation of our understanding of eternal marriage. The destiny of mankind is to become like Heavenly Father and Heavenly Mother in an eternal covenant and creative union. This capacity is part of our premortal, mortal, and postmortal nature. The First Presidency of Heber J. Grant, Anthony W. Ivins, and Charles W. Nibley taught, "Man is the child of God, formed in the divine image and endowed with divine attributes, and even as the infant son of an earthly father and mother is capable in due time of becoming a man, so that undeveloped offspring of celestial parentage is capable, by experience through ages and aeons, of evolving into a God."[19]

In an article on same-gender attraction, Elder Oaks taught that "the purpose of mortal life and the mission of The Church of Jesus Christ of Latter-day Saints is to prepare the sons and daughters of God for their destiny—to become like our heavenly parents."[20]

We are God's children. Through a comprehensive understanding of the nature of God, we are enabled to better understand our own nature and the privileges that come with it. This understanding is essential if we are to live up to the potential within us. President Packer taught that "we all live far below our privileges."[21] Part of the challenge is that at times we lack a correct understanding of our nature. The corresponding doctrine to God being our Father is that we are His children. Few doctrines are more apparent through a study of the scriptures. In the beginning, the Lord declared to Adam: "Behold, thou art one in me, a son of God; and thus may all become my sons" (Moses 6:68). God refers to Moses, and Moses refers to himself, as a son of God seven times in the book of Moses. In the same book, as the Lord introduces Himself to Enoch, He calls him "my son" (Moses 6:27). And in the book of Abraham, the Lord refers to Abraham as "my son" (Abraham 1:17).

President Marion G. Romney explained that this is "the most important knowledge available to mortals. Such knowledge is beyond the ken of the uninspired mind. Neither logic, science, philosophy, nor any other field of worldly learning has ever been, or ever will be, able to find it out. . . . Fortunately for us, as has already been shown, it has been so revealed repeatedly from Adam until today.

"The aspirations, desires, and motivations of one who accepts, believes, and by the power of the Holy Spirit obtains a witness to the truth that he is a begotten son or daughter unto God differs from the aspirations of him who believes otherwise, as the growing vine differs from the severed branch (2 Timothy 3:7)."[22]

As stated at the beginning of this chapter, hope is often the child of desire. President Romney taught that the knowledge that we are children of a God who loves us and gave His only begotten Son for us helps us to change our desires, aspirations, and motivations.

However, some who know this to be true still struggle. Once we gain a basic knowledge of our divine heritage, we must deepen our understanding of what it actually means in our daily life.[23] How often have members of the Church sung the words to the children's hymn "I Am a Child of God" without really drinking deeply from its meaning? President Gordon B. Hinckley asked us if we really understand the significance of this doctrine:

"I challenge every one of you who can hear me to rise to the divinity within you. Do we really realize what it means to be a child of God, to have within us something of the divine nature? . . . We can either subdue the divine nature and hide it so that it finds no expression in our lives, or we can bring it to the front and let it shine through all that we do."[24]

A deep and abiding testimony that we are children of God will help us live up to our "infinite capacities to grow spiritually and become more like [God]."[25] It is a knowledge that protects as well as directs. Our spiritual security increases as we come to more deeply sense our identity as children of God. Sheri Dew taught that "the more clearly we understand our divine destiny, the more immune we become to Satan" and ultimately to Satan's counterfeits to Heavenly Father's plan.[26]

Understanding our nature. Through understanding the nature of God and our relationship to Him, we come to understand that our nature is nothing less than His nature in embryo. Because God by nature is a heterosexually creative being, we too must have the seeds of that same eternal nature within us. If our eternal destiny depends on our being eternally married to someone of the opposite sex, our deepest, most innate spiritual nature—buried within the human development and experience that LDS psychologist Allen Bergin calls our "mortal overlay"[27]—must be in line with that destiny. As President Howard W. Hunter taught, "My spiritual reasoning tells me that because God is an exalted being, holy and good, that man's supreme goal [and destiny] is to be like him."[28] Being like Him means that our supreme goal and destiny is linked to our relationship with our future spouse. Elder Oaks taught that "attraction between man and woman was instilled by the Creator."[29] This is true even if that attraction is temporarily hidden or absent.

Understanding this aspect of our nature helps us understand that we can never find real happiness in this life or in the next by living contrary to that nature. Jesus explained why those who allow their nature to become carnal can never find lasting happiness (see Alma 41:10–11). It is true that there can be momentary pleasure and even a sense of joy "for a season," but that season always ends in pain and sorrow (3 Nephi 27:11). Alma taught that those who give into their carnal nature "are without God in the world, and they have gone contrary to the nature of God; therefore, they are in a state contrary to the nature of happiness" (Alma 41:11). God's nature (and our true nature as His children) is the nature of happiness. This is why Helaman taught that those who were living contrary to God's nature and commandments could never truly be happy. He explained that they seek "for happiness in doing iniquity, which thing is contrary to the nature of that righteousness which is in our great and Eternal Head" (Helaman 13:38). Hence, any attempt to live contrary to our divine nature will unavoidably fail to bring the eternal happiness we seek.

Implications for Those Struggling with Same-Gender Attraction

It's not easy. Understanding our true nature does not make everything easy when our current fallen nature seems to be telling us that we are different from what the scriptures and prophets tell us we are. Many of Heavenly Father's children for one reason or another do not feel an attraction to members of the opposite sex. This chapter does not discuss what we know about the reasons for this. But by truly understanding what our eternal nature and destiny is, we can begin to live, or continue our efforts to live our life in such a way as to make our eternal destiny a reality. The following discussion contains principles that can assist those who seek to live their lives in accordance with Heavenly Father's plan for them.

Do not label yourself. One of the sophistries often used to justify inappropriate behavior connected with same-gender attraction is that you shouldn't deny your true nature. In other words, some would claim that if you are attracted to those of the same-gender, you are going against your true nature by not granting romantic or sexual expression to those feelings. However, as explained above, our *true* nature can never be homosexual—it is to become like God. But for reasons beyond our current understanding and often through circumstances outside of our control, a God-instilled attraction to members of the opposite sex may be temporarily absent from our life. The Lord has not given us a full understanding of why this is so. It likely involves social, psychological, and biological issues. Though they may wish it were otherwise, some people do feel attracted to persons of the same gender. The answer is not to deny this reality but to see it for what it is: a temporary condition or part of one's nature in mortality that will eventually be fully understood and resolved.

Understanding this truth does not make dealing with the challenge of same-gender attraction easy, but it helps those struggling with it to avoid the mistake of labeling or defining themselves in a way that is characteristic of a permanent, eternal state of being. Elder Oaks said:

"We should note that the words *homosexual, lesbian,* and *gay* are adjectives to describe particular thoughts, feelings, or behaviors. We should refrain from using these words as nouns to identify particular conditions or specific persons. Our religious doctrine dictates this usage. It is wrong to use these words to denote a *condition,* because this implies that a person is consigned by birth to a circumstance in which he or she has no choice in respect to the critically important matter of sexual *behavior.*

"Feelings are another matter. Some kinds of feelings seem to be inborn. Others are traceable to mortal experiences. Still other feelings seem to be acquired from a complex interaction of 'nature and nurture.' All of us have some feelings we did not choose, but the gospel of Jesus Christ teaches us that we still have the power to resist and reform our feelings (as needed) and to assure that they do not lead us to entertain inappropriate thoughts or to engage in sinful behavior."[30]

As we refuse to accept the world's labels, we are subsequently free to choose what will define us. Speaking of those who refuse to give in to such labeling, one author wrote, "They are those who, recognizing we are not named by what tempts us, eschew the label 'gay' to take upon them the name of Christ instead."[31]

Have hope for the future. As stated earlier, one of the most important things any person can do is to nurture hope. In an interview with Elder Oaks and Elder Lance B. Wickman of the Seventy, Elder Wickman explained: "The good news for somebody who is struggling with same-gender attraction is this: 1) It is that 'I'm not stuck with it forever.' It's just now. Admittedly, for each one of us, it's hard to look beyond the 'now' sometimes. But nonetheless, if you see mortality as now, it's only during this season. 2) If I can keep myself worthy here, if I can be true to gospel commandments, if I can keep covenants that I have made, the blessings of exaltation and eternal life that Heavenly Father holds out to all of His children apply to me. Every blessing— including eternal marriage—is and will be mine in due course."

He also stated: "What we look forward to, and the great promise of the gospel, is that whatever our inclinations are here, whatever our shortcomings are here, whatever the hindrances to our enjoying a fulness of joy here, we have the Lord's assurance for every one of us that those in due course will be removed. We just need to remain faithful."[32]

Even if, as with Paul's "thorn in the flesh" (2 Corinthians 12:7), same-gender attraction is not immediately removed or ever removed in this lifetime, it is important to continue hoping for all that Heavenly Father has promised us. We must understand that it is within our realm of control, our agency, to choose what we will do and who we will be.

Agency is the key. Agency is one of the most essential characteristics of premortal, mortal, and postmortal life. Since the beginning, Satan has sought to destroy the agency of man, but our Father in Heaven has never allowed him to succeed. A third of the hosts of heaven were lost over this battle in the premortal realm. Surely we must understand that Heavenly Father wouldn't allow anything to rob us of our agency now.

Elder Oaks taught: "Satan would like us to believe that we are not responsible in this life. That is the result he tried to achieve by his contest in the pre-existence. A person who insists that he is not responsible for the exercise of his free agency because he was 'born that way' is trying to ignore the outcome of the War in Heaven."[33] The scriptures teach that "there hath no temptation taken you but such as is common to man: but God is faithful, who will not suffer you to be tempted above that ye are able; but will with the temptation also make a way to escape, that ye may be able to bear it" (1 Corinthians 10:13). Understanding this principle enables us to realize that even in the challenge of same-gender attraction, we still have our agency and must use that agency to choose the path that will ultimately lead us back to our Heavenly Father and to ultimate happiness.

Agency and marriage. God would have us use our agency to help bring to pass our eternal life as well as that of our brothers and sisters. But how can I use my agency in relation to eternal marriage when I face this challenge? What is my responsibility when it comes to eternal marriage? First and foremost, it must be understood that getting married, eternally or otherwise, is not a method for overcoming same-gender attraction. Elder Jeffrey R. Holland said, "Marriage is not an all-purpose solution. Same-gender attractions run deep, and trying to force a heterosexual relationship is not likely to change them."[34]

But the time may come when a person feels ready to begin dating members of the opposite sex. The decision as to when a person is ready for such a move is deeply personal and likely to involve personal revelation.

The closer we can come to living the ideal, the better off we will be. This does not mean we seek unrighteous alternatives to marriage. It means that we live our lives as close to the ideal as we can. We live the gospel of Jesus Christ to the fullest. We develop and enjoy healthy relationships with people of both genders. We value and seek to strengthen our commitments to marriage and families, including our birth families. We learn all we can about marriage and family from the words of the living prophets and apostles. We invite the Atonement of Jesus Christ to help remake us in the image of our Redeemer. Elder Scott counseled us to come as close to the ideal as possible because that will result in the greatest happiness:

"Throughout your life on earth, seek diligently to fulfill the fundamental purposes of this life *through the ideal family.* While you may not have yet reached that ideal, do all you can through obedience and faith in the Lord to consistently draw as close to it as you are able. Let nothing dissuade you from that objective. If it requires fundamental changes in your personal life, make them. When you have the required age and maturity, obtain all of the ordinances of the temple you can receive. If for the present, that does not include sealing in the temple to a righteous companion, live for it. Pray for it. Exercise faith that you will obtain it. Never do anything that would make you unworthy of it. If you have lost the vision of eternal marriage, rekindle it. If your dream requires patience, give it. . . . Don't become overanxious. Do the best you can. We cannot say whether that blessing will be obtained on this side of the veil or beyond it, but the Lord will keep His promises. In His infinite wisdom, He will make possible all you qualify in worthiness to receive. Do not be discouraged. Living a pattern of life as close as possible to the ideal will provide much happiness, great satisfaction, and impressive growth while here on earth regardless of your current life circumstances."[35]

Overcoming loneliness. Those who are currently not ready for marriage are not destined to a life of loneliness even though some loneliness is likely a part of everyone's life, even those who are married. The same counsel the Brethren give to all of us regarding overcoming loneliness applies equally well to those struggling with same-gender attraction. Counsel given by President Hinckley to single women has strong application here. He taught that we should not wait for marriage to make us happy:

"Do not give up hope. And do not give up trying. But do give up being obsessed with it. The chances are that if you forget about it and become anxiously engaged in other activities, the prospects will brighten immeasurably.

"I believe that for most of us the best medicine for loneliness is work, service in behalf of others. I do not minimize your problems, but I do not hesitate to say that there are many others whose problems are more serious than are yours. Reach out to serve them, to help them, to encourage them."[36]

Elder Oaks taught similar principles when he said: "If you are just marking time waiting for a marriage prospect, stop waiting. You may never have the opportunity for a suitable marriage in this life, so stop waiting and start moving. Prepare yourself for life—even a single life—by education, experience, and planning. Don't wait for happiness to be thrust upon you. Seek it out in service and learning. Make a life for yourself. And trust in the Lord. Your dedication of a lifetime should follow King Benjamin's advice to be 'calling on the name of the Lord daily, and standing steadfastly in the faith of that which is to come' (Mosiah 4:11)."[37]

Each of us is able to find meaning in our lives as we choose to live according to the gospel that Jesus Christ gave us. As the Savior taught, the best way to find ourselves is to lose ourselves in love and service to others (see Matthew 10:39).

A broader definition of intimacy. Each of us longs for the type of intimacy that gives meaning and purpose to life. Those who experience same-gender attraction but who are committed to the gospel will choose not to take part in sexual intimacy until they are married to someone of the opposite sex. However, every other aspect of human intimacy is available and worthy of our cultivation in our relationships with both men and women. Dr. Charles Beckert has identified ten different kinds of intimacy available to us all. Only one of them involves sexual intimacy. The other facets of intimacy include:

- Emotional intimacy: being on the same wavelength and feeling close
- Intellectual intimacy: sharing thoughts and ideas
- Aesthetic intimacy: sharing the beauties of the world
- Creative intimacy: sharing acts of creating together
- Recreational intimacy: playing together
- Work intimacy: sharing common tasks in closeness
- Conflict intimacy: facing and struggling with challenges and differences
- Crisis intimacy: coping together with problems and pain
- Spiritual intimacy: experiencing the "uniting of spirits"[38]

Even physical intimacy of a nonsexual nature is an important and beautiful part of life that all can appropriately enjoy. Sexual intimacy is important and sacred, but each of us, married or single, is capable of greater intimacy with friends and loved ones. In truth, sexual intimacy without the other aspects of human intimacy is devoid of true beauty and meaning. Outside of marriage, sexual intimacy can be nothing but selfish and degrading. The day may come when sexual intimacy is a part of our life, but we need not await that day before we experience the many forms of closeness and intimacy that cast away the shadows of loneliness.

Learning from personal experience. The reality of mortal life is that we all have many experiences we would not necessarily choose for ourselves. Each of us has personal challenges, our own "thorn in the flesh" that we have to cope with. This does not mean we are broken. Though each of us is fallen and subject to the fall of Adam, we can approach wholeness now through a covenant relationship with Jesus Christ.

Alma promised that "now is the time and the day of your salvation; and therefore, if ye will repent and harden not your hearts, immediately shall the great plan of redemption be brought about unto you" (Alma

34:31). Through this knowledge, we can seek to learn from our experiences as we move forward in life. We can pray to the Father that He will help us see what we can learn and how we can grow—not despite our trials but through our trials. He can whisper peace to our troubled souls and teach us how to experience peace and fulfillment now.

Conclusion

No sacrifice is too great when exaltation and eternal life are the goal. Through living righteously, through striving to lose ourselves in service to the Lord and to our brothers and sisters, everyone, including those who struggle with same-gender attraction, is able to live richly and experience joy in this life and a fulness in the life to come. A thorough understanding of eternal marriage is one of the keys by which we unlock the vision and ability to live our life to the fullest and ultimately overcome every challenge we face, including challenges with same-gender attraction.

An Unlikely Gift

Jason G. Lockhart

Jason Lockhart (pseudonym) lives in the Pacific Northwest with his wife and children. He was married three months after returning from his mission to South America and has now been married for nine very happy years. He graduated from BYU in education and has enjoyed working in schools for most of her career.

When I was nineteen, after a long and entertaining day together, my girlfriend (now my wife) gave me a very interesting gift. We were sitting in my room when she looked at me and said, "I have something for you . . . but I'm worried about giving it to you because it's kind of *different*." I laughed and of course tried my best to persuade her to give it to me anyway. And so she did.

It was her birthstone set in a white stud. It was just one earring— nothing terribly fancy. However, knowing its significance immediately, I leaned over, gave her a sincere hug and kiss, and thanked her for it. It was one of the only gifts she ever received from her late grandfather. It's one of the most genuinely appreciated and significant gifts I've ever received.

When I was in eighth grade (she was in ninth), we used to eat lunch together at the same table. At the time we were just friends, though she later admitted, and her journals attest, that she had had a crush on me. I was initially interested in sitting by her mostly because she was popular, and I wanted to impress her. As the year progressed, we became pretty good friends.

One day she came to lunch and sat in her usual place. She had recently been to her grandpa's funeral, I discovered. As I talked to her, however, I realized that this was not your run-of-the-mill, average LDS funeral. Her grandpa, you see, had been gay. His body had been cremated, which had been required at that time because he had died of AIDS.

By this time I had already realized a horrific truth about myself: my feelings of attraction to girls weren't just late in coming but were being *replaced* by compelling feelings for guys. I had even gone so far as to tell my parents. So, understandably, I was fascinated by the story behind her grandpa's death. However, it was too soon to ask. It was a story I would hear later. But first I need to explain what happened with *us*.

After that school year, she moved to a different state. Our friendship should have ended. I wrote her one letter, which I never sent, and saw her once or twice when her family came to visit our ward on vacation. Besides this, we had no contact. Under typical circumstances, that would have been the end of things, and I would have had that one little nugget of knowledge about her grandpa. I would have known that some girl I knew in junior high had had a grandpa who died of AIDS, and that would have been the end of it.

However, two years after her family moved, my family—for reasons unexpected and different from hers—moved to the exact same city. My family stayed with hers while we looked for a house. Her mom was the one to find the house my family moved to—a mere ten-minute drive from their home. And, to top it all off, my dad had the distinct impression that our move, in part, occurred so that one of his children would marry the right person. Clearly, there was some serious spiritual finagling going on.

But . . . I was *gay*. And not just kind of. I was attracted entirely to guys and had no sexual stirrings for women. At all. Not even a little bit. So the spiritual finagling would have to continue for a few years.

Because we were both relatively new to the area, my friend and I resumed our friendship and became close. Thankfully, I was sixteen, so I was allowed to date. One evening during a long, deep discussion, I insinuated that I had a secret I wasn't sure I should share but that I thought she might understand because of her family history. I had never shared my secret with anyone outside of my parents, so I was scared. Naturally, she wanted to know. And I wanted her to know, but I was hesitant. After lengthy deliberations, I finally said a prayer in my heart that if she was supposed to know about me, she would guess my secret. So I asked her to.

"What?" she asked. "Guess your secret?"

"That's right," I said. "I want to see if you can guess it."

Part of me so hoped she would, and another part of me dreaded the thought.

"Well," she said and then paused. "If I had to guess it—and this doesn't mean anything if it's not true; it's just a guess based on what you've said so far—I wonder if . . . maybe you're gay?" She had hit the nail on the head.

"Nope," I replied with a smile. I couldn't quite go there—couldn't quite own it right then, right there in the passenger seat of her car, right at that moment.

And then she exhaled deeply and said, "Oh, I'm so relieved. Whew! I'm so glad that wasn't it!"

I didn't know what to say. Her reaction stung—not because it was in any way cruel but because it echoed my own pain at the time. She was visibly relieved to know that her friend didn't suffer under that burden, but I *did* suffer under it. And it was very, very painful at times—a deep, dark, horrible hurt that followed me wherever I went.

I couldn't let it slip past. I needed her to know, but I couldn't say the words. "Why did you say that?" I asked, looking troubled. "Why did you say you were so relieved?" And from the look on my face—and probably from the way I uttered those words—she knew. And I knew she knew.

"Because that would be an awfully, awfully difficult trial to have to go through, and I wouldn't wish it on anybody," she said.

From there the conversation took off. I poured out my soul, relishing in the catharsis. She shared her own insights and asked what my plans were for the future. I told her I wanted to go on a mission and I wanted to get married and have children. She said she believed those goals were totally possible.

We met up a lot over our remaining high school years. We discussed this issue constantly—so much that her parents worried about her a little bit. We wanted to figure it out. We were determined to figure out just what this particular trial meant for somebody within the context of the plan of salvation, and just what somebody facing this trial could expect out of life. By the time we were in college, we were convinced that I had every reason to believe I could fulfill my dream of getting married and having kids. But she was also quick to point out that she could never marry someone who was same-sex attracted—she had too much libido. She *wanted* sex, and she was sure she'd want it often.

"But," I'd protest, "if you're not willing to marry me, why should I expect somebody else to?"

She'd deflect this question with a shrug and an "I don't know," but then once again she'd affirm that she knew marriage would be possible for me. And I believed her. I felt it to be true as well.

By then I had made my own personal decision. The summer before that first year of college, I'd pondered "the choice." I had weighed my testimony and the many personal assurances of the veracity of the Church I had felt in my soul over the course of my life (a very tender and personal thing) on one end of the scale, with my desires for men and the romantic dreams and sexual desires of my mind, body, and even parts of my heart (another very tender and personal thing) on the other end of the scale.

I was at a crossroad. The two paths seemed mutually exclusive. I knew that if I went to a Church school, I'd be signing the honor code—and I intended to live by it and mean it. I also knew that if I chose the other end of the scale, I wouldn't fit in at that school and I would need to take an alternative path. Weighing carefully what I knew at that time and trying my hardest to be honest with myself, honest with my parents and leaders, and honest with the Lord, I made the choice that felt correct to me. I decided to live the gospel for the rest of my life and forego that other very tempting, very personal path.

But even so, marriage in some ways seemed far-fetched. I hadn't yet gone on a mission, for one thing, and that was one heck of a hurdle. For another, I'd *never* seriously dated anyone, male or female. Never kissed anyone. Never pursued anyone romantically at all.

Despite all of this, I decided to start entertaining the idea of getting a girlfriend. And the surprising thing was that shortly after allowing the idea to rest in my mind, it happened. I began a relationship with a girl who was one of my friend's roommates and best friends. Our relationship lasted several months, during which time I told her about my same-sex attractions, had my first kiss, and experienced my first budding romance. And it was promising. She didn't break up with me when she found out about my same-sex attractions. I ended up enjoying kissing. And I liked being in a relationship.

Though things didn't work out between this girl and me, our relationship, which I had thrust myself into with great faith, ended up having great impact on my life. Because of it, my wife-to-be—who was then my best friend—was able to see me in an entirely new light. Instead of seeing me as a great friend who was off limits because of same-sex attraction, she saw me as a part of a heterosexual couple. Suddenly she knew what she would lose if I married someone else. She wouldn't just lose her gay best friend, she would lose a true potential partner, someone capable of being in a romantic relationship who happened to be same-sex attracted but who was also her closest comrade.

This was it. When my relationship with the other girl came to an end, my best friend and I shared several months together before I went on my mission. And our friendship morphed. It became something deeper and richer and more intense. Our touches meant something new. Our words began to be laced with a certain longing. I didn't just love to be with her, I *loved* her. And she *loved* me. In a way that was more powerful for both of us than anything in our pasts.

And then . . . we let it go. It was extremely difficult for both of us. It was hard for me because I thought for sure that this beautiful, wonderful girl would be married when I got back. But when my time to serve a mission came, we turned our newly burgeoning love over to the Lord and completely let it go. We had faith that if we were supposed to be together, we would end up together.

The story didn't end there, of course—there are a million beautiful little details that make it *our* story, that make it tender and special and personal and private. But in the end we did end up together. To my utter joy, we were married in the temple. And our marriage has been a wonderful experience. I would never imply that it has been without its hard moments or even that those hard moments haven't, at times, had to do with my same-sex attraction. But we are happy together and have been for nine years. We've never contemplated a split. We are in love—truly and deeply.

Which brings me back to the earring and the story behind that gift she gave to me on that summer day back when I was nineteen, preparing for my mission. It wasn't long after I received that gift that I finally heard the whole story behind her grandfather's tragic death. It's a story that has great import in our lives, and it's a private story that we don't often share but that we feel connected to on a deep level. I share it in this context because it helps to explain why, even with our eyes wide open, we still have perfect faith that our marriage is not only viable but also can be lasting and in every way fulfilling.

When my wife's grandparents had had two children, her grandpa began to feel the brunt of his discontent. He started wanting to veer from his idyllic little life—the wife, the children, the life he'd so conscientiously constructed. He started seeing a therapist. He was searching for *something*. He was considering his entrance into the gay world. In an interview he had with a prominent Church leader, he received direction. This leader, who commiserated with him and was understanding of his plight, said something that persuaded him to make his family his priority. What he said was to this effect: "I know it's hard. I know. I don't envy your lot in life. You have made certain decisions, though, and it is your responsibility to follow through with them. There comes a point in every married man's life when he has to simply decide where his priorities lie and raise his family."

The words struck her grandpa as did, I suspect, the Spirit. He knew it was true. He girded up his loins and decided not to leave his wife and children. He decided to stay and *be* their father. In a sequence of events that I am grateful for in the grandest way, it was only a month or so after this that they found out they were expecting their third child, my wife's mother. Had he left, she and my amazing spouse would not have been born into that family.

He did well. He worked hard and supported his growing family, which eventually included two additional children. They say he was a pleasant influence in the home, that their home was a home of love, that the cousins always wanted to stay with them because there was such a wonderful feel to their household. He did a good job of controlling his ulterior urges. However, after nearly two decades of living happily with his wife, he started looking heavily at pornography—the vice that led to his demise. His children found some in the basement but couldn't fathom why it was there. His wife, lamentably, had only a small idea of his attractions. Out of nowhere he told her that he had been feeling that something was missing. He told her that he felt that the gay lifestyle held some allure for him and that he didn't think he'd ever be satisfied if he didn't satisfy that one part of himself. He told her that he was leaving. She, of course, loved him and begged him to stay. Their children were mostly raised, though, and he felt that he had waited long enough.

My wife's aunt, who was one of two children still at home, told me that one day she came home from school and found him sitting at the kitchen table eating cherries. She sat down with him. She was fourteen years old. He sat pensively a moment, looked at her, and then told her he was gay and that he was leaving. She started to cry. There was a honk in front of the house—it was his sister, whom he had called to come get him. With no further explanation (at least then), he got up, left his daughter sitting at the kitchen table, and walked out. She says she sat there and wept for hours until her older brother came home and hugged her and told her it wasn't her fault.

He lived his dream. He moved to Hawaii, fell in love with a man, and they became companions. He paid little regard to the fact that his wife now had to support her remaining children alone. Little regard for the fact that his youngest daughter was so traumatized that she slept every night in the same bed as her mom, yearning for comfort. Little regard for the fact that he had abandoned his wife. He was busy with his exciting new existence—with the fantastic vistas of his newfound home, with the exhilaration of living out this fantasy.

My wife at this time was nearly a year old. When she was ten, her grandpa gave her one of the only Christmas presents she ever remembers getting from him: a pair of earrings. By this time he had moved back to the mainland and was living in an apartment with his most recent lover. Ironically, because he was low on funds, his wife, who still loved him, paid for his apartment. My wife remembers visiting him there once. He had invited her and her parents to dinner. They went and ate (his roommate didn't stay for the meal), and when he took them on a tour of the apartment, my wife, a perceptive and precocious little girl, noticed there was only one bed. On the way home she asked about the bed. After receiving an unsatisfactory answer, she simply asked, "Mom, is Grandpa gay?" Her mother turned to her in the back seat, started crying, and said, "Yes. But he loves you very, very much."

When the HIV developed into AIDS, he thought about not telling the family. He talked to his youngest daughter (the one he had abandoned at the kitchen table who had made diligent efforts to maintain a relationship with him) and asked her if she thought that would be all right. She was appalled. She convinced him that after all he had put his children through, he owed it to them to let them know he was dying so they could tell him good-bye before it was too late. So he told them.

By this point he had begun a rapid deterioration and was almost immediately hospitalized. And there, multiple times, his children had the opportunity to say good-bye. Each child handled it differently. My wife's mom took it hard, looked at him, and demanded, "Are you happy now? Is *this* what you gave *us* up for? This?" One of his sons, feeling so betrayed by his leaving, refused to see him.

And then, surrounded by the solemn faces of the family he had left behind, he humbly admitted that the happiest years of his life were the years he had spent with them—years spent in his home, loyal to his wife and surrounded by a family who loved him. He spoke of family home evenings, of singing Christmas carols, of playful nicknames long forgotten. He spoke of pleasant times. He said that those were his only truly contented years, and he noted that all the friends he had made since leaving his family had since abandoned him.

I, as a same-sex-attracted man raising a family, believe him—someone who's been there and seen the aftermath play out in its entirety. He had no reason to lie. He was staring death in the eyes. This wasn't philosophical. This wasn't the opinion of some heavy-handed, hot-headed propagandist saying, "Oh, don't leave your family or you'll regret it." This was a man who had done it—had opted to leave those he loved to "find himself" and to "be true to his sexuality"—and was simply observing the realities of his personal past as viewed from the twilight of his existence. The choice he had made was not worth the consequences. It literally brought him nothing but death. And worse than that fate even, it brought his family immeasurable pain—pain that, nearly thirty years later, I see playing out in the lives of his children, grandchildren, and great-grandchildren.

So when I take out that earring occasionally, palm it gently, think of where it was purchased, think of a man giving it to a beautiful granddaughter who, because of his choices, he barely knew, I thank God for that man who attempted with such diligence to remain with his family for all those years and thus provided me with my loving wife. And then I ache for his grand mistake, for the consequences of it, and I thank God again that I am aware of it and that I don't have to or want to make the same mistake myself.

And so my wife and I move forward with faith in Heavenly Father. We knew what we were giving up, and we knew what we were getting when we knelt across the altar of the temple. But despite the inherent complexity of our union, our marriage doesn't just survive—it thrives. Our love is strong. It is real. Our romance is real. Our intimacy is real. It is enough—more than enough—for both of us. It is amazing—our cup runneth over.

I don't know what the Lord has in store for other men and women who experience same-sex attraction. But I know that He is intimately involved in our lives and wants us to be happy. I know that He took care of me and continues to do so with great care and obvious miracles. I know that my wife and I were supposed to find, follow, and marry each other. We love each other and always will—and I don't say that with some sophomoric naiveté.

I may not be able to convince others of our love or of the inevitable longevity of our union. But without hesitation—and as I would have done if asked during any of the years of our marriage that have ticked by—I declare that our love will continue. Nine years will become ninety. Ninety will become eternity—and we will be side by side through it all, watching our progeny, enjoying being in the company of our best friend and lover, and rejoicing in the Lord. To us, ours is the world's greatest and purest love story. It is the most unlikely gift.

For Time and All Eternity

Katharine Matis Adams

*Katharine Adams was married for five years before losing
her husband to a heart attack. Before meeting her husband, she
served in the Wisconsin Milwaukee Mission and then graduated from
BYU in music dance theater. While at BYU she also performed
with the Young Ambassadors, traveling throughout Southeast
Asia and North Africa. She now resides in Highland, Utah,
with her three beautiful and energetic daughters.*

I was married to Christian for five years to the day. He died on our
fifth wedding anniversary, leaving behind two beautiful little girls and
another on the way. Our time together was short, from our courtship
to our engagement to our marriage. As I look back, it is clear to me the
Lord had His hand in our life together from even before we met, and
the Spirit was a driving force throughout our relationship.

While at Brigham Young University, I became well acquainted
with many LDS men who experienced same-gender attraction. And,
of course, I had crushes on several of those men only to have my heart
broken. During those years I developed a finely tuned "gay-dar" (gay
radar) and even developed a mantra of sorts when it came to dating: so
I could avoid history repeating itself, if I had *any* suspicion that a guy
experienced same-gender attraction, he was guilty until proven innocent. Given the great friendships I developed over time with many of
these men, I became intimately familiar with the struggles experienced
by Latter-day Saints who have gay feelings. I didn't have any sense how
important that understanding would be, however, until well after I had
left BYU.

Christian and I met online through an LDS dating website (he
never wanted people to know that we met online, but he can't do

anything about it now), and it was a good thing we did. Because Christian and I started conversing online, my gay-dar wasn't registering. We hit it off immediately, and it wasn't long before we talked on the phone. That was when the red flags started to wave and the bells and whistles went off. But something inside of me said strongly not to worry—that I needed to continue to get to know him. So I did. In our second phone conversation, I told him about my brother Stuart.

Stuart was my older brother. He and I were very close. It wasn't until I had gone through my experience at BYU that I thought he might be struggling with same-gender attraction. After offering many subtle hints so that he knew he could feel safe to confide in me, he did. I was the first one he told in the family. Even though I had suspicions about Stuart's attractions before he told me, the reality of it still caught me off guard. It was as if everything had gone gray, and I was suddenly watching a movie or a TV show. But because we were so close—we always had been—we were able to joke about it almost immediately.

But along with the laughter and the "gay or not gay" game we would play while people-watching, there were dark times as he struggled with his insecurities and the fact that he hadn't been successful in trying to fast or pray away his feelings. And no amount of scripture reading or temple attendance had seemed to change anything, as he hoped it would. During the year that followed, I saw him go from what I perceived to be confident and spiritually strong to insecure and lost. He had tried in secret for years—since admitting his attractions to himself at age twelve—to have his feelings taken from him. The more time passed, the more he doubted his worth. Then, in the midst of the negative energy and often-cruel rhetoric of a heated political battle over same-sex marriage where we lived in California, he got so depressed that he took his life.

Knowing Stuart as I did, and having watched right in front of me the downward spiral that ended in his suicide, further influenced my views of Latter-day Saints who have same-gender feelings. Through that experience, it was reconfirmed to me that there are many, many individuals who do not choose their attractions. Stuart never acted on his attractions sexually because he knew it would be wrong to do so, but I learned how discouraging those feelings can be to someone who is taught his whole life that an eternal marriage to someone of the opposite sex is the ultimate goal. Because Stuart and I were so close, and because I knew him long before I was aware of his inner struggle, I came to appreciate that same-gender attraction is only one aspect of a person; it does not define the person as a whole. Many people see someone who experiences same-gender attraction, and all they seem to see is a gay person. I loved my brother, and to me he will always simply be my brother Stuart—not my *gay* brother Stuart.

So, during that second phone conversation, when Christian told me he was gay, I had already learned much about same-gender attraction. Having the background I did, accompanied by the Spirit's guidance at the moment Christian revealed his secret, I was surprisingly calm about it. The big question was how my parents would react to it. In the past, my father had been fairly protective of me regarding the gentlemen (for some of them, I use the term loosely) I dated. He even tracked down the bishop of a guy from Canada I had dated! Yet somehow, when I told him about Christian, he was fine with it. My parents knew what I knew. And I felt that the Spirit was at work on them as well. That was a big confirmation to me that I was making the right choice to continue pursuing my relationship with Christian.

I think he was rather surprised when I didn't flinch at the news, especially when he told me he had spent the previous nine years or so living as an openly gay man. Christian had been a great kid growing up—good student, friendly, cross-country runner, member of the seminary presidency in high school, and a great older brother. Then, after being put in a vulnerable position toward the end of his senior year of high school, he made a mistake. Because of the guilt and confusion he felt, one mistake led to another and another until he had two feet firmly planted in everything that came with the worst stereotype of a gay lifestyle. Yet, throughout it all, he never lost his testimony. He told me of an experience when he and a friend were smoking pot. There they sat in a smoke-filled room, heads buzzing, as he bore testimony of the truthfulness of the restored gospel to her. She was baptized a few years later.

Then one day he decided it was time to make a change. He did a complete 180 and stopped everything. It wasn't long before he was going back to church. By the time we met, he was well on his way in his preparation to go through the temple.

That was the Christian I knew. I didn't know the other Christian. I've seen pictures of him from that time in his life, and he seemed like a completely different person. The Christian I met was active in the Church, had a calling, was guiding his youngest brother off the path of a wild teen and on to the road toward a mission, was actively studying—not just reading—his scriptures every day, and had played a huge part in the baptism of one of his friends. She is still an active member to this day. These were all of the things I fell in love with. It didn't hurt that he was cute, funny, smart, musically inclined, and, very important, hilarious.

Initially there was a small part of me that wondered if I was just a beard for him (a beard is a woman a same-sex-attracted guy dates—or marries—strictly to give the appearance of being straight or to meet social expectations). I wondered if he really was attracted to me and wanted to be with me for the right reasons. I knew our personalities clicked, but I had many gay friends in and out of the Church with whom I clicked. Although I loved hanging out with them and loved them as friends, I wouldn't have married a single one of them. My ideal was to marry someone who was in love with me and with whom I was in love—and all signs pointed to marrying Christian.

When we met, he was living in Oklahoma. I was in Utah and in a position that would make moving to Oklahoma impossible. After talking on the phone and e-mailing almost daily for a couple of weeks, I told the Lord (as if He needed me to point this out to Him) that the relationship would only work if Christian moved to Utah. That night in our phone conversation, Christian told me he had just received a job working in Salt Lake City. He had taken a pay cut and a demotion so he could move to Utah, knowing that was the only way to move forward with our relationship. We both were pretty sure within those two weeks that we were going to get married. It was a scary thought for both of us, perhaps for different reasons, but we also continued to feel the Spirit's comforting assurance.

The more I talked to him about his past and our relationship, and the more I prayed about it all, the clearer it became to me that he really was attracted to me and that we were supposed to be together. He told me on several occasions that I was the only woman he had ever been genuinely attracted to. We always joked that at least I didn't have to worry about him being a skirt chaser. When he signed up for the LDS dating website, he did it to prove to his friend (who had been using the website) that there were only stalkers and crazy people who used the Internet as a dating tool. I was the first and only person he actually contacted. He had looked at other profiles but never felt a desire to write to anyone—that is, until he saw mine. I wish I could tell you why he took the next step and wrote to me. He only told me that he thought I was cute and seemed like I'd be fun to talk to. He also told me he never thought anything would come of it, especially because I was in Utah. Boy, was he wrong—five years and three kids wrong.

Our courtship felt just like any other. Because I had had my moments of wandering off the strait and narrow, he felt that I understood him more than those who had never had to find their way back to the gospel. That brought some peace to his mind that I wouldn't judge him. He wondered, however, what I would do if I ever came face to face with his past. What would I say if someone confronted me about his previous lifestyle? I told him I wouldn't care. If that happened, I would tell them that I was aware of everything and that I loved him and that he loved me and that we were sealed for eternity in the temple—and that's all I cared about. I knew what our relationship was. I married him because of so many things I loved about him. His stereotypical gay qualities were part of what I loved so much. He was my best friend.

But whether or not he had made some poor choices in his past, I don't think it would have made a difference in how I viewed him. I believe strongly in the transforming power of the Atonement of Jesus Christ. I always have. I felt that if I really believed in the Atonement and that if a person is truly washed clean from past transgressions and that if the Lord has forgiven and forgotten, how could I judge Christian for choices that were no longer a part of his life? That said, I did feel plagued by story after story of same-gender-attracted men getting married only to cheat on their wives. So I continued to make our relationship a matter of prayer. I always felt at peace about his attraction; any of the issues that may have come up in our marriage seemed to be less directly related to that.

I say *directly* because it seems that the insecurities that often accompany men who experience same-gender attraction affect other aspects of their life. There were times when he seemed to have an especially strong reaction to something, and looking back, I can see how his emotional reactions were directly affected by how he was feeling about himself. And how he was feeling about himself had a great deal to do with the patterns of self-deprecating thoughts he had developed over the years. I had to learn to adjust to those moods, and I admit it was rather hard at times—though that's not to say I was never to blame. I'm sure I made thoughtless comments that would be hurtful to someone whether that person had the same sensitivities or not. The difference here was how my comments seemed to be like pouring salt in an already painful wound.

Christian's insecurities seemed to be deeply rooted in both his silent childhood and his past as an openly gay man. It's amazing how hurtful people can be when they don't know the real reasons that another person acts or thinks the way he or she does. So many hurtful and homophobic comments were made to and around Christian throughout his life. Many of the difficult experiences Christian had in his family and predominantly LDS community, and then during his out years, continued to haunt him. Those experiences shaped how he thought and how he dealt with people, including me. Out of our past grows our present.

A lot happened in our five years of marriage: we created three beautiful little girls (I was seven months pregnant with our third when he died), he had three open-heart surgeries and two other significant surgeries, and we lived in four different cities (two different states) due to his job changes. Changes can be hard, and we had our share of them. Of all the changes, the hardest one for Christian was the addition of a new child. We had children rather fast. Our first daughter was born the day before our nine-month anniversary (I promise, our temple marriage was legit). Our second daughter came twenty-one months later. When I was pregnant with our third child, I was adamant the baby was going to be a boy. I was so convinced, in fact, that I gave all of our girl baby clothes to my brother- and sister-in-law.

The idea of having a boy sent Christian into a panic. He had always had deep insecurities about his manhood. He had four younger brothers—all of whom were typical alpha males, as was his father. And then there was Christian—playing piano, singing in musical theater. He didn't feel he would measure up as a man, as a father to a boy. He had friends who had attended and recommended a weekend retreat called "Journey into Manhood," which helps men who experience same-gender attraction identify more fully with their masculine self and feel more secure and confident in who they are as men. Much of this is done through intensive emotional-healing work and in exploring and resolving past and present relationships. Christian was skeptical and reluctant to go, fearful of what might come up for him, but the idea of having a boy made him willing to try anything.

He returned from that weekend a completely new man. While he honestly felt that he had previously fully dealt with his past issues, he realized he had not. Upon returning, he stepped out of the car and met my mother on the curb. Embracing her, he said, weeping as he spoke, "I am not *ashamed* anymore, for the first time in my life! I took my shame into my marriage, my work, my Church callings, my relationships—but I'm not *ashamed* anymore!" It was a complete transformation. He truly seemed like a new Christian. I had never known this Christian. He was more at peace, less reactive, calmer. His play with the kids was freer. He came home from work happier. He handled daily stress better. I only wish he had done this retreat five years earlier.

Prior to the "Journey into Manhood" weekend, I don't think Christian had ever truly forgiven himself for his past. I know he felt extreme guilt for not serving a mission. He always talked about serving one with me when we were older. That would be his chance to make right what he had done wrong. I often wonder what his self-image would have been like had he never taken that first step into a gay life-style. Once he did, though, the guilt had pulled him farther and farther in. It had happened quickly and subtly.

I knew that part of Christian's story long before I agreed to marry him. I didn't realize, though, how much it would affect other aspects of our life together. That is not to say that his feelings of same-gender attraction caused his guilt; it was related partly to the poor decisions he had made and partly to his seeming difficulty in really accepting the grace and forgiveness of a loving Savior.

I have known people who have struggled with accepting the gift of Christ's grace and Atonement, but I never watched it so up close and personal until Christian. When, without all his shame, he finally accepted the gift of the Atonement and believed he was worthy of it, he was transformed. In turn, everything in his life changed for the better. We worked out the issues in our relationship related to his previous insecurities and feelings of shame, and when he died, things were better than they'd ever been. I was amazed at how much better they *could* be. I had never realized how much his shame and insecurities related to same-gender attraction had seeped into other aspects of his life. I wish I had known that earlier. It would have changed my reactions to him. I would have been more sensitive.

My mother told me that as she hugged him on the curb, she felt so clearly the magnitude of his soul. I had had moments through-out our courtship and marriage when I had that same experience. I believe that same-gender attraction is one of the greatest difficulties some people have to work through in this life, one they may have even agreed to before coming to this world. To be willing to work through the difficulties associated with such an experience says something to me of their incredible goodness and strength.

Going into my marriage to Christian, I wondered how much his same-gender attraction would affect our marriage. I found it interesting the ways it did *not*. Christian was my husband—not my *gay* husband. There may be some differences between men who experience same-gender attraction and those who don't—chances are, a straight husband won't know which musical won the Tony last year or be able to pick out a fabulous pair of heels for his wife—but, at the core, there are many more similarities than differences. Those similarities are what I chose to focus on—the differences were just perks. I thoroughly enjoyed the clothes he bought me for my birthday and watching *Project Runway* together. I chose to have those things over a live-in handyman. It's a trade-off. For me, the trade-off paid off.

Christian always told me our relationship was better than any other he had been in. He had been in love with men. He had even been in a committed relationship (though from what he told me, many committed gay relationships are not monogamous—there is often mutual, agreed-upon infidelity). He also told me that there was something in our relationship that was inherently different than the gay relationships he had been in. It was intangible, he said, but it made it so much better—it just felt more right. I always thought that was interesting.

I think when a man and a woman love each other and then commit to each other, sealing those commitments in the Lord's holy temple, there is a Spirit that accompanies the relationship that other relationships aren't blessed with. He told me that on several occasions, and I know he meant it. And that was one of the reasons I never worried about his commitment to me or our marriage. He knew what we had was special—not because of some storybook romantic notion of being the one and only for each other but because our relationship was blessed with temporal and eternal promises.

I recognize that any marriage requires hard work to realize both temporal and eternal blessings. The ultimate decision for me when contemplating marriage to Christian came down to listening to the

Spirit. To me, that's how it should be when anyone is trying to decide if marrying someone is the right choice. The Spirit told me yes, so I said yes. I had confirmation that because the Lord agreed with my decision, I would have Him there to help me through any of the bumps or hurdles we would face in our life together.

After several years of heart problems and several open-heart surgeries, Christian passed away from a heart attack on our fifth wedding anniversary. His first surgery had occurred when our oldest daughter was two weeks old. None of the doctors or nurses working with him knew whether he would survive, but Christian received a priesthood blessing from his father making it clear to him that he still had a purpose to fulfill on earth. In addition to helping bring two more beautiful girls into this world, he touched many lives by his genuine love and concern for others and by his natural ability to make people laugh. People just felt good around him.

In September 2008, two days before our anniversary, Christian left on a business trip to Los Angeles—we looked forward to celebrating when he got back. On his second night there, he decided to go for a run. (Each of his health episodes seemed to happen when he was on a health kick. I used to tell him, "Sit back, relax, eat some Häagen-Dazs, get fat, and live longer!"). While he was running, his heart rate began to rise, and he couldn't catch his breath. He made it to the emergency room, where emergency personnel were able to stabilize him—only to later have his heart rate drop dramatically.

A friend of Christian's father lived in the area and came quickly to the hospital to give him a priesthood blessing. He reported that as he laid hands on Christian's head, he felt strongly impressed to release him—that Christian had completed what he needed to do here on earth. Shortly afterward, Christian silently slipped away. It all happened so fast. I wasn't able to fly out to see him. The last time I saw him was when I kissed him good-bye at the airport. The next time was at the funeral home.

Minutes after I found out on the phone that Christian had passed away, the Spirit flooded over me. I felt so calm and at peace. I knew it was his time to go. When someone so close to you passes away, the reality of the next life becomes clearer. Seeing how Christian was prepared to move on has brought clarity to the doctrine that our work continues on the other side. I was one of those fortunate enough to learn from Christian here on this earth. He now has many others on the other side of the veil to teach, and the lessons he learned before he died have prepared him to do so. He played the role of friend and mentor to many men who experience same-gender attraction. He might now be counseling others about how to deal with difficult experiences on this earth. I'm happy that he was finally able to meet Stuart. I always wished they'd had a chance to meet in this life; I knew they would have gotten along incredibly well. They were so much alike.

In the time since Christian passed, it's become increasingly clear to me that those five years together had been divinely mapped out. Seeing how things played out, I really feel I was prepared throughout my life to marry him, to be sealed to him. Because our time together would be so short, I needed to be completely ready to meet him when I did, and all my previous life experiences prepared me. It's been hard for me that things ended when they did, particularly as a single mother to three energetic girls. But Christian was ready to move forward, and *we* were ready for him to move forward. Now, as he is serving that mission he always wanted to serve, I look forward to our eternity.

Resolution: The Unexpected Miracle

Jeff Bennion

*Jeff Bennion was born and raised in the Salt Lake area.
He served a full-time mission in northeastern France and graduated from
the University of Utah in psychology. He has served in the Church as a
teacher in the Primary, Sunday School, and elders quorum, and he has*

served in elders quorum presidencies and in bishoprics. He loves to read,
travel, and swim. When not doing one of those things, he works
as a project and property manager for a real estate holding company
in the Salt Lake area. He and his beautiful wife, Tanya, have been
married for seven years and are the parents of one son (see "Creating a
Whole Marriage," p. 348).

"If we could see the miracle of a single flower clearly,
our whole life would change."
—SIDDHARTHA GAUTAMA[39]

Many people wonder whether change is possible. My experience is that change is inevitable. The challenge for me was to figure out what I wanted and then to make sure my life's changes were ones that would lead me where I wanted to go.

After being led by the Spirit while on my mission to admit to myself that I dealt with same-sex attraction, I initially made a lot of progress. I learned how to jettison the unnecessary shame about my attractions—the feelings themselves weren't a sin; only inappropriate thoughts and actions were. That dramatically improved my relationship with God, which had been harmed by my feelings of constant unworthiness.

Then, thanks to many useful books, individual therapy, and group therapy, I learned how to diminish the homosexual feelings, identify underlying emotional issues that led to those feelings becoming dominant, and employ strategies for eliminating spiritually harmful behavior.

Probably most important of all was finding a group of faithful Latter-day Saints who were happily dealing with this challenge. I didn't feel so isolated knowing there were others who had similar feelings and wanted to respond to them in a way that was compatible with gospel ideals. Seeing others have success in these efforts gave me hope. This wonderful community gradually dispersed, however; it seemed that I was the only one still stuck in between.

I dated many women and was interested in a few, but more often than not I broke things off. This left me feeling guilty for not being attracted enough to these women and doubtful that I could make a normal life in the Church work. These feelings became more acute with each passing year, each breakup, each dud of a first date.

Even good things like going to the temple would send me into despair if I saw an attractive and happy couple about my age there, because it seemed that I would never have that. My singles ward was difficult at times, particularly because of the pressure to date and marry from some well-meaning leaders who seemed to think the answer to everything was to date, date, date and then marry the first woman who was minimally acceptable.

After one breakup while in my mid-twenties, I went to the temple, praying for some comfort that I would find someone else to marry quickly. Instead, the Spirit unmistakably told me that it would be a while before I got married. Instead of feeling comforted, I was so angry that I couldn't return to the temple for several months, and scripture reading became a strain. The promises in the scriptures seemed for someone else or for me only after I was dead. I felt the opposite of Paul: if I could only have joy in the next life but never in this one, then I would be "most miserable" (1 Corinthians 15:19). About the only parts I could read without wanting to hurl my scriptures across the room in anger were Lamentations and some of the Psalms. However, I remained committed and active in the Church and in my callings, and I prayed and read my scriptures regularly, though I didn't see how this was doing me any good.

After my next breakup with a woman, I felt even more lost. And this time, the needed comfort arrived unbidden. I had a powerful spiritual experience that assured me that I would have a wife and at least one child, a son. But as my romantic drought with women continued for several more years, that promise seemed less like a comfort and more like a cruel divine joke. How long could I live on that promise? Would I go to my grave waiting for it to be fulfilled and feel like God's chump, wasting my life waiting for the fulfillment of a promise that would only be fulfilled when it was too late to do any good? How long did the Lord really expect me to keep hanging on?

As I passed thirty, I felt that I was rapidly running out of steam. And when I looked in the scriptures for clues as to how long I was expected to endure, I didn't find much comfort (see Isaiah 6:11 and Hebrews 11:13, for example). I related to the melancholy poet Gerard Manley Hopkins when he complained:

> *Oh, the sots and thralls of lust*
> *Do in spare hours more thrive than I that spend,*
> *Sir, life upon thy cause. See, banks and brakes*
> *Now leavèd how thick! lacèd they are again*
> *With fretty chervil, look, and fresh wind shakes*
> *Them; birds build—but not I build; no, but strain,*
> *Time's eunuch, and not breed one work that wakes.*
> *Mine, O thou lord of life, send my roots rain.*[40]

I not only felt that I would never get married but also that no part of my life had any lasting purpose. I was time's eunuch; nothing I touched would outlast my existence. Much of this, I see now, was just a bad attitude; I denigrated the consolations of friendship and over-looked how much good I was doing in so many areas of my life.

I began to dabble more seriously than ever before with romantic relationships with men. My experiments with same-sex relationships were never serious, but they didn't make things any easier. I found that the only thing harder than living one life is trying to live two mutually incompatible ones. One night after going further with a guy than I ever had before, I felt horribly guilty. I knew I had seriously grieved the Spirit. I had put myself in a very dangerous situation and, while I didn't get burned, I had come out badly singed. Had I gone so far that I had forfeited the powerful promises God had made to me? Beyond this specific incident, had I been too double-minded, too bitter and faithless, to still qualify for those promises? Was it too late for a wife and family? My dream of having an ordinary life with a wife and kids seemed more remote than ever.

In answer, the Spirit brought to my remembrance that day in the temple many years before—that it would be a while before I would be married. What had been such a source of sadness was now one of comfort. While I was sure that the Lord at times wasn't happy with my attitude, or my actions certainly, He knew and, in fact, had told me that it would be a while. It was not too late! I had not yet sold my birthright for a mess of pottage. After this incident, as in other cases, I kept my bishop informed of what I was doing and how I was feeling.

I was encouraged by this but still unclear if what I thought I wanted was what I *should* want. Should I, as urged by so many of my former LDS friends who were gay, adjust my moral and spiritual outlook beyond Church teachings and practices? They claimed they were as spiritually fulfilled and morally upright as ever, if not more so, as well as much happier than they were when they were following Church standards regarding homosexual behavior. That's not how they seemed from my perspective, but I didn't want to arbitrarily limit the path God might want me to tread.

One day in my scripture reading, I came across some verses in Romans, chapter 8. A phrase in verse 24 caught my eye: "For we are saved by hope." I felt that I had run out of faith, but I still had some hope, even though I wasn't waiting with the kind of patience Paul admonished the Roman Saints to have in verse 25. Paul continues in verses 26 and 28: "Likewise the Spirit also helpeth our infirmities: for we know not what we should pray for as we ought: but the Spirit itself maketh intercession for us with groanings which cannot be uttered. . . . And we know that all things work together for good to them that love God, to them who are the called according to his purpose."

As I read this, I felt impressed that the Spirit could help me know what to pray for. And until I did know, I at least knew I loved God, so I could have faith and hope in the idea that all things would work together for my good.

For several months that's all I really prayed for. I told Heavenly Father I didn't know what I should want; I didn't fully trust my desires, but I did trust Him to tell me what I should want. The answer came in one word: *resolution*. I was to pray for resolution. Just hearing the word in my mind brought peace to me. This was an idea that I could get behind: resolving two fundamental but apparently irreconcilable desires—my testimony, love for the Church, and desire for a wife and family on one hand and my deep-seated homosexual feelings on the other. That's what I wanted—resolution! I wanted the struggle and conflict to end. I wanted to be at peace.

I went to the dictionary and looked the word up. Its etymology evokes the idea of being loosed or released. Its meanings include the process of reducing something complex to something more simple, the act of answering, becoming determined to do something (as in a New Year's resolution), finding a solution to a problem, moving from a dis-harmonious to a harmonious chord in music, and the point in the plot of a dramatic work where the complication is worked out.

These were all things I ardently desired. I began earnestly praying for resolution. As I acted on my hope and faith, gradually those parts of my life that made it difficult to maintain gospel standards fell out of my life. These things included some people I spent a lot of time with, places I would go, things I would read, and even music I would listen to.

Not long after I began praying so, I went on a blind date with a woman named Tanya. It had been a long time since I'd been out with a woman like Tanya. We had an enjoyable first date, but she was de-manding and clearly expected a level of affection and attention I wasn't used to giving women. I wasn't sure how I felt about her, and it seemed that she really wasn't sure about me either.

One date turned into two and then ten. But even after several months, I was far from the conventional boyfriend. I wasn't sure I even wanted to be any woman's boyfriend. Tanya let me know that I wasn't measuring up: by this point most guys call every day, she said, if they aren't dropping by every night. I called barely once a week, and we went out twice a month. Not to mention the lack of hand-holding or kissing.

She wasn't sure I was really all that attracted to her, so she was un-certain why I kept asking her out (which wasn't all that often at first).

At this point my attraction for her, which was mostly based on non-physical traits, was certainly not why I stopped my dabbling in same-sex dating. With Tanya, it wasn't a case of love at first sight.

For a long time I thought I would have to feel a powerful physical attraction to a woman in order to feel motivated and convinced that I could make a traditional marriage work. In hindsight, I now realize that this was the wrong reason; no physical attraction is powerful enough to motivate someone to maintain standards he is not internally motivated to keep. Furthermore, physical attraction can obscure working through issues that are better explored before marriage. What kept me going was a determination to learn and experience everything I could—to see if I could take the risks necessary for long-lasting love. Even if things didn't work out with Tanya, I thought those lessons would be useful in future relationships.

After six months or so I was getting hints from Church leaders, roommates, family members, and Tanya herself that I wasn't moving very fast. That was bad enough, but it wasn't anything compared to what I was telling myself. I knew I wasn't measuring up. I knew I wasn't a very good boyfriend, and I was sure that I would make an even worse husband. So the first concept I had to throw out was that I had to conform to someone else's arbitrary timeline and social standard. I realized I was going to do this backward: where most relationships start with physical attraction and then proceed to emotional intimacy, I was going to start with friendship and emotional intimacy and then, I hoped, move to physical attraction.

At this point I realized something I wish I had done earlier. Relating to a woman romantically is totally different than relating to her as an intimate friend, which I had *plenty* of experience with. I thought that because I was close to many women that I would know how to relate to them romantically as well. I had believed this wasn't happening because I wasn't *able* to. In fact, I didn't know *how* to. That brought hope, because while I might not be able to change an innate tendency, with effort I certainly could learn how to do unfamiliar things.

However slowly, our relationship was deepening. I did get to a point that I held her hand and even kissed her, and I found both enjoyable, but on *my* schedule. My physical attraction to her was growing bit by bit. Some observers felt that the relationship was stagnant because I was afraid to commit (a male-bashing bromide familiar to many), but I was moving as fast as I could. Tanya eventually became supportive of this learning process because she saw me making progress. Once that happened, my relatively slow pace didn't bother me as much, though I would still get discouraged when I compared myself to others whose relationships seemed to move toward marriage more quickly and easily.

At this point, my biggest fear was being stifled by a wife or girlfriend. I knew heterosexual men who felt trapped in their relationships, bound by a sense of duty and the physical and financial support their wives and children expected from them. These men seemed to have no freedom, were deeply unhappy, and had wives who did not respect them or allow them any autonomy. Some of these men envied my bachelorhood even as they were most strident about how I was shirking my priesthood duties by remaining single.

The longer Tanya and I dated, the larger the marriage question loomed. We were in *some* kind of relationship, but was she the one I should marry? How could I decide that? The more I agonized over this question, the less I knew and the more anxious I became. I took these concerns to a good friend of mine who also experienced same-sex attraction and had recently married after his own long courtship. He gave me some excellent advice: "Rather than asking yourself if you should marry her," he counseled, "ask yourself, 'What is the next step I can take in this relationship? What more am I willing to do with her? How much more of myself am I willing to share?' Rather than worrying so much about the scary, ultimate question 'Is she the one?' focus more on what the next steps are in the relationship and whether you're willing to take them."

That really helped me calm down. Shortly after that conversation, Tanya planned a daylong excursion for just the two of us. It was going to be four hours each way in the car together, plus many hours together as we toured the area. It had been a long time since I'd spent such a long stretch of time with a girlfriend. I was worried I'd be climbing the walls trying to meet all these impossible expectations. And in my mind, that was just the beginning. If things worked out, I would be doing more of these. And if we got married, I might have to go on lots and lots and lots of excursions like these, probably *for the rest of my life.*

I knelt down to pray, feeling a bit overwhelmed but recalling the words of my friend. And a Voice outside of me asked, "Can you spend tomorrow with Tanya?" *Yes, I can do that,* I thought. "Well then," the Voice replied, "why don't you have a nice time tomorrow and worry about all those future trips when the time comes?"

I realized I was biting off more than I needed to chew at that moment. I went on the trip, and we both had a very nice time. Thanks to that reminder from the Spirit, I kept following my friend's advice, taking each aspect of our relationship one step at a time.

Finally, after a year and a half of dating, I decided it was time to disclose to her my same-sex attraction. In hindsight, I had waited too long—to the last possible moment until there was nothing else to do to advance the relationship. It was either tell her or break up. Because I wasn't ready to break up, late one evening after an enjoyable day together, I laid it all out to her. I also left her with a couple of books and the phone numbers of some friends' wives who might be of help to her.

I was tremendously relieved to finally share this major aspect of my life I had been keeping from her. But she was just now *beginning* to deal with it. Things got intense for me answering all her questions, some of them very personal. I had to deal with my hurt feelings at having her question my motives and trustworthiness. But gradually things got better, and then we decided to take a break from talking about same-sex attraction. She told me that I could bring it up if I wanted to but that she wasn't going to bring it up for an entire month. Without needing to discuss anything else, that month became three months. At that point I decided I wanted to marry her, so long as we could cross one more hurdle.

Tanya came home with me to my parents for Christmas. I remember we were sitting in the hot tub. There is an old joke that goes,

"Women marry men hoping they will change. Men marry women hoping they will not change. Both are inevitably disappointed." I wondered if Tanya would marry me with an unacceptably low level of physical affection and attention, hoping I would change. Or was the way things were now enough to ensure that her needs would be met and she would be happy being with me the rest of our lives? If I didn't improve at all with my level of hand-holding, cuddling, and kissing, would she be able to live with that the rest of her life? Would she feel that she was *settling* and always pine for something better or more?

As we sat in the hot tub under the cold starlight, I explained that, for my part, I thought I had developed a sufficient attraction to be reasonably confident that I could function, and even enjoy, the sexual part of our relationship. I couldn't be sure, of course, but I had as much confidence as I could within worthy LDS courtship standards. She said yes, it was enough—more than enough. With that answer, we began making wedding plans.

A few months later I made an appointment with my therapist for the two of us. I wanted to have a third party help us make sure we both understood what each of us was getting into and if our expectations were realistic. One of the things Tanya brought up was about our future sex life. "I want a husband who is a husband in all aspects, including our sexual relationship," she said.

"You know," my therapist replied, "I deal with a lot of adoptions in my practice, and a few of these couples will come in and say to me, 'We want to start our family.' I always stop them right there. I say, 'Hold on. You two are married and made sacred covenants to each other. That's what a family is. You already *are* a family. If you don't think you are a family already, then an adoption won't make you any more of one. Now, if you want to *expand* your family, I can help with that.'

"In the same way," he continued, "if your husband has made commitments to you, and he is keeping them, that makes him your husband even if he doesn't meet all of your expectations. If he has made that commitment to you, he *is* your husband."

I think she took that conversation to heart, because a few weeks before our marriage, Tanya said, "Jeff, I want sex to be a good experience for you. If it takes you a few days, a few weeks, a few months, that's fine. I'll be here, and I'll give you as much time as you need."

I was relieved to hear that. It took so much pressure off. I replied that I obviously didn't know how things would go, but if it was unpleasant or unsatisfying for either of us, I promised that I would work on it. I obviously couldn't know beforehand if things were going to work out, and my therapist had encouraged us not to assume it was going to be a problem before it became one, but I could at least commit to working on it.

A few weeks later we were married. Much to my surprise, our physical relationship became very satisfying. At first it was enjoyable but not very fulfilling. We continued to talk and work on things, and I have to say, it is now very satisfying—more satisfying than I ever thought possible. I didn't expect it to replicate the intensity of how I imagined homosexual experiences to be, and it does not. I never wanted to replicate that, and I have not attempted to through fantasy during sexual intimacy with my wife. I had met plenty of people who had experienced intense homosexual sex, but it seemed mostly to only leave them wanting more. My sexual relationship is more fulfilling and nourishing for both of us than what is depicted about sex (even the heterosexual variety) in the worldly culture.

One day after we had been married a few years, Tanya asked me a question: "Do you miss being single and being able to explore same-sex romantic relationships?" Since our dating time, we have had a rule that if one of us has been brooding over a question for a while, the other gets just as much time to brood over the answer. So after thinking about the question for a while, I replied, "I think that's the wrong question. Sometimes I'll still see attractive men and feel strongly attracted to them, though this depends on my mood and what is going on in my life. Sometimes I'll remember past experiences with a pang of nostalgia. Some better questions I think you should ask are, 'Have you ever regretted being married to me?' 'Have you ever seen an attractive guy and wished you were with him instead of me?' 'Have you ever

wished you were with one of the guys you dated rather than with me?'
And the answer to all of those questions is 'Absolutely not.' I have never
felt that way."

Even for me, it is surprising after almost ten years together that
enough really is enough. I had one or two crushes on other women
growing up and many more on men. Those relationships were intense:
having my infatuation reciprocated, being so swept away in the relationship's intensity that I abandoned myself and my obligations. The
irresistible thrill of clasping hands with that incredible someone and
running off into the sunset together is something I yearned for and occasionally experienced over many years of being single. Did I have that
with Tanya? Not at first. What we have is better, I contend, because it
is more solid. It is built on a kind of love that isn't often sung about,
that they don't often make movies about, but that is true. It's a love that
lasts, that you can count on. It is reassuring. It fulfills and comforts
and strengthens and understands. It is not just focused on itself. Most
important, it is a love that you can build two lives around, and even
many more.

The other kind of love—the intense, infatuated kind I yearned for
and felt deprived of for so long—I now realize cannot last. Though it
seems harmless, the problem is that ninety-nine times out of one hundred, it eventually burns out. Then the parties in the relationship either
break up or somehow have to build a more enduring relationship out
of its ashes.

Tanya and I both feel that same-sex attraction has been a minor
issue in our marriage. For several years we dealt with infertility, moves,
job changes, and financial instability, and all of these so far have been
more difficult than same-sex attraction has proven to be. That our challenges are so ordinary is a miracle.

Despite these challenges that have arisen in our marriage, I feel
abundantly blessed. Next to my marriage, the birth of my first child,
a son, was a miracle on so many levels. I know that fatherhood brings
its own challenges. I know I am certainly not out of the woods when it
comes to same-sex attraction and other weaknesses and behaviors that, in

my case, have come with that. I also am aware that I have just taken on a whole set of new challenges, though I feel I still have some work to do on the old ones, and that is terrifying at times. But I am also profoundly grateful for this blessing of marriage and fatherhood. On so many levels, I feel resolved. What was cloudy is now clear. What was confusing is now simple. What was discordant is now a beautiful harmony.

Any narrative makes an experience seem neat and tidy, with the outcome foreordained. My journey was anything but—it was messy and confusing, and the outcome was uncomfortably uncertain. How I got where I am is still a bit of a mystery to me, as I suppose most miracles are, though I have shared here some valuable lessons I learned along the way as I was guided by the Lord, even (or perhaps especially) when He seemed most distant. It involved more than hard work because I was lazy at times. It involved more than persistence because I did not always endure my trials, or endure them well. It involved more than my intellect because my life is happier and more fulfilling than I could have planned for myself. Above all, the credit goes to God's grace, which no one gains by merit alone. Like Job confronted by God in the whirlwind, I fall silent at last, certain in the knowledge that God can "do every thing . . . things too wonderful for me, which I knew not" (Job 42:2–3).

Creating a Whole Marriage

Tanya Bennion

Tanya Bennion was born in St. Louis, grew up in Wyoming, and spent most of her adult life in the Washington, D.C., area, where she earned her bachelor's degree. Her interests include photography, travel, and making jewelry. She has served in several callings in both the Primary and Relief Society within the Church. She served in the Japan Fukuoka

Mission. She works from home as a freelance graphic designer and website developer. She volunteers as a support group leader for wives of men who experience same-sex attraction. She and her husband, Jeff, are the parents of one son (see "Resolution: The Unexpected Miracle," p. 336).

It had been a wonderful fall day. The sun was shining brightly over the waterfalls, and the temperature was pleasant. After spending all day together, we went back to his place with take-out, ready to watch a movie. As we sat on his couch, he said there was something he needed to tell me. My stomach leapt because I thought he was finally going to tell me that he loved me. Instead, he told me that he was attracted to men.

My heart was racing but now for a different reason. What did this mean? How did this affect our relationship? What was I supposed to do with this information? I had never heard the term "same-sex attraction" (SSA), so the ensuing conversation was all new to me. I listened and learned, and my mind reeled for the next few hours before I headed home. Fortunately, he sent me home with a couple of books, which helped keep me occupied during that nearly sleepless night. For the next several hours, I devoured everything I read.

Over the next days and weeks, as I sat reading the books, I had millions of questions running through my head, sparked mostly by what I was reading. Each time I had another question for him, I wrote it on a Post-it note. After a couple of days, the books were filled with Post-it notes, as were many pads filled with questions. We now jokingly refer to this as the "Post-it note" phase of our relationship.

Unfortunately, I didn't always approach him with my questions very well. He sometimes felt I was attacking him or didn't trust him—which was probably true. But I was upset, scared, and confused. I wanted to understand everything right then, and I wanted to save our relationship. In my desperation, I didn't realize that what I was doing was pushing him away. He felt so attacked that by the fourth day he was ready to end our relationship. That's when I really understood the harm I was causing. For the next week, before and after work, I dropped off cards at his door, telling him how much he meant to me.

We had been together for a year and a half, and I didn't want to lose him. This new information was significant, but it didn't change what I already knew and loved about him.

The Spirit taught me a lot during this time in our relationship. On one occasion, while I was asking Jeff all of my Post-it note questions, he didn't want to answer some of the questions. I was upset because I had been stewing about these questions all day, and I wanted to know the answers! Not only did I want him to give me the answers right then, but they had better be the *right* answers as well! The Spirit whispered to me in that moment that I had been thinking about these questions all day, and that it was only fair that he be given some time to think about the answers before replying to me.

I paused in my questions, took a deep breath, and began again. I told him that I had many questions for him and that some of these questions I needed to know the answers to right away; others he could take his time on. If he didn't want to answer one of the questions at that moment, I handed him the paper, and he was able to think about it for a few days before coming back to me with his explanation. Consequently, there have been times when this form of communication has extended into other areas of our marriage, and it's been beneficial. I've learned to be patient for answers, and when I am, I am much more satisfied by the answers I receive.

Obviously we didn't break up, but things were really rocky for a few weeks. Two weeks after he told me, I went with him to a conference sponsored by Evergreen International, which helped me understand the issue better. I was scared to go, but a friend convinced me that if I wanted to be with Jeff, I should learn all I could about this issue as quickly as possible. I attribute the success of our relationship—at least as it relates to same-sex attraction—to being open-minded, learning all I could through books and conferences, asking questions, and communicating.

During this unstable time I asked Jeff if he was attracted to me. His answer was that he was attracted to me "enough." Enough? What did that mean? I thought that was a *horrible* answer. In no romantic fantasy does a girl dream of her man being attracted to her "enough." I wanted him to tell me that he thought I was beautiful and that he was completely and utterly drawn to me. But that wasn't the case. He was attracted to me . . . enough. It took me a long time for "enough" to be enough for me. Over time I have learned that both of us didn't have to be attracted to each other equally. I had to be enough for him, and he had to be enough for me. It may not be true for everyone, but, in our relationship, his attraction to me has grown throughout our marriage—until "enough" is no longer part of the equation.

By the end of the first month of my knowing about his SSA, our relationship was in shambles. There wasn't any joy left when we were together. I was obsessed with talking about this issue and asking questions, and thus the subject became our only topic of conversation. At this point I realized that I was the cause of the pain in our relationship. I was so focused on his attraction to men that I had forgotten about everything that I loved about him. It was time to make a change. I told him that I wasn't going to bring the topic up for one month. He was welcome to talk about it, but I wasn't going to bring it up in hopes that we could get back to where we had been in our relationship before he told me. Amazingly, one month became two months, and at the end of the third month, he realized that this was something that I could handle and told me for the first time that he thought I was someone he could marry.

A couple of months later we were engaged. I was doing so well with the subject now, that he was worried that I didn't really understand what this was all about. He also worried that I thought marriage would fix him and resolve some of these things that weren't resolved from our courtship. So before we got married, he asked me to go with him to his therapist. He wanted his therapist to talk to me, and if it didn't seem that I "got it," then I could meet with the therapist alone.

I did get it. Jeff just didn't understand how much I really did get it. My understanding was that there are emotional, mental, and physical components to same-sex attraction, and I saw that so many other issues in life manifest themselves the same way. I had been married previously and dealt with a lot of issues in that marriage as well. My first husband was diagnosed with cancer six weeks after we were married. He had lost several jobs because of his health problems. He had almost died on numerous occasions for several reasons. All of these things I found out *after* I was married. At least in the case of Jeff, I got to choose whether I wanted to sign up. I didn't have that luxury the first time.

The way I looked at it was this: Was Jeff trustworthy? Have we demonstrated to one another that we could work through problems? Did Jeff have a testimony of the gospel of Jesus Christ, and did he honor his priesthood covenants? Those were the things that were most important to me. With this knowledge, I knew that we could work through anything that came our way. If one of us was unfaithful to the other (and it is not fair to assume that just because of his different feelings that *he* would automatically be the one who was unfaithful), we had tools in our relationship to work through it. I trusted Jeff that he would be honest with me. I trusted that Jeff loved the Lord and would strive to be an honorable husband, father, and son of God. That is how I knew our relationship would work—if not thrive.

The meeting with the therapist went well, and we left with one important piece of advice. Jeff and I were worried about the "what if's." What if [fill in the blank] happens? The therapist said, "The surest way to make sure something is going to be a problem is to assume it's going to be a problem. If you approach whatever it is with a positive attitude, chances are it won't be a problem. And if it is, there's always help." Jeff and I both wholeheartedly agree with this statement and have tried to make this a policy in our marriage—with everything, not just his SSA feelings.

Shortly after getting married, we had an issue arise, and my first reaction was to attach it to his same-sex attraction. As we talked about it, however, I quickly realized it had nothing to do with his SSA but rather with other aspects of his life experience. This experience taught me to be careful of my judgments. It's easy for me to blame all the problems in our relationship on his SSA, but when I take the time to talk to Jeff about them, I often find that his SSA plays little to no role in the issue.

One of the books Jeff gave me that first night was a compilation of stories of people telling their loved ones about their same-sex attraction.[41] Unfortunately, one of the common themes I recognized through reading these stories was that once the person experiencing SSA confided in his or her loved one about it, the subject wasn't discussed again. What then seemed to follow was that when another problem arose regarding the SSA, it was like having to come to terms with the issue all over again. I didn't want to go through that. Coming to terms with it once was hard enough! This book led to the implementation of the most important tool we have in our marriage: companionship inventory.

It isn't good for me to be my husband's accountability partner (and I can't be an effective one anyway), his therapist, or his warden, but I do desire to know generally how things are going for him in regards to his feelings and attractions. However, if I ask him about them out of the blue, it makes him feel that he's done something that made me suspicious.

I heard an analogy once that if I hold a piece of paper in front of my face, that's all I see. However, if I put it at arm's length in front of my face and off to the side, I can see it through my peripheral vision, but I can also see everything around me. This is what I wanted to do with this issue in our marriage. I didn't want to make it the only issue we talked about, but I didn't want to avoid the subject either. And I especially didn't want Jeff to be defensive when we did talk about it.

To solve this problem, we resurrected companionship inventory from our missions. We make sure that ours is held at a regular time so that each of us has prior notice well in advance. It isn't companionship inventory if one of us springs it on the other. We also make sure we are both in a positive and open state of mind. If we are not, we postpone it a day.

During these discussions, which don't have to take longer than ten minutes, we don't make my husband's attractions the focus. We focus on all aspects of our companionship: the household, our jobs, our Church callings, and our son. We make sure to touch on the SSA, but it is only a minor aspect—this is an opportunity for *both* of us to be accountable.

These inventories have shown us patterns in our marriage. After several years of holding these inventories, we have noticed a rhythm when certain issues crop up in our relationship. Noticing these patterns has helped us to address problems before they arise because we can anticipate their arrival.

My relationship with Jeff has taught me a great deal about patience. As we were dating, I felt that our relationship was moving forward at a snail's pace. There were so many times I wanted to call it quits. Unbeknownst to him, I tested him over and over, and I set deadlines for relationship progress markers. But the Lord knew better and helped me grow through this process. One of the wonderful things I learned was not to judge our relationship by other people's timetables. So many people around us were wondering why we weren't moving our relationship forward faster. This wasn't their relationship! They didn't know what was going on! I learned to tune them out. The only opinions that mattered belonged to Jeff, the Lord, and me.

So I finally dropped all of my timetables and told Jeff that I was in this for the long haul. I told him that as long as our relationship was moving forward, I wanted to be with him. Little did I know that while I thought our relationship was moving at a turtle's pace, Jeff felt that he was the rabbit in the race. I learned that each of us can have vastly different perspectives about the same thing. I have tried to remember this in my marriage, and that I need to honor his perspective as much as I honor my own.

Relationships don't come easily. I feel, however, that one critical reason we have such a healthy relationship is that we have separately worked to become healthy individuals. Jeff had been working through his issues, actively addressing his same-sex attraction, for twelve years before we were married. I had been working on my own growth and healing for five years.

After the death of my first husband, I was a wreck. I was coming to terms with being a twenty-six-year-old widow, feeling lost and having my hopes and dreams of what my future would be ripped away from me. I went to grief counseling and started a grief group to help me understand and work through my feelings. I began serving in the temple two weeks after his death. For the next six years, I served in the temple, and it served as the ideal place for me to work through my emotions. In fact, once Jeff and I had worked through the major portion of my concerns about his same-sex attraction and began making wedding plans, some of my insecurities regarding my status as a widow arose, and we needed to address how that made Jeff feel. We spent the next several months working through my stuff before we were finally married.

I was told once that a whole marriage can't consist of half of two people but rather two whole people coming together. That is why I believe our marriage is a success. We continually work separately to be whole individuals so that we can give everything we have to one another and to our marriage.

Our marriage has been wonderful. We have our trials, but we work through them. I had a good first marriage too, but we didn't talk about the hard subjects that came up. Jeff's experience with same-sex attraction has been a real blessing in our marriage because it's forced us to communicate. Our marriage is stronger than many, ironically *because* of his challenges. We have had to learn how to talk about hard subjects together, and that has made it easier for us to talk about *any* subject in our marriage.

Also, as we move forward with our marriage, Jeff and I continue to be involved with helping others affected by SSA. We have found that helping others has helped our marriage *and* us. As we each learn new things through our associations with other men and women (and their spouses, if married), we are able to bring those things back, discuss them, and strengthen our marriage through the process. The story of the ten lepers (see Luke 17:11–19) teaches the importance of gratitude to the Lord for our blessings. One of the ways Jeff and I have tried to thank the Lord for our fulfilling and happy marriage is through helping others achieve the same thing.

Jeff told me about his same-sex attraction at a time in my life when I personalized too many things. I was an emotional wreck and cried constantly. But the Spirit taught me that I couldn't handle this situation the same way. As we approached things defensively, neither Jeff nor I communicated clearly, and the meaning of what we said to one another was always distorted through the murky filter we were wading through. I knew I loved Jeff and wanted to work on this together, and, in order to do so, I needed to handle this in a very clear manner. Through constant nudges from the Spirit, I learned how to approach our relationship with a clear head rather than leading with my hurt feelings.

The Spirit taught me that if I took time to calm down and make sure the Spirit was with me when I approached Jeff, the outcome would be significantly different, and we would be able to understand what each other was saying. Over the years the Spirit has taught me to be still and listen to His advice before reacting. He has taught me that with His help, Jeff and I can make it through any trial that may come our way.

I know Jeff loves me, and my heart no longer races when I hear the term *same-sex attraction*. My first husband was attracted to women, and my second husband is attracted to men. I have learned that the gender my partner is attracted to makes no difference if we are committed to our relationship. I know Jeff is committed to me, and I am to him. I know that if we continue to keep the Lord present in our daily lives, as we communicate with one another and as we make sure we are both growing, there isn't any trial too large that Jeff and I can't make it through together.

Before I met Jeff, when I was still unsure if I would ever marry again, or even if I would *want* to marry again, I had a spiritual experience that confirmed to me that Jesus Christ saw and loved me perfectly. When the veil is taken away, and we too partake of this perfect love, we will see each other perfectly, in pure love, the way the Savior sees each of us (see D&C 76:94). For a brief moment I caught sight of that vision, and I knew that everything would be all right, that the Lord with His perfect love would take care of all of us.

I testify that the Lord knows and loves each of us perfectly. I need that perfect love and understanding from Him, and I need to reflect it in my marriage and in all my relationships. I have felt His love and been blessed beyond measure by it—not just in the promise of the next life but in this one as well. I know that each of us, no matter our circumstances here in mortality, can rely on the Lord. His promises are sure.

Epilogue

As we come to the end of this volume, I would like to leave you with a couple of concluding thoughts. As part of my own broader spiritual journey of seeking to know the Lord and to live His teachings, the process of compiling these chapters and essays has been one of the most enriching and rewarding projects I've ever engaged in. I feel such a deep sense of gratitude for each of those who were willing to be a part of it, as well as the many more who I would have liked to include but couldn't because of natural limitations of length. I also can't sufficiently thank each of you who has traveled this journey with us.

It's also been one of the most heart-wrenching projects I've ever engaged in, with such a broad range of conflicting emotions. I stepped into this project with the encouragement of a couple of spiritual mentors whose lives and examples have been a great inspiration to me. At the same time, I had never participated in anything like this so I had some fear and feelings of inadequacy. I knew I would have to rely "wholly upon the merits of him who is mighty to save" to see me see through it (2 Nephi 31:19). There were even numerous occasions when I wanted to quit.

Given the sensitive and controversial nature of this topic, there were times I wanted to get as far away from it as I could and just live the quiet life of faith I'd only ever wanted. I began the project in the fall of 2006, well before any of the more recent highly public and controversial events that have brought so much attention to The Church of Jesus Christ of Latter-day Saints and its positions and teachings regarding homosexual behavior and same-sex marriage, particularly Church leaders' encouragement of members in California to help pass Proposition 8. As opinions become more passionate and debates more heated, it's hard to say *any*thing on this topic without some form of backlash by *some*one. And I imagine that we've seen still only a glimpse of the cultural tensions Latter-day Saints will face as gay and lesbian issues rise to greater prominence on the socio-political landscape of the many countries wherein we have a presence.

At the end of the day, however, this book is very much nonpolitical. While there are certainly times when the call to build up Zion requires Latter-day Saints, individually or collectively, to speak up in socio-political arenas, a living faith in Jesus Christ can never be legislated. It is just such a living faith, and how it shows up in the lives of believing Latter-day Saints dealing with same-gender attraction regardless of socio-cultural context, that this book is about. This book is an exploration into the life of faith born of the Spirit—a faith that Latter-day Saints must nurture with ever more care and attunement to the things of eternity, things which transcend the increasingly secular smog of contemporary cultures and philosophies.

My belief is that homosexuality represents one of the last great generational Abrahamic tests—a spiritual sifter, if you will—before the great Second Coming of our Savior. It presents a spiritual crucible that will try our allegiance to the testimony of those prophetic witnesses whom God has called to be spiritual watchmen (see D&C 101:44–62) in a long-prophesied day when men and women would increasingly "call evil good, and good evil" and "put darkness for light, and light for darkness" (Isaiah 5:20).

Whether the Abrahamic tests that try our faith are individual or collective as a people, Joseph Smith taught that Latter-day Saints "will have all kinds of trials to pass through. And it is quite as necessary for you to be tried as it was for Abraham and other men of God . . . God will feel after you, and he will take hold of you and wrench your very heart strings, and if you cannot stand it you will not be fit for an inheritance in the Celestial Kingdom of God."[1] The Prophet also taught that before any individual can be exalted or have his calling and election made sure, he must learn to "liv[e] by every word of God" and be "thoroughly proved" until the Lord "finds that the man is determined to serve Him at all hazards."[2]

It is my belief that the Church's doctrinal stance on homosexual relations will prove to be a potent force in the sifting of those who stand with the prophets and those who do not. The questions Latter-day Saints have about homosexuality should be as much about unconditional worship and what constitutes a fully consecrated life as they may be about anything else.

I would also like to reiterate some feelings expressed in the introduction. Each of you reading this book is coming from a very different place and has very different needs. Some of you may experience same-gender attraction yourselves and are seeking ways to respond to your feelings that are in harmony with the restored gospel of Jesus Christ. To you, my hope is that you've felt something akin to the three key human needs President Hinckley spoke of: that you know you are not alone either in your feelings or in your efforts to live the gospel; that you've gained a deeper appreciation for the truth that you belong in the Church and have a vital role in the growth and perfection of the Lord's kingdom; and, finally, that you've felt the love, spiritual nourishment, and power that come only in and through the life-giving word of Jesus Christ.

Others of you are parents or family members or friends who have loved ones who are dealing with these issues, some of whom are currently participating in the Church and living gospel standards while others are not. Still others of you are priesthood or other auxiliary leaders who are seeking to know how to minister more effectively and with greater care and compassion to those within your stewardship. Whoever you are and whatever your circumstances might be, my hope and prayer is that you have been uplifted, enlightened, and edified by the contributions to this volume and that you feel greater direction concerning how the Lord might have you respond within your spheres of stewardship.

More broadly, I hope this volume will help all of us respond more compassionately to those who are dealing with issues relating to same-gender attraction, whether or not they are presently choosing to live in harmony with the principles of the restored gospel. In a recent statement from Church leadership, they note, "This Church has felt the bitter sting of persecution and marginalization early in our history, when we were too few in numbers to adequately protect ourselves and when society's leaders often seemed disinclined to help. Our parents, young adults, teens and children should therefore, of all people, be especially sensitive to the vulnerable in society and be willing to speak out against bullying or intimidation whenever it occurs, including unkindness toward those who are attracted to others of the same sex. This is particularly so in our own Latter-day Saint congregations. Each Latter-day Saint family and individual should carefully consider whether their attitudes and actions toward others properly reflect Jesus Christ's second great commandment—to love one another."[3]

Finally, and most important, I hope the many voices and testimonies shared in this volume have helped you to feel a greater desire to come closer to our Lord and Savior Jesus Christ as they have witnessed of Him, our ultimate Voice of Hope. I have an ever-growing testimony of His love for me and for each and every one of us as our Father's children, that He is holy and full of grace and wants us home, and for that reason a ransom was made—for that reason did He say, "I will be merciful to them . . . if they will repent and come unto me; for mine arm is lengthened out all the day long" (2 Nephi 28:32). I am eternally grateful for the peace and perspective and purpose I have felt as He has helped me through His Spirit to better understand the divine purposes of all we experience here in mortality. As I ponder the many ways I've felt His love in my life, I feel to echo the words of Nephi: "I glory in plainness; I glory in truth; I glory in my Jesus, for he hath redeemed my soul from hell" (2 Nephi 33:6).

Notes

Introduction
"A Seal of Living Reality"

1. Hinckley, "Stand Strong," 99.
2. Hinckley, "Converts and Young Men," 47.
3. Dew, *No Doubt about It,* 74–76.
4. McConkie, "The How and Why of Faith-promoting Stories," 5.
5. McConkie, "The How and Why of Faith-promoting Stories," 4, 5.
6. Scott, "Acquiring Spiritual Knowledge," 86.
7. Packer, "Little Children," 17.
8. Packer, "The Mediator," 56.
9. Maxwell, "Hope through the Atonement," 63.
10. Thomas, in George, *Classic Christianity,* 7; also quoted in Millet, *More Holiness Give Me,* 20–21.
11. Brach, *Radical Acceptance,* 46.
12. Young, in *Journal of Discourses,* 2:301.
13. Whitney, in Kimball, *Faith Precedes the Miracle,* 98.
14. Hinckley, "A Conversation with Gordon B. Hinckley," interview.
15. Nibley, *The World and the Prophets,* 134.
16. Maxwell, "'Brightness of Hope,'" 35–36.
17. Holland, "Helping Those Who Struggle," 42.
18. Holland, "The Mormons," interview.
19. Keller, "Authority and Worldwide Growth," 307.

20. For contemporary application of these ideas, see Oaks, "Love and Law," 26–29.
21. Richards, "Bringing Humanity to the Gospel," 43; emphasis added.
22. Uchtdorf, "The Love of God," 21.
23. Jensen, "The Mormons," interview.
24. Holland, "Helping Those Who Struggle," 45.
25. Uchtdorf, "'You Are My Hands,'" 68–69.
26. Wirthlin, "Concern for the One," 19–20.
27. Smith, *From Prophet to Son*, 42–43.

Chapter 1
Seeing the Big Picture

1. Stott, *Life in Christ*, 109.
2. See also Hafen, *Spiritually Anchored in Unsettled Times*, 32–33.
3. See Smith, *Lectures on Faith*, 38–44.

Becoming

4. Oaks, "The Challenge to Become," 32–34.

Chapter 2
A Gift of Love: Perspectives for Parents

1. Maxwell, "But for a Small Moment," in *Speeches*, 444.
2. Smith, *Gospel Doctrine*, 13.
3. Maxwell, *But for a Small Moment*, 98–99.
4. McConkie, *A New Witness for the Articles of Faith*, 512.
5. Whitney, in Conference Report, April 1929, 110–11.
6. McConkie, *A New Witness for the Articles of Faith*, 513.
7. Cannon, *Gospel Truth*, 304.
8. Scott, "Obtaining Help from the Lord," 86.
9. Holland, "Lessons from Liberty Jail," 28–29.
10. Maxwell, "But for a Small Moment," in *Speeches*, 448.
11. Holland, "Lessons from Liberty Jail," 30.
12. Holland, "The Mormons," interview.
13. The reader may find helpful a book the author has written on the issues

surrounding troubled thinking called *Light in the Wilderness: Explorations in the Spiritual Life.*

14. Authors such as Eckhart Tolle, Byron Katie, and Eugene Gendlin propose variations and extensions of this method for dealing with troublesome thoughts and feelings.

15. Holland, "Lessons from Liberty Jail," 32.

16. Maxwell, "But for a Small Moment," in *Speeches,* 449.

17. "Don't assume you are the reason for those feelings. No one, including the one struggling, should try to shoulder blame. Nor should anyone place blame on another—including God. Walk by faith, and help your loved one deal the best he or she can with this challenge" (Holland, "Helping Those Who Struggle," 44).

18. Scott, "Trust in the Lord," 16–17.

19. Peck, *The Road Less Traveled,* 81.

20. Hawkins, *Power vs. Force,* 90–91.

21. Jensen, "The Mormons," interview.

22. Oaks and Wickman, "Same-Gender Attraction," interview.

23. Scott, "Trust in the Lord," 17–18.

24. There are many good books on opening communication lines and avoiding pitfalls. One that deals with how parents can reestablish a loving relationship with a child dealing with same-gender attraction is Richard Cohen's *Gay Children, Straight Parents: A Plan for Family Healing.*

25. Holland, "Helping Those Who Struggle," 44.

26. Oaks and Wickman, "Same-Gender Attraction," interview.

27. Stauffer, *Giants,* 111.

28. Barzaghi, "Red Thread Zen."

29. "I do know that this will not be a post-mortal condition. It will not be a post-mortal difficulty. . . . I just say . . . to people struggling with gender identity: 'Hang on, and hope on, and pray on, and this will be resolved in eternity.' These conditions will not exist [in] post-mortality" (Holland, "The Mormons," interview).

30. Brown, "Live the Questions."

31. Oaks and Wickman, "Same-Gender Attraction," interview; paragraphing altered.

32. Oaks and Wickman, "Same-Gender Attraction," interview.

33. Smith, *Teachings,* 191.

34. Whitney, in Conference Report, April 1929, 110.

35. Packer, "Our Moral Environment," 68.

36. Snow, "Discourse by Lorenzo Snow," 52–53.

"Trust in the Lord"

37. "I Know That My Redeemer Lives," *Hymns,* no. 136.

38. See Nelson, "Divine Love," 20.

Chapter 3
"Come Unto Me": Exploring the Heart of Christian Discipleship

1. Same-gender attraction has been variously attributed to or associated with genetic predisposition, early experience, hormonal processes, family dynamics, abuse or trauma, brain chemistry, temperament, peer relations, certain talents and interests, identity disorders, addictive processes, birth order, and societal factors. This list will probably grow as we learn more.

2. One translation of the Lord's prayer, "Give us this day our daily bread," would be "Give us today today's bread," or in other words, "Give us in this hour the sustenance we need for this hour."

3. If we have been sexually abused by a person who was older or more powerful than we, we are not responsible or guilty of sin. Nor should we be concerned if we participated in sexual play or experimentation when we were children. Such involvement can affect us negatively or make us feel tainted, but we are not morally accountable for sin because of these experiences.

4. Smith, *Lectures on Faith,* 69.

5. Benson, in Staheli, "Obedience—Life's Great Challenge," 82.

Being My True Self

6. Valéry in Tillich, *The Essential Tillich,* 198.

Chapter 4
A Church for All, A Gospel of Inclusion

1. Packer, *"That All May Be Edified,"* 134–35; see also Packer, "Children," 7.

2. Yancey, *The Jesus I Never Knew,* 147–48.

3. Holland, "Helping Those Who Struggle," 42; see also Packer, "Ye Are the Temple of God," 74.

4. Groberg, "Writing Your Personal and Family History," 49.

5. Eyring, "That We May Be One," 68.

6. "O Savior, Thou Who Wearest a Crown," *Hymns,* no. 197.

A Christ-Centered Gender Identity

7. Scott, "To Acquire Spiritual Guidance," 6.

8. "The Family: A Proclamation to the World," 102.

9. Holland, "Broken Things to Mend," 70.

10. McKay, *Pathways to Happiness,* 291–92; see also Uchtdorf, "The Influence of Righteous Women," 8.

11. See also Maxwell, "Consecrate Thy Performance," 37.

Chapter 5
Feeding the Flock of God:
The Vital Role of Sensitive and Loving Priesthood Leaders

1. "O God, the Eternal Father," *Hymns,* no. 175.

2. See Packer, "The Choice," 20–22.

3. Smith, *Teachings,* 191.

4. Kimball, *Faith Precedes the Miracle,* 175.

5. Hinckley, "What Are People Asking about Us?" 71; see also Hinckley, "Why We Do Some of the Things We Do," 54.

6. Kimball, "Listen to the Prophets," 77.

7. Hinckley, "Reverence and Morality," 47.

8. Hinckley, "Why We Do Some of the Things We Do," 54.

9. Oaks, "Same-Gender Attraction," 8.

10. Oaks, "Same-Gender Attraction," 7–8.

11. Smith, *Teachings,* 296.

My Shepherd Will Supply My Need

12. Watts, "My Shepherd Will Supply My Need," audio CD.

My Journey as a Priesthood Leader

13. *Preach My Gospel,* 188.
14. Smith, *Teachings of Presidents of the Church: Joseph Smith,* 428.

The Atonement Can Fix That Too!

15. Wayne and Sherman, *Big Jake.*

Chapter 6
Eternal Marriage: Principles, Possibilities, and Promises

1. Scott, "Receive the Temple Blessings," 27.
2. Packer, "Marriage," 15.
3. Kimball, *Teachings,* 305.
4. See Packer, "Marriage," 13.
5. *God Loveth His Children,* 3–4; emphasis added.
6. Packer, "Do Not Fear," 79.
7. Eyring, "That We May Be One," 66.
8. Smith, *The Way to Perfection,* 251.
9. McConkie, *Doctrinal New Testament Commentary,* 1:546.
10. Young, *Discourses of Brigham Young,* 195.
11. Kimball, "The Family Influence," 15.
12. Snow, "Devotion to a Divine Inspiration," 656.
13. Smith, *Lectures on Faith,* 38.
14. Cannon, *Gospel Truth,* 102.
15. Snow, in *Journal of Discourses,* 19:270–71.
16. Lee, *Teachings,* 22.
17. Oaks, "Focus and Priorities," 83–84.
18. Simmons, "But If Not . . . ," 73.
19. Grant, Ivins, Nibley, in Clark, *Messages of the First Presidency,* 5:244.
20. Oaks, "Same-Gender Attraction," 7.
21. Packer, in Staheli, "Obedience—Life's Great Challenge," 81.
22. Romney, "Man—A Child of God," 14.
23. See Ballard, "One More," 71.
24. Hinckley, "Each a Better Person," 99.
25. Morrison, "'Come and See,'" 12.

26. Dew, *No Doubt about It,* 47.

27. Bergin, *Eternal Values,* 29.

28. Hunter, *Teachings,* 15.

29. Oaks, "Same-Gender Attraction," 7.

30. Ibid., 9.

31. Name Withheld, "Compassion for Those Who Struggle," 59.

32. Oaks, "Same-Gender Attraction," 10.

33. Ibid.

34. Holland, "Helping Those Who Struggle," 44.

35. Scott, "First Things First," 7.

36. Hinckley, "Women of the Church," 68.

37. Oaks, "The Dedication of a Lifetime."

38. Beckert, in *Living a Covenant Marriage,* 221–22.

Resolution: The Unexpected Miracle

39. Gautama in Holden, *Be Happy,* 221.

40. Hopkins, in *The Major Works,* 183.

Creating a Whole Marriage

41. See Hyde and Hyde, *A Place in the Kingdom.*

Epilogue

1. John Taylor in *Journal of Discourses,* 24:197.

2. Smith, *Teachings,* 150.

3. Ottersen, "Statement on Same-Sex Attraction."

Sources

Articles by General Authorities

Ballard, M. Russell. "One More." *Ensign,* May 2005, 69–71.

Conference Reports of The Church of Jesus Christ of Latter-day Saints. Salt Lake City: The Church of Jesus Christ of Latter-day Saints, 1898–.

Eyring, Henry B. "That We May Be One." *Ensign,* May 1998, 66–68.

"The Family: A Proclamation to the World." *Ensign,* November 1995, 102.

Groberg, John H. "Writing Your Personal and Family History." *Ensign,* May 1980, 48–49.

Hinckley, Gordon B. "Converts and Young Men." *Ensign,* May 1997, 47–50.

———. "Each a Better Person." *Ensign,* November 2002, 99–100.

———. "Reverence and Morality." *Ensign,* May 1987, 45–48.

———. "Stand Strong against the Wiles of the World." *Ensign,* November 1995, 98–101.

———. "What Are People Asking about Us?" *Ensign,* November 1998, 70–72.

———. "Why We Do Some of the Things We Do." *Ensign,* November 1999, 52–54.

———. "Women of the Church." *Ensign,* November 1996, 67–70.

Holland, Jeffrey R. "Broken Things to Mend." *Ensign,* May 2006, 69–71.

———. "Helping Those Who Struggle with Same-Gender Attraction." *Ensign,* October 2007, 42–45.

———. "Lessons from Liberty Jail." *Ensign,* September 2009, 26–33.

Kimball, Spencer W. "Listen to the Prophets." *Ensign,* May 1978, 76–78.

———. "The Family Influence." *Ensign,* July 1973, 15–18.

Maxwell, Neal A. "Brightness of Hope." *Ensign,* November 1994, 34–36.

———. "But for a Small Moment." In *Speeches of the Year: BYU Devotional and Ten-Stake Fireside Addresses 1974.* Provo, Utah: Brigham Young University Press, 1975, 443–57.

———. "Consecrate Thy Performance." *Ensign,* May 2002, 36–38.

———. "Hope through the Atonement of Jesus Christ." *Ensign,* November 1998, 61–63.

McConkie, Bruce R. "The How and Why of Faith-promoting Stories." *New Era,* July 1978, 4–10.

Morrison, Alexander B. "'Come and See.'" *Ensign,* November 2000, 12–13.

Nelson, Russell M. "Divine Love." *Ensign,* February 2003, 20–25.

Oaks, Dallin H. "The Challenge to Become." *Ensign,* November 2000, 32–34.

———. "The Dedication of a Lifetime." CES Fireside for Young Adults, May 1, 2005. Available at http://lds.org/library/display/0,4945,538–1–3100–1,00.html

———. "Focus and Priorities." *Ensign,* May 2001, 82–84.

———. "Love and Law." *Ensign,* November 2009, 26–29.

———. "Same-Gender Attraction." *Ensign,* October 1995, 7–14.

Packer, Boyd K. "Children." *Ensign,* May 2002, 7–10.

———. "The Choice." *Ensign,* November 1980, 20–22.

———. "Do Not Fear." *Ensign,* May 2004, 77–80.

———. "Little Children." *Ensign,* November 1986, 16–18.

———. "Marriage." *Ensign,* May 1981, 13–15.

———. "The Mediator." *Ensign,* May 1977, 54–56.

———. "Our Moral Environment." *Ensign,* May 1992, 66–68.

———. "Ye Are the Temple of God." *Ensign,* November 2000, 72–74.

Richards, Stephen L. "Bringing Humanity to the Gospel." *Sunstone,* May–June 1979, 43–46.

Romney, Marion G. "Man—A Child of God." *Ensign,* July 1973, 11–14.

Scott, Richard G. "Acquiring Spiritual Knowledge." *Ensign,* November 1993, 86–88.

———. "To Acquire Spiritual Guidance." *Ensign,* November 2009, 6–9.

———. "First Things First." *Ensign,* May 2001, 6–9.

———. "Obtaining Help from the Lord." *Ensign,* November 1991, 84–86.

———. "Receive the Temple Blessings." *Ensign,* May 1999, 25–27.

———. "Trust in the Lord." *Ensign,* November 1995, 16–18.

Simmons, Dennis E. "But If Not . . ." *Ensign,* May 2004, 73–75.

Snow, LeRoi C. "Devotion to a Divine Inspiration." *Improvement Era,* June 1919, 653–62.

Snow, Lorenzo. "Discourse by Lorenzo Snow." *Millennial Star,* January 22, 1894, 49–53.

Staheli, Donald L. "Obedience—Life's Great Challenge." *Ensign,* May 1998, 81–82.

Uchtdorf, Dieter F. "The Influence of Righteous Women." *Ensign,* September 2009, 5–9.

———. "The Love of God." *Ensign,* November 2009, 21–24.

———. "'You Are My Hands.'" *Ensign,* May 2010, 68–70, 75.

Wirthlin, Joseph B. "Concern for the One." *Ensign,* May 2008, 17–20.

Books by LDS Authors

Cannon, George Q. *Gospel Truth: Discourses and Writings of President George Q. Cannon.* Edited by Jerreld L. Newquist. Salt Lake City: Deseret Book, 1987.

Beckert, Charles B. "The Couple Connection." In *Living a Covenant Marriage.* Edited by Douglas E. Brinley and Daniel K Judd. Salt Lake City: Deseret Book, 2004.

Bergin, Allen E. *Eternal Values and Personal Growth: A Guide on Your Journey to Spiritual, Emotional, and Social Wellness.* Provo, UT: BYU Studies, 2002.

Clark, James R., comp. *Messages of the First Presidency of The Church of Jesus Christ of Latter-day Saints.* 6 vols. Salt Lake City: Bookcraft, 1965–75.

Dew, Sheri. *No Doubt about It.* Salt Lake City: Bookcraft, 2001.

Eldridge, Erin. *Born That Way?: A True Story of Overcoming Same-Sex Attraction with Insights for Friends, Families, and Leaders.* Salt Lake City: Deseret Book, 1994.

Hafen, Bruce C. *Spiritually Anchored in Unsettled Times.* Salt Lake City: Deseret Book, 2009.

Hunter, Howard W. *The Teachings of Howard W. Hunter.* Edited by Clyde J. Williams. Salt Lake City: Bookcraft, 1997.

Hyde, Garrick, and Ginger Hyde, eds. *A Place in the Kingdom: Spiritual Insights from Latter-day Saints about Same-Sex Attraction.* Salt Lake City: Century Publishing, 1997.

Journal of Discourses. 26 vols. London: Latter-day Saints' Book Depot, 1854–86.

Keller, Roger R. "Authority and Worldwide Growth." In *The Worlds of Joseph*

Smith: A Bicentennial Conference at the Library of Congress. Edited by John W. Welch. Provo, Utah: Brigham Young University Press, 2006.

Kimball, Spencer W. *Faith Precedes the Miracle.* Salt Lake City: Deseret Book, 1972.

———. *The Teachings of Spencer W. Kimball.* Edited by Edward L. Kimball. Salt Lake City: Bookcraft, 1982.

Lee, Harold B. *The Teachings of Harold B. Lee.* Edited by Clyde J. Williams. Salt Lake City: Bookcraft, 1996.

Maxwell, Neal A. *"But for a Small Moment."* Salt Lake City: Bookcraft, 1986.

McConkie, Bruce R. *A New Witness for the Articles of Faith.* Salt Lake City: Deseret Book, 1985.

———. *Doctrinal New Testament Commentary.* 3 vols. Salt Lake City: Bookcraft, 1977.

McKay, David O. *Pathways to Happiness.* Compiled by Llewelyn R. McKay. Salt Lake City: Bookcraft, 1957.

Millet, Robert L. *More Holiness Give Me.* Salt Lake City: Deseret Book, 2001.

Nibley, Hugh. *The World and the Prophets.* Salt Lake City: Deseret Book, 1987.

Packer, Boyd K. *"That All May Be Edified."* Salt Lake City: Deseret Book, 1982.

Smith, Joseph. *Lectures on Faith.* Salt Lake City: Deseret Book, 1985.

———. *Teachings of Presidents of the Church: Joseph Smith.* Salt Lake City: The Church of Jesus Christ of Latter-day Saints, 2007.

———. *Teachings of the Prophet Joseph Smith.* Selected by Joseph Fielding Smith. Salt Lake City: Deseret Book, 1976.

Smith, Joseph F. *From Prophet to Son: Advice of Joseph F. Smith to His Missionary Sons.* Compiled by Hyrum M. Smith III and Scott G. Kenney. Salt Lake City: Deseret Book, 1981.

Smith, Joseph Fielding. *Gospel Doctrine: Selections from the Sermons and Writings of Joseph F. Smith.* Salt Lake City: Deseret Book, 1971.

———. *The Way to Perfection.* Salt Lake City: Genealogical Society of The Church of Jesus Christ of Latter-day Saints, 1931.

Thomas, M. Catherine. *Light in the Wilderness: Explorations in the Spiritual Life.* Salt Lake City: Digital Legend, 2010.

Yancey, Philip. *The Jesus I Never Knew.* Grand Rapids, Mich.: Zondervan, 1995.

Young, Brigham. *Discourses of Brigham Young.* Compiled by John A. Widtsoe. Salt Lake City: Deseret Book, 1976.

Books by Other Authors

Brach, Tara. *Radical Acceptance: Embracing Your Life with the Heart of a Buddha.* New York: Bantam Books, 2004.

Cohen, Richard. *Gay Children, Straight Parents: A Plan for Family Healing.* Downers Grove, Ill.: IVP Books, 2007.

George, Bob. *Classic Christianity: Life's Too Short to Miss the Real Thing.* Eugene, Ore.: Harvest House, 1989.

Hawkins, David. *Power vs. Force: Hidden Determinants of Human Behavior.* Carlsbad, Calif.: Hay House, 2002.

Holden, Robert. *Be Happy! Release the Power of Happiness in You.* Carlsbad, CA: Hay House, 2010.

Hopkins, Gerard Manley. "'Though Art Indeed Just, Lord, If I Contend.'" In *The Major Works.* Oxford: Oxford University Press, 2009.

Peck, M. Scott. *The Road Less Traveled: A New Psychology of Love, Traditional Values and Spiritual Growth.* New York: Simon & Schuster, 1978.

Stauffer, John. *Giants: The Parallel Lives of Frederick Douglass and Abraham Lincoln.* New York: Twelve, 2008.

Stott, John. *Life in Christ: A Guide to Daily Living.* Grand Rapids, Mich.: Baker Books, 2003.

Tillich, Paul and F. Forrester Church, eds. *The Essential Tillich: An Anthology of the Writings of Paul Tillich.* Chicago: University of Chicago Press, 1999.

Church Publications

God Loveth His Children. Salt Lake City: The Church of Jesus Christ of Latter-day Saints, 2007. This Church-published booklet provides counsel for individuals who experience same-gender attraction. It is helpful for their priesthood leaders and family members as well.

Hymns of The Church of Jesus Christ of Latter-day Saints. Salt Lake City: The Church of Jesus Christ of Latter-day Saints, 1985.

Preach My Gospel: A Guide to Missionary Service. Salt Lake City: The Church of Jesus Christ of Latter-day Saints, 2004.

Interviews and Online Sources

Barzaghi, Subhana. "Red Thread Zen—the Tao of Love, Passion, and Sex." In *Spiritual Concepts: Hidden Mysteries*. Available at www.hiddenmysteries. org/spirit/menu.shtml.

Brown, Phillip. "Live the Questions." In *North Star* (November 2007). Available at http://northstarlds.org/voices_full_2007–11.php.

Hinckley, Gordon B. "A Conversation with Gordon B. Hinckley, President of The Church of Jesus Christ of Latter Day Saints." Interview by Larry King. *CNN Larry King Live* (December 26, 2004). Available at http:// transcripts.cnn.com/TRANSCRIPTS/0412/26/lk1.01.html.

Holland, Jeffrey R. "The Mormons: Interview with Jeffrey Holland." Interview by PBS (March 4, 2006). Available at http://www.pbs.org/mormons/interviews/holland.html.

Jensen, Marlin K. "The Mormons: Interview with Marlin Jensen." Interview by PBS (March 7, 2006). Available at http://www.pbs.org/mormons/interviews/jensen.html.

Oaks, Dallin H., and Lance B. Wickman. "Same-Gender Attraction." Interview by Public Affairs Department of The Church of Jesus Christ of Latter-day Saints Church. *LDS Newsroom* (2006). Available at http://beta-newsroom. lds.org/official-statement/same-gender-attraction.

Ottersen, Michael. "Church Responds to HRC Petitions: Statement on Same-Sex Attraction." News release, 12 October 2010. The Church of Jesus Christ of Latter-day Saints Newsroom. Available at http://newsroom.lds. org/article/church-mormon-responds-to-human-rights-campaign-petition-same-sex-attraction.

Audio CD and DVD

Watts, Isaac. "My Shepherd Will Supply My Need." In *The Southern Harmony*, 1835.

Wayne, M. A., prod., and G. Sherman, dir. *Big Jake* (motion picture). United States: Cinema Center Films, 1971.

Resources
Specific to Same-Gender
Attraction

Church Publications

God Loveth His Children. Salt Lake City: The Church of Jesus Christ of
Latter-day Saints, 2007. This Church-published booklet provides counsel for individuals who experience same-gender attraction. It is helpful for
their priesthood leaders and family members as well.

Articles by General Authorities

Hafen, Bruce C. "Same-Sex Attraction." Address delivered at the Nineteenth
Annual Evergreen Conference. http://newsroom.lds.org/ldsnewsroom/
eng/publicissues/elder-bruce-c-hafen-speaks-on-same-sex-attraction.

Holland, Jeffrey R. "Helping Those Who Struggle with Same-Gender
Attraction." *Ensign,* October 2007.

Mason, James O. "The Worth of a Soul Is Great." Address delivered at the
Fifteenth Annual Evergreen Conference, September 17, 2005. http://
www.evergreeninternational.org/Worth_of_a_Soul.htm.

Morrison, Alexander B. "Some Gospel Perspectives on Same-Gender Attraction." Address delivered at the Tenth Annual Evergreen Conference,
September 16, 2000. http://www.evergreeninternational.org/morrison
.htm.

Oaks, Dallin H. "Same-Gender Attraction." *Ensign,* October 1995.

Oaks, Dallin H. and Lance B. Wickman. "Same-Gender Attraction." Church
Public Affairs Interview, *LDS Newroom,* August 2006.

Ensign Articles

Name Withheld. "The Best Thing I Can Do for Leigh." *Ensign,* September 2009.

Name Withheld. "Compassion for Those Who Struggle." *Ensign,* September 2004.

Name Withheld. "I Won't Give Up On Them!" *Ensign.* February 2004.

Name Withheld. "My Battle With Same-Sex Attraction." *Ensign,* August 2002.

Price, Joanna Stephenson. "Disagreeing without Being Disagreeable." *Ensign,* March 2005.

Books by LDS Authors

Byrd, A. Dean. *Mormons and Homosexuality: Setting the Record Straight.* Orem, UT: Millennial Press, 2008.

Dahle, Dennis V., A. Dean Byrd, et al., eds. *Understanding Same-Sex Attraction, Where to Turn and How to Help.* Salt Lake City: Foundation for Attraction Research, 2009.

Eldridge, Erin. *Born That Way?: A True Story of Overcoming Same-Sex Attraction with Insights for Friends, Families, and Leaders.* Salt Lake City: Deseret Book, 1994.

Hyde, Garrick, and Ginger Hyde, eds. *A Place in the Kingdom: Spiritual Insights from Latter-day Saints about Same-Sex Attraction.* Salt Lake City: Century Publishing, 1997.

Matis, Fred, Marilyn Matis, and Ty Mansfield. *In Quiet Desperation: Understanding the Challenge of Same-Gender Attraction.* Salt Lake City: Deseret Book, 2004.

Park, Jason. *Helping LDS Men Resolve Homosexual Problems: A Guide for Family, Friends, and Church Leaders.* Salt Lake City: Century Publishing, 1997.

_____. *Resolving Homosexual Problems: A Guide for LDS Men.* Salt Lake City: Century Publishing, 1997.

Pearson, Carol Lynn. *Goodbye, I Love You: The True Story of a Wife, Her Homosexual Husband, and a Love That Transcended Tragedy.* New York: Random House, 1986.

Books by Other Authors

Chambers, Alan. *God's Grace and the Homosexual Next Door: Reaching the Heart of the Gay Men and Women in Your World.* Eugene, OR: Harvest House, 2006.

Cohen, Richard. *Gay Children, Straight Parents: A Plan for Family Healing.* Downers Grove, IL: IVP Books, 2007.

Dallas, Joe and Nancy Heche. *The Complete Christian Guide to Understanding Homosexuality: A Biblical and Compassionate Response to Same-Sex Attraction.* Eugene, OR: Harvest House, 2010.

Gagnon, Robert A. J. *The Bible and Homosexual Practice: Texts and Hermeneutics.* Nashville, TN: Abingdon Press, 2002.

Goldberg, Arthur. *Light in the Closet: Torah, Homosexuality, and the Power to Change.* Beverly Hills, CA: Red Heifer Press, 2009.

Hallman, Janelle. *The Heart of Female Homosexuality: A Comprehensive Counseling Resource.* Downers Grove, IL: IVP Books, 2008.

Hill, Wesley. *Washed and Waiting: Reflections on Christian Faithfulness and Homosexuality.* Grand Rapids, MI: Zondervan, 2010.

Jones, Stanton L. and Mark A. Yarhouse. *Homosexuality: The Use of Scientific Research in the Church's Moral Debate.* Downers Grove, IL: IVP Academic, 2000.

Marin, Andrew. *Love Is an Orientation: Elevating the Conversation with the Gay Community.* Downers Grove, IL: IVP Books, 2009.

Medinger, Alan. *Growth into Manhood.* Colorado Springs, CO: Shaw Books, 2000.

Paris, Jenell Williams. *The End of Sexual Identity: Why Sex Is Too Important to Define Who We Are.* Downers Grove, IL: IVP Books, 2011.

Satinover, Jeffrey. *Homosexuality and the Politics of Truth.* Grand Rapids, MI: Baker Books, 1996.

Thompson, Chad. *Loving Homosexuals as Jesus Would: A Fresh Christian Approach.* Grand Rapids, MI: Brazos Press, 2004.

Whitehead, Briar. *Craving for Love: Relationship Addiction, Homosexuality, and the God Who Heals.* Mill Hill, London: Monarch Books, 2003.

Yarhouse, Mark A. *Homosexuality and the Christian: A Guide for Parents, Pastors, and Friends.* Minneapolis, MN: Bethany House, 2010.

Yarhouse, Mark A. and Erica S. N. Tan. *Sexual Identity Synthesis: Attributions,*

Meaning-Making, and the Search for Congruence. Lanham, MD: University Press of America, 2004.

LDS-Oriented Organizations

North Star International—NorthStarLDS.org

"North Star is a nonprofit community-based organization that assists Latter-day Saints looking for spiritual and social support that will empower them to live within their covenants, values, and beliefs as members of the Church. North Star takes no official position on the origin or mutability of homosexual feelings and attractions but supports all efforts consistent with the gospel that help individuals live with greater fulfillment and integrity within their covenants."

Evergreen International—EvergreenInternational.org

"Evergreen is a nonprofit organization that provides direction and support to Latter-day Saint men and women who want to diminish their same-sex attraction and free themselves from homosexual behavior. It is also a resource to family and friends, professional counselors, and religious leaders. The organization provides referrals to affiliated support groups and therapists, publishes a newsletter, maintains an online bookstore, and sponsors an annual conference (307 West 200 South, Suite 3004, Salt Lake City, UT 84110, phone 1-800-391-1000)."

Other Organizations

People Can Change—PeopleCanChange.com

"People Can Change is a nonprofit, nonreligious educational organization whose mission is to support and guide men who seek to transition away from unwanted homosexual attractions and behavior. PCC also provides information and support to family members, especially wives. Founded in 2000, PCC is best known for its life-changing 'Journey into Manhood' weekend experience, offered throughout the United States and in England."

Contributors

Brad Wilcox

Brad Wilcox is an associate professor in the Department of Teacher Education at Brigham Young University. Brad and his wife, Debi, recently lived in Santiago, Chile, where Brad served as a mission president of the Chile Santiago East Mission from 2003 to 2006. He is the author of *Growing Up: Gospel Answers about Maturation and Sex* and *The Continuous Atonement*.

M. Catherine Thomas

M. Catherine Thomas is a professor emeritus of ancient scripture at Brigham Young University. She and her husband, Gordon, recently returned from serving a full-time mission in Spain. She is the author of *Spiritual Lightening: How the Power of the Gospel Can Enlighten Minds and Lighten Burdens; Selected Writings of M. Catherine Thomas,* in the Gospel Scholars Series; and *Light in the Wilderness: Explorations in the Spiritual Life.*

Wendy Ulrich

Wendy Ulrich was a psychologist in Michigan before serving with her husband, David, while he was president of the Canada Montreal Mission. They now live in Alpine, Utah, where she founded Sixteen Stones Center for Growth, offering seminar retreats on forgiveness, loss, spirituality, and personal growth. She is a former president of the Association of Mormon Counselors and Psychotherapists (AMCAP) and the author of *Forgiving*

Ourselves: Getting Back Up When We Let Ourselves Down and *Weakness Is Not Sin: The Liberating Distinction That Awakens Our Strengths.*

Camille Fronk Olson

Camille Fronk Olson is a professor of ancient scripture at Brigham Young University and a former dean of students at LDS Business College. She has served on the Young Women general board and the Church's Teacher Development Curriculum Committee. She is the author of *Women of the Old Testament; In the Hands of the Potter; Mary, Martha, and Me: Seeking the One Thing That Is Needful;* and *Too Much to Carry Alone.*

Robert L. Millet

Robert L. Millet is Abraham O. Smoot University Professor and professor of ancient scripture at Brigham Young University. He earned a master's degree in psychology from BYU and a Ph.D. in religious studies from Florida State University. Brother Millet has served in the Church as a bishop, stake president, temple worker, and member of the Church Materials Evaluation Committee. A prolific speaker and writer, his works include *Men of Valor, Men of Influence, Are We There Yet? Grace Works, More Holiness Give Me,* and *When a Child Wanders.*

Michael Goodman

Michael Goodman is an associate professor of Church history at Brigham Young University. Brother Goodman served a full-time mission to Bangkok, Thailand, and returned to serve there as mission president from 1997 to 2000. He completed a Ph.D. in marriage, family, and human development. He has worked for the Church Educational System since 1989 and with the BYU College of Religious Education since 2000.

Index

About the Author

Ty Mansfield is a marriage and family therapist in Lubbock, Texas, where he is also currently completing a PhD in that field at Texas Tech University. Well-acquainted with the dichotomy faced by Latter-day Saints who experience same-gender attraction, Ty chronicled his own spiritual journey as a coauthor of *In Quiet Desperation: Understanding the Challenge of Same-Gender Attraction,* published by Deseret Book in 2004. He is a cofounder of the nonprofit organization North Star, a faith-affirming support organization for LDS individuals and families affected by homosexuality.

Ty enjoys playing racquetball, training for and competing in triathlons, eating Thai food, and hails the invention of the iPhone as one of the greatest technological advancements of the twenty-first century. He loves to travel and has lived or studied internationally in Japan, China, Israel/Palestine, and Egypt. Ty married his lovely wife, Danielle, in 2010 and they recently welcomed a beautiful baby boy into their family in the spring of 2011. Ty has served in the Church as a Gospel Doctrine teacher, ward mission leader, institute instructor, and temple ordinance worker.